MW01677479

WAKEFIELD PRESS

GREAT CENTRAL STATE

Jack Cross grew up in the lower Flinders Ranges amid the influences of the German Lutheran community. He holds qualifications from Adelaide Teachers College, the University of Adelaide, the University of Melbourne and Stanford University in California, and has worked as a teacher, free-range poultry farmer and associate professor.

Jack spent five years as a Research Fellow in Australian History at the University of Adelaide. For twenty years he was Head of Studies in Education at the Underdale campus of what is now the University of South Australia. He was a founder of the Aboriginal Tauondi College at Port Adelaide and the Anangu Teacher Education program at Ernabella in the APY Lands. A special edition of *The Teachers' Journal* acknowledged him as 'an inspirational educator'. He was author of *Schooling the Conflict of Belief*, and a member of the Classification Board.

Since semi-retirement, Jack has been awarded life membership of the WEA and the University of the Third Age Adelaide for his contribution to adult education. He is now a teacher in the History of Ideas at the Adelaide Central School of Art and the University of South Australia.

Jack Cross is married to Jillian and has no children.

Great Central State

The Foundation *of* the Northern Territory

Jack Cross

Wakefield Press

Wakefield Press
1 The Parade West
Kent Town
South Australia 5067
www.wakefieldpress.com.au

First published 2011

Cover design by Liz Nicholson, designBITE
Typeset by Wakefield Press
Printed and bound by Hyde Park Press, Adelaide

National Library of Australia Cataloguing-in-Publication entry

Author:	Cross, Jack.
Title:	Great central state: the foundation of the Northern Territory / Jack Cross.
ISBN:	978 1 86254 877 0 (pbk.).
Subjects:	Northern Territory – History. South Australia – History.
Dewey Number:	994.29

Publication of this book was assisted by the Commonwealth Government through the Australia Council, its arts funding and advisory body.

CONTENTS

To Jillian B

‘The past is never dead.
It’s not even past.’

William Faulkner

PREFACE

The opening of the overland railway from Adelaide to Darwin in 2004 –as well as looking forward – refers back to an earlier history of the Northern Territory: the attempt by South Australia to develop the Territory as a bridge to Asia.

This is several histories wrapped into one. At one level it is the colourful story of the foundation years of the Northern Territory – that vast tract of Australia facing Asia which is so attractive to tourists and investors. At another level it is the tale of South Australia's attempt to replicate its own planned colonisation on the north coast – part of South Australia's, or more particularly some South Australians', bid to become the premier colony of Australia. Suggested names for this premier colony were Albert, Adelaide, Australia (being at the heart of Australia) and Shakespeare, but the name that eventually stuck was Great Central State. As such it is a case study in planned colonisation, a world wide movement in the mid-19th century, which, at its most ambitious, aimed at spreading civilisation around the world.

There are many ways of writing the history of the Territory. This approach involved a detailed study of the South Australian context, and uses some of the recurring themes in South Australian historiography. It is as much a history of the South Australian way of doing things as it is a history of the foundation of the Northern Territory. I have been particularly interested in the way South Australians, because they saw themselves as different from other colonials, tended to go back to experiences from their own history for the solutions. Take the way George Goyder and Charles Todd were asked to draw a second Goyder Line, separating agricultural and pastoral lands, for the Territory. I have also been interested in the interaction between forward planning and the intervention of apparently chaotic chance variables. A continuing theme in South Australian history was the conflict between grand vision and numerous petty disputes among an inner circle of leading citizens – what Douglas Pike, of the Department of History at the University of Adelaide, with a twinkle in his eye, liked to call 'the paradise of dissent'.

As well as representing events, a deliberate attempt has been made to represent some of the constructions of reality used at the time by the selective use of contemporary words, images, and stories, especially in relation to race and geography. At the time, race was the most common way of constructing knowledge about people of different cultures. Unlike our current view of geography, North-West Arnhem Land (the name is no longer used) tended to be seen as on the southern perimeter of the Indies Archipelago and much like Java, and therefore should be incorporated in the sphere of South-East Asia. The rhetoric of progress – the so-called March of Civilisation – was also widely invoked, with its preference for heroic language full of hyperbole and alliteration – words like 'egregious' and 'imbroglio'.

Many of these narratives may well seem strange or prejudiced when viewed from another vantage point in history. But (as with relativity in physics) reference points of history are forever changing.

My method has been to support generalisations with 'judiciously chosen examples' (quoting Douglas Pike) in order to fill out the story and make the history live. Similarly many of the illustrations have been chosen because they are symbolic. Visual images of the time were particularly expressive (especially faces), consisting mainly of drawings, engravings and cartoons. No attempt was made to go beyond 1911. In general I have taken the view that more recent history would best be written by Territorians.

CHAPTER 1

THE GREAT CENTRAL STATE

'The worst that can be said against the Government of 1863 is that they encouraged the dream of a self-supporting colony.'

Register, 28 March 1868

The strangest part of the history about to be related is that no one seemed to know when it first began.

In 1863 the representatives of the struggling colony of South Australia acquired a huge tract of so-called wasteland which they called the Northern Territory. But when the question was raised, no one seemed to know with any certainty how the idea of taking over such a large area of land had come about. 'The thing has grown upon us', wrote the *Advertiser* columnist. It had grown until it was too much trouble to turn back.[1]

What kept the northern issue alive was a preoccupation by a number of South Australians – some of whom already had links with parts of Asia – with the idea of 'The Unlimited Asian Market'. This meant gaining entry to the Indies Archipelago, particularly the Dutch East Indies and the Malay States, as well as the Indian sub-continent, but most of all China. At this stage trade with Japan was not an issue.

Linked to the dream of an Unlimited Asian Market was a second dream: of extending South Australia's northern boundary right across the continent to the north coast to form what later came to be known as 'The Great Central State'.

When it came to the Asian market, a Great Central State would be particularly advantaged, being at the centre of the Australian colonies, while its north coast was uniquely joined to Asia by the monsoon winds blowing from the north-west in the wet season and

1 *Advertiser* 25/4/1864.

bringing ships from Asia – and then switching to the south-east in the dry and taking ships back to Asia. In the era of sail the map of the world was read differently from today.

The Dream of the Great Asian Market

According to William Hutt, one of the surviving planners of South Australia, whose letter appeared in the *South Australian Register* in 1864, the founders of the home colony in the 1830s had always wanted a northern boundary beside the Indian Ocean. The idea of a northern boundary facing Asia was, on his single evidence, older even than the Adelaide settlement itself.[2]

Hutt (who once applied to be governor) had served on two of the three associations formed successively in London in the first half of the 1830s to force under the notice of the Colonial Office Edward Gibbon Wakefield's new revolutionary method of colonisation as well as the feasibility of trying it out near the mouth of the River Murray, on the central south coast of Australia. Each of these associations did, in fact, want the northern boundary left open or, failing that, pushed north as far as possible. The first association of 1830–1831, the National Colonisation Society, laid down in its 'Proposal to His Majesty's Government for founding a colony on the southern coast of Australia' a southern, eastern and western, but not a northern boundary.[3] The second association, the South Australian Land Company, proposed the use of a chartered company to pilot colonisation as in early Virginia 'between the 132nd and 141st degrees of East longitude, without any assigned boundary towards the north or interior'.[4]

It was later explained how the association wanted incorporated in their charter the right to extend the colony at the choice of the company.[5] Some time between 16 April 1832, when a deputation presented the company's scheme to Lord Goderich of the Colonial Office, and 28 May, when a revised scheme was sent in, this hope received a severe set-back. The revised draft abandoned the idea

2 *Register* 15/3/1864, Hutt's letter to Hart.

3 *Proposal to His Majesty's Government for founding a colony on the southern coast of Australia*, Nicol, London, 1831, p. 20.

4 *South Australian Land Company Prospectus 1832* (C.O. 13/1 Folio 83).

5 Statement concerning revision of the company (C.O. 13/2 Folio 35 *seq.*).

G.W. Goyder 'in pursuit of rainfall'. That is, land for agriculture.
(Courtesy of the State Library of South Australia – B 14851)

of an open north for a definite boundary at the twentieth parallel, thus still including all of Central Australia in the proposed colony.[6] The change was probably made at the hands of James Stephen, the energetic Counsel to the Colonial Office, who was consulted during the interval and who believed that extravagant grants of land once almost ruined the chartered colonies of America.

Still Stephen thought the dimensions too extravagant. The third association, the South Australian Association of 1833–1834, started out by withdrawing the boundary approximately three-and-a-half degrees to the Tropic of Capricorn.[7] The revised line was carefully incorporated in the 1834 Bill to create South Australia as a separate colony. But in the House of Commons, the Calcutta-born Francis Thornhill Baring, who possessed large areas of land for sale in

6 Whitmore to Goderich 28/5/1832 (C.O. 13/1 Folio 88); Enclosure (C.O. 13/1 Folio 92 *seq.*).

7 *South Australia Outline of the Plan of a Proposed Colony to be founded on the South Coast of Australia; with an account of the Soil, Climate,* Ridgway, London, 1834, p. 6.

America and did not want competition, was influential in having it reduced still further to the 26th parallel.[8]

No sooner was the new colony settled after 1836 than some South Australians began to draw the boundary northwards again in their own imagination. They had been planted in the driest colony in the driest inhabited continent on earth. By the mid 1850s it was clear to far-seeing individuals like George Goyder that the amount of land suitable for agriculture in South Australia would always be limited. On the other hand, the country above the 26th parallel was seen as a 'No Man's Land', a wasteland and all that those words implied – an uncivilised wilderness, little used by the existing inhabitants and beckoning to be explored and developed. In this context, No Man's Land did not so much mean that the land was unoccupied, but that hunter gathering by the traditional inhabitants was an inferior use of a precious commodity.[9]

Agitation to alter the existing boundaries began as early as the 1850s, and was centered mainly on the activities of four men: James 'Jemmy' Chambers, a shrewd pastoralist; William Finke, his partner; John McDouall Stuart, their surveyor and explorer; and Governor Richard Graves MacDonnell, graduate with distinction in classics and science at Trinity College Dublin, who represented the public interest. As it turned out, the reasons for their interests were not always compatible.

Chambers' vision was to open up a practical stock route across the continent linked by a chain of wells to the far north-west coast, from where, in the dry season, April to October, the trade winds would carry surplus stock to China and India, particularly horses to India. The whole concept was closely connected with the contemporary notion that commercial greatness awaited the country breaking into the Great Asian Market, coupled with the belief that North Australia and the coast of Asia were uniquely linked for trade by the monsoon winds which blew steadily towards Australia

8 H.P.D. (3) Vol. XXV c.701.

9 The legal term *Terra Nullius* may have been implied, but as far as I can discover was never used in South Australia in reference to the Northern Territory. For a comparison of Yolngu and European approaches to land see: Nancy M. Williams, *The Yolngu and their Land*, Stanford University Press, California, 1986.

in the wet season and away from Australia towards South-East Asia in the dry.

In 1853 Finke obtained the services of Stuart to spy out and survey runs reaching into the interior – and with luck, eventually through to the north coast itself. By this method Chambers and Finke aimed to lay open a path across the continent safe for cattle and sprinkled with stations and mines, while also taking first bite into any choice country then selling it at an enormous profit to those who followed.

This ambition seemed plausible in the late 1850s. South Australians were among the pioneers in dry pastoral management, as they were also to become in dry agriculture. With great ingenuity, individual pastoralists had already managed to invade the low rainfall areas by making use of every range and water-hole, and there was no reason to doubt that, by continuing the same practices, they could traverse the entire continent step by step to the Timor and Arafura seas.

Governor MacDonnell, on the other hand, represented a second interest in the efforts to acquire the northern wastelands. As well as strongly supporting pastoral expansion through to the north coast, he had visions of an overland telegraph line across the centre to connect with an undersea cable from Singapore – and thence linked all the way to London. This required getting control of all the country through to the north coast to prevent other colonies (especially New South Wales and Queensland) blocking its path. MacDonnell's interest in an overland telegraph reflected the fact that Adelaide had recently become the telegraph capital of Australia; and he wanted to make sure that it did not lose its pre-eminent position when an undersea cable eventually was extended to Australia.

South Australia's pre-eminence in telegraphy had begun with the recruitment from the Royal Observatory Greenwich of Charles Heavitree Todd in 1855, as government astronomer and superintendent of the electric telegraph. Even before leaving England Todd had dreams of linking Australia to the mother country with an electric telegraph. Soon after his arrival Todd, backed by Governor MacDonnell, took the lead in proposing and building the first inter-colonial overland line between Adelaide and Melbourne, started in April 1857 and opened in July 1858. This made Port Adelaide the first important port of call for sailing ships using the Westerlies and bringing news from Europe, feeding into a telegraph network which eventually joined Adelaide, Melbourne, Sydney, Brisbane, Hobart and numerous provincial towns. (Perth, the first possible port of call, was isolated because of the Nullarbor.) News from English and European newspapers was summarised in Adelaide then tapped out by morse through a series of repeater stations to Melbourne and from there on to other capitals. But no sooner was the commercial advantage and prestige of this arrangement won, than it came under threat. In 1858–1859 a representative of the Red Sea and India Telegraph Company approached various colonial authorities in eastern Australia about their sharing the cost of a direct cable link to Brisbane. MacDonnell's response, aided by Todd and individual politicians with commercial interests, was to set in motion a vigorous campaign by South Australia (lasting for 12 years in all) to prevent Queensland getting the cable route because it put South Australia at the tail end of all commercial intelligence coming from overseas.

Whatever the ambitions of his supporters, such as Chambers, Finke and MacDonnell, John McDouall Stuart's epic explorations were in large part a working out of his private demons. Socially frustrated and fighting back alcoholism he drove himself beyond endurance to conquer the forces of Nature. He was a classic colonial hero. Like many heroes popular adoration for him rose quickly and doubts followed almost as fast. He represented yet another element in the move to take over the Territory. At the height of his fame, between about 1860 and 1863, there was a popular feeling in South Australia that the colony deserved the wastelands as a reward for the exertions of its great explorers such as Stuart, Sturt and McKinlay. Stuart's main reputation rested on three expeditions: in 1860 to the centre of Australia, where he hoisted the British flag on Central Mount Sturt and then proceeded to Tennant Creek, but failed to find a way to the Victoria River; then in 1860–1861 a largely government-sponsored expedition to the dry lands around Newcastle Waters (over two-thirds of the way across the continent) before he was forced to turn back; finally in 1862 another mainly government expedition, successfully through to what he erroneously thought was the mouth of the Adelaide River. But within a few months of his triumphant return to a hero's welcome in the streets of Adelaide, the doubts were beginning to circulate. He had three times failed to penetrate the dry country north-west of Tennant Creek to the Victoria River which had been his express instruction. Every time Stuart tried to veer to the north-west, the harshness of the country drove him north.

Just as the ambition of the four men promised rewards, their luck left them. In 1862 Chambers died in his prime at the age of 49. Seventeen months later Finke dropped dead off a stool in a pub in Currie Street at 48. With Chambers and Finke gone, a reaction set in – especially to trusting their judgement. Stuart returned from crossing the continent a broken man and soon left the country. In 1862 Governor MacDonnell was transferred allegedly because of his connection with the Great Northern Copper Mine scandal. MacDonnell had arrived in 1855 prior to South Australia gaining self-government in 1857, and could never step down from being the master. With MacDonnell's departure an era ended, democracy took hold and the Northern Territory question soon became secondary to local issues such as schools, roads, and the conflict between farmers and pastoralists over land with adequate rainfall – a conflict which reached its peak in 1865.

A Confused Acquisition

Competition between Chambers and MacDonnell complicated moves to acquire the Territory. Chambers' aim was to take advantage of his prior access to the lands in the north discovered by Stuart, and sell pastoral and mining lands to anyone willing to buy. In 1859, Finke, using J.B. Neales, Commissioner of Crown Lands, as link man, tricked the governor into lending his name to the bogus Great Northern Copper Mine Company. Consequently, Chambers, Finke, John Baker and Captain John Hart immediately made an alleged fortune selling 'illegal mining leases' and 'exhausted holes' (to quote the governor) to unsuspecting capitalists in London. Governor MacDonnell was so upset by the scam that he donned explorer's clothes and travelled to the dry north as far as William Creek to investigate the bogus sites for himself. Neales was made to resign for abuse of office.

The tensions continued after Stuart returned from his first

major exploration to the centre of Australia in 1860. Chambers forbade Stuart to reveal details of his trip, even to the governor when he was invited to Government House – an exclusion which annoyed the Queen's representative. Chambers also took possession of all Stuart's maps, even changing some of the explorer's names of places to those of his family. MacDonnell believed he was working for the public good and resented Chambers' and Finke's narrow focus on making money.[10]

In October 1860, soon after Stuart's return from the centre of Australia – and without access to Stuart's journal – Governor MacDonnell made the first move to acquire the Northern Territory. On 26 October he despatched a letter to the Colonial Office, with little or no reference to his advisers in government. Parliament knew little about the approach, except that the governor intended to write home to England (for a second time, the first was in 1857) about the so-called 'Western Territory' (which still belonged to New South Wales), the three-degree gap between the borders of South and Western Australia.[11]

The main point of Governor MacDonnell's letter was that South Australian pastoralists were about to infiltrate across the existing western and northern boundaries. To counter this situation MacDonnell proposed that the Western Territory should be annexed permanently to South Australia, while the Northern Territory above the 26th parallel should be temporarily annexed to South Australia until a separate tropical colony existed on the north-west coast, perhaps centred on the Victoria River. In pressing South Australia's special claim to the Northern Territory MacDonnell stressed *convenience of administration* as the major justification, as well as South Australia's proven record in opening up the region. No other government at the time (he argued) was so conveniently situated to protect and administer it. He then went on to refer to the recent discoveries made by Stuart in finding a natural path far into

10 Perhaps the worst scam in South Australian colonial history. For years after, those implicated blamed one another – and all blamed Finke because he was German. See S.A.P.P. 111, 115, 116 of 1859; 83 of 1860; 234 of 1862. For a recent study of Stuart (including the scam) see J. Bailey, *Mr Stuart's Track*, MacMillan, Sydney, 2006, Chapter 6.

11 S.A.P.D. 1860 c.1046; *Register* 13/10/1860 Parliamentary Proceedings. The *Constitution Act* was passed in 1856 and the new parliament met in 1857.

Governor Dominick Daly successfully backed South Australia's bid to take over the Northern Territory. He wanted the Plains of Promise from Queensland as well. (*Illustrated Sydney News* 25/3/1868. Courtesy of the State Library of South Australia)

the interior; the relentless movement of pastoralists from south to north; and the hope of eventually establishing a trade in horses via the north coast to India.[12]

The Secretary of State in London decided these were better arguments for shifting the existing northern boundary northwards in stages ahead of settlement, than for handing over all the country through to the north coast.[13]

In his letter to London, MacDonnell also made a brief reference to an overland telegraph. He conceded that the line might not follow Stuart's route – while behind the scenes he shared with Todd and others the hope that once they gained access to all the land to the north coast, a direct route across Australia to Adelaide was exactly what would happen.

At the time, the centre of Australia attracted most attention among the general public because Stuart's discoveries in Central Australia in a favourable season had led to a wave of optimism. In a series of articles, the *Register* argued that South Australia was no longer now a poor colony wedged between desert to the north and

12 MacDonnell to Newcastle 26/10/1860 (S.A.P.P. 29 of 1861); Extension of Western Boundary of South Australia (S.A.P.P. 27 of 1858).

13 Newcastle to MacDonnell 26/2/1861 (S.A.P.P. 29 of 1861).

the sea to the south. One of the politicians wanting them to acquire Stuart's land straightaway was Boyle Travers Finniss.[14]

The governor's letter reached London at a time of a national crisis caused mainly by the situation in Europe which brought Palmerston to power for life and with him the Duke of Newcastle, Henry Pelham (now in the twilight of his career), in charge of the colonies. The main problem in Europe in 1859–1860 was the change in the balance of power almost leading to war caused by the attempted unification of Italy. When difficulties appeared near to home, the distant colonies were generally the first to be pruned, and Newcastle, with failing health, became distinguished for the ingenuity by which he avoided any action that added to the cost of his department. According to one British journal his 'do-nothing policy' was seen best of all in the handling of the North Australia question.[15]

'Do nothing' reflected the domestic policy (in contrast to the foreign policy) of the second Palmerston government from 1859–1865. In his reply to MacDonnell, the Duke of Newcastle stressed that the annexation of North Australia was not a pressing affair. He pointed out that South Australia, separated as it was by the whole breadth of the continent, seemed of all colonies the least conveniently situated to administer it. Turning to the immediate question of the infiltration of pastoralists into a No Man's Land, he promised with the preparation of suitable legislation to extend the western boundary to meet Western Australia and to allow the northern boundary to be gradually shifted as the need arose.[16]

Not long after Newcastle had responded to Governor MacDonnell he received another approach, this one stressing how Queensland squatters were about to invade the No Man's Land on its eastern boundary. The new move came from Sir Charles Nicholson, first speaker of the Legislative Council of New South Wales, first president of the Legislative Council of Queensland,

---

14 Examples, *Register* 26/10/1860 leader; 26/12/1860, p. 4.

15 *Australian and New Zealand Gazette* 9/1/1864 (in *Register* 14/3/1864, p. 2). Newcastle died 18/10/1864, Palmerston died exactly a year later.

16 Newcastle to MacDonnell 26/2/1861 (S.A.P.P. 29 of 1861). The western boundary now corresponded to the Pope's famous line of demarcation between the Portuguese world to the west and the Spanish to the east.

a founding father of Queensland then resident in London and a spokesman for great capitalists and companies, whom South Australians accused of 'panting for a governorship'. Nicholson apparently acted on his own initiative. But he also had a shadowy link to certain parties hoping to settle the north coast with a joint stock company.

Sir Charles Nicholson argued in a large submission – reflecting his status – that North Australia was so important it deserved to be colonised straight from Britain, if necessary on borrowed money repayable as the lands were sold or rented out. If, however, the Colonial Office still felt apprehensive about the cost he advised as the last resort to hand it temporarily to Queensland,[17] a colony which at the time gave concessions to powerful capitalists and companies. The suggested arrangement insulted the southerners and was little welcomed by the fledgling over-extended colony of Queensland with an adult European population of only about 30,000. But the idea of the colonials having to pay if they encroached upon a No Man's Land appealed to Newcastle. After seeking the counsel and assurance of his advisers, the Emigration Commissioners, he decided to annex the country below the Tropic of Capricorn permanently to South Australia and that above for a few years only to Queensland. The southerners were at last to get the boundary ordered in the 1834 Bill setting up South Australia, but it did not please them much. 'It is probable that it will be one of the last portions of Australia to be occupied,' complained the Executive Council in Adelaide, referring to the proposed added area.[18]

One event tended to precipitate another. The affront of being passed over in favour of another colony made the South Australian government and its backers more determined to gain the Northern Territory.

In November 1862 a second and stronger South Australian bid was made, this time by the full elected government led by George Marsden Waterhouse, and the Pastoral Association, a pressure group of pastoralists then at the height of its influence, backed

17 Nicholson to Newcastle July 1862 (S.A.P.P. 37 of 1863).

18 Newcastle to Daly 21/9/1862; Rogers to Emigration Commissioners 11/8/1862; Murdoch to Rogers 19/8/1862; Minutes of Executive Council 25/11/1862 (S.A.P.P. 37 of 1863).

by a covering plea from the new governor, Dominick Daly. As it turned out, the petitions from the government and the pastoralists were not entirely compatible. By 1862 the focus had shifted from the centre to the north. The explorer McKinlay had recently returned from crossing the continent to the Gulf of Carpentaria and Stuart was resting at Mount Margaret Station near Lake Eyre after making his epic journey to the Van Diemen Gulf. Between 1860 and 1862 further explorations by the two great Scots explorers had disillusioned everyone about the value of the interior. South Australia was still, alas, a poor country of limited fertile land in between desert and the sea.

George Marsden Waterhouse, who led the move, was a canny businessman. In 1863 he came under scrutiny by a select committee of parliament for shady dealings involving the Moonta Mine. He later became premier and acting governor of New Zealand. The Pastoral Association of South Australia had been formed in November 1859 with Clement Sabine as secretary to lobby against increased pastoral rents, and to agitate for more land for pastoralists.

The Waterhouse Government reasoned that two distinct areas – geographers would have called them 'natural regions' – existed on the north coast, one centred on the Victoria River near the Western Australian border, the other on the Albert River in the Gulf of Carpentaria, and that South Australia could establish a pastoral settlement on the Victoria River with *greater expedition* than Queensland. For one reason South Australian grazing lands were saturated and its pastoralists land hungry while Queensland's were not, and between the settled areas of Queensland and the Victoria River there stretched a thousand miles of grasslands which would take 20 years for stock to use up. South Australia was separated from the north by semi-desert which could be bridged in a few jumps. The Victoria River region had two natural advantages. It was within range of the trade winds to aid ships carrying horses for export to India and China, as well as being an intermediate location where the undersea cable coming from Europe, via the East Indies, could meet an overland telegraph line 'across the Continent' – route and destination unclear.[19]

19 Daly to Newcastle 26/11/1862 with enclosures (S.A.P.P. 37 of 1863). The concept of Natural Regions was used in geography at the time.

About a month later, the pastoral firm of Levi and Co. appealed direct to London for pastoral blocks on the Victoria River – on behalf of seven capitalists including Waterhouse himself – with each capitalist contributing £1000 to support sending 10,000 ewes across the continent to the Victoria River district, using 16 to 18 drovers.[20]

But not everyone agreed with the narrow focus on the Victoria River. The Pastoral Association, in an attached submission supported by Governor Daly, pressed their claims to the Gulf of Carpentaria country as well by the extension of the existing eastern boundary of South Australia straight north to the coast. The governor explained in his covering dispatch:[21]

> A strong and general feeling exists in this Province that South Australia having made great and successful exertions in exploration and from geographical position, has a strong claim to an extension of territory to the Gulf of Carpentaria.

The attention of many pastoralists was shifting from the north-west to the north-east because of the explorations of John McKinlay, who unlike Stuart travelled with sheep and cattle. In August 1861 McKinlay had set out from Adelaide for the north-east corner of the colony on a relief expedition to find the Victorian explorers Burke and Wills. Having found what he considered to be the remains of Charley Gray, a member of Burke's expedition, he proceeded to the Gulf of Carpentaria by making use of the river systems on the eastern side of the dry interior, reaching it on 20 May. This discovery of an alternative route, coupled with Stuart's difficulties in crossing the centre, had by late 1862 convinced many South Australian pastoralists like John Baker that McKinlay's was now the best, if not the only, practical stock route to the north coast. The Pastoral Association had met to agitate for the Gulf Country on the day McKinlay's journal was made public.

Between about 1858 and 1864 the pastoralists in South Australia were at the zenith of their influence. But because most leases came up for review at the end of June 1865 they feared that much of their best land was about to be resumed for farmers. The *Register*

20 Daly to Newcastle 26/1/1863 with enclosures (S.A.P.P. 127 of 1863); *Advertiser* 27/1/1863, p. 2.

21 Daly to Newcastle 26/11/1862 (S.A.P.P. 37 of 1863, p. 4).

later commented on the reasons for this second bid, pointing to the fact that South Australia had been passed over in favour of another colony, and the pressure exerted by the Pastoral Association 'and other persons interested'[22] possibly referring to land speculators (the so-called 'sharks') in Adelaide. The emphasis on concentrated settlement had encouraged a culture of land speculation in South Australia from the beginning.[23]

Newcastle would have rejected the persistent South Australians had not the Queensland government refused to entertain his idea that they take sole temporary responsibility for all the territory above the Tropic of Capricorn. In a shrewd move the Queenslanders decided to accept only the eastern portion to the 138th line of east longitude which they had already received some months earlier after putting pressure on the Colonial Office. This added strip included the so-called Plains of Promise between the Albert and Flinders rivers eulogised by John Lort Stokes of the *Beagle* in two volumes back in 1846. Having got their Plains of Promise the Queensland government, as represented by Governor Bowen, supported South Australia's right to the rest. According to South Australian sources the Queensland government had refused to take the whole of the territory on the advice of its famous explorer and surveyor-general, Augustus Charles Gregory.[24]

The prospect of an uncontrolled squatting expansion like that which had occurred in early New South Wales, and the cost of a new colony, was unthinkable. Newcastle was left with one alternative, to give it to South Australia for a few years only. In May 1863 he sent a curt note to inform the colonials of his decision. The South Australians had gained No Man's Land at last.[25]

The Territory carved out of New South Wales was transferred on

---

22 *Register* 21/7/1863 leader.

23 According to the Wakefield plan South Australia was to be a paradise for small business people. But it is one of the many ironies of South Australian history that (perhaps more than any other colony and state) it later came to be dominated by old established wealth, many of whom without regard for the spirit of the thing, had made their money by deliberately misusing the Wakefield system.

24 Bowen to Newcastle 13/1/1863 with enclosures 1 and 2 (Queensland Legislative Assembly, Votes and Proceedings, 1st Session 1863, pp. 539–545).

25 Newcastle to Daly 26/5/1863 (S.A.P.P. 70 of 1863).

6 July 1863 by Letters Patent which made it plain that the acquisition was provisional. Twenty years later when the South Australian government petitioned the Colonial Office for a more permanent arrangement than by Letters Patent, the request was rejected.[26]

From the beginning there were disagreements among politicians between those who supported an enlarged South Australia and those who believed it was beyond their means to manage. No sooner had this strong bid been made than many parliamentarians (especially those who had not been involved in the moves such as George Fife Angas and George Strickland Kingston) began to have second thoughts about the colony's cupidity. It was one thing to gain access to the Unlimited Asian Market, quite another to pay for it.

Waterhouse and his supporters had acted while parliament was in recess. When in March 1863 (after a parliamentary election) the Houses got down to business, their efforts became the centre of a first-class political row. The opposition was led by Captain John Hart (aided in the Upper House by Henry Ayers) who objected to the way Waterhouse had committed everyone to the cost of conducting a remote sub-colony on the far side of the continent. Hart had operated as a trading captain off the south coast of the continent before Adelaide was settled and later moved into the shipping business at Port Adelaide with great success. He insisted it would have been more beneficial to help Vice-Consul Owen (a former Port Adelaide merchant) colonise the Fiji Islands.[27] Ayers, who had made his fortune from the Burra copper mines and saw himself as a statesman (he read Macaulay and Carlyle), pronounced the acquisition a White Elephant, a name that unfortunately stuck. Supporting those not wanting the added land, he said: 'Like the man who was offered the white elephant, they said thank you, but it would be more expensive than useful.'[28] Many others in parliament were also doubtful. The idea of a frontier settlement on the northern outskirts of South Australia had not been unpopular. It was seen as

26 Newcastle to Daly 16/7/1863 with Letters Patent as enclosure (S.A.P.P. 113 of 1863); Jervois to Kimberley 19/7/1882 with enclosures; Derby to Robinson 6/1/1883 (S.A.P.P. 113 of 1883–1884).

27 *Register* 5/3/1863, pp. 2 and 3 Parliamentary Proceedings.

28 *Register* 4/3/1863 Parliamentary Proceedings. For a biography of Ayers, see *Henry Ayers*, Jason Shute, Tauris, London 2011.

a vindication of South Australia's right to the lands ordered in the 1834 Bill, as well as a reward for the exertions of South Australian explorers and the enterprise of local pastoralists. But the idea of a 'separate settlement' 2000 miles distant by an overland route on the north-west coast, was a different matter because it made South Australia in effect a coloniser at a time when it needed all the means of colonisation for itself. A motion was entered in the Lower House of Parliament to remove all mention of the Victoria District from the traditional reply to the governor's speech. This was defeated when the government threatened to resign if it was carried, and by it giving an assurance that only a rudimentary pastoral settlement was contemplated under a stipendiary magistrate and a few mounted troopers.[29] Thus, the Northern Territory Question began its parliamentary career as a political crisis.

In London a group of powerful capitalists was unhappy with Newcastle's easy surrender to, what seemed to them, very poor arguments. For some time the group had been planning to colonise North Australia direct from England with a chartered company, and had formed the North Australian Association to put pressure on the Colonial Office after the style of the South Australian Association in 1834. In June 1863 they confronted Newcastle with an influential deputation, organised by Sir Charles Nicholson and led by Lord Alfred Churchill, of prominent politicians (Tite, Marsh, Vansittart, Potts) in a final effort to induce Newcastle to change his mind. They urged him to create a new colony called 'Northern Australia' (to emphasise that it might eventually extend right across the top of the continent) under a governor and the Colonial Office, an arrangement which they said would provide prospective shareholders with a sense of security. Since the 1830s there had been a succession of proposals to colonise so-called North Australia and so compete with the Dutch in the Indies.

Newcastle repeated his objection that his department could not afford it. But he invited the association to proceed with settlement immediately using what he called the 'Laissez-Faire Principle'.

---

29 *Register* 5/3/1863 Parliamentary Proceedings. For a study of some earlier proposals to colonise North Australia see K.T. Borrow, *Prince Alfred Land (and some other proposed North Australia colonies 1853–1876)* privately printed, Adelaide, 1961.

He thought a separate colony under control of the Colonial Office would need to be founded two or three years later. Heartened by the assurance, the group then wrote to Adelaide asking for a grant of 250,000 acres which would be divided and sold to the company's colonists as the mainspring of colonisation.[30] Newcastle enclosed with the Letters Patent, formally giving the Territory to South Australia, a strong hint to copy Queensland's land laws devised to encourage company settlement.[31] But because of the Wakefield tradition of championing small business, South Australians had a prejudice against large company colonisation. Once they gained possession of the Northern Territory the South Australians embarked on a contrary line, introducing laws levelled against large joint stock companies and deliberately delaying a formal response to the august association for a year.[32]

There were further misgivings over Newcastle's decision when the news reached Adelaide by the July mail steamer. The first public information in Adelaide came from Sir Richard MacDonnell, the former governor, who had been independently lobbying the Colonial Office and who in a lecture to the Dublin Young Men's Christian Association on 7 May 1863 had been able to give a preview of Newcastle's intention. MacDonnell was delighted that the added country made South Australia the largest colony in the British Empire reaching, as it did, right across Australia.[33] There was a brief spate of newspaper talk over changing the name 'South Australia' to something more apt. According to the novelist Anthony Trollope (Australia's first celebrity visitor), when he later visited Australia, South Australia had become 'northern as much as southern'.[34] The newspapers championed the name 'Adelaide'; the ministry thought about 'Albert' as a gesture to the mourning queen; others suggested 'Australia', 'Alexander' and 'Adel-land'. (The proposer of the last

30 E.A. Oppen to the Minister of Crown Lands 24/7/1863 (C.C.L.I.L. 2353/1863); *Register* 10/8/1863, p. 3 Anglo-Australian news section; *Advertiser* 10/8/1863, p. 3 miscellaneous section.

31 Newcastle to Daly 16/7/1863 (S.A.P.P. 113 of 1863); *Register* 11/9/1863 leader.

32 *Register* 6/11/1863 Parliamentary Proceedings; E.A. Oppen to Minister of Crown Lands 24/7/1863 Minute (C.C.L.I.L. 2353/1863).

33 Sir Richard G. MacDonnell, *Australia: What It Is, and What it May Be, A Lecture*, Hodges Smith and Co., Dublin, 1863.

34 *Chronicle* 18/1/1873, p. 5.

was urged to take the name 'Addle-head'.) Yet another wanted 'Shakespeare' with all districts and divisions named after his main characters, South Australia being about to celebrate the Shakespeare Tercentenary. Apart from discussions about the name, all of which overlooked the temporary nature of the annexation, the reception was mixed because the acquisition had been led by pressure groups rather than a groundswell from the general population. Faced by a choice between the Territory and roads and schools most citizens would have preferred the latter.[35]

Thus began a pattern of ambivalence, based on whether South Australians felt they were over-reaching themselves, that characterised almost half a century of South Australian control.

The Pastoral Association was disgruntled to discover that the Duke of Newcastle had not given them the Albert and Herbert River country, the so-called Plains of Promise, which they had especially wanted. Instead he had given it to Queensland possibly until a separate tropical colony facing Asia extended along the north coast of Australia.[36] They were even less pleased, when details of the Waterhouse petition became public, to find the government had not supported their request but rather seemed to suggest that Queensland had better claims to the border country which adjoined it.

The months between applying for and receiving the Territory were marred by the second worst political crisis in the colony's history (the first was after gaining self-government in 1857) culminating in the defeat of the Waterhouse Government in July and its eventual replacement by the Ayers–Hart opposition party. A main reason for the confusion was a general election held in November 1862 leading to a new parliament which met at the end of February. Thus, by chance, the Northern Territory had to be settled by the men (especially Hart, Ayers and Glyde) who had opposed its acquisition as a waste of public money.

Their valiant efforts to reconcile their new commitments with their old criticisms produced the Northern Territory Plan.

---

35 *Register* 14/7/1863 leader and also p. 2; 22/7/1863, p. 2; 27/7/1863 leader; *Advertiser* 3/8/1863 leader.

36 *Register* 16/7/1863, p. 3 Sabine to Editor; *Chronicle* 18/1/1873, p. 5.

The Northern Territory Plan

The day after taking office Hart, who believed in minimal government and low taxation, foreshadowed the terms under which his government would colonise the northern acquisition. He could not conceal his apprehension, his resentment, even his embarrassment. Referring to the government's apprehension the *Register* wrote:

> It is not surprising that Mr Hart should now take this view of the subject, for when it was first brought forward some months ago he was amongst those members of the House of Assembly who strenuously objected to the proposal for placing Stuart's country under the guardianship of this colony.[37]

The main condition laid down was the principle of separate development. This insisted that the north-west territory must be kept separate from South Australia in public finances and by not competing for the means of colonisation. 'If it was only proposed to send from our own flocks and herds there, and to settle it with drafts from our own population,' said Hart in parliament, 'the acquisition of this new country would be an unmitigated evil.'[38] 'I will say, further, that it would not be politic for the Government to undertake the management of these lands unless they were assured that no loss should thereby accrue to South Australia.' Both statements were followed by a chorus of 'Hear, hear.'[39] As a surety against loss the South Australian government intended to take the same precautions as the home government took with South Australia in 1834. They would not allow settlement to begin until a set portion of the lands had been sold and paid for in advance and the money was in hand ready to tide the Territory over the first difficult years, after which it would have to pay its own way.[40] The reasons for the precautions were clear. Now that the worst (in the view of the detractors) had happened, and South Australia was saddled with the new Territory

---

37 *Register* 21/7/1863 leader.

38 *Register* 17/7/1863 Parliamentary Proceedings. Statement changed back to first person.

39 *Register* 17/7/1863 Parliamentary Proceedings.

40 *Register* 17/7/1863 Parliamentary Proceedings; *Advertiser* 17/7/1863 Parliamentary Proceedings.

Captain John Hart, former whaling captain at Encounter Bay and adviser to Colonel Light on navigating the South Australian coast.
Chief architect of the Northern Territory Plan.
(*Illustrated Sydney News* 15/2/1873, p. 16.
Courtesy of the State Library of South Australia)

and acting the part of a coloniser, all a government could do was to ensure that it did not compete for the limited supply of migrants and capital. A few days later Henry Ayers made a parallel ministerial statement to the Upper House. Ayers and Hart would not serve under the other, so like Spartan kings they ruled together, each watching the other out of the corner of his eye.

The principles came as a shock to those who knew and had shared the vision of James Chambers and Company. Would this have happened, they asked, had Chambers and Finke been still alive? It was clear that the local squatters, for whom the Territory had been primarily obtained, would no longer be the mainspring of colonisation, but unknown outsiders knowing nothing of the new country or its prospects. The Hon. John Baker in the Upper House, a prominent member of the Pastoral Association who had once been associated with Chambers and Finke, called for a Select Committee to investigate the most appropriate way of settling the country.[41] His action was well received by the newspapers, but Ayers and Hart took the attitude that such an inquiry would interfere with plans already in hand. Baker withdrew the motion but for years after kept reminding parliament about his original doubts over the method of colonisation.[42]

Baker argued an alternative theory of colonisation: pastoralists must come first, followed by agriculture. He suggested grants of one acre for each sheep introduced, up to 10,000 acres.[43]

Between July and October 1863 the Northern Territory Plan matured with the passing of winter, and the government's confidence improved especially as 1863–1864 turned out to be a period of prosperity, particularly in agriculture.[44] They decided to restage the original South Australian experiment used at the foundation of the home colony but – and this is the important point – with *improvements*.

But they were deluding themselves. In the 1830s the initiative to set up the parent colony of South Australia came from outside the government, from the advocates of colonisation or from the colonists themselves. In 1863 the initiative had to come from the government because they had passed over pastoralists ready to go to the Territory, in favour of attracting putative land investors. But the government would need to find those investors – probably in Asia.

These different starting points impacted on what followed. The British government in the 1830s could remain detached; the South Australian government, though they tried to do the same, became more and more enmeshed with every event. The ministers found it insufficient just to restage the land system which Wakefield held to be the beginning and secret of all good colonisation; they then had to creep behind the scenes and to prod private enterprises into action as well.

In October 1863, Hart introduced into parliament a Bill to set Northern Territory colonisation in perpetual motion, after which Commissioner of Crown Lands Lavington Glyde, who a few months

41 *Register* 12/9/1863, p. 2.

42 *Register* 16/9/1863 Parliamentary Proceedings.

43 *Advertiser* 5/11/1863, p. 3.

44 *Register* 2/3/1868, p. 4 Review of Governor Daly period.

earlier had opposed the acquisition, was entrusted with explaining it at the second reading.[45] In his speech the commissioner set out to explain how the Territory would be transformed into a second South Australia. Instead of opting for a simple pastoral settlement his government had decided to re-employ South Australia's complex method of systematic colonisation used at its birth in the 1830s but, as the original scheme had run into difficulties, improved upon as a result of first-hand experience.

Here then was something new in the world history of systematic colonisation: a systematic colony planned around the direct experience of the colonists themselves.

The centre of the original South Australian scheme had been to attract capitalists to the proposed colony by selling land, even in advance of settlement, in a concentrated geographic area at a price sufficient to ensure that the labourer did not immediately become a landowner, so guaranteeing a regular supply of labour; and then to use the total revenue thus raised from the sale of land to pay the cost of bringing in a steady stream of new immigrants – who would then wait their turn to become landowners themselves. Other costs, including the first costs of government, were to be financed from loans, repayable as the infant settlement generated its own income.

The aim of the new Northern Territory scheme was to attract capitalists in the same way: by selling land, some in advance of settlement, at a sufficient price in a concentrated geographic area, but then to use the increased revenue thus generated to pay *all the first costs of establishing the new colony.* The public cost of first establishing South Australia after 1836 was the point at which the original scheme had broken down, and, as colonials themselves, they could not now risk a repetition. The net result, it was claimed, would be a system even less expensive to the taxpayer than the pastoral colony suggested by Waterhouse.

The Wakefield Background

Behind the proposed legislation lay a genealogy of ideas and practices (half-remembered) going back to those of Edward Gibbon Wakefield and other systematic colonisers such as Robert Torrens

45 *Register* 2/10/1863 Parliamentary Proceedings. Hart, Ayers, Glyde seem to have led the opposition to taking over the Territory.

and Robert Gouger, who a generation before had developed the well-rounded theory of so-called Systematic Colonisation. By the 1860s only fragments of their theory were in use in South Australia – such as the sacred doctrine of survey before selection and the prejudice against large company colonisation. Also surviving were the leading immigrants Wakefield's ideas had originally attracted to South Australia who believed they did things in a superior way to other colonial Australians. Surviving, too, was an addiction to land speculation brought about by concentrated settlement.

Underlying the Northern Territory Bill now introduced into parliament lay two key principles, one pragmatic and the other more idealistic, which had caused problems between Wakefield and Torrens even in the 1830s. The first was the principle of a 'Self-Supporting Colony' emphasised by Torrens and Gouger in 1835 in an effort to reassure the Colonial Office that the proposed experimental colony of South Australia would never become a drain on the British taxpayer. Although it had failed and the British government had been forced to bail out the colony in 1842, the experience gained was now thought sufficient to make a self-supporting colony work in the future. Wakefield had distrusted emphasis on a self-supporting system because he felt it detracted from more important aspects of his theory. especially the key principle of 'Concentrated Settlement' – what Bentham called the 'dispersion preventing principle' – made famous by Wakefield between 1829 and 1834 in a series of persuasive books and articles. It was an idea that had survived in South Australia which, as it happened, was well-suited to concentrated development, with its rich agricultural land to the north, south and east of Adelaide, hemmed in by a vast dry hinterland.

Because by the 1860s there was little interest left in Wakefield's theories as a whole, it is doubtful if many politicians understood the full implications of the legislation they were now passing – and what legal responsibilities they were letting themselves in for.

Wakefield had been part of a revolutionary movement in the early 19th century which saw the private ownership of land by individuals – what Adam Smith called 'the sacred rights of private property' – as the key to great social progress, providing the right formula was found for sub-dividing, selling and developing this precious commodity. It was revolutionary because it marked the final victory of private ownership over the European traditions of common land and land held on trust. Wakefield and his followers believed this private ownership could be used to found a model colonial society providing the land could be disposed of and mixed with capital and labour in exactly the right formula, leading to a 'New British Empire'. For Wakefield the key to getting these three elements of land, capital and labour in a perfect relationship was the principle of concentration – though one suspects that he used the word in several overlapping senses. Failing to recognise different meanings of the word 'science', Wakefield apparently thought he had produced a true science with precise powers of prediction.[46]

By concentrating the settlement in a limited prescribed area he hoped to attract capitalists who would purchase land secure in the belief that their assets would keep increasing in value due to the forced development and concentrated division of labour around them. By then fixing the price of this land in a concentrated area at a carefully calculated 'Uniform and Sufficient Price' (calculated according to the Golden Mean) he hoped to use the increased revenue generated to bring in superior labourers in the right numbers – particularly young married couples in the prime of life – instead of shovelling out the paupers and convicts of England, which was the common practice – especially in places like New South Wales. By maintaining this sufficient price at a level just above the reach of these superior immigrants he then hoped to guarantee a regular supply of quality labour for the capitalist. Yet the price would not be so high as to prevent the hard-working thrifty labourer, after serving and saving for several years, stepping up the class ladder to join the small landowner class. And so there would be a constant renewal in the investment of capital and the supply of labour through the careful control of the sale of land. By preventing too much dispersion he hoped to short-circuit the

46 In early South Australia the predicted perfect relationship between land, labour and capital never eventuated – the import of labour outstripped the survey of land, while many capitalists failed to develop their property, preferring instead to sit on it for speculation. That is, when put to the test, land, labour and capital acted as separate variables not a system. See J.D. Young, 'South Australian Historians and Wakefield's Scheme', *Historical Studies*, Melbourne, October 1969.

years of pioneering barbarism conspicuous in North America and eastern Australia because the instruments of civilisation such as the school, the chapel and the rule of law could be established from the start with the frontiers of settlement. It also made it possible to plan the lay-out of the landscape, including reserves for the indigenous people, in a rational way. The result would be a new kind of society that took from the Old and the New Worlds, all that was orderly, socially mobile and civilised, avoiding the inequities of the Old World as well as the dislocations and crass materialism of the New. Only when this new social substructure was firmly in place and the population had reached a certain size, would the new colonials be given the right to rule themselves, self-government being a precondition for all future progress in a civilised society. At its most ambitious it would be a kind of petty bourgeois utopia at a time when utopias were in fashion.

Such a theory implied considerable government supervision, especially at the beginning, much more than most politicians considering the legislation in 1863 anticipated.

This was Wakefield's social vision – much grander in scale than just a method of colonisation. But in the view of his famous critic Karl Marx, Wakefield misunderstood the true nature of capitalism. Writing in *Das Kapital* Marx argued that the whole scheme was an attempt to manufacture the wage-labour system in the colonies. The 'Sufficient Price' was 'a euphemistic circumlocution for the ransom which the labourer pays to the capitalist'. Marx shared with Wakefield belief in certain revolutionary starting points such as the growing polarisation of society in England and the need to get the social and economic substructures right. But whereas one turned to socialism for the solution, the other hoped to make use of the violent up-rooting of emigration to a new land to set up an ethically superior form of capitalism.

Finally, as a kind of second-order benefit – and here the ideas of concentration and a self-supporting colony begin to merge – the advantages of getting land early under conditions of forced concentration were so great that some colonists could be induced to purchase blocks *in advance*, even before the settlement took place, instead of waiting as usual to see where and how the wind blew. The parent government could therefore play absolutely safe

Karl Marx who thought that Wakefield misunderstood the true nature of capitalism.

by avoiding any steps towards colonisation until there was money in hand to pay for it. The self-supporting system would be self-supporting from the start. It was this last benefit that particularly appealed to Hart and the planners of 1863.

Among the ministry now steering the legislation through parliament, there is no doubt that the main architect of the new Northern Territory scheme was the 'other premier' Captain John Hart, who had acted as a navigation adviser to Colonel Light in 1835 and knew the South Australian experiment well. Hart's approach was pragmatic. Having originally opposed the acquisition of the Territory his main interest now was in a self-supporting colony that would not put a burden on taxpayers. And if the self-supporting colony happened to make money for him (and others) then that was a bonus.

Plan in Detail – in Parliament

The second reading of the Bill was introduced in the House of Assembly on 13 October 1863 by Lavington Glyde, opposer of pastoralists because he thought they wanted to turn South Australia into one big sheep station. Most members seem not to have studied the Bill in advance, and it was left to the *Register* and *Advertiser* newspapers on the following day to provide the commentary and to consider the main details of the legislation.

With a view to gaining money in advance the original South Australian practice of taking preliminary orders for lands so as to give first and cheapest access to them would now be revived. The first offering would be 781 lots in Adelaide and the same number offered at the same time in London, entitling each acceptor to a 160-acre country block plus a half-acre city block at the never-to-be-repeated price of 7 shillings and 6 pence an acre. This was to be followed by a second offer in Adelaide and London of 781 lots, with the same conditions but at 12 shillings an acre, after which land would be disposed of in the customary way at less advantageous rates. Given the wages of the time, all blocks were thus well beyond the reach of the typical South Australian worker. The size of the blocks had also been carefully chosen so as not to be attractive to South Australian farmers. As those getting hold of the best-placed parcels of land could look forward to a ten or even hundred-fold increase in value, the order of choice first for city and then for country blocks was to be decided scrupulously by casting lots. If this sounds suspiciously like a lottery it is worth noting that questions were asked about whether the ballot infringed the colony's gambling laws.

Those who decided to wait as long as they could before they made a choice, must do so inside five years. This five-year limit was seen as a great improvement. It was intended to catch out the likes of those preliminary buyers in earlier South Australia who, without regard for the spirit of the enterprise, had deliberately waited for many years then used their preliminary purchase orders to claim choice spots as the country was opened up. As events turned out, it caught only the catchers themselves.

The revenues thus gained from the sale of land were to be deployed solely for the day-by-day administration (especially in setting up the colony), the general improvement of the colony, and to meet a five per cent (finally 10 per cent) commission on all public incomes charged by the home colony to cover its costs. The self-supporting system was thus taken a step further. Instead of South Australia paying for the Territory, the Territory had now to pay South Australia for the privilege of being colonised. The distribution of the money would have seemed to Wakefield, who had died a year earlier in New Zealand, a rank heresy. It was he who had led the insistence that *all* income from land should be spent on immigration, so much so that the infant South Australia started out with too many migrants and starved of funds for surveying and various government services. In fact, by 1841 the government in South Australia was bankrupt. By emphasising public finances the planners now tried to patch up the weakness in the original South Australian experiment but at the expense of its real strength – the provision of superior immigration. Some purists saw it as the final rejection of the central principle of Wakefield's philosophy.

The new planners, however, did not believe they were neglecting immigrants any more than Wakefield himself. They fixed the price of land 'at a sufficient price', minus the cost of the landholders importing their *own* workers as the need arose. This had several advantages over the former South Australian practice. It avoided risking a repetition of the unemployment in early Adelaide when the importation of labourers outstripped the speed of surveying and the desire of land-owners to employ them. It lessened the chances of parent and child colony bidding against each other for settlers, for the northern planter would tend to employ the nearer Indonesians (to use a term before its time) and Asians to the north. About the same time, it was noted with enthusiasm in Adelaide, the Dutch were developing the Netherlands India line around the Indies, along which plantation owners with their workers could gravitate down to Australia.

Though the members of the government thought they had provided for all the needs of immigration, the first serious outside criticism of their scheme, in eastern colonies and British newspapers, focused on the lack of specific provision for migrants. The decision to abandon the so-called Wakefield Principle, meaning the expenditure of *all* the land money for immigration, followed changes already made in South Australia proper in 1862 when Sutherland's Act reduced to a third the amount of money from the sale of public land that could be spent on immigration, the remainder to be spent on public works.

The reception in the Lower House – the House of Assembly – to the Northern Territory Plan was very restrained. It was damned with faint praise. Members followed the complicated scheme to the point of it costing the parent colony nothing and then lost interest. The only opposition came from several lawyers who tried to prove that the House was wasting its time, that having received the Territory lands only by Letters Patent they had insufficient legal authority to sell off land in this way. In the *South Australia Act* of 1834 the governor of South Australia had been restricted to set boundaries and nothing short of a special Act of the Imperial Parliament could change the situation. Unimpressed, the laymen of the House decided that even if the Duke of Newcastle did not give them full power to colonise the Territory, that was his intention and for practical purposes the intention was as good as law.[47]

In the Legislative Council the former chief minister, or premier, Waterhouse, complained that the Bill did not reflect his intention when asking for the Territory, nor Newcastle's intention in giving it to them and, in fact, it amounted to a breach of faith with the home government. He saw the annexation as 'provisional'. He believed that Newcastle decided to hand over the Territory only after Nicholson had startled him with the prospect of Queensland's pastoralists about to invade a No Man's Land. Waterhouse claimed his government, interpreting Newcastle's wishes, had intended to do no more than supervise the spread of stock in a manner similar to northern South Australia, using revenue from rents to pay for law and order. It was never its policy to sell the lands, least of all in a speculative way. He believed, too, there would be difficulties in getting settlers when vast tracts of unopened tropical land abounded elsewhere in the world and with labour at hand. Waterhouse's original hope of benefiting from the Territory's pastoral industry had come to a sudden halt.

Most honourable members in the Council House followed the lead of Waterhouse. Between them they predicted nearly every catastrophe which later overtook the Northern Territory Plan. Some wanted to seek Newcastle's approval before starting out on such a course. To ensure South Australia against loss in the possible event of failure, they increased the colony's commission to an exorbitant ten per cent and then passed the Bill.[48] It was honoured with the

47 *Register* 14/10/1863 Parliamentary Proceedings and leader; *Advertiser* 14/10/1863 Parliamentary Proceedings with leader.

48 *Register* 5/11/1863; 6/11/1863 Parliamentary Proceedings; *Advertiser* 5/11/1863; 6/11/1863 Parliamentary Proceedings.

governor's stamp on the 12 November 1863.[49] In the same month the colony's agent-general in London, Gregory Walters, was instructed to arrange for the first round of preliminary sales.

The doubts did not stop. When he sent the legislation to London, Governor Daly expressed concern over the self supporting principle – which he thought had been adopted by the legislature because of fears over whether the colony's finances could carry the extra load.[50] When details of the legislation became public in London there was conjecture about Newcastle approaching the Queen to have it disallowed. And there were renewed concerns as to whether under the terms of the Letters Patent South Australia had the legal right to sell the land even before settlement took place. Fearing that unless these rumours were stopped at once the plan was doomed, the agent-general and his London advisers decided to go straight to the Colonial Office for guidance.

Newcastle with characteristic caution called in his advisers, the Colonial Land and Emigration Commissioners, to report on the Act before he himself passed an opinion.[51] In their considered report the commissioners advised that South Australia under the terms of the annexation had the right to do whatever it liked with the Territory lands, but they warned Newcastle to make it plain that the colony alone was responsible for the consequences.[52] When Ayers and Hart heard that the agent-general, a mere public servant, had by-passed the governor and sought advice directly from the Colonial Office they were embarrassed, particularly because the Colonial Office took the doubts seriously.[53] But Governor Daly's reprimand was mild, forced on him by his advisers, and the Colonial Office praised Walters for his initiative.[54]

With the approach of summer 1863 parliament went into recess and the Northern Territory Plan could be unpinned from the drawing board. For Ayers and Hart it was a welcome haven; several times they were almost defeated by Waterhouse and the Opposition

---

49 S.A.P.A. 23 of 1863.

50 Daly to Newcastle 26/11/1863 (G.O.D. [Governor's out despatch] 76 of 1863).

51 Walters to Glyde 15/1/1864 with enclosures (S.A.P.P. 89 of 1865, pp. 77, 78, 79).

52 Emigration Board report 26/1/1864 (C.O. 13/116 Folio 39 *seq.*).

53 Glyde to Walters 26/3/1864 (S.A.P.P. 89 of 1865, p. 79).

54 Daly to Newcastle 24/3/1864 with Minutes (C.O. 13/114 Folio 153 *seq.*).

who attacked them on a range of policies. As the detailed planning got under way the Adelaide planners, especially Hart and Ayers, disagreed over the question of the site. At the time the Territory was thought to comprise three natural regions: the dry interior, the so-called 'Home of the Hot Winds'; the pastoral grasslands extending around the Victoria River; and Arnhem Land (especially North-West Arnhem Land) suitable for tropical agriculture.[55] Arnhem Land (sometimes called Arnhem Peninsula) was a key concept in 19th-century thinking about the north coast. It reached out towards the Indies and included most of the country above the Victoria River on one side and the Roper River on the other.[56] The Victoria River was the only region seriously considered as a pastoral colony. But once a concentrated agricultural settlement was considered attention moved in the direction of the Van Diemen Gulf area, on the north-west tip of Arnhem Land, nearest the Indies. This left the two Spartan kings moving in contrary directions, Ayers favouring Arnhem Land and Hart, who had sympathies towards the pastoralists, stubbornly supporting the Victoria River.

Ayers chose North-West Arnhem Land because he was convinced that it was a natural extension of the Indies Archipelago down which migrants would 'naturally flow' in a kind of gravitation. The *Register* called it a 'spontaneous migration' from the north to the south (that is from the top of the globe to the bottom), and from over-populated areas to under-populated areas.[57] Malay sailors were already known to come there. Also he assumed that the climate and soil was much like Java due to its location on the southern perimeter of the Indies. First he had to persuade his Cabinet.

In January 1864 a stroke of luck came Ayers' way: George Windsor Earl arrived in Adelaide with his wife and daughter

---

55 *Register* 5/11/1863 Waterhouse's speech in Parliamentary Proceedings.

56 I have decided to keep this 19th century construction of geography because it was so central to planning. Distinguish from modern Arnhem Land. Because of a professional interest in the history of ideas, throughout this book I have selectively used 19th century discourses, for example on geography and race, to communicate contemporary constructions of reality.

57 The emphasis on 'natural flow' is an example of the 'bewitchment of language', caused by using words like 'top' and 'bottom' of the world; *Register* 31/3/1864, p. 2. In answer to the London *Examiner*'s criticism of a lack of provision for migrants.

from the Straits Settlements, allegedly for the benefits of his health. Earl had been Commissioner of Crown Lands and collector of information in the former Port Essington settlement on the north coast and was considered *the* world authority on questions of North Australian colonisation. In 1846 he had published a book based on his experiences there.[58] In 1862, hearing of the revived interest, he published a sequel: a detailed handbook for intending colonists.[59] He was also an authority on the Indies Archipelago, stretching from Indochina to North Australia, which he saw as one great natural region – sometimes called by others The Asiatic Mediterranean. His book *The Eastern Seas* (1837) was, and still is, considered a classic on the subject.[60]

At the time the geographic concept of the Indies – incorporating the Indies Archipelago reaching from the Malay States to Timor and including India itself – was seen as a place of magic, abounding with spices, exotica and almost unlimited potential.

Earl could set South Australian minds at rest on many scores. He could explain away the failures of the three earlier British outposts in North Australia: at Melville Island, Raffles Bay and Port Essington (the first two failed in the 1820s and the third in the 1840s) as spurious attempts and hence unfair tests of its potential. He could quote the Colonial Office telling the officers quietly to discourage settlers to Port Essington so that it would stay an inexpensive outpost against trespassers. He promised that North Australia had unlimited opportunities for labour: Indians for herdsmen, horse keepers and shepherds; Chinese for agriculture

---

58 G.W. Earl, *Enterprise in Tropical Australia*, Madden & Malcolm, London, 1846; see also R.H.W. Reece, 'Introduction' in G.W. Earl, *Enterprise in Tropical Australia*, Northern Territory University Press, Darwin, 1846 (reprinted 2002).

59 G.W. Earl, 'A Handbook for Colonists in Tropical Australia', *The Journal of the Indian Archipelago and Eastern Asia* Vol. IV Pt. I, ed J. Logan, Penang, 1862.

60 Contemporary names which conceptually joined Australia and the Indies Archipelago together were 'Austral India', 'Austral Asia' and 'Australind' (and much earlier 'Java La Grande' and 'Java Major'). The idea that parts of North Australia are on the southern end of the archipelago is still taught in some Indonesian schools. For a recent edition of Earl's book see G.W. Earl with introduction by C.M. Turnbull, *The Eastern Seas*, Oxford University Press, Singapore, 1971.

The noble head of George Windsor Earl, Britain's expert on the Indies Archipelago. He recommended that the Finniss expedition should proceed direct to Adam Bay. (Courtesy of Earl's great great-grandson, Ranald Noel-Paton, Perthshire Scotland)

and business; Malays for labourers and fishermen.[61]

> When it is considered that the population of China is upwards of three hundred millions, that of the British possessions in India seventy millions, and that of the Indian Archipelago between twenty and thirty millions, it may be safely stated that the supply of labour from these sources is likely to prove inexhaustible.[62]

Most significantly he could show that North-West Arnhem Land better suited their plan because it jutted out towards the populous Indies and was most influenced by the tropics. He thought that cotton could become the early staple, for the demand was high and production low owing to the disruptions of the American Civil War.

Earl's authority steamrolled most people, but not Hart. The press (especially the *Register*) quoted him as an oracle. South Australia's official handbook for intending colonists (published in

61 I have kept the generic name Malay which was loosely used at the time for all the Malay speaking peoples of the Indies Archipelago and sometimes even more loosely used for any native inhabitant of the Indies Archipelago.

62 G.W. Earl, *Enterprise in Tropical Australia*, p. 127, a work often cited in 1863 and 1864.

November) repeated Earl's works copiously.[63] In February Ayers, having won over the rest of Cabinet, petitioned him to recommend a site and Earl drew up a detailed memorandum which pointed to Adam Bay on the estuary of the Adelaide River.[64] Hart then made a last effort to work upon the leader of the expedition, B.T. Finniss, to choose the Victoria River after he had been chosen by Cabinet to lead an expedition and to select a site.[65] The disagreement between Hart and Ayers was a serious weakness in the planning which later proved disastrous. In the end the Northern Territory expedition set out with members and investors beginning to have doubts about the best site for the capital.

After complaints six months earlier about the lack of provision for migrants, the confusion over the site caused a second round of outside criticism against South Australia's colonisation, especially in the eastern colonies, the Indies and the British press. Even Governor Richard MacDonnell was moved to criticise.[66] The criticisms were unpropitious because the South Australian prototype had shown how faith in the site was a first prerequisite for compact colonisation. In fact the scheme was premised on an excellent location acceptable to those who had risked their money in advance, and after settlement capable of attracting migrants and capital as the need arose. Having switched to attracting migrants from the nearby Indies, the government then made no effort to advertise the sale of land-orders in places like Calcutta and Batavia. Stranger still, they did not seriously advertise the sale in the other Australian colonies – probably because they wanted the benefits for themselves.

An Unequal Partnership

In 1835–1836 South Australia's preliminary land sales had shown that unless prospective buyers were confident of others buying they refused to risk their money. A certain density was needed before

63 *The Northern Territory of South Australia,* W.C. Cox Government Printer, Adelaide, 1863.

64 Memo: Recommending a site for new settlement on Northern Coast 29/4/1864 (C.S.O.I.L. $265^{1/2}$/1864).

65 B.T. Finniss's statement of his defence (State Records Finniss Papers, p. 32 G.R.G. 35/643/57).

66 *Register* 29/3/1864 leader; *Advertiser* 26/3/1864, p. 4.

the concentrated colony bore fruits. To meet this, in January 1836 a wealthy promoter named George Fife Angas formed almost single-handedly the South Australian Company which bought 13,700 acres of preliminary lands, advertised the new colony abroad and through many enterprises (particularly in land) succeeded in quickening the colony's pulse at the same time as making a profit. As no wealthy promoter was available in 1864 the individual ministers themselves had to go behind the scenes to see what they could encourage. Two companies were finally arranged: one to stimulate preliminary land sales in Adelaide and the other in London; each, like the South Australian Company, neither so weak as to be impotent nor so strong as to be a law unto itself, but substantial enough to become a *participating partner* in the business of colonisation. In their demand for something similar to the South Australian Company, the ministers even turned down outside offers of help. The powerful North Australian Association, seeking monopolistic land grants as in Africa, was rejected as too strong. Another company mooted by the artist and writer, William Cawthorne, was passed over as too weak because it concerned itself only with settling poor people using the co-operative principle. (Cawthorne later became famous for his early studies of the Kaurna people around Adelaide.)[67]

There were, however, two fundamental differences which made unlikely a partnership as agreeable as the alliance that had existed after 1836 between the colonial officers and the South Australian Company. Having been created by the action of the ministers, these two new companies started out with a bargaining power over successive South Australian governments that their precursor never held over the Colonial Office. Also, the 1860s proved a period of party instability during which 17 separate ministries occupied the treasury benches. As one wag wrote:

> Rejoice all ye who read my lay,
> The crisis now is o'er:
> And Ministries won't go astray,
> Till – they go wrong once more.[68]

---

67 *Register* 2/11/1863, p. 3; 9/11/1863, p. 2.

68 *Register* 25/7/1863, p. 2.

Party politics at the time was centred on factions loosely congregated around prominent politicians like Ayers, Hart, Waterhouse, and Strangways. With this kind of arrangement the possible political combinations, permutations and conspiracies were legion. Between July 1863, when the colony first received news of the annexation, and November 1868, when it was finally decided to send George Goyder straight to Port Darwin, governments changed at an average rate of every 177 days – which led the founding father, George Fife Angas, to complain that self-government had been the ruination of the colony. The various ministries were insecure, timid and divided against themselves and never a fit match for the single-minded company directors bonded in a common desire to make money. From the first the alliance between company and government augured to become an unequal partnership.

The Northern Territory Company was formed behind the scenes to act as a secret stimulus by Ayers, Hart and others to help the first round of preliminary land sales held in Adelaide between 1 and 29 March 1864. There were 781 lots offered in Adelaide, and the same number at the same time in London. The opening day of the Adelaide market started well when about half of all the lots eventually ordered were applied for by local and some English land buyers.[69] Fifty-three were taken out under the name of the Thorngate family of England. As a private investor Hart took ten. No sooner did the newspapers begin boasting in anticipation and the ministry decide it was safe to fit out an expedition than the demand almost ceased. However the clandestine company, under the guise of private names like Levi and Ayers, continued to buy until all up it had taken out 150 orders for 24,075 acres. At the end of sales about 40 allotments still remained untouched,[70] and the ministry was left with the consolation that its foresight had saved the sales from complete dishonour. It did not risk its luck by putting on the market in Adelaide the second lot of preliminary lands provided for by the Act.

---

69 *Register* 2/3/1864 leader also p. 3; 30/3/1864, p. 2. Details about the formation of the company are still unclear. For information about the Thorngate's links to South Australia see Churcher v. Martin, 1889, Supreme Court, Vol. XLII – courtesy of Vern O'Brien.

70 For final list see: *Register* 16/5/1870, p. 6; Purchasers of Northern Territory Allotments (S.A.P.P. 104 of 1866–1867).

A few days after sales closed the underground Northern Territory Company emerged, like a mole, into the open and the promoters met in the Mining Association's rooms to elect a committee to draft its rules. Those chosen included Hart, who presided, Ayers, Samuel Tomkinson (a banker) and two leading members of the Pastoral Association, Thomas Elder and Philip Levi. Two other members were Arthur Blyth (a founder of the Adelaide Club) who would soon join the government as Commissioner of Crown Lands and immigration, and Thomas Graves who intended to trade with the East. The secretary was Clement Sabine, also secretary of the Pastoral Association. The only project foreshadowed at this stage was to overland stock and to take up large holdings on the north coast. The promoters boasted a respectable clientele which included most of Adelaide's first businessmen – many of whom had made their money from the Burra and Moonta copper mines and were looking for somewhere to invest it.[71] The lone voice of a land-order holder complained in the local newspapers of it being such a select club and called for an association of those excluded, such as small investors and the 'industrial classes'.[72]

The calling of a public meeting to approve the committee's drafted rules was delayed until May 1864, when news reached Adelaide of the success of the London sales. At the meeting Henry Ayers took the chair before an influential gathering and outlined the objectives of the proposed company. The first was to buy, lease and sell agricultural and pastoral lands, in the manner of the successful South Australian Company. The second was to lease and develop mines, for minerals, *especially gold*, were expected to abound up north. The third aim, after the dream of Chambers and others, was to purchase, breed and sell stock to Eastern markets. Four thousand £12 10/- shares were to be offered with the right to double the capital should the need arise. The two main productive enterprises were stated as stock-raising and mining. The prospectus was judiciously silent on the contentious question of importing migrants.[73]

Meanwhile in London, a council of advice formed by 'friends of South Australia' to help Agent-General Walters launch the first

71 *Register* 4/4/1864, p. 2.

72 *Register* 15/6/1864, p. 2.

73 *Register* 16/5/1864, p. 2.

George Kingston helped supervise the order of selection by lot of Preliminary Lands in South Australia in 1837. In 1864 he did much the same for the Northern Territory. (George E. Loyau, *Representative Men of South Australia*, Howell, Adelaide, 1882, wood engraving by Jeffrey Bruer)

round of preliminary sales there, had saved the other half of the land sales from a similar dishonour. As in Adelaide, there was a good start in March when old friends of the colony took up most of 151 allotments purchased. But then the sales flagged sensationally and it became clear that the time had passed when English speculators grew excited over distant colonisation projects. Walters, fearing that complete failure would damage South Australia's reputation on the loan market, consulted the council of advice he had formed consisting of other prominent South Australians then resident in London – particularly Alex Elder (whose brother Tom took a leading part in the Adelaide company), Captain Bagot, George Anstey and Governor MacDonnell – and it was agreed to launch 'a provisional company' to give an artificial impetus to the sales.[74] Elder and Bagot had made a fortune in South Australia from copper mining and pastoral pursuits and had returned to

74 Walters to Glyde 23/3/1864 (S.A.P.P. 89 of 1865, p. 82); *Register* 23/11/1867, p. 2. Anstey's account of formation of the North Australian Company; Research Notes Shirley Thamm of the Burra Historical Society 2/8/2006. Walters was South Australia's first agent-general.

London as successful colonials. In 1863 Bagot even published a book emphasising to the British *The National Importance of Emigration*. The ambition of the company was to publicise itself noisily in the hope that it would never be formed. If private English investors could be persuaded by news of the proposed company into taking out all the preliminary 781 offers, then the promoters would quietly abandon the company. Here was a land sales promotion in contrast to the more secretive methods associated with the Adelaide group.

The advertised company got away to a good start, though not so early in March 1864 as the promoters would have liked. MacDonnell, prior to taking up an appointment as acting governor in Nova Scotia and soon after that governor in Hong Kong, attached his name as first chairman of directors. The capital was fixed at a respectable £200,000 (in £10 shares), equal in size to the original South Australian Company of 1836 and four times the opening capital of its Adelaide counterpart. Its stated object was to act as agent for absentees investing in the new territory. This was a much-needed amenity because the problem of finding agents to represent the interests of investors was known to deter them from investing in the colonies. The company also intended to take up land and resell it when the virgin wastes blossomed as the head of an overland telegraph and export trade. As advertising the actual sale was their main concern at this stage, they appeared very optimistic.

Meanwhile, Agent-General Walters (close friend of Captain Hart and a former smelting authority and managing director of the Patent Copper Company, Burra, who in London gave most of his services free) set to work with scissors and paste making sure that the British newspapers got the right (expurgated) picture of the Northern Territory's prospects. He tried hard to win over the snubbed North Australian Association by inviting its honorary secretary, Professor Edward Oppen, to prepare a handbook giving information about the Territory and the proposed company. The booklet stressed South Australian's fine record as colonisers and the special situation of North Australia; facing Asia it was the least isolated of all the British colonies in the south and confronted a vast labour potential.[75] Walters was so intent for Oppen to say

75 E.A. Oppen, *A Description of the Northern Territory of South Australia*, Austin, Hertford, 1864.

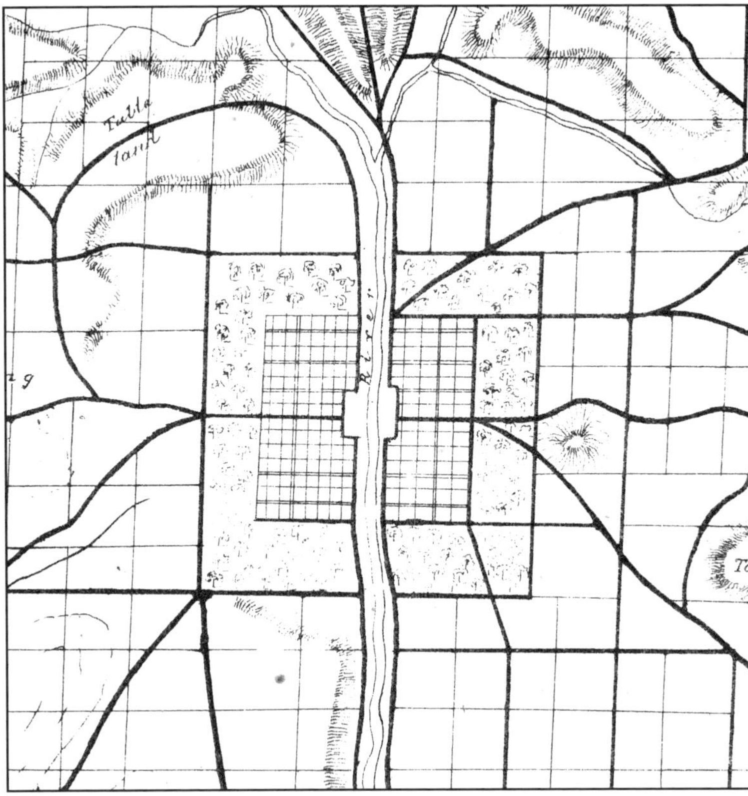

An example of the South Australian habit of following precedents laid down during its foundation in the 1830s. The proposal for the northern capital, based on the Adelaide city square with a large river down the equivalent of King William Street big enough to carry ocean-going shipping. (S.A.P.P. 36 of 1864)

these things that he offered to pay him from his own pocket should Cabinet disapprove.[76]

The publicity did succeed in reviving the becalmed sales, but time ran out. More than 40 per cent still remained unsold at the end of March, and the North Australian Company then entered the market taking out 328 land-orders. Many of the buyers attracted, independently or in company shares, were not astute speculators but unsophisticated investors who trusted implicitly in the counsel of men like Anstey, Bagot and Elder. The directors had staked their

76 Walters to Glyde 23/3/1864 (S.A.P.P. 89 of 1865, p. 82); *Register* 23/11/1867, p. 2. Anstey at deputation to Chief Secretary.

personal reputations on delivering quality land in a good location.[77]

Once forced into existence, the London company took the initiative from its Adelaide counterpart. In June the directors broached the question of sending out a vessel with migrants and goods to the new country. This, the agent-general pointed out, would have caused a 'sensation'. Unaware that the government in Adelaide had decided not to offer the second lot of preliminary lands, he had made the mistake of putting the second 781 preliminary blocks on the market and only one had been sold (eventually two were sold). The good intention was short lived. Agent-General Walters held no authority to help the directors arrange for emigrants and the directors had no site to which to send the vessel.[78] Once the drama of the Northern Territory began to unfold there was no more mention of sending out migrant ships. Another important step taken by the London directors was for an amalgamation with the Adelaide group by offering them 3000 of their 10,000 shares. The prospect of an amalgamation had always been in the wind. The London directors also wanted the Adelaide group to nominate suitable agents who could represent both parties in the Northern Territory, before they laid on a ship to the new settlement.[79] Two names were suggested by the Adelaide directors, but beyond that little was done.

The only serious enterprise in which the two companies eventually joined forces was in a common, intense drive to get their money back without losing a single penny.

77 Walters to Glyde 25/4/1864 (S.A.P.P. 89 of 1865, p. 83); *Register* 23/11/1867, p. 2. Anstey at deputation to Chief Secretary.

78 Walters to Hart 22/6/1864 (Agent-General O.L. Volume III, p. 663).

79 *Register* 13/7/1864, p. 2.

CHAPTER 2

CAESAR AND HIS FORTUNE

> 'The large practical experience in colonization which Englishmen have had during the last century has left little to be learnt in the art of planting new settlements; and the pioneers who now sail for North Australia have acquired their knowledge of the subject in one of the best schools.'
>
> *Register,* 23 April 1864

By a circuitous route the representatives of South Australia had arrived at a 'plan'. How then did it work out?

The Banquet

By April 1864 the preparations were advanced and the government decided to launch the northern expedition with a banquet. They wanted a banquet for two main reasons: to gain public support for the colonisation venture, and to calm the recent rumours about the suitability of the men.

The rumours alone guaranteed a good attendance. To reduce costs the government had kept wages low and tried to attract skilled men on the understanding that they would get the first plums of office in the new settlement.

It was rumoured that the method had attracted instead a motley crowd of known individualists pushed forward by friends and relations above the leader's plea for more say in choosing his men, and that some officers in particular were totally unsuited. Many guests were sure to come to see the evidence for themselves.

Arrangements were made in the grand style. The date was set as 16 April. Invitations were issued, cuisine arranged, and a large marquee decked with flags and bunting was set up at Port Adelaide on the South Australian Company wharf beside the expedition's principal ship, the *Henry Ellis*. The government had called for tenders and the *Henry Ellis*, the tender of Elder Smith and Co., had won. Her master, John Philipps, had already taken several similar expeditions to the coast of Africa, or so it was claimed.

On the day of the event most of the 150 influential guests who had accepted – politicians, department heads, foreign consuls and gentlemen – were taken to the Port in royal fashion by a special train that was cheered along its route by straggling groups of well-wishers. The guests crowded under the large marquee like ants under a mushroom, and the celebration began.

The dinner ran the usual course, first the eating and drinking, then the speeches and toasts. The speakers each sought to justify what they were now celebrating by referring to South Australians' past endeavours. A colony with their achievements, said the governor, would make small fry of the Territory. South Australia had, said another, in proportion to its population 'produced greater results than any other country on the face of the earth'. It had also, suggested Henry Ayers and the governor, inspired Stuart to cross the continent. When the epic explorer's name was first mentioned by Ayers there was loud applause.

Not far away, probably sheltering at John Chambers' farm in nearby Richmond, the other Stuart – ill, alcoholic and excluded – was packing his bags to leave for England, where two years later he died. The story that he had been promised one of Chambers' daughters if he crossed the continent was never a possibility. Governor Daly also opposed him being given a knighthood because of his 'habits of intemperance'.

The company being farewelled consisted of one leader, 10 officers and 30 men, but to make room for the guests none of the men was allowed to attend. Because of the conflicts between officials and private settlers in early South Australia, private settlers had been excluded from the expedition. When it came to convincing the public about the new empire builders, the speakers found it difficult to maintain their tone of confidence. Most were anxious to counter accusations that jobbery had occurred in filling some of the best places. As the senior ranks alone were present, they in particular were the centre of attention. Captain Hart called them the 'Surveyor-Generals and Auditor-Generals and Registrar-Generals' of the future. One pioneer of 28 years standing urged

Boyle Travers Finniss, as he liked to be seen in 1864 – looking much younger than he really was. A product of that great age of conservatism that followed the French Revolution and an expert on the South Australian method of colonisation. (*Illustrated Melbourne Post* 25/5/1864, p. 4. Courtesy of the State Library of South Australia)

them to follow the example of his generation, who 'drew the sword and cast away the scabbard'. Even the leader eventually got carried away and trapped himself into praising his officers and men. He later came to bite his tongue many times.

The leader of the expedition was Lieutenant Colonel Boyle Travers Finniss. His choice demonstrated the intention to follow out the South Australian system of planned colonisation. He was 56 and not a bushman, but no man alive had such an insight into the South Australian experiment. He was ideologically a conservative, a product of that so–called Age of Conservatism that followed the French Revolution, and a man of considerable principle. He sat at the head of the gathering with Ayers, Hart, the governor and several others, behind whom was painted an old Latin proverb, turned into a pun, which read: FINIS CORONAT OPUS (the end – that is Finniss – crowns the work).[80]

Finniss's task was to choose an ideal site for a capital which would set the scheme in perpetual motion – at a time when the concept of perpetual motion was still a common idea.

Most of the after-dinner speakers could not resist referring to one or other of his achievements. Educated at Sandhurst Military College to become a gentleman officer, he seems never to have lost the soldier's reaction to a tight situation. At the foundation of South Australia in 1836, the colonisation commissioners had used him as their expert to teach intending settlers the arts of self-defence against Aborigines – a fortunate qualification now that the Territory faced a parallel situation and fierce Malay pirates were also thought to frequent the north coast. To take advantage of this skill the government had, on the previous day, made him a Lieutenant Colonel and before that fitted the expedition out as an expeditionary force. In the days leading up to the farewell, there had been two hours drill a day at the barracks, which was possibly why four of those chosen deserted. Finniss was also a first-class surveyor, again trained at Sandhurst, with three years army experience in Mauritius in tropical surveying with Indian convict gangs. In 1836 the young Finniss, having sold out of the army, joined Colonel William Light in laying out Adelaide and its surroundings – another fortunate qualification, seeing that the government intended to make the northern capital as much as possible like Adelaide and to lay out the land in a similar way to South Australia. Finniss was also a most industrious civil servant; though one famous contemporary considered him hard working but 'decidedly slow'.[81] In 1843, much of the surveying around Adelaide completed, he took up public office and became in turn commissioner of police, registrar-general and treasurer, colonial secretary, nominee legislative councillor, acting governor of South Australia and first chief minister (or premier) under self rule. Meanwhile, he had lived to see his friends grow rich while he slaved at his desk for his colony's good, but he

---

80 *Register* 18/4/1864 leader also p. 3; *Advertiser* 18/4/1864 leader also p. 3. For a quote by J.P. Boucaut describing them as 'pets of the government' see Boucaut to Finniss 26/10/1864 (S.L.S.A. Mortlock P.R.G. 527/148).

81 Torrens to Forster 16/5/1858 (S.L.S.A. Mortlock P.R.G. 526/6).

hoped to redress the mistake in the next colony he helped to found.[82]

The celebration had been held on a Saturday. On Monday the *Register* observed with pride:

> Mr Finniss now resumes in North Australia the task which he commenced twenty-eight years ago in South Australia.
>
> Like a shipbuilder who has already helped to turn out one noble vessel out of hand and has seen her sailing away on a prosperous voyage, he now prepares to lay the keel and to build up the sides of another.[83]

The second appointment announced to the press had been that of Ebenezer Ward, Finniss's right-hand man and confidential aide. His presence brought a tingle of excitement to the celebration. If jobbery had occurred, then he was the prize exhibit, being, so it was said, the special protégé of Cabinet itself.

Ward was such a fiery individualist that many doubted the wisdom of his going at all. He was a man not to be ignored, with 'eagle eye, combative nose, upstanding hair, defiant pose of the head, magnificent swagger, and frenzied gestures'.[84] If Adelaide society was dominated by an inner circle of businessmen, then Ward was the chief minister for all opposition. He saw himself as a liberal, perhaps even as a radical – particularly when it came to the land question – and spent a distinguished life testing himself against first his superiors, and later his equals. As a boy he had broken with devout parents who wanted to give their son to the church, run away to London and joined the godless worlds of journalism and the theatre. He went to Melbourne as a journalist in 1859, and as an actor he first came to Adelaide in 1860. He soon became the centre of scandal when he eloped with a 17-year-old girl – later he became one of the first public figures in South Australia to get a divorce.

---

82 *Observer* 30/12/1893, p. 15; Extracts from the Reminiscences of The Hon. Boyle Travers Finniss (S.L.S.A. Mortlock P.R.G. 527/1); B.T. Finniss Biographical Sketch by G.C. Morphett (S.L.S.A. Mortlock A891).

83 *Register* 18/4/1864 leader.

84 *Observer* 3/10/1891, p. 41.

List of the Officers and Men of the Northern Territory Expedition

Name	Appointment	Salary
		per annum
Boyle Travers Finniss	Government Resident	£1000
James Thomas Manton	Engineer and Surveyor	£500
Francis Edward Goldsmith	Surgeon and Protector of Aborigines	£400
Ebenezer Ward	Clerk in charge, Accountant, and Postmaster	£350
William Pearson	Surveyor	£350
Stephen King, Snr	Storekeeper and Superintendent of Stock	£280
John Davis	Assistant Storekeeper	£200
Richard Watson	Draftsman	£160
John William Ogilvie Bennett	Draftsman	£120
James Wadham	Junior Surveyor	£120
Arthur R. Hamilton	Junior Surveyor	£120
		per day
William McMinn	Chainman	6s.
Frank J. Packard	Chainman	6s.
T. Railton Atkinson	Chainman	6s.
Frederick Robe Finniss	Chainman	6s.
David Bowen Wiltshire	Chainman and Able Seaman	6s.
Charles W. Machell	Chainman and Able Seaman	6s.
Michael Edward Fitch	Chainman and Able Seaman	6s.
William Reid	Chainman and Able Seaman	6s.
William Moorshead	Carpenter	7s.
John Absolom Howe	Carpenter	7s.
Thomas Brennan	Blacksmith	7s.
Bastin Boucaut	Laborer	5s.
James Gilbert	Laborer	5s.
Robert J. Ware	Laborer	5s.
John F. Roberts	Laborer	5s.
William Stephen Murray	Laborer	5s.
Charles Hake	Laborer	5s.
Frederick Henry Litchfield	Laborer	5s.
William Patrick Auld	Laborer	5s.
Heinrich Christian Conrad Baumgurtel	Laborer and Miner	5s.
Samuel Baker	Laborer	5s.
Alaric Ward	Laborer	5s.
Francis Edwards	Laborer	5s.
Henry Thomas Styles	Laborer	5s.
John Bohn	Laborer and Able Seaman	5s.

Thomas King	Laborer and Able Seaman	5s.
John Cowie	Shoemaker and Laborer	5s.
William Smith	Laborer	5s.
John Dyer	Laborer and Bullock Driver	5s.
Stephen Chandler	Laborer	5s.

The whole of the party under Mr Finniss have been enrolled under the Volunteer Act, and are to receive rations in addition to pay for twelve months, during which period they are severally bound by Agreement, to obey the orders and directions of the Government Resident.

Based on South Australian Parliamentary Paper 36 of 1864, p. 5.

In 1863 Ward joined the *Telegraph*, a minor Adelaide newspaper, as a sub-editor, and gave readers the first taste of his vitriolic pen.[85] He soon showed himself 'an extraordinary partisan' of the Ayers–Hart ministry which contrived the Northern Territory scheme. Throughout the latter half of the 1863 session he 'wrote the Opposition off their legs' and received credit for helping pilot the ministry through a treacherous session. Parliament in recess, the ubiquitous journalist turned his energies across the border. Prior to Treasurer Hart going to Melbourne and Sydney for a proposed inter-colonial conference on lighthouses, Ward went to Melbourne and promoted the South Australian politician in the press of both eastern capitals; when Hart proved a personal success, he sent back despatches telling what a figure the Treasurer had cut in the more established colonies. Later still, when sections of the Melbourne and Sydney press began to poke fun at the Northern Territory Plan he hastened to the government's aid by praising and explaining the scheme in eastern newspapers.[86] No doubt most saw which way Ward's mind tended, for he soon gained a reputation as an indefatigable seeker for public office. What they did not anticipate was the openness with which he received his reward when in 1864 he obtained a prized billet in the northern expedition. Mr Ward's energies in two colonies, noted another journalist, was doubtless the reason why he was thought worthy of a plurality of offices in the new Territory.[87]

Ward's appointment put the expedition's leader in a delicate

85 Ebenezer Ward Biography (S.L.S.A. Mortlock D7909(Misc), p. 13).

86 *Register* 22/6/1864 leader and Parliamentary Proceedings.

87 *Register* 22/6/1864 leader.

spot. Though he had right of veto, how could he refuse the protégé of Captain Hart and the ministry? From the first the ambitious young upstart seems to have irked Finniss. As early as December 1863 Ward took the liberty to introduce himself in a city street and to announce to Finniss the latter's appointment as Government Resident. As this was three months before appointments were due to be known, Finniss retorted that the young journalist appeared to have inside information to Cabinet secrets. The conversation which followed was later disputed, Ward claiming to have asked Finniss if there were objections to his applying for office, Finniss claiming that Ward actually introduced himself as the chief officer.[88] Whichever was true, the coming leader certainly suspected the young newspaper-man of being foisted upon him.[89] The suspicion grew as events unfolded. Soon after the meeting, Ebenezer Ward tendered a curt application without a single credential.[90] He then took himself off to Melbourne to sing the praises of the Treasurer. In March 1864 he was given the three key appointments of Clerk and Private Secretary, Accountant and Postmaster. This made young Ward, as Hart explained, the leader's right-hand man and confidential aide.[91] Perhaps Finniss could be pardoned for noticing just how convenient the arrangement was for spying on him. Later it was found that Ward did in fact supply Hart with secret private letters from the Northern Territory[92]; indeed, he even boasted of his special connection.[93]

As the preparations got under way, the leader grew to suspect that his clerk was not going to pull his weight. When work was most hectic Ward was still occupied in Melbourne with his family, and a temporary secretary had to be employed until he could be

88 *Register* 30/3/1868, pp. 2 and 3 Finniss's speech at Town Hall Meeting; South Australia Report of Commission to Inquire into the Management of the Northern Territory Expedition. Questions 1681; 1682; 1877 to 1883 (S.A.P.P. 17 of 1866–1867).

89 *Register* 30/3/1868, pp. 2 and 3 Finniss's speech at Town Hall Meeting.

90 Ward to Ayers 29/12/1863 (C.S.O.I.L. 1238/1863).

91 *Register* 30/3/1868, pp. 2 and 3 Finniss's speech at Town Hall Meeting.

92 Northern Territory Commission. Questions 1703 (S.A.P.P. 17 of 1866–1867).

93 Northern Territory Commission. Questions 1937 to 1943 (S.A.P.P. 17 of 1866–1867).

Ebenezer Ward with his eagle eye, combative nose and upstanding hair.
He spent a distinguished life crossing swords with someone or other.
(*Frearsons Weekly* 6/7/1878, p. 144. Courtesy of the State Library of South Australia)

brought at the beck of a telegram.[94] But the real clash between the two men occurred on the eve of departure, when the commander ordered all aboard for fear of infringing the *Henry Ellis*'s charter. Ward, in his usual devil-may-care manner, was indolent in obeying until Finniss sharply ordered him aboard in front of the other men.[95] Ward obeyed, but he did not forget the insult to an officer in the presence of the lower ranks.

Most politicians would have known of the circumstances surrounding Ward's appointment and of the tensions between the two men. But not until the *Henry Ellis* had left and was out of ear-shot did the criticisms break out in parliament. One elder statesman questioned the propriety of ever giving public positions to journalists, especially to one who smeared and vilified gentlemen in the Opposition. The *Telegraph* was branded a government organ,

94 Finniss to Ayers 9/3/1864 (C.S.O.I.L. 316/1864).

95 Northern Territory Commission. Questions 1705 to 1709; also p. XVIII (S.A.P.P. 17 of 1866–1867).

with the inference that the reputation of the whole press had been somehow compromised. Even the staid old *Register*, doyen of the newspapers, linked his name to Artemus Ward, the American humorist famous for 'putting his foot in it'.

In parliament Treasurer Hart tried his utmost to stem the criticisms, emphatically denying that Ward had ever been given special patronage. 'That this is true,' he vowed, 'I declare upon my …' But he did not finish the oath, and the House broke into loud laughter.[96]

No hint of these criticisms, however, was heard at the Grand Dinner of 16 April 1864, which was followed by a tour of inspection of the ship *Henry Ellis*, which in the words of the *Register* was to bear 'not only Caesar and his fortune, but the fate of this new colonization scheme'.

The celebration seems to have given satisfaction all round. It was particularly satisfying for Henry Ayers who, because he could not delegate, had arranged most of the expedition. There were toasts to the Queen, her family, the governor, Finniss, the officers present, local pioneers, and the chairman. 'God Save the Queen' was played three times and, for the Irish present, 'Saint Patrick's Day in the Morning' once. On Monday there was even a ceremony, attended mainly by the ladies, to christen the life-boat which was called *Julia*, after the Government Resident's daughter. The only public complaint came from people worried that the gathering had forgotten to thank a Higher Power for the blessing they were about to receive.

'Thus ended' wrote the *Register*, 'a demonstration to the men on whom the attention of thousands is concentred, and on whose success or failure will probably depend the future of the vast territories in the North.'[97]

First Northern Territory Expedition: 1864

Three vessels were laid on to carry Caesar and his fortune and the fate of the Northern Territory expedition. Each was despatched separately for an agreed rendezvous at Adam Bay, though Finniss wanted them to proceed as a fleet.

96 *Register* 22/6/1864 leader and Parliamentary Proceedings.

97 *Register* 18/4/1864, p. 3; *S.A. Government Gazette* 19/4/1864, pp. 313–327 for a detailed list of instructions given to the expedition.

First there was a surveying schooner, the *Beatrice*, jointly owned by South Australia and the British Admiralty and reluctantly released by the Admiralty to aid in finding a suitable port. She arrived at Adam Bay on 31 May 1864 after an uneventful journey by the quicker east-coast route. Thirty-two miles up the Adelaide River its crew was welcomed by local Aborigines 'throwing themselves in all manner of shapes and singing "Semoy, Semoy" at the very tops of their voices'. While awaiting the main expedition the *Beatrice*'s commander, Captain John Hutchison – who held a medal for distinguished sailing in the Arctic region – busied himself on preliminary duties, sounding out Adam Bay at the mouth of the river, surveying up the Adelaide River for more than 50 miles, and exploring friendly relations with the local Djerimanga or Woolna people. To break the ice the crew staged a concert complete with tin whistle, fiddle, concertina and drums. They also taught the Aborigines how to do jigs and polkas.[98]

Three weeks later on 21 June, the principal vessel, the *Henry Ellis*, entered the bay, having come by the western route after insurance companies had refused to insure its passage through Torres Strait.[99]

The voyage of the *Henry Ellis* had been more eventful. More than half of the expedition's 150 sheep smothered in the holds and had to be consigned at regular intervals to watery graves.[100] Then an epidemic of insubordination erupted in the calm horse latitudes off the Western Australian coast, the crew taking exception to the brutal behaviour of the Yankee mate and striking twice before being ordered below on bread and water.[101] The first signs of a dissident

98 Extract from the Remark Book of Her Majesty's Surveying Schooner 'Beatrice' whilst employed in the Northern Territory of South Australia, in 1864 (S.A.P.P. 18 of 1865). For a quotation on meeting the Aborigines see the Journal of Alfred Charles Webling 4/6/1864 (S.L.S.A. Mortlock D3058/1(L)). Woolna was the common name used by the Europeans. All names of Aboriginal groups and individuals in the records are very approximate.

99 F. Finniss: Recollections of the First Expedition to the Northern Territory, paper II (State Records Finniss Papers G.R.G. 35/643/292).

100 Ebenezer Ward's Official Journal 23/3/1864 to 21/6/1864 *passim* (S.A.P.P. 89 of 1865, pp. 10, 11, 12).

101 Ebenezer Ward's Official Journal 29/5/1864 *seq.* (S.A.P.P. 89 of 1865); F. Finniss: Recollections of the First Expedition to the Northern Territory,

spirit appeared too among the members of the expedition, over the mildly contentious question of military exercises. Finniss thought the calms beyond Cape Leeuwin at the south-west corner of the continent provided an excellent opportunity to improve the shoddy skills of his force and test out his arsenal of weapons, so he set them to work, dressed in their red garibaldis, with drill in squads of ten, sword fighting and shooting at a target astern. A few felt this a genuine hardship, arguing that the brilliance of their uniforms combined with the roll of the ship made fools of them before the captain's wife and crew, though one old Trafalgar veteran thought they went out of their way to exaggerate the staggering.[102] The disaffected few tried to infect the others by renaming the colonel the B.T.F., or Bloody Tom Fool.[103] On the positive side, the expeditioners did manage one edition of a hand-written newspaper, the *Northern Pioneer.* Then, to cap off irritations, the *Henry Ellis* became stuck on a reef in sight of Adam Bay on 20 June and took on a precarious list at low tide, so that the men, unaccustomed to the vagaries of the sea, could not stand up without hanging on to a rail. Eventually the vessel was freed,[104] but the accident made the captain so conscious of reefs that he refused to unload close in to shore, even where it was shown to be safe, so that most of the stock had to be taken ashore via the *Beatrice.*

The last and smallest vessel, the schooner *Yatala* under Captain Francis Humbert (former chief officer of the *Henry Ellis*), who had experience in the Indies, was a run-about ship for making quick contacts with the outside world, especially nearby Koepang in Timor. She hobbled into Adam Bay on the 29 June without her rudder and false keel. Coming via the eastern route, she had gone aground on Cobourg Peninsula, which Finniss complained was about the best-charted part of the coast. A few months later, when time allowed in October, the *Beatrice* gingerly escorted her for

paper II (State Records Finniss Papers G.R.G. 35/643/292).

102 Northern Territory Commission. Question 3687 (S.A.P.P. 17 of 1866–1867).

103 Northern Territory Commission Questions 1781 to 1789. (S.A.P.P. 17 of 1866–1867).

104 Ebenezer Ward's Official Journal 20/6/1864 (S.A.P.P. 89 of 1865, p. 12); F. Finniss's Recollections of the First Expedition to the Northern Territory Paper III (State Records Finniss Papers G.R.G. 35/643 /292). Because of the mishap, the date of arrival is open to different interpretations.

repairs to Timor[105], where she fell to pieces on the beach and was sold for scrap. The expedition had not made a confident start.

Finniss's first pressing need on reaching Adam Bay at the mouth of the Adelaide River was to uncover a well-watered place for the rest of the stock before they went the way of the wasted sheep. As Captain Hutchison had failed to find good water, except on the fresh-water reaches beyond the influence of the saltwater tides, Finniss decided to make a temporary depot about 40 miles upstream, near where the explorer Stuart claimed to have passed along the river. With the shipping at hand, this made unloading a hazardous and drawn-out business. The master of the *Henry Ellis* refused point-blank to move inside the river unless Finniss would indemnify his ship, the crippled *Yatala* staggered and lumbered from one bank to the other, and the lion's share consequently fell on the British survey schooner *Beatrice*.[106] The first serious effect of these prolonged operations was that the *Henry Ellis* could not be discharged before her contract expired, a delay which cost £464 for another month's hire and cut well into Finniss's short allowance of ready money with which to pay his men.[107]

As soon as the animals were safely settled up the river, Finniss, with time to deliberate, chose a more convenient site near the mouth at Escape Cliffs which was easily accessible from the sea and above the markings left by the floods.[108] Thus for its first months the new colony on the north coast consisted of two depots: upriver under the second in command, James Thomas Manton who was backed by officers like Ebenezer Ward and Dr Francis Goldsmith, and downriver under Finniss himself.

So far the primitive needs of finding shelter and protection had kept the party working together like ants. 'Up to this time,' observed the Resident later, 'it would be difficult to accuse me of inertness or

---

105 Finniss to Ayers 10/8/1864 (S.A.P.P. 89 of 1865, p. 4).

106 Ebenezer Ward's Official Journal 21/6/1864 to 11/8/1864 (S.A.P.P. 89 of 1865, pp. 12 to 15); Finniss to Ayers 10/8/1864 (S.A.P.P. 89 of 1865, pp. 4 and 5); Northern Territory Commission Proceedings p. XVIII (S.A.P.P. 17 of 1866–1867).

107 Finniss to Ayers 6/10/1864 (S.A.P.P. 89 of 1865, p. 42). The lack of money was later seen as a deliberate strategy to prevent the men deserting.

108 Finniss to Ayers 10/8/1864 (S.A.P.P. 89 of 1865, pp. 4 and 5).

negligence.'[109] But once these first needs were met the differences of temperament sparked bitter feuds between the commander and his supporters on one side and the officers on the other. Soon all positive colonisation was paralysed.

In the period before relief arrived in December (about five months) these disputes centred on three main points of disagreement.

The first arose from a skirmish with the local Woolnas that took place at the upriver camp on the 9 August. The inter-linked tribes[110] between Van Diemen Gulf and the Gulf of Carpentaria had traded for at least two centuries with sailors from the port of Macassar in the East Indies who came in large numbers every year to fish for trepang. With these sailors the local people had established elaborate protocols. Even the inland tribes (according to E.O. Robinson, later collector of customs on Cobourg Peninsula) seemed to have well-established trade links with the Macassan fishers who they called 'Ballangers'.[111] As soon as the upriver camp was established the local Aborigines began to follow what appears to have been a pattern: first, two Aboriginal men visited the camp acting with studied decorum; next day 12 arrived and fraternised with the visitors; a few days after that 40 arrived, removing the Ballangers' property in an open and friendly manner; then 70 armed warriors arrived with their families, demonstrating how they could throw their light spears 150 to 200 yards; then finally with innumerable sounds, like poltergeists, they closed in around the camp at night.

The response of the Europeans was genuine alarm. Their preconception was that they were dealing with primitive people whose motives were far more elemental than their own.[112] Sentries

109 Northern Territory Commission Proceedings p. XIX (S.A.P.P. 17 of 1866–1867).

110 'Tribe' was the common English word used at the time for groups of Aborigines. I have used it sparingly because it has overtones of exclusiveness which does not match the Aboriginal pattern of interlocking language groups and family groups.

111 Robinson to Little 30/3/1882 (N.T.I.L. 346/1882). Ballanger probably from Hollander.

112 This was a time when the European sense of cultural superiority was at its height, partly due to their success with technology, including military technology. It was also a time when the new ideology of race was rising towards its peak, which ascribed all kinds of psychological attributes like savagery on one side and intelligence on the other to racial origins. Nowhere

were mounted and then doubled and a line put round the camp over which the Aborigines must not step. Before taking up his position permanently at the Escape Cliffs depot Government Resident Finniss left complicated military instructions turning the out-bush camp into a barracks:

> A guard, consisting of a sergeant and three privates of volunteers, will mount guard every day in front of the tent of the Government Resident …
>
> When the guard is relieved, the men will discharge their pieces at a target for practice, and then carefully clean their rifles.
>
> Sentries will challenge all persons approaching their post between sunset and sunrise.
>
> The answer should be 'Friend'.
>
> The sentry then calls out in a loud voice 'Pass friend, and all's well'.[113]

The ceremony was not wasted. Watching through the mangroves the Aborigines, who liked to laugh at the unusual customs of the visitors by mimicking them, were soon marching up and down too, with sticks over their shoulders.

The end came tragically in a brief trial of strength, about six weeks after the upriver camp was made. During the day of 8 August some Woolna men showed interest in bags of grain and flour placed on the bank for return downriver but were deterred from handling the bags by armed guards. At evening the Woolnas disappeared and Manton foolishly removed the guards. No time, and the obvious had happened. Barely half an hour later two of the party caught a crowd of eager Aborigines slashing open the food sacks and promptly opened fire.[114]

Next morning a horse party was organised to retrieve

---

in the numerous references consulted on early contact with the indigenous peoples in the Territory is there the slightest inkling by the invaders that they were confronting a society as complex as their own. As an example, not even did they hear their ancient deeply moving music as anything more than noise.

113 Ebenezer Ward's Official Journal 2/7/1864 to 11/7/1864 (S.A.P.P. 89 of 1865, p. 13); Ebenezer Ward's Diary, pp. 34–42 (S.L.S.A. Mortlock P.R.G. 1000); General Order (S.A.P.P. 89 of 1865, p. 15).

114 Ebenezer Ward's Official Journal 8/8/1864 (S.A.P.P. 89 of 1865, pp. 14 and 15); Manton to Finniss 9/8/1864 (S.A.P.P. 89 of 1865, p. 7).

The Up River Camp on the Adelaide River, 1864. The Aborigines began marching up and down too, with sticks over their shoulders. (*Illustrated Melbourne Post* 18/2/1865, p. 29. Courtesy of the State Library of South Australia)

what property it could find, but scarcely did the men round the mangroves outside the camp when they were met by a hail of spears accompanied by 'a most hideous and horrid yell, sounding as if emanating from a single voice'.[115] In the brief battle that followed one officer, Pearson, was seriously wounded in four places, a subordinate, Litchfield, in the arm, and one of the horses in the rump, before the Woolnas were forced to withdraw.[116] The Woolnas' casualties included one man who suffered a shattered hip joint, another who floated across the river on a piece of bark and died in the reeds, while a third man (who had earlier been a guest on the *Beatrice*) was left behind dying with a bullet wound in the head.[117]

That evening Ebenezer Ward and Dr Goldsmith, the medical officer and Protector of Aborigines, held an extraordinary inquest

115 F.H. Litchfield's Statement 16/9/1864 (S.A.P.P. 89 of 1865, p. 23).

116 Ebenezer Ward's Official Journal 9/8/1864 (S.A.P.P. 89 of 1865, p. 15); F.H. Litchfield's Statement 16/9/1864 (S.A.P.P. 89 of 1865, p. 23).

117 Manton to Blyth 3/12/1866 (S.A.P.P. 16 of 1867, p. 2); Journal of Alfred Charles Webling 9/8/1864 (S.L.S.A. Mortlock D3058/1(L)).

on the captured body of the man shot in the head, arranged solely to bring censure on Colonel Finniss. Ever since landing, the bond between the leader and his officers (in particular Ward) had become increasingly strained. When Finniss maintained that there was no immediate prospect of fresh water on the coast, Ward claimed to have found some there; when Finniss claimed that the water upstream was fresh, Ward maintained it to be salt at high tide and brackish at low[118]; when Finniss expected his men to stay together for mutual protection, Ward decided to try his hand at exploration[119]; when Finniss ordered drill on the Sabbath, Ward had conscientious objections to Sunday work. He read Shakespeare instead.[120] The officers now saw in the tragic skirmish with the Woolnas an excellent opportunity to embarrass the leader by blaming him directly for the death of the Aboriginal man they had shot. After all, who had chosen the upriver camp in the first place? The inquest set to work with Ward, though but an ordinary juror, dragooning the reluctant chairman and non-officer jurors into investigating the location of the depot as the cause of the accident. After proceedings strange and irregular to behold, such as the foreman Stephen King being pushed into the background, a verdict of justifiable homicide was returned, to which was attached a rider, proposed by Ward, blaming Finniss for his choice of such a mangrove-ridden site in the first place. Ward then proceeded down the river to deliver the package containing the verdict to the Government Resident.[121]

The upheaval his arrival caused could be heard as far distant as London. 'Why – this – is – a positive – vote of censure upon me!' stormed the angry Government Resident, to the messenger's

118 Northern Territory Commission. Questions 1685; 1686; 1687 (S.A.P.P. 17 of 1866–1867); Ebenezer Ward's Diary pp. 22 and 27 (S.L.S.A. Mortlock P.R.G. 1000).

119 Ward to Finniss 28/7/1864 (S.A.P.P. 89 of 1865, pp. 3 and 4); General Order 26/7/1864 (S.A.P.P. 89 of 1865, p. 16).

120 Northern Territory Commission. Questions 1687; 1750; 1751 (S.A.P.P. 17 of 1866–67); Ebenezer Ward's Diary pp. 49 and 50 (S.L.S.A. Mortlock P.R.G. 1000).

121 Finniss to Ayers 11/8/1864 with enclosures (S.A.P.P. 89 of 1865, pp. 6 to 9); Finniss to Ayers 21/9/1864 (S.A.P.P. 89 of 1865, pp. 18 and 19); Ward to Ayers 5/9/1864 (S.A.P.P. 89 of 1865, p. 22); F.H. Litchfield's Statement 16/9/1864 (S.A.P.P. 89 of 1865, p. 23).

delight.[122] Most serious of all, the events of early August invited open war with the indigenous tribes. The upriver depot was hastily wound up by Finniss to consolidate defences, and at the end of the month the last of the camp, the sheep and cattle, were driven north along the river shadowed by a concourse of unseen warriors seeing them off the grounds. The post-mortem on the deceased man had been performed with a mallet and chisel so that the head was left in a shockingly mutilated condition.[123] His people, who dug up the body to give it a proper burial in a tree[124], did not overlook this mutilation; about a year later young Alaric Ward, the same European who shot the man, was found mutilated in the mangrove scrub in sight of the base camp with upper jaw and nose hacked off in the same crude manner, and three spears in the heart. This event showed the tragedy of the situation; for after shooting the Aboriginal man, as a gesture of peace, Alaric had decided not to carry his hand gun.[125]

In Adelaide, the South Australian government absolved Finniss of all blame and criticised the officers for their carelessness and insubordination.[126] 'It would be amusing,' noted one journal, 'if the matter were not serious, to find a small exploring party first shooting a black-fellow and then holding an inquest upon his body.'[127]

Back at Escape Cliffs, the master of the *Beatrice*, finding that six of his own sailors had put their names to the offensive rider, brought them to order before the Government Resident in person, where with quavering voice they tried to explain how the officers had assured them that no possible harm was intended.[128] Finniss accepted their apologies with grace, but took every step to report his own officers to Adelaide. 'There is an ungenerous spirit of mischief apparent in these proceedings,' he wrote, 'emanating chiefly from

122 Ebenezer Ward's Diary, p. 110 (S.L.S.A. Mortlock P.R.G. 1000).

123 *Register* 16/12/1864, p. 2 Hutchison interview.

124 Manton to Blyth 3/12/1866 (S.A.P.P. 16 of 1867, p. 2).

125 *Register* 16/12/1865, p. 2 N.T. Correspondent; William Dougall to John Dougall 10/8/1865 (S.L.S.A. Mortlock A583); Alaric Ward to Family. Four letters plus covering note (S.L.S.A. Mortlock D3697/1–4 (L)).

126 Ayers to Finniss 10/2/1865 (S.A.P.P. 89 of 1865, pp. 61 and 62).

127 *Register* 18/10/1864 leader.

128 Government Resident's Minute 12/8/1864 with enclosures (S.A.P.P. 89 of 1865, p. 7).

the doctor; and I believe, from the statements of the men of the *Beatrice*, who attribute the speaking part of the ceremony to Mr Ward, from him also …' He then began the protracted dismissal of Ebenezer Ward who, unlike the doctor, was dispensable.[129]

At first Finniss lost the initiative by not packing Ward out of the Territory by the first vessel going. Because of the former journalist's political connections, Finniss hesitated for 40 days before merely suspending him and even then wrote to Adelaide for approval.[130] Ward therefore remained in the camp until December, pending certain dismissal, making himself personally objectionable to the leader and stirring up dissension in the officers' mess. He sent long complaints through the Government Resident to the ministers in Adelaide, directing attention to the colonel's weaknesses. He acted as chief news-reader for a scurrilous camp paper called *Court Circulars,* reciting each edition in the presence of Finniss's supporters in the hope they would convey the contents back to the leader. He openly took to composing a book, which he boasted would be published by a reputed London firm[131], that portrayed the commander as small-minded, cowardly, brutal and lazy in the last degree:

> The great Mogul Cock Lofty
> Was a fat and foolish fellow;
> He sat all day on his ottoman gay
> Squat under a big umbrella.[132]

The diatribe ended on a patriotic outburst:

> Sorry shall I be if they fail to erase from the fair page of South Australian history the foul blotch with which Mr Finniss has besmeared it.[133]

Finniss retaliated by making the author's stay as cheerless as he could. After Ward's suspension in April, the store was ordered to

---

129 Government Resident's Minute 12/8/1864 (S.A.P. P. 89 of 1865, p. 7).

130 Finniss to Ayers 21/9/1864 (S.A.P.P. 89 of 1865, pp. 18 and 19); Finniss to Ward 20/9/1864 (S.A.P.P. 89 of 1865, p. 24).

131 The reputed publishers Sampson Low, Marston, Searle & Rivington of London have no record of entertaining publication.

132 Ebenezer Ward's Diary, p. 47 (S.L.S.A. Mortlock P.R.G.1000).

133 Ebenezer Ward's Diary, p. 156 (S.L.S.A. Mortlock P.R.G. 1000).

stop feeding him, his tent was repossessed and he was urged to find his own way home. As Ward drew only a small part of his salary in the Territory, he must have been compelled to live in the bush with the Woolnas or to start walking as advised, had he not managed to come to terms with the captain of the *South Australian* for a passage home.[134] He eventually got to Adelaide on New Year's Day 1865, turning up, as one columnist noted, 'like a bad shilling'.[135]

The second main incident between the commander and his officers occurred a month after the first, on 8 September, and again involved the local people. Finniss stated his views on Aborigines with a candour that embarrassed his masters in Adelaide, who contrived to hush him up. Their embarrassment would have been less felt had not the Colonial Office in London made the treatment of Aborigines its special interest. Finniss had no patience with such idealists, whom he accused of not knowing what they were talking about. Experience by Europeans along the overland routes into South Australia and especially in the earlier outposts on North-West Arnhem Land *proved* the original inhabitants to be treacherous individuals who repaid generosity and kindness with murder and theft.[136] But they could be taught to respect civilisation if appropriate force was used – after which they could then choose to contribute to society or retire to reserves. Until this respect for civilised life was reached, Protectors of Aborigines were useless. Notwithstanding these theories Finniss was made to accept the help of just such a Protector, who happened to be Dr Goldsmith, one of his worst enemies. In his original instructions, Finniss was also urged, out of respect for the Colonial Office, to treat the native inhabitants with every kindness, fairness and firmness, and to impress on them their rights as British subjects protected by the constitutional prerogatives of the Crown.[137]

---

134 Ward to Ayers 5/1/1865 (S.A.P.P. 89 of 1865 pp. 91 and 92).

135 *Register* 3/1/1865 leader.

136 Finniss to Ayers 5/10/1864 (S.A.P.P. 89 of 1865, pp. 31 and 32); Finniss to Ayers 1/5/1865 (S.A.P.P. 15 of 1865–1866, pp. 10 and 11); Northern Territory Commission. Proceedings, pp. XXII to XXIV (S.A.P.P. 17 of 1866–1867).

137 Instructions to Boyle Travers Finniss: Instruction 18 (S.A.P.P. 36 of 1864, p. 3); Instructions from Commissioner of Crown Lands to Protector of Aborigines (S.A.P.P. 36 of 1864, pp. 10 and 11). Such as the right to vote at elections, a right which in effect lapsed in South Australia with Federation.

By September 1864 the single depot at Escape Cliffs had been consolidated and fortified, and the Government Resident, always the soldier, resolved to forestall any more skirmishes by taking the offensive. Already, according to Finniss, the Aborigines had shown a taste for plunder and a party of upriver men were hovering in the bush behind the camp, some daubed in red war paint and others in white mourning paint, put on when they had a death to avenge. He thought that the Aboriginal peoples were about to combine into a well-organised army, as the Maoris had recently done in New Zealand and various tribes tended to do in Africa. The choice, as Finniss saw it, was to take the offensive or surrender the country back to the opposing side.

> Their attitude was that of war – they had plundered our stores, both here and at the detached camp, at the very moment we were making presents to them, and endeavoring to conciliate them, under every disgusting concession on our part …
>
> I determined at once to give the natives a lesson, and to treat them as armed bushrangers acting against the laws and property of the men of the expedition.[138]

On 8 September, he took the initiative and despatched a punitive expedition under his loyal son Fred and 15 of the best-trained horse and foot volunteers with unwritten instructions to shoot every 'sanguinary native' in sight and by looting their property to give them a taste of their own medicine. The expedition eventually found some Aborigines resting on the beach at Chambers Bay and, opening fire like a sudden storm, sent them racing toward the mangroves. One old man, injured and too slow afoot, was found lying on the ground pleading for mercy with his yam stick in hand and a basket around his neck. He was promptly shot in the chest from point-blank range. 'Shot in cold blood', wrote a crewman of the *Beatrice*. When the old man began to stagger about, someone then shot him in the head to put him out of his misery. Next the party turned their attention to the Aborigines' camp, burning or

138 Finniss to Ayers 5/10/1864 (S.A.P.P. 89 of 1865, pp. 31 and 32); Northern Territory Commission. Proceedings, p. XXIII (S.A.P.P. 17 of 1866–1867).

confiscating everything in reach, before returning to Escape Cliffs for a round of sherry and an extra ration of spirits.[139]

After this the Djerimanga – or Woolna – people disappeared for eight months,[140] adding to the sense of apprehension. In the mind of Edward Hodgson of the *Beatrice* they 'were numerous, warlike and well-built and powerful men'.[141] Only after the English sailors of the *Beatrice* renewed friendships with the Aborigines did they dare come near Escape Cliffs to resume with renewed energy the practice of carrying off whatever they could move.

The punitive raid played right into the hands of Finniss's enemy Dr Goldsmith (the two men could not get on), who, as well as being Protector of Aborigines, had a vested interest in rejecting Escape Cliffs. A former naval doctor, he was planning to marry Emma Hallett, daughter of a prominent pastoral family on the look-out for good land in the Territory. As the Halletts' prospective real-estate agent, he had come to the conclusion that the land around Adam Bay would be useless for a capital or almost anything else. History was repeating itself. His future father-in-law, John Hallett, had taken a similar lead in agitating against William Light's selection of the site for the South Australian capital in 1837.

Taking his duties as Protector with a seriousness he'd not shown before, immediately after the punitive expedition, Goldsmith took the first steps to charge all those involved with wilful homicide. If by no other means, then he would have Finniss brought to ground as a murderer. This the Government Resident refused to accept on the ground that it would terminate the whole expedition, with the leader and 16 of his men inside the Adelaide gaol pending trial and most of the others outside held as witnesses. Goldsmith then switched his line of attack, writing to Adelaide with the

139 Finniss to Ayers 5/10/1864 with enclosures (S.A.P.P. 89 of 1865, pp. 31 to 34); Ebenezer Ward's Diary, pp. 143 to 156 (S.L.S.A. Mortlock P.R.G. 1000); Northern Territory Commission. Proceedings p. XXIII; Questions 1608 to 1649; 2695 to 2699; 2916 to 2945 (S.A.P.P. 17 of 1866–1867); R. Edmund's Diary 11/4/1865 (S.L.S.A. Mortlock D8043(L)); Journal of Alfred Charles Webling, 2/10/1864. (S.L.S.A. Mortlock D3058/1(L)).

140 Northern Territory Commission. Proceedings, p. XXIII (S.A.P.P. 17 of 1866–1867).

141 Diary of Edward Hodgson 13/5/1865 to 30/7/1865, p. 46 (Northern Territory Archives).

suggestion that the authorities should take the necessary steps to prosecute them; after which he set to work in anticipation gathering incriminating evidence.[142] Meanwhile, other members of the officers' clique saw to it that the Adelaide newspapers were only too well informed. There were sensational reports that Finniss's punitive party had looted the native camp for Macassan axes, nets, bags and tools, and stories of puppies snatched from the breasts of native women.[143] Other reports told of the festivities which followed: 'When they returned and told their horrid tale, Finniss said "Well done, Freddy; I knew you'd teach them a lesson. Gentlemen, will you take a glass of sherry?"'[144] Ebenezer Ward added his own brand of melodrama (almost certainly untrue) by carefully recording in his book how the men had taken turns to bayonet the Aborigine's body and cut off locks of his hair as souvenirs.[145]

The people of South Australia were not accustomed to their officers acting in such a manner, and Governor Daly and his advisers were made to feel extremely embarrassed. A delegation from the Aborigines' Friends Association called on Daly and demanded an

---

142 Finniss to Ayers 5/10/1864 with enclosures (S.A.P.P. 89 of 1865, pp. 31 to 34); Goldsmith to Ayers 4/10/1864 with enclosures (S.A.P.P. 89 of 1865, pp. 35 to 39).

143 'Native', meaning born in the place, or with ancient roots in the place, or original, was the most common word used at the time to describe the indigenous peoples. Also used for Europeans—'native of Devon', 'South Australian Natives' being the first intercolonial football team, Australian Natives Association (the ANA) used by native born white Australians as a mark of superiority over other Australians born in the Old World, etc. A similar meaning still survives in the term 'Native Americans' used by some North American Indians. Also still used by descendants of early European settlers in America. Because 'Native' has now acquired some negative connotations in Australia I have used it carefully, only when I am trying to communicate contemporary constructs of reality. When it came to defining themselves the indigenous peoples on the north coast rarely went beyond their own localised hunter gatherer groups and their immediate neighbours. Before publication of the book, I wrote to the Northern Territory Land Council asking if there was a general Aboriginal word acceptable to all Aboriginal groups in the Top End. I was advised that as many different Aboriginal languages were actively in use there was no prospect of agreeing on a common word for the foreseeable future. Southern Aboriginal names were clearly not acceptable.

144 *Register* 16/12/1864, p. 2.

145 Ebenezer Ward's Diary, p. 153 (S.L.S.A. Mortlock P.R.G. 1000).

inquiry into this 'peculiar atrocity'. There was no hiding this latest action from the Colonial Office in London.

'It was his duty,' replied the governor to the delegation, 'from instructions received from his Sovereign and otherwise, to look after the welfare of the aborigines, and he hoped that he had not neglected that duty, for it was his intention that it should not be neglected.'[146] After handing over the Territory, the main concern of the Colonial Office in London had been to protect the indigenous peoples and he well knew it was the governor's duty to see that this was carried out. On being notified of the first skirmish upriver, Frederick Rogers of the Colonial Office had attached a wry comment:

> Express hope that every endeavour will be made to establish amicable relations with the natives (a vain hope I am afraid) ...[147]

A strongly worded despatch was sent by Ayers reprimanding Colonel Finniss for his action and setting up a three-member board of inquiry into the killing of the old man.[148] Over a year later a Royal Commission, formed by the colonists themselves without outside pressure reproved him for being 'highly indiscreet'.[149] In August 1865, Patrick Auld (from one of the 'superior Adelaide families') who shot the Aboriginal man in the chest, was charged with murder. But here the governor and his advisers overstepped their zeal for justice and landed themselves in more trouble than they had bargained for.

The trouble came when Auld's defence counsel disputed South Australia's right to try him, and broke the uneasy silence on whether or not the Duke of Newcastle had ever granted with the Territory the appropriate powers to make laws for its peace, order and good government. Auld's lawyers denied that he had ever done so. *The South Australian Act* of 1834, they argued, limited the governor to govern within certain boundaries and nothing in the Letters

---

146 *Register* 14/1/1865, p. 3.

147 Daly to Cardwell 24/10/1864 with Minute J.R. (C.O. 13/115 Folio 95).

148 Ayers to Finniss 10/2/1865 (S.A.P.P. 89 of 1865, p. 63); Ayers to F. Howard, B. Ninnis, R.H. Edmunds 10/2/1865 asking them to form a board of inquiry (S.A.P.P. 89 of 1865, p. 91); R. Edmund's Diary 11/4/1865 (S.L.S.A. Mortlock D8043 (L)).

149 Northern Territory Commission. Report (S.A.P.P. 17 of 1866–1867, p. 3).

Patent altered this restriction. If the accused was to have a fair trial, they argued, he must be tried in New South Wales whose laws still applied in the Territory.[150] The thought of a free-born South Australian going to a convict colony for justice gave many citizens a considerable shock.

The government soon had good cause not to forget this first Northern Territory murder trial, which lasted 12 months and became more disconcerting as time went by. It started in the Adelaide Police Court in August 1865, only to be postponed pending the apprehension of two accomplices in the alleged murder and eight witnesses, all in the Northern Territory.[151] Early in the next year the two accomplices were acquitted in the same court in Adelaide, to the accompaniment of cheers.[152] Then in May the trial of Auld began in the Supreme Court, only to be again postponed when the presiding judge, Benjamin Boothby, always a fly in the ointment for successive governments in South Australia, doubted the jurisdiction of the court to try the case.[153] The government ministers now found themselves in a dilemma. If they let Auld go free they acknowledged an inability to try him; if they went ahead they risked a collision with Boothby and the Supreme Court. In the end a combination of circumstances came to their aid. Of the three key witnesses, Chandler died in a brawl in a Flinders Street brothel, Packard was drowned in the Murray, and Dougall left the country. When the case came up for the last time in August 1866 the government with all honesty could plead it had been deprived of its main evidence, and Auld was acquitted for want of witnesses.[154] But the complications were not yet over. Auld, heartened by events, and backed by his family, petitioned parliament for compensation for the suffering and expense the protracted delays had cost him. In parliament Attorney-General J.P. Boucaut replied that he had let

150 Minutes and Proceedings of the Executive Council relating to the conduct of Mr Justice Boothby (S.A.P.P. 22 of 1867, p. 17).

151 *Register* 26/8/1865, pp. 2 and 3 Police Court proceedings.

152 *Register* 16/2/1866 Police Court proceedings.

153 *Register* 19/5/1866, p. 3; 23/5/1866, p. 3 Supreme Court proceedings; *Register* 23/5/1866, p. 2; Queen v. Auld (State Record G.R.G. 1/18). Boothby's ruling was complicated by the fact that Finniss had supported Boothby.

154 *Register* 29/8/1866, p. 8 Supreme Court proceedings.

proceedings drop only with misgivings, and threatened to reopen the case should Auld continue with his campaign.[155]

The Auld case revived doubts as to whether South Australia did in fact have full power to colonise the Territory. For the second time the question was raised in parliament when the Legislative Council sought reassurances from the governor, which he obligingly gave. After that the subject was brought up from time to time, generally to the embarrassment of the government in power.[156]

Boothby's judgement in the Auld case was also not forgotten. It was one of the cases cited when in 1867 the Executive Council controversially 'amoved' Mr Justice Boothby from office for being obstructive in the Supreme Court.[157]

The third and gravest point of disagreement between Colonel Finniss and his officers was over the situation of Escape Cliffs and most of all its healthiness as a site for a northern capital.

Finniss chose Escape Cliffs as a preliminary winter depot in late July 1864.[158] By the end of August, with the upriver camp abandoned, he had concentrated all his forces there. On the 11 October he finally announced his intention to make it a permanent settlement.[159] His many critics jumped to the conclusion that he had made up his mind prematurely. But Finniss read his instructions to mean that unless the Adelaide River was found altogether unsuitable, he was to save time and restrict his searching exclusively

---

155 S.A.P.D. 1866–1867 c. 1370.

156 S.A.P.D. 1866–1867 c. 1475 and 1505. As late as the 1970s descendants of Finniss were defending Boothby's judgement on the Northern Territory. For continuation of the debate by descendants of Finniss see: Travers Borrow, *The Northern Territory of Australia and Federation* (Proceedings of the Royal Geographical Society of Australasia, South Australian Branch Vol. 57, pp. 15–24); K.T. Borrow, *The Northern Territory of Australia, North Australia and Alexandra Land* (1862–1900) (The Australian Law Journal, Vol. 28, pp. 148–151); K.T. Borrow, Additional Research Notes to the author 1972.

157 See Minutes of Proceedings of the Executive Council relating to the conduct of Mr Justice Boothby (S.A.P.P. 22 of 1867 pp. 17, 18, 19, 20). Benjamin Boothby (1803–1868) was the second judge of the Supreme Court and appointed by the Colonial Office. He had many clashes with successive South Australian governments and was 'amoved' from office in 1868. He died soon after.

158 Ebenezer Ward's Official Journal 29/7/1864 (S.A.P.P. 89 of 1865, p. 14).

159 Finniss to Walters 10/10/1864 with postscript of 11/10/1864 (S.A.P.P. 89 of 1865, p. 74).

How Escape Cliffs got its name. Confronted by a large group of Aborigines, they danced until help arrived.
(*Discoveries in Australia* by J. Lort Stokes, London 1846, frontispiece. Courtesy of the State Library of South Australia)

to its upper and lower reaches.[160] Before fixing on Escape Cliffs, he made only two serious explorations: the high ground about 50 miles inland and the low coastal plain near the river's mouth. The first journey, made in July by Finniss and a few men, was from the upriver camp toward Beatrice Hill about ten miles further inland, a site recommended by Captain Hutchison. After three days in the mud Finniss's party was unable to penetrate the swamps and so the hill was discounted as inaccessible.[161] As though to embarrass the colonel, Ebenezer Ward and his cronies then hastened to organise an unauthorised expedition to the same hill and reached it without much trouble, an achievement they never let the Government Resident forget.[162] Meanwhile Finniss, turning his eyes towards the river's mouth, had despatched a party under Patrick Auld (one of

160 Finniss to Ayers 1/5/1865 (S.A.P.P. 15 of 1865–1866, p. 11).

161 Finniss to Ayers 10/8/1864 (S.A.P.P. 89 of 1865, pp. 4 and 5); Ebenezer Ward's Official Journal 8/7/1864 to 11/7/1864 (S.A.P.P. 89 of 1865, pp. 13 and 14).

162 Ebenezer Ward's Diary pp. 61 to 82 (S.L.S.A. Mortlock P.R.G. 1000); Ward to Finniss 28/7/1864 (S.A.P.P. 89 of 1865, pp. 3 and 4).

Stuart's men) to examine Adam Bay and the fertility and possible elevated ground between the Adelaide and Alligator rivers. Auld's report proved generally favourable and left Finniss much impressed with Escape Cliffs on Cape Hotham Peninsula at the mouth of the Adelaide River.[163]

Perhaps this was an omen. Escape Cliffs had been named by Captain Stokes of the *Beagle* when he discovered the Adelaide River in 1839. The cliffs were named to commemorate the escape of two of his men who, caught on the beach below the cliffs by warriors with spears raised, kept the Aborigines at bay by 'dancing for their lives' various jigs until relief arrived.[164]

What pleased Finniss most about Escape Cliffs was the 'healthy, cheerful habitation'. Leaning on the experience of the neighbouring Dutch, Finniss considered avoidance of fevers the first essential for successful settlement in the tropics[165]. The site was elevated 30 feet above the prevailing coastline, had a cool, insular climate, being perched on a peninsula, and was open to the north-west monsoon in the wet season and to daily sea breezes all the year round. Even the rapid tides and currents regularly swept its shores clean like a broom and the high tides submerged the marshes to prevent the breeding of malaria. Added to these advantages was Auld's assurance that it could be linked to the hinterland by a practical road.[166] 'In my selection,' wrote Finniss, 'I have regarded health as a *sine qua non* to successful settlement; and I am sure that I shall be found correct in my assumption that the peninsula of Cape Hotham is the healthiest part of the north-west coast, within reasonable proximity to a secure harbour.'[167] When his many critics complained that the area was too limited, he countered crossly 'I have not made selection of this site with a view to its becoming a sheep run or a cattle station, but chiefly for the convenience of health and commerce'.[168]

163 Northern Territory Commission. Proceedings, p. XIX (S.A.P.P. 17 of 1866–1867); Instructions to Auld 20/7/1864 (S.A.P.P. 89 of 1865, p. 16).

164 J. Lort Stokes, *Discoveries in Australia,* Vol. 1, pp. 413, 414, Boone, London 1846.

165 Finniss to Ayers 10/8/1864 (S.A.P.P. 89 of 1865, pp. 4 and 5); Finniss to Ayers 1/5/1865 (S.A.P.P. 15 of 1865, p. 12).

166 Finniss to Ayers 15/4/1865 (S.A.P.P. 15 of 1865–1866, p. 4 to 6).

167 Finniss to Ayers 1/5/1865 (S.A.P.P. 15 of 1865–1866, p. 12).

168 Finniss to Ayers 15/4/1865 (S.A.P.P. 15 of 1865–1866, p. 5).

Unfortunately no sooner had Colonel Finniss gathered together his men at this 'healthy, cheerful habitation' than their health broke down. There was one main reason for the setback: between August and December fresh food ran out and the doctor, seizing his chance to undermine his leader, demoralised the camp into thinking that they were all being 'weeded out' by the unhealthy location.

From the start the South Australian government's provisioning had been skinflint. Finniss had asked for 300 sheep and 7800 pounds of salt meat (exclusive of supplies for the journey up) for an expedition of 30 men. The government gave him 40 men, 150 sheep and 7800 pounds of salt meat (inclusive of supplies for the journey). They deceived him into believing that the necessary extras would be sent on the *Beatrice* when it picked up supplies in Sydney, followed by a relief vessel in two or three months. When the colonel's ship reached Adam Bay only 52 miserable, bald sheep remained, and the salt meat smelt like a carcase. The *Beatrice* was found to have no extra supplies and its captain held out no hope for immediate relief. So the expedition set to work sustained principally by a basic diet of flour, tea, sugar and grog. Inside two months many members of the party were showing the effects.[169]

The food shortage would not have become half so bad had Finniss been luckier with his little fleet. The *Yatala* had been given to him for just such emergencies and he never forgave her captain (he later had him dismissed) for accidentally running aground on the way up. The *Henry Ellis* might have taken her place as a foraging ship, but funds were too low to keep such a large vessel and in mid August she took her leave. Everything was thus left to the surveying schooner *Beatrice*, which in late August 1864 did in fact make a saving run to Koepang in Timor for fresh supplies, returning on the first day of October with vegetables (mainly yams), buffaloes and plants. Then misfortune struck her too: the captain's health broke down and it was decided to head post-haste for Adelaide. The *Beatrice* finally left on 9 October by way of Timor so as to escort the *Yatala* there for urgent repairs. The party was now left entirely isolated watching for the speedy return of a refitted *Yatala* and the

169 Northern Territory Commission. Proceedings, p. XX (S.A.P.P. 17 of 1866–1867).

long promised relief from the south. But the *Yatala* never returned, and the relief steamer arrived only in December.

Meanwhile, the expedition had to turn to the melancholy task of extracting fresh food from the Australian environment. Now the thriving Aborigines all around seemed the superior race. A permanent party was sent off to scrounge along the creeks and lagoons for fish. 'We have cleared the vicinity of Escape Cliffs of lizards, rats, etc,' wrote one young man, 'and thought them deuced good eating when we could get nothing else.'[170] All this time the spirits and health of the expedition deteriorated. Already in September two men had died, one from liver disease and the other, young Bastin Boucaut from one of the best Adelaide families, of remittent fever. They were buried with military honours.[171] From time to time, most believed they themselves would come to the same end.

The anxiety had several compensations for the malcontents in the officers' mess, a place once described as worse than any shearing shed. Dr Goldsmith capitalised on it by attributing the sickness and depression to the poisonous condition of the water at Escape Cliffs, giving force to his diagnosis by boasting of his expert experience as a naval doctor in the West Indies.

Finniss was furious. Not six or seven weeks before, the doctor had approved of the water, which had been taken into account in selecting the site. Ebenezer Ward dramatised the scene which followed:

> Dr Goldsmith '... I don't consider our lives are safe, while we have nothing but poisonous water to drink.'
>
> Mr Finniss (complacently) 'Very well Dr then we must all lie down and die. I can do nothing.'
>
> Dr Goldsmith 'Do you really mean to say that Sir?'
>
> Mr Finniss (still complacently) 'Yes Dr. I can do nothing. I cannot get better water and I cannot move the Camp. We must all lie down and die.'

170 *Register* 4/1/1865, p. 3 N.T. correspondent.

171 Medical Journal, Northern Territory from August 9th to October 1st, 1864 (S.A.P.P. 89 of 1865, p. 40).

> Dr Goldsmith (with great emphasis) 'Then Sir! I have not hesitation in saying you are an imbecile and unfit for your position!'[172]

Having announced his diagnosis the doctor did all in his power to make it appear true. 'He frightened many of the men into sickness,' complained the Resident, 'he invited them to place themselves on the sick list, and announced all illness as originating in the use of deleterious water.'[173] 'The alarm created and excited was sufficient to cause despondency, and I have no doubt that it had such an effect.'[174] The doctor even had an unauthorised notice pinned on a tree outside his tent which read:

> Dr. Goldsmith being painfully aware of the deleterious state of the water now in use at camp, wishes to caution the members of the expedition, and requests them to observe the following rules –
>
> 1 To drink as little water as possible.
> 2 To drink water which has been boiled, in preference to water in its natural state.
> 3 By filtering water through charcoal, some of its deleterious properties may be arrested!
> 4 Should any symptoms of illness occur, apply at once for medical advice.
>
> Dr. Goldsmith will issue quinine daily, at 6 a.m.[175]

The Government Resident tried to shrug off this new attack. The party had neither the site nor the ships nor food enough to move and the leader thought best to stay put. But the doctor refused to be ignored and kept pushing complaints about the poisonous state of the water under Finniss's nose until he lost his temper and vowed never again to accept medical help from such a man even if he was struggling on his last legs.[176]

---

172 Ebenezer Ward's Diary pp. 136 and 137 (S.L.S.A. Mortlock P.R.G. 1000).

173 Finniss to Ayers 5/10/1864 (S.A.P.P. 89 of 1865, pp. 40 and 41).

174 Finniss to Ayers 6/10/1864 (S.A.P.P. 89 of 1865, p. 42).

175 Copy of Memorandum posted on a tree, copied 17/9/1864 (S.A.P.P. 89 of 1865, p. 49).

176 Finniss to Ayers 5/10/1864 (S.A.P.P. 89 of 1865, p. 41); Finniss to Ayers 2/12/1864 with enclosures (S.A.P.P. 89 of 1865, pp. 48 to 50).

A bottle of the allegedly poisonous water was sealed by Finniss or his representative and sent all the way to Adelaide, where eventually government analysts found it free from all poisonous impurities.[177] Finniss also told the Adelaide authorities that a new medical officer would be welcomed as soon as one could be found.[178] Unfortunately doctors were hard to get[179], and when Dr Goldsmith got news of their search he packed his medical bags and left in May 1865 by the *Bengal* bound for Batavia, abandoning the expedition without a permanent medical officer to the mercy of the Woolnas and the poisonous water. He eventually got to Adelaide in July 1865, welcomed by scorn in the newspapers for breaking medical ethics and leaving his post.[180] The second 'bad shilling' had come home.[181]

When the long-awaited relief vessel finally did head into Adam Bay near the end of 1864, the officer in charge of it was astounded by what he saw:

> I found the settlement was not besieged by blacks, nothing had been done in the way of surveying the town. The Government Resident's house was put up and a very roughly built store ... There appeared to be very little control over the men at the settlement, who were nearly all drunk before noon.[182]

The party's efforts to bring each other down over the Aborigines had put the fear of the hangman's rope into everyone. They were hungry, lean and lonely. Even had they quarrelled less fiercely, 'the provisions which the men had before the arrival of the *South Australian* were not such that they could work upon,' said one of Finniss's strongest critics.[183]

In Adelaide accusations flew thick and fast. One wit criticised Finniss for making an exhibition of himself by needing a bodyguard against the Aborigines thus:

---

177 *Register* 14/2/1865, p. 2. Dr Goldsmith had claimed it was impregnated with copper.

178 Finniss to Ayers 2/12/1864 (S.A.P.P. 89 of 1865, pp. 48 and 49).

179 Reynolds to Walters 24/3/1865 (S.A.P.P. 89 of 1865, pp. 70 and 71).

180 *Register* 27/7/1865 leader.

181 He died in 1875, after suffering from a well-concealed illness leading to gradual paralysis, by committing suicide. In 1897 his son Fred became a doctor in the Territory.

182 R. Edmund's Diary 5/12/1864 (S.L.S.A. Mortlock D8043 (L)).

183 Northern Territory Commission. Question 828 (S.A.P.P. 17 of 1866–1867).

And even here, it seems quite hard
He should require a bodyguard.
Who were from useful work debarred,
To form an Exhibition.[184]

Henry Ayers put the failure in a nutshell. After consolidating Escape Cliffs for

> more than 100 days – nothing of importance had been accomplished. No report of the interior had been furnished, no shelter provided for men and stores, although the wet season had commenced: no attempt to form a garden, no paddock fenced in for the protection of the stock, and not the slightest effort made to commence the survey of either town or country land.[185]

Thus stood the much-vaunted Northern Territory colonisation at the end of 1864, the first year in which it was set up for trial.

Relief Ships – 1865

News that the Northern Territory scheme was not operating to plan reached Adelaide in October and December 1864 and took many good citizens by surprise. Unfortunately for Finniss the officers' side of the story got there first, and he seems never to have made up the leeway.

The first communications came in October 1864, via the *Henry Ellis*, which after departing North Australia had connected by chance with the English mail at Colombo. This batch of letters contained only private correspondence (some critical of Finniss) except for a cursory personal letter from Finniss to Chief Secretary Ayers.[186] The second batch came to hand in mid-December when the *Beatrice* unexpectedly appeared off Port Adelaide with her ailing captain. It included Finniss's first detailed despatches to reach Adelaide, he having preferred to wait for safer channels than the *Henry Ellis*. It also brought private letters so violently critical of him that they caused an immediate sensation and were hustled

184 *Advertiser* 12/1/1865, p. 3.

185 Ayers to Finniss 10/2/1865 (S.A.P.P. 89 of 1865, p. 64).

186 *Register* 14/10/1864 leader also p. 2; Finniss to Ayers 13/8/1864 (S.A.P.P. 163 of 1864, p. 1).

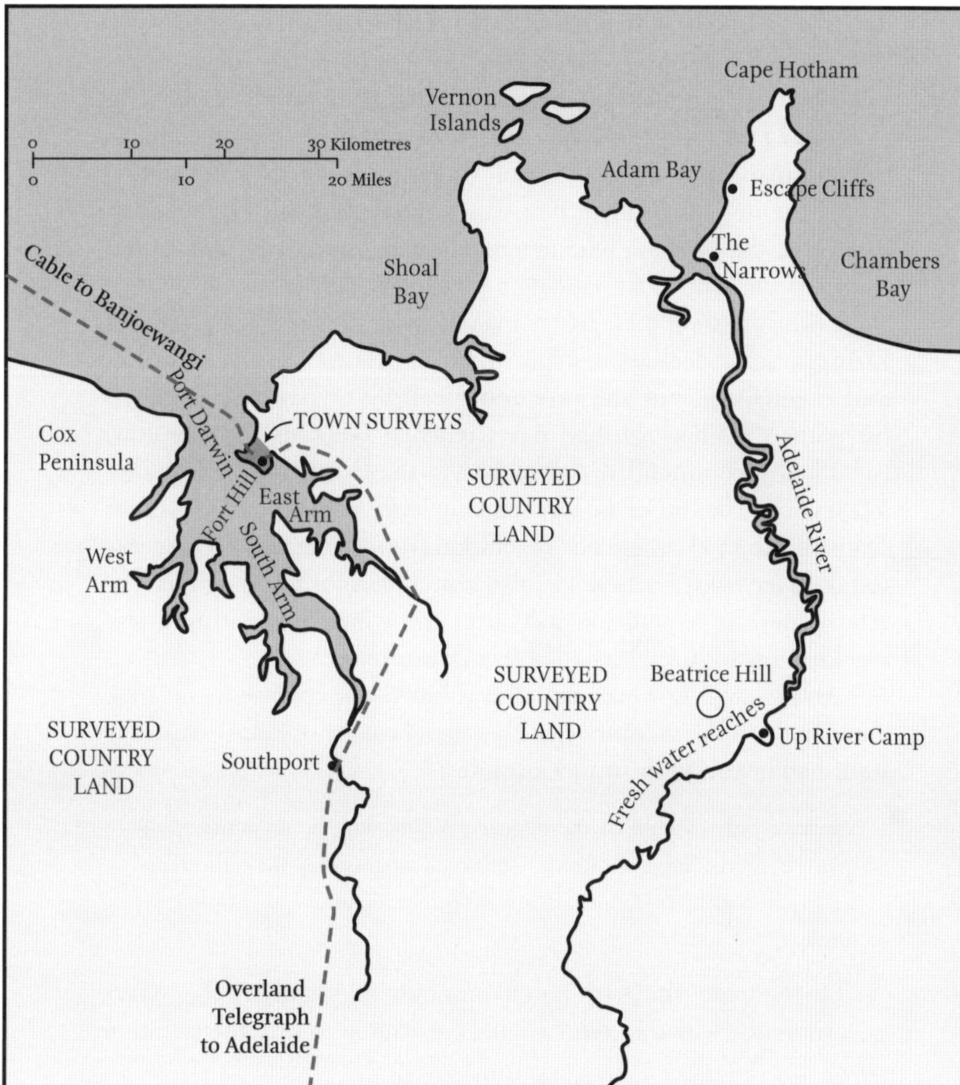

Palmerston – the bridge to Asia

(Based on map C80, State Library of South Australia)

around the city from person to person. As a counter, the officers were described by Finniss's supporters as 'Old Women'.[187] The Ayers government, taken aback by the failure of its expedition, was slow to make Finniss's despatches public, while the newspapers published every private letter they could lay their hands upon. '... it is not our fault,' wrote the *Register* piously, 'that their publication is unaccompanied by the antidote of Mr Finniss's official statement.'[188] About the only antidote at first was Captain Hutchison, the ailing captain of the *Beatrice*, who defended the commander publicly and criticised the officers for lacking a pioneering spirit.[189]

The impression these letters made can be gauged from Governor Daly's personal decision to go to Adam Bay himself as a peacemaker and cheerleader, but the premature calling of parliament ended his plans.[190] When the bad news reached George Windsor Earl (who had recommended Adam Bay in the first place) in Province Wellesley in the Indies, he wrote a long letter to his friend Governor Daly offering to lead a relief expedition from the Straits Settlements to take over from Finniss. He also sent a plan for a fort against the Aborigines, to be built on stilts over the water. But within a few weeks of his writing, Earl died from dysentery.[191]

At this stage, however, not all was lost. Some commentators took comfort from the memory that the model colony of South Australia itself had begun with similar disputes:

> We have only to read in the *Register* of that day the accounts of the quarrels, proceeding from words to blows, among some of the early official settlers in South Australia to see what a remarkably happy family they formed.[192]

On hearing the first batch of news in October, the Ayers government decided to send a relief expedition to save the situation

187 *Register* 15/12/1864 leader and p. 3; 16/12/1864, p. 2.

188 *Register* 16/12/1864, p. 2.

189 *Register* 16/12/1864, p. 2; 17/12/1864 leader also p. 2.

190 Daly to Cardwell 25/10/1864 (G.O.D. 52/1864); *Register* 31/10/1864, p. 3 governor's speech.

191 Information courtesy of Bob Reece, Murdoch University; Reece, 'Introduction' in G.W. Earl, 1846, *Enterprise in Tropical Australia*, Northern Territory University Press, Darwin, 1846, reprinted 2002, pp. 18, 20 to 23.

192 *Register* 15/12/1864 leader.

in the Territory, to be followed by a second relief ship with supplies over the next few months.

The first and main vessel, the *South Australian*, put out on 29 October 1864 bearing 40 selected men (to save money, they were not to be paid until they reached Adam Bay) with Robert Edmunds as leader, and a few private settlers, the first permitted. Seven rabbits, chosen to populate the north, were not taken at the last moment. Before leaving, the governor gave the men a sermon on the subject of discipline. 'There could be neither prosperity nor happiness,' he said, 'unless they acknowledged their superiors; and those gentlemen who set themselves up against the proper authority deserved to go down, would go down, and should go down.'[193]

Next day prayers were held in churches for the party's safety and strength in the trials ahead. Hopes were high for a new start. When his Excellency prorogued parliament after the main party left he was so bold as to congratulate them on the prospects of the Northern Territory expedition.[194]

Unlike earlier ships to the Territory, the *South Australian* was a paddle-driven steamship with sails. She could afford to defy Torres Strait and so take the east-coast route. The crew could therefore delay final loading of stock and perishables until reaching the last major port at Brisbane. The gallant steamship was followed some weeks later by two more relief vessels: the *Beatrice* returning 9 April under a new captain, Frederick Howard, with important instructions to guide the Government Resident, and 12 days later the Swedish barque, *Bengal,* arrived carrying extra supplies of working stock, sheep and poultry.[195]

When the *South Australian* reached Adam Bay on the 5 December 1864, she brought a transitory burst of optimism. On seeing the steamship head into the bay, Finniss in his excitement treated everyone to a holiday, which was spent getting thoroughly drunk instead of unloading the animals. There were ample grounds for festivities: fresh food for the first time in months, new supplies of grog, letters from loved ones.

The *South Australian* also brought a gardener, Alfred Smith,

193 *Register* 31/10/1864, p. 3.

194 *Register* 10/12/1864 Parliamentary Proceedings.

195 Howard to Daly 1/5/1865 (S.A.P.P. 15 of 1865–1866, p. 18).

Men appointed to reinforce the Northern Territory Party, 29 October 1864

Name	Appointment	Salary
Robert Henry Edmunds	Surveyor	£350 per annum
Harrison Daniel Packard	Surveyor	£280 per annum
Clement Young	Postmaster and Clerk	£200 per annum
		per day
John Varley	Mason	7s.
John Wadham	Carpenter	7s.
Robert Charles Burton	Laborer	5s.
George Thomas Cottrell	Laborer	5s.
James Davis	Laborer	5s.
Firmin Deacon	Laborer	5s.
J. Dodson de Skelton	Laborer	5s.
William W. de Bathe	Laborer	5s.
James Douglas	Laborer	5s.
Thomas S. Gillman	Laborer	5s.
Charles S. Hulls	Laborer	5s.
David Johnston	Laborer	5s.
Stephen King, Jnr	Laborer in charge of stock	5s.
John G. Kirby	Laborer in charge of stock	5s.
Gilbert R. McMinn	Laborer	5s.
John Ryan	Laborer	5s.
Jeremiah Ryan	Laborer	5s.
Walter Rowland	Laborer	5s.
James Ross	Laborer in charge of stock	5s.
Alfred Smith	Laborer and Gardener	5s.
Edward Strawbridge	Laborer	5s.
Wycliffe Stow	Laborer	5s.
Alfred John Todd	Laborer	5s.
Edward Tuckwell	Laborer	5s.
Frederick Wadham	Laborer	5s.
John White	Laborer	5s.
Edward J. Wilson	Laborer	5s.
John Young	Laborer	5s.
Christian Schmid	Laborer	5s.
Charles Edwin Neal	Laborer	5s.
George Francis Edmunds	Laborer	5s.
George Kersley	Laborer	5s.
William Henry Walker	Laborer	5s.
Frank Hood	Laborer	5s.
Henry Martin	Laborer	5s.
Edward Burford	Laborer	5s.
George Warland	Laborer in charge of stock	5s.

HENRY AYERS, Chief Secretary.
Based on South Australian Parliamentary Paper 36A of 1864, p. 2.

who set about building a garden and testing plants brought back on the *Beatrice* from Koepang.

There was even the arrival of two wives, Mary Packard and Eliza Bauer, to moderate a society 'unchastened by women'. The Woolnas were noted for not wearing clothes, except head-dress. As soon as the two women could manage it they tried to get their black sisters to cover themselves up, but without success.[196] The Woolna women wore the thick skirts made for them on their shoulders or heads.

For Finniss there was a despatch from Henry Ayers tacitly accepting (by not rejecting) his choice of the site for the capital on Cape Hotham Peninsula, and a request from Governor Daly to name it 'Palmerston' in honour of the Imperial Prime Minister. And besides bringing blessings to the colonel, the *South Australian* spirited trouble away. She left immediately on unloading, taking with her the long suspended Ebenezer Ward as well as Captain Humbert, the disgraced master of the *Yatala,* and 'a few of the most insubordinate and idle of the men'.[197] Most important of all the size of the expedition was about doubled and the men could set to work at once, wet season or not, at the long-postponed business of laying out the town. On 14 December, just nine days after he arrived, Robert Edmunds took the first active steps to survey the metropolis of Palmerston.[198]

When it came to laying out the northern capital, Finniss leaned upon the precedents of his old master and friend, Colonel William Light, who dared to separate the port from the city of Adelaide in order to obtain the best possible location for both. The original plan (suggested by Surveyor-General Goyder) was for a city laid out just like Adelaide, but with a large river down the equivalent of King William Street. As he could find no site on the Adelaide River suitable for both port and capital, Finniss situated the port near the Narrows where the river met Adam Bay 'for the

196 R. Edmunds' Diary 1/1/1866 (S.L.S.A. Mortlock D8043 (L)).

197 When it came to the Territory, for a description of the activities of the relief party see: R. Edmunds' Diary 27/10/1864 to 14/1/1866 (S.L.S.A. Mortlock D8043 (L)); Ayers to Finniss 28/10/1864 (S.A.P.P. 36A of 1864, p. 2); Finniss to Ayers 1/5/1865 (S.A.P.P. 15 of 1865–1866, p. 10).

198 R. Edmunds' Diary 14/12/1864 (S.L.S.A. Mortlock D8043 (L)).

convenience of *shipping and wharfage*' and the city at Escape Cliffs as far out on Cape Hotham Peninsula as possible '*for health and cheerfulness*'. These were to be linked by a low country road similar to the roadway which connected Adelaide's port with its city. Any dispersion of the town allotments interfered with the benefits of forced concentration and was never popular with land speculators, even in Light's day. Finniss wrote to Ayers:

> I recollect the opposition made in the selection of the site of Adelaide by Colonel Light by those who wished the capital at the present Port. 'Bring the ships to our doors,' was then the cry. The Land Company at Port Adelaide [however] has made a large profit by investments in a swamp of which the water has to be banked out for four feet at high tides and south west winds ...[199]

'Escape Cliffs is Port Adelaide duplicated' – explained the critical journal *Pasquin* in a slightly confused statement.[200]

Throughout the rainy season the surveyors, sometimes knee-deep in alluvial mud, laid out the town acres in two towns according to Finniss's plan. Then in June 1865, as the oncoming dry season baked the shallow lagoons, they started on the country lands west of the river and stretching towards Port Darwin. Always at the centre of Finniss's vision was the rich, navigable Adelaide River, eulogised by Stuart, which was to give sustenance, an outlet and cohesion to the new colony in much the same way (according to Finniss) as the Mississippi gave life and cohesion to the old French settlement at New Orleans.[201]

When the *South Australian* first hove in sight, Ebenezer Ward (in a parting shot) had said to Finniss, 'Old man you may smile, but as soon as the Despatches are landed you will smile on the other side of your mouth.'[202] He was anticipating news that the government had repudiated the Escape Cliffs site. But a letter from Chief Secretary Ayers contained nothing revolutionary. The criticisms Ward so confidently expected arrived 9 April 1865 along with the

---

199 Finniss to Ayers 1/5/1865 (S.A.P.P. 15 of 1865–1866, p. 12).

200 *Pasquin* 11/1/1868, p. 323.

201 Finniss to Ayers 15/4/1865 (S.A.P.P. 15 of 1865–1866, p. 6); Northern Territory Commission. Proceedings, p. XXI (S.A.P.P. 17 of 1866–1867).

202 Northern Territory Commission. Question 3810 (S.A.P.P. 17 of 1866–1867).

second relief vessel, the returning *Beatrice,* by which time Ward was safely removed from the Territory.

As it turned out, the despatches by the *Beatrice* did indeed partly repudiate Finniss's choice – but not completely, and this was the cause of much confusion to follow.

On the one hand Finniss was instructed to give up the idea of making Escape Cliffs the capital and to look further afield for a more spacious site down the north-western side of Arnhem Land – that is, still in the same general area. The government had decided on this course because the complaints against Escape Cliffs were legion. This would have pleased Ward, who had complained loudest of all.

On the other hand Finniss was ordered to push ahead with the country surveys while the exploring was going on. Escape Cliffs was not to be ruled out as a secondary town, or even as the primary town if all the other sites turned out worse.[203] This pleased Finniss, who was convinced that the chances of getting a better site on North-West Arnhem Land were slim.

His faith in the superiority of the Adelaide River made him reluctant to leave Escape Cliffs until everything was first in order.[204] For nine or 10 weeks after receiving his instructions he continued to supervise the new surveys, taking every advantage of the dry season as if nothing had happened; which appeared to his critics sheer block-headedness and disobedience. Then, after an eight months respite, the Aborigines renewed their depredations and he built a solid stockade (known as Star Fort) around the public offices on top of the cliff, made of 12-foot upright logs fitted with slits for hand weapons and three cannon placements, carefully positioned to cover all angles.[205] He formed a red-shirt constabulary – 'to scour the country and catch or shoot blacks', to quote one of its members.[206] Finniss also took a second look at two other likely sites for a capital on or near the Adelaide River country, the upper Adelaide and, via

203 Ayers to Finniss 10/2/1865 (S.A.P.P. 89 of 1865, pp. 63 and 64).

204 Finniss to Ayers 1/9/1865 (S.A.P.P. 83 of 1865–1866, pp. 8 and 9).

205 R. Edmunds' Diary 5/7/1865 (S.L.S.A. Mortlock D8043(L)); Finniss to Ayers 31/7/1865 (S.A.P.P. 83 of 1865–1866, p. 7).

206 William Dougall to John Dougall 10/8/1865 (S.L.S.A. Mortlock A583); R. Edmunds' Diary 5/7/1865 (S.L.S.A. Mortlock D8043(L)).

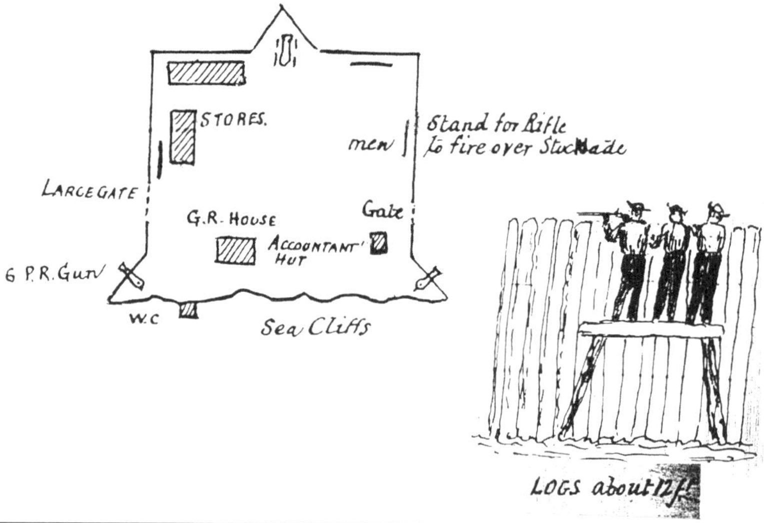

The stockade at Escape Cliffs, symbol of the first Palmerston on the Adelaide River.
(*Top:* adapted from Robert H. Edmunds Diary 5/7/1865.
Bottom: pen and brush copy of S. King's sketch by Sidney Wellington Herbert,
State Library of South Australia (D6995 (L), p. 26)

an expedition led by Patrick Auld, Port Darwin,[207] – of which he wrote:

> I find Port Darwin a magnificent harbor, as far as shipping and landing conveniences are concerned … The main objection, however, is that the

207 Finniss to Ayers 2/5/1865 with enclosure (S.A.P.P. 15 of 1865–1866, pp. 13 to 16); Finniss to Ayers 19/6/1865 with enclosure (S.A.P.P. 83 of 1865–1866, pp. 1 to 5).

> harbor is land-locked, shut in by rocks on the north side, and encompassed in the form of a horseshoe, towards all other quarters by low mangrove shores … [208]

In general, neither site matched Escape Cliffs at the mouth of the Adelaide River.

Only in August 1865 did Colonel Finniss find time to carry out his main instruction brought by the *Beatrice* by looking further afield for an alternative site along the north-west coast of Arnhem Land. His approach was two-pronged. As Ayers' letter had stressed the need for a good hinterland as well as a suitable harbour, he despatched a party on foot down the coastal plain toward the south-west keeping well inland while he himself took the *Beatrice* and the small boat named *Julia* down the coast. The land party under Fred Litchfield, a capable young man originally from India, succeeded between mid September and mid October in trudging across about half of the north-west side of Arnhem Land. Litchfield was generally impressed by what he saw, but his most exciting discovery was traces of alluvial gold on the Finniss River, which reminded some of his party of the rich workings in New Zealand.[209] Meanwhile, the Government Resident with the *Beatrice* and the *Julia* had canvassed the coastline itself all the way to the Victoria River estuary. He too had made an exciting discovery: a new river about half way down which he named the Daly in honour of the South Australian governor. He found the Victoria River just what he expected it to be: 'For navigable purposes, the river may be pronounced one of the worst and most unsafe on the coast.' Though he admitted the upper reaches of the Victoria River were 'fit for all the purposes of settlement, its estuary was gloomy and dangerous'.[210] The sea expedition then returned to Adam Bay via Timor, lying opposite, where Finniss met the governor; much-needed fresh stores were taken aboard and despatches reiterating the superiority of the

---

208 Finniss to Ayers 2/5/1865 with enclosure (S.A.P.P. 15 of 1865–1866, pp. 13 and 14).

209 Finniss to Ayers 16/10/1865 with enclosure (S.A.P.P. 83 of 1865–1866, pp. 12 to 15); J. Dickinson, *Litchfield's Gold: The Life of Fred Litchfield*, Darwin N.T., 1988, Chapter 10.

210 Finniss to Ayers 1/9/1865 (S.A.P.P. 83 of 1865–1866, pp. 8 to 10).

Adelaide River were posted south.[211] This deviation to a foreign land later got Finniss into trouble.

Two positive effects had followed the arrival of the relief expeditions: a temporary revitalising of the party leading to the start of the surveys after the *South Australian* arrived with 40 men and good food; and further explorations after the arrival of the *Beatrice* with new instructions. These were, however, more than outweighed by the negative effects centred in the person of Jefferson Pickman Stow.

Stow was one of a little band of gallant private citizens who came north in the *South Australian*. A man of influential connections, he might have given the leader the help he needed had not the two men fallen out straightaway over the Escape Cliffs site. Now the third major vendetta broke out, led – as Finniss admitted – by a far more formidable adversary than Ward or Goldsmith. As a private citizen Stow was beyond official discipline, and he confidently told everyone how the place would be repudiated on his own good judgement. He was a special journalist for a leading Adelaide newspaper, the *South Australian Advertiser* (he later became editor), his brother was the attorney-general, and most important of all, he officially represented 200 southern land-order holders and was held in respect by many more.[212] Stow's understudy (when he wasn't drunk) was another private citizen, John Stuckey, an intending shopkeeper and spokesman for 40 more land-order holders.[213] Stuckey in turn was supported by a third private settler, Jacob Bauer, a meteorologist from Melbourne who represented only himself. As land agents they were the first representatives of the land-order holders to be allowed to see the site.

Stow took exception to Escape Cliffs as soon as he saw the place. Inside three days he had posted a despatch by return mail to his newspaper, which published it three weeks later. Among Stow's many complaints was that the site reminded him too much of Sydney Harbour, with the good country about 20 miles inland,

---

211 Finniss's return via Timor was later exaggerated into a charge of leaving his post. See Northern Territory Commission. Charges No. 6 (S.A.P.P. 17 of 1866–1867, pp. 2 and 3).

212 Northern Territory Commission. Question 1491 (S.A.P.P. 17 of 1866–1867).

213 His brother was attorney-general July 1864 to March 1865. Northern Territory Commission, Question 1957. (S.A.P.P. 17 of 1866–1867).

and here there would be no convict gangs to break the back of settlement.[214] A few days later he sent a complaint through the Government Resident to the authorities in Adelaide:

> … while the capital of a new settlement requires everything to attract, the proposed site of Palmerston has everything about it to repel settlers … neither open country, pastoral land, elevation, agriculture, commerce, surface water nor building materials.[215]

Constant criticism had made Finniss sensitive about his cherished selection, and with this a state of war broke out between the two men. When the next mail went south four months later, Stow sent violent despatches to the two main newspapers, as well as a customised version for the chief secretary:

> Fancy a ship from England landing 300 or 400 people at Adam Bay. They would huddle on the edge of the Cliffs for the sake of fresh air … They would be surrounded by swamps and tortured by misquitoes. They would find that the land in the neighbourhood was worthless, and that scarcely anything would grow.

As for Finniss:

> I distinctly and formally charge him with gross selfishness, inhumanity, scurrilous and abusive conduct.[216]

In his newspaper articles he painted Finniss as a petty little man issuing 'Orders full of bombast, bunkum and bad English'.[217]

Why this strong antipathy towards the Adelaide River? Stow's objections seem to have rested on three grounds. Before setting eyes on Escape Cliffs he had been converted to the Victoria River party. He then became influenced by those in the expedition who doubted if this was the fair country discovered by Stuart at all. Lastly, a man of genteel tastes, he happened to arrive in the wet season, the worst possible time of year.

---

214 *Advertiser* 3/1/1865 leader also p. 2.

215 J.P. Stow, J. Stuckey, J. Bauer to Finniss 16/12/1864 (S.A.P.P. 15 of 1865–1866, p. 6).

216 Stow to Ayers 25/4/1865 (State Records Finniss Papers G.R.G. 35/643/215). 'Misquitoes' was an occasional 19th-century spelling.

217 *Register* 31/7/1865, p. 2 *seq*.

The dismal failures on the Adelaide River had probably given secret joy to those who, with Captain Hart, had always advocated the Victoria River. At any rate, there had been renewed talk about the Victoria River district just as Stow was preparing to leave Adelaide. When the *South Australian* put into Moreton Bay to take on stock, Stow immediately sought out Augustus Charles Gregory, the discoverer of the Victoria River country and surveyor-general of Queensland, to gain first hand information. Gregory, who strongly resented the way Earl had dissuaded South Australia away from the Victoria River, welcomed the opportunity to describe the superior qualities of his own discovery. He promised the men of the relief party a good site and a fair harbour, saying that the dangers to navigation had been much exaggerated.[218] The men lapped it up: it mattered hardly at all that the old explorer had never set eyes on the Adelaide River to make a fair comparison.

When Finniss went aboard to greet the party at Adam Bay he was taken aback to find most of them convinced that they had come to the wrong place. John Stuckey demanded to be taken to the Victoria River straight away, and was astonished when told that the capital had already been fixed where they stood.[219] Stow and Stuckey then became crusaders for the view that they were on the inferior site. (Nor did Augustus Gregory lightly abandon his hope. Later he wrote to the government in Adelaide urging them to exchange the 'worse than useless' site of Adam Bay for the Victoria River, 'the only place on the Coast where healthy pasture is accessible'.)[220]

John McDouall Stuart's admiration for the Adelaide River had influenced the decision to go there in the first place. Unfortunately by December 1864 most members of the expedition were convinced that Stuart had either fabricated the exciting climax to his journey to the north coast or had lost his way and reached the sea somewhere else. In Ebenezer Ward's opinion: 'Stuart has no more seen the Adelaide River than he has bathed his feet in the waters of the moon'.[221]

These doubts first arose earlier in 1864 when the upriver

218 *Advertiser* 3/1/1865 leader also p. 2

219 Finniss to Ayers 15/4/1865 (S.A.P.P. 15 of 1865–1866, p. 1).

220 A.C. Gregory to Andrews 31/12/1866 (C.C.L.I.L. 156/1867).

221 Ebenezer Ward's Diary p. 80 (S.L.S.A. Mortlock P.R.G. 1000).

party, who had been indoctrinated with Stuart's journals, noticed inconsistencies between the explorer's Adelaide and the river as it really was. Stuart's river, for instance, was wider than the real Adelaide and not subject to the same strong tidal rise and fall in its upper reaches. Most telling of all, Stuart's veterans in the party, Auld, King and later Thring, could recognise no landmarks at all. The Government Resident tried to disarm these rumours with various unconvincing arguments until on 18 July he decided to scotch the doubters forever by despatching Patrick Auld with a few men to the latitude where Stuart claimed to have discovered the river.[222] They came back on the same day without finding the slightest traces of the explorer's tracks. Undaunted, Finniss next day sent Auld down along the coast to recover the flag (made by James Chambers' daughters Elizabeth, Catherine and Anna, and presented to Stuart by Elizabeth) and bottle Stuart left behind to prove he had reached the sea. Auld found neither flag nor bottle.[223] In November Finniss himself tried his hand at the mystery and skirted the coast – without joy.[224] Doubts about whether Stuart was a fraud were only settled in 1870.

Jefferson Stow, a gentleman by profession, had landed at Escape Cliffs in December 1864 just when the monsoon seemed ready to flood everyone out. He found the expedition practically shelterless, the surrounding mangrove swamps dismal and the insects unbearable. Most inconvenient of all, the *Yatala* was gone and there was no comfortable way left by which a gentleman could view the country lands for the land-order holders he represented. Frustrated and bored, he would withdraw to the *Beatrice* and get drunk daily. In the time he was there, from December to May, only once did Stow dare to examine the countryside in detail. Soon after arriving he set out to try his own hand at finding Stuart's flag on

222 Ebenezer Ward's Official Journal 18/7/1864 (S.A.P.P. 89 of 1865, p. 14); Research notes by Margaret Blacker, Secretary, John McDouall Stuart Society, 21/7/2009.

223 Ebenezer Ward's Official Journal 19/7/1864; 27/7/1864 (S.A.P.P. 89 of 1865, p. 14); Instructions to Auld 20/7/1864 (S.A.P.P. 89 of 1865, p. 16).

224 *Register* 4/1/1865, p. 3. No one seems to have thought to consult the report of the scientist in Stuart's expedition, Frederick George Waterhouse, that they had not reached the coast at the Adelaide River. It turned out that they had arrived on the mud flats of the Mary River.

Chambers Bay, but instead he became hopelessly lost in a labyrinth of swamps. His horse fell into a creek and was drowned or taken by crocodiles,[225] and Stow himself lost his pants and gun in a desperate struggle to regain the bank. Stockmen eventually found him flitting in and out of the trees sorely sunburnt.[226] After that Stow stayed at home, making himself thoroughly objectionable to the Government Resident and plotting ways of destroying the settlement.

In May 1865 he almost achieved his ambition by sparking a secession of officers and men. Tired of being cooped up, Stow purchased a long-boat from the barque *Bengal* (the third relief vessel which arrived 21 April), christened it the *Forlorn Hope*, hoisted a calico flag reading 'N.T. FINIS CORONAT OPUS' and, accompanied by six men, including several branded by Finniss as deserters, set out to sail the open boat to Champion Bay 2600 miles down the west coast. The inscription on the flag referred back to the banner used at the farewell banquet, but now translated: 'Finniss finishes off the work'. The party would have departed without the most elementary charts and instruments had not one of the senior surveyors intervened. As there was a safe passage available by orthodox means, Stow's decision was surely a contrived piece of martyrdom.

The *Forlorn Hope*, much overloaded, took its leave on the 7 May, most of those left behind believing they had seen its sailors for the last time. The Adelaide papers first passed the men off as daft, but when they turned up at Swan River two-and-a-half months later they were greeted by the same journals as heroes and fugitives from oppression. Stow even sold the story of his epic journey in instalment form to the newspapers, and when that proved successful he published it as a book, which ran into two editions.[227]

One secession encouraged another. About the same time, 6 May, three officers and about a dozen men, including more so-called deserters, left by the departing *Bengal* to return home via

225 Crocodiles were generally called alligators in the Northern Territory in the 19th century. They were seen by most Europeans as manifestations of evil. The word 'alligator' seems to have had more sinister connotations than 'crocodile'.

226 *Register* 14/8/1865, p. 2.

227 R. Edmunds' Diary 1/5/1865 to 7/5/1865 (S.L.S.A. Mortlock D8043(L)); J.P. Stow, *The Voyage of the Forlorn Hope and Notes on Western Australia*, W. Hay, Adelaide, 1865.

Henry Ayers who saw himself as a statesman. He regularly read Macaulay and Carlyle. (*Australasian Sketcher* 8/7/1876, p. 61. Courtesy of the State Library of South Australia)

the Indies.[228] By September (according to Captain Howard of the *Beatrice*) about two-thirds of all the men left behind were making preparations secretly or in the open to quit by the first transport going.[229] Up to this time (according to his accusers) Finniss had deterred desertions by withholding wages. In October the surveyors up country built themselves a rough-hewn craft called the *Independent* and headed downriver to Escape Cliffs ready to make their escape. When they were met at the mouth by the Government Resident he sacked all six men on the spot so that they could return home by more orthodox transport.[230] News of these defections gave people in Adelaide the impression the Northern Territory settlement was about to disband itself, each man heading south according to his own peculiar fashion. Parliament went into recess for the government to review the situation.

Back up north, only Finniss had grounds for joy. He had rid himself of the more brazen elements of insubordination and now, by depriving them of cooking and messing facilities, he encouraged

228 Finniss to Ayers 2/5/1865 (S.A.P.P. 15 of 1865–1866, p. 14); S.A.P.D. 1865 c.921.

229 Howard to Daly 9/9/1865 (S.A.P.P. 84 of 1865–1866, p. 8).

230 Finniss to Ayers 16/10/1865 (S.A.P.P. 83 of 1865–1866, p. 13); Finniss to Ayers 14/11/1865 (S.A.P.P. 134 of 1865–1866, p. 1); Northern Territory Commission. Questions 1257 to 1265 (S.A.P.P. 17 of 1866–1867).

private citizens Stuckey and Bauer to follow suit.[231] 'The party generally seem to have behaved much better since the departure of the *Bengal* and *Forlorn Hope*,' noted the *Beatrice's* captain, 'and especially since the supply of spirits was expended.'[232] But Finniss's days at Adam Bay were numbered. Already the *Ellen Lewis* was sailing north to bring him back, too.

The Winding Up

Throughout 1866 Palmerston-on-the-Adelaide drifted hopelessly through its last months of existence.

In November 1865 Finniss received orders to place the expedition under his second-in-command, James Manton, and to travel by the same vessel home (on what Finniss called 'special duties'), where he would be given an opportunity in person to counter the charges being heaped against him in his absence. Accompanying the instructions was the famous explorer John McKinlay, who was to undertake 12 months thorough investigation before the proper site for Palmerston was settled upon.[233]

The intelligence sealed the break-up of the Northern Territory expedition. Thirty-eight men, almost two thirds of the remaining members of the expedition, headed south by the return trip of the *Ellen Lewis*, escorting their recalled leader.[234] Most of those left behind would have departed as well, had not they been up country working while the vessel was in port. At the prospect of leaving and an impending quarrel with the government in Adelaide over their wages, relations between the leader and his officers and men thawed. He even issued an official order thanking them for their 'unvarying respect and obedience'.[235] This gracious attempt to bury the hatchet was grasped upon by Finniss's enemies to prove him an inveterate liar.[236]

---

231 Northern Territory Commission. Question 2049 (S.A.P.P. 17 of 1866–1867).

232 Howard to Daly 9/9/1865 (S.A.P.P. 84 of 1865–1866, p. 8).

233 Ayers to Finniss 21/9/1865 (S.A.P.P. 15 of 1865–1866, p. 19); Ayers to Manton 21/9/1865 (S.A.P.P. 15 of 1865–1866, pp. 19 and 20); Ayers to Howard 20/9/1865 (S.A.P.P. 15 of 1865–1866, p. 20); Ayers to McKinlay 20/9/1865 (S.A.P.P. 15 of 1865–1866, pp. 20 and 21).

234 *Register* 14/2/1866, p. 2.

235 General Order 155, 9/11/1865 (S.A.P.P. 134 of 1865–1866, p. 3).

236 Northern Territory Commission. Proceedings. p. XII (S.A.P.P. 17 of 1866–

The party reached Adelaide without fame and honour about ten weeks later. One of their first acts was to organise a dinner for themselves in the Criterion Hotel in King William Street, where Finniss was greeted with cheers and the men demanded the government should pay the cost of their unauthorised exodus from the Territory.[237]

Meanwhile, on the lonely shores of North Australia, Manton was left with nine officers and ten men, one private citizen (regularly drunk) plus his wife and child, and the family of one of his surveyors, whose wife soon became pregnant. When born, this first white child was called Adam Manton Finniss Packard (after Adam Bay).[238] In order to consolidate so small a band Manton gathered them around him at Escape Cliffs like a large family.[239] The South Australian government, failing to anticipate the exodus, had left him with instructions quite beyond his means to carry out. He had to push ahead with the country surveys, do supplementary exploring to McKinlay's, and guard the property and animals at Escape Cliffs against the Aborigines – which proved in itself a full-time occupation and a half.[240]

Whereas Finniss the soldier tried to blunderbuss the local people, Manton the civilian (no doubt remembering the Auld case) set out to appease them by kindness, sugar and weevilly flour. His methods produced unexpected results. Soon he was overrun by about 200 old men, young men, women and children, all seeking to trade and be friends. The whites decided to take shelter behind Finniss's stout log stockade. In return for the flour and sugar, the tribe was quick to supply the whites, whose clumsy methods of rod fishing caused great hilarity, with mullet, salmon, turtle, goose eggs and leeches. When the visitors did not reciprocate by opening up their solid log store house, the Woolnas tried to dismantle the store themselves.[241]

1867).

237 *Register* 22/2/1866, p. 2.

238 *Register* 14/2/1866, p. 2; Daly to Cardwell 23/2/1866 (G.O.D. 10 of 1866).

239 Manton to Blyth 21/7/1866 (S.A.P.P. 80 of 1866–1867, p. 1).

240 Ayers to Manton 21/9/1865 (S.A.P.P. 15 of 1865–1866, pp. 19 and 20).

241 Clement Young's Official Journal 13/11/1865 to 10/8/1866 (S.A.P.P. 80 of 1866–1867, pp. 7 to 11); *Register* 27/9/1866, p. 2.

These developments ruled out any thought of surveys or exploration. Meanwhile, the Europeans were blessed by the arrival on the *Ellen Lewis* of a new permanent doctor, Dr James Stokes Millner, who combined the role of medical practitioner and Protector of Aborigines with that of a lay clergyman blessed by the Lord Bishop of Adelaide.[242]

The tension of being cooped up behind the stockade paved the way for more brawling. The greatest single vendetta arose between Manton and McKinlay, each of whom kept hurling their separate instructions back and forth and doing all in his power to hinder the other's work.[243] The quarrel ended abruptly in August 1866 when McKinlay, having failed dismally in carrying out his instructions, hastened south to accuse Manton before the South Australian government. Manton retaliated by posting a letter to the agent-general in London, advertising McKinlay's failures to all and sundry.[244] McKinlay returned to Adelaide by the *Beatrice* which, much to the relief of the Admiralty and at the governor's request, was now relieved of duties on the north coast.[245] The little party were left without way of escape should the Aborigines ask them to leave.

Now Manton could concentrate on harassing his second main enemy: the sole surviving private settler, a German named Jacob Bauer. Their enmity developed in late 1865 after the camp was overtaken by an outbreak of drunkenness traced eventually to Bauer who, having purchased barrels of spirits from the *Ellen Lewis*, was dispensing the contents on the black market to the officers and men. Manton was at first satisfied only to take charge of the barrels, but as the irritations grew he regretted that he had been so lenient and issued orders to stop the German's supply of food, which he was obtaining on credit from the Government store. Bauer and his family had to fall back on the alms of others – until one day he was

---

242 *Register* 26/9/1865, p. 4; Millner's first report 23/7/1866 (S.A.P.P. 80 of 1866–1867, p. 4).

243 Manton to Blyth 21/7/1866 with enclosures (S.A.P.P. 80 of 1866–1867, pp. 1 to 11); McKinlay to Blyth 3/10/1866 (S.A.P.P. 82A of 1866–1867, p. 1).

244 Manton to Dutton 18/7/1866 (S.A.P.P. 80 of 1866–1867, pp. 3 and 4).

245 John McKinlay's Journal 11/8/1866 to 25/8/1866 (S.A.P.P. 82A of 1866–1867, pp. 6 and 7).

drowned scrounging for food along the Adelaide River.[246] All this time relations between the leader and his own men slowly worsened to the point where most of his officers refused to mess with him. Not a few looked back nostalgically to the good old days when 'Bloody Tom Fool' was in charge rather than 'Cautious Tommy'.[247]

Between September and November 1866, Manton had second thoughts about how the ministers in Adelaide would take his shelving of their instructions. He therefore decided to undergo three exploring expeditions (a part-time journalist present called them recreational shooting trips) in the vicinity of the Adelaide River, using as his means of travel the small boat, *Julia*. With only seven horses to his name he could hardly contemplate anything more ambitious.

The first voyage was inland to where the upper limits of the Adelaide lost itself in a chain of small ponds.[248] Here Manton found just what he wanted: evidence to justify his discontinuance of country surveys. 'To survey land in the lower part of the Adelaide River district,' he wrote:

> would be utterly useless work, for the land is nothing but sand, scrub, and swamps ... for there is no land within fifty miles of Escape Cliffs that I should think of surveying for agriculture.[249]

Next he tried his hand at the fascinating riddle of proving whether Stuart was a fraud or not. Taking Thring, one of Stuart's men who had arrived by the *Ellen Lewis,* and nine others he examined the Wildman River and the various Alligator rivers with no result but for a brisk and close brush with the 'wild blacks'.[250] The expedition proved nothing except, as one cynic said, that the place was fit only for the wild man and the alligator.[251] His final shooting trip was to Port Darwin 'to examine Point Emery in an engineering point of view'. Again not much was proved, though later Manton

246 Manton to Blyth 21/7/1866 (S.A.P.P. 80 of 1866–1867, pp. 1 and 2); *Register* 5/2/1867, p. 2; *Advertiser* 5/2/1867 leader.

247 *Register* 5/2/1867, p. 2; *Advertiser* 5/2/1867 leader.

248 Manton to Blyth 3/12/1866 (S.A.P.P. 16 of 1867, pp. 1 and 2).

249 Manton to Blyth 11/1/1867 (S.A.P.P. 16 of 1867, p. 7).

250 Manton to Blyth 10/12/1866 (S.A.P.P. 16 of 1867, pp. 3 to 6).

251 *Register* 5/2/1867, p. 2.

claimed that it was he and not George Goyder who first suggested Port Darwin as the best site for the capital. Later again Patrick Auld made a similar claim, having been sent to explore Port Darwin in April 1865.[252]

At the end of 1866 the Northern Territory settlement on the Adelaide was wound up, symbolically enough, with an all round brawl. In December a small vessel called the *Eagle*, a paddle steamer converted to a screw steamer, arrived from Sydney bearing orders to disband the expedition and for the party to return to Adelaide, via Sydney, as quickly as possible.[253] As the South Australian government was too stingy to afford a larger vessel, the cattle had to be turned out, the little *Julia* abandoned and the buildings left where they stood – 'like another Tadmore in the Wilderness,' said a devotee of the Old Testament. Stores were buried and the gunpowder and rockets destroyed in a spectacular display that left the Aborigines gaping. They had long resented the whites' habit of hoarding possessions and must have been amazed by this change of heart. As it was, the stowage proved still inadequate, and the party spent the last weeks in bitter disputes over what should be left behind. Manton ordered the men to throw away their cherished souvenirs and demanded the right to search them to see that they did. The men refused to part with their collections unless Manton would do the same. Defying him, they piled their goods on the beach ready for shipment. The deadlock was settled in part through an accident involving the loading punt *Cautious Tommy*. The punt had been purchased from the *Ellen Lewis* and privately named by the men after their leader. The leader swore she was seaworthy while the men swore she was not. Manton insisted on proving his point by loading the punt high with their possessions. The men, alas, were right: *Cautious Tommy* sank gently with its cargo while the party watched helplessly on shore. Hearing the derogatory comments, the commander turned on the party, and challenged one man to a fight.[254] As acceptance would have meant hitting a

252 Manton to Blyth 20/12/1866 (S.A.P.P. 16 of 1867, pp. 6 and 7); *Register* 11/8/1873, p. 5, Manton to Editor; *Register* 16/8/1873, p. 5.

253 Blyth to Manton 6/11/1866 (S.A.P.P. 133 of 1866–1867, pp. 1 and 2); Manton to Blyth 11/1/1867 (S.A.P.P. 16 of 1867, p. 8).

254 *Register* 5/2/1867, p. 2; *Advertiser* 5/2/1867 leader.

superior officer the man, Hulls, refused to join issue, biding his time until they reached Adelaide when he tried to charge the leader and magistrate with intended assault and conduct unbecoming.[255]

After near three weeks stuffing and cramming, the *Eagle* finally got away so full that most of the party had to sleep on deck. The Woolnas immediately took possession of the stockade, but some gashed their bodies in grief as the party sailed away.[256] When Captain Cadell visited Escape Cliffs later in 1867 he found Old Mira, still keeping the ghost settlement in good order, anticipating the return of what must have been the strangest lot of traders from the sea the north-coast people had ever seen.[257]

Retribution

Meanwhile, Finniss had been in Adelaide facing charges of having caused the ruin of the settlement. In February 1866, a few days after his return, the government announced the establishment of a Royal Commission to investigate his mismanagement of affairs on the Adelaide River.[258]

At the time Royal Commissions were widely used by ministers to bypass being criticised in parliament and to off-load controversial decisions. The *Commission to inquire into the management of the Northern Territory* was set up mainly to white-wash the South Australian government, and this fact holds the key to most of the events that followed, which honoured the well-known advice to government: 'Never set up a Royal Commission unless you think you already know the answer.'

Architect of the Commission was the leader of the government, Captain John Hart, who had been the chief planner behind the original scheme. Hart, an astute politician (who happened to be the chief minister), realised there would need to be a scapegoat for the Territory failures and was taking steps to ensure that it would not be him. The inquiry's terms of reference were carefully restricted so that the original method of colonisation could not be considered. The six charges focused on events which occurred *after*

255 *Register* 8/2/1867, p. 2; 11/2/1867, p. 2.

256 *Register* 5/2/1867, p. 2; *Advertiser* 5/2/1867 leader.

257 *Register* 7/1/1868, p. 3. Telegraphic News.

258 *Register* 20/2/1866, p. 2.

the party left Adelaide, when the expedition was taken out of the direct control of the Ayers–Hart ministry. In addition, the terms of reference were focused only on the person of Finniss himself. There was no instruction to investigate the character and selection of the other senior officers, some of whom had been nominated by Cabinet in the teeth of the leader's request for more say in choosing his men.[259] As a final precaution, and despite the newspapers' pleas for impartiality, each appointed royal commissioner was in some way beholden to Hart and his government. The chairman, Captain O'Halloran, was head of a department under Hart's direct control. The other two members were William Milne and Charles Goode, ambitious politicians determined to make an impression in a parliament dominated by elder statesmen such as Hart and Ayers. Milne had almost certainly been promised a place in a future ministry. When someone came to Hart's office threatening to expose the chicanery, the wily Chief Minister bluffed him, noting wryly in his diary: 'he certainly was under a mistake if he supposed that the Govt. were to be tried on this occasion which his objection to Milne would seem to infer.'[260]

Having set up the Royal Commission, Hart soon resigned from Cabinet (bringing down his ministry) and headed off for England on a business trip – avoiding the chance that he might be called in to give evidence. Milne joined the re-organised government.[261]

A few radical critics saw the Royal Commission as the final act in a giant public fraud operated by some senior politicians. Finniss himself once said that the course taken in recalling him was to fabricate a collapse, force the small investor to sell out to the large investors in the Northern Territory Company and so strengthen the Company's hold over Territory history.[262] The critical newspaper *Pasquin* (always a defender of Finniss) claimed 'that the expedition was a sham, and the leader a scapegoat. The indignation of the people at his inevitable failure was to cover the frauds of responsible

259 Finniss to Ayers 26/3/1864 (C.S.O.I.L. 427/1864).

260 Diary of Captain John Hart 19/2/1866 (S.L.S.A. Mortlock P.R.G. 218).

261 *ibid.* April 1866.

262 Notes on choice of capital site, Finniss Papers (State Records G.R.G. 35/643/72).

George Fife Angas, one of the true founders of South Australia and of the South Australian Company. He approved of the Northern Territory Plan, but thought it could be better organised.
(George E. Loyau, *Representative Men of South Australia*, Howell, Adelaide, 1882, wood engraving by Jeffrey Bruer)

slop-sellers'.[263]

The inquiry opened on 7 March 1866 and dragged on for ten weeks. Finniss asked to conduct his own defence with his loyal son, Fred, as clerk and, according to standing practice, a non-legal gentleman was appointed to oppose him. The arrangement gave the chief minister further opportunity to choose another man under his thumb: Frank Rymill, of Hart's Post Office Department, whom he carefully briefed and provided with the full resources of the government and the lion's share of the witnesses headed by the formidable trio of Stow, Stuckey and Ward.[264]

Despite the arms ranged against him, Finniss made a far better showing than his prosecutor, who was content mainly to pile up personal testimonies that condemned the leader's acts. Part way through the inquiry William Milne retired to join the reshuffled government as Commissioner of Crown Lands and immigration.

263 *Pasquin* 8/5/1869, p. 150.

264 Diary of Captain John Hart 12/3/1866 (S.L.S.A. Mortlock P.R.G. 218).

His place on the Royal Commission was taken by another ambitious politician, Henry Bright, who had to make his judgement without hearing half of the witnesses. On the 16 May 1866 the commissioners finally handed down their report.

The six accusations made against the Government Resident involved three main issues. The first was that he displayed 'an utter want of management of the men under his charge, leading to the total disorganisation of the party, the destruction of stores, and other great waste of the funds of the settlement.'[265] Rymill heaped together evidence, reliable and unreliable, accusing Finniss of being lethargic, block-headed, set in his ideas and notoriously tactless in the handling of men under such trying conditions – in fact, of lacking all the qualities of dynamic leadership. After considering evidence from both sides the commissioners found him guilty.[266] Not even Finniss's supporters in parliament (men like John Tuthill Bagot) denied that he was a slow-thinking, slow-acting man.[267] He also lacked experience in managing men in field conditions – and could be very blunt. The terms of reference however deflected the blame from where it should *also* have been laid: on the architects of the Northern Territory colonisation scheme. Most of Finniss's weaknesses were those of an older man beyond his prime continually undermined by ambitious younger men who deliberately set out to aggravate him. Yet in 1863 the government had sought out Finniss's services precisely because he was from an older generation and experienced in South Australian colonisation, virtues which were accounted more important than tact or vigour, though both were expected. He was also accused of being petty in his military practices. But again, the government of 1863 had chosen him for his training and disposition as a gentleman officer of the old school. Finniss himself complained that he was sent out as a soldier, then accused of pettiness when he acted like one.[268]

He was also accused of destroying the discipline by passing over

---

265 Northern Territory Commission. Charges No. 1 (S.A.P.P. 17 of 1866–1867, p. 2).

266 Northern Territory Commission. Report. (S.A.P.P. 17 of 1866–1867, p. 3).

267 S.A.P.D. 1866–1867 c. 663.

268 Northern Territory Commission. Proceedings, p. XVII (S.A.P.P. 17 of 1866–1867).

the normal officers for defacto ones, appointed from the ranks of his followers and chosen mainly because of their good breeding and superior education. His tendency to rely on his supporters had given the officer clique a permanent grudge on which to build their insubordination. The Commission brought out the intensity of the hatred some of the officers had shown Finniss's supporters – how they were persecuted as toadies and informers, how obscene pictures of Finniss and his supporters (drawn by Railton Atkinson, who had links to the government) were hawked under their noses, how one supporter was even threatened with being dumped over the cliffs to the crocodiles.[269]

The restricted terms of reference, however, discouraged the three commissioners from concentrating too much on other possible causes for the insubordination, such as the party's lack of bushmen, so that the leader eventually had to write home for hardy labourers,[270] or the fact that many in the party had gone with an eye to future promotion and were less suited temperamentally than the commander himself.[271] As a side comment the commissioners did observe, at least, how the expedition 'included many persons unfitted for the work for which they had been engaged'.[272]

South Australians were sometimes accused of being 'a paradise of dissent', in the negative sense of disagreement. Given that arguments started so early, perhaps the pattern was set even before the departure of the *Henry Ellis* in April 1864.[273]

The second main complaint against the Government Resident (made with the Colonial Office in mind) was that he broke the spirit of his instructions by using armed, aggressive tactics against the native inhabitants.[274] Again Finniss was judged guilty by the

269 J.W.O. Bennett to T. Bennett 22/4/1865 (S.L.S.A. Mortlock D7425(L)); Northern Territory Commission. Questions 3778 to 3781; 1895 to 1916; 4159 (S.A.P.P. 17 of 1866–1867).

270 Finniss to Ayers 6/10/1864 (S.A.P.P. 89 of 1865, p. 43).

271 Northern Territory Commission. Proceedings, p. XX (S.A.P.P. 17 of 1866–1867); B.T. Finniss's statement of his defence (State Records Finniss Papers G.R.G. 35/643/57, p. 43).

272 Northern Territory Commission. Report (S.A.P.P. 17 of 1866–1867, p. 3).

273 Douglas Pike, *Paradise of Dissent* Melbourne University Press, Melbourne, 1957, for an analysis of the origins of this culture of dissent.

274 Northern Territory Commission. Charges No. 4 (S.A.P.P. 17 of 1866–1867,

Commission. As a military man he was always over-hasty to employ force, and he also believed that the 'Aboriginal question' could be solved mainly by using accredited army methods. Here again, he was made singly to blame for a complicated situation, for which the government was at least partially responsible. No mention was made in the verdict of how, before leaving Adelaide, his party was organised as a miniature expeditionary force equipped with an arsenal of weaponry, and that he was told to be ready for hostile Malays to seaward and treacherous Aborigines to landward. No mention was made, either, of the part played by the officers, whose carelessness invited Aboriginal thefts and friction, nor of Finniss's strange position in strict law. He was ordered to treat the native inhabitants as British subjects and then ordered to take their land in a manner contrary to the spirit of British law, especially as it related to property.[275]

The third charge and the one regarded as the most serious was that Finniss had ignored his instructions by prematurely fixing the capital at Escape Cliffs against the better advice of his men and the various agents and without sufficient previous exploration of the coast and adjacent country.[276] On this, the commissioners disagreed. Captain O'Halloran, an old army man and civil servant of Finniss's generation, held that the Government Resident 'almost literally' carried out his orders to make a settlement on or near the Adelaide River, and only to abandon the locale if he was personally convinced that no suitable site existed there.[277] O'Halloran's opinion was overruled by the other two commissioners, who decided that, even if there was no better site, Finniss still disregarded his orders by fixing it before first examining other likely places.[278]

The weight of the evidence so clearly lies with O'Halloran that it is difficult to see how the others reached their conclusion except

---

p. 2).

275 Northern Territory Commission. Proceedings, p. XXIII (S.A.P.P. 17 of 1866–1867).

276 Northern Territory Commission. Charges No. 3 (S.A.P.P. 17 of 1866–1867, p. 2).

277 Northern Territory Commission. Minority Report (S.A.P.P. 17 of 1866–1867, p. 4).

278 Northern Territory Commission. Report (S.A.P.P. 17 of 1866–1867, p. 3).

that they misunderstood the case or were prejudiced by outside pressures. Finniss's original instructions plainly directed him to the Adelaide River, which he knew Stuart, Earl, Ayers, the governor and the majority of his ministers preferred – though Governor Daly first needed some convincing. He knew also that his expedition was mainly equipped for surveying and deficient in horses for proper explorations. He had been ordered to study selected explorers' journals (especially Stuart's) on the journey north, and they had favoured the Adelaide River site. He understood that the 'Territory was to be settled on the faith of the reports of previous explorers'[279], and that his real task was to choose and lay out a metropolis, not to waste his resources trying to improve on the expert explorers who had gone before. True, the South Australian government had added the proviso that if there was no site suitable in his own estimation on the Adelaide River, he was then to look around at other places in the vicinity. In his own estimation, and backed by Captain Hutchison who was sent to advise him, Finniss decided that Escape Cliffs on Adam Bay suited the needs of the new metropolis. Had he persisted in exploring after deciding on the matter, he would most certainly have been guilty of disobeying his instructions. The majority opinion of the two younger commissioners is suspect in that Goode and Bright privately accredited Escape Cliffs with advantages, and were in general impressed by the soils on the Adelaide River, yet they still condemned him for not first taking the elementary precaution of looking further afield.[280]

Finniss did not help his cause by the unfortunate, stilted official language with which he made known his preference for Escape Cliffs. 'My mind is strongly determined in favor of making this the capital,' he wrote in his first letter to reach Adelaide, 'with Adam Bay for an outer, and the mouth of the river for an inner harbor.'[281] This looked like a personal predetermined bias. His next despatch suggested worse: a preference for it on faith. 'I am of opinion, therefore, that we shall not find a more suitable place,

279 Northern Territory Commission. Proceedings, p. XXIV (S.A.P.P. 17 of 1866–1867).

280 Northern Territory Commission. Report (S.A.P.P. 17 of 1866–1867, p. 3); S.A.P.D. 1866–1867 c. 688 and 696.

281 Finniss to Ayers 13/8/1864 (S.A.P.P. 163 of 1864, p. 1).

on the whole, than this; but I shall see other places first.'[282] In his third and subsequent despatches he became too eloquent in favour of his choice and too quick to put down other sites, some of which he had never seen. All this deflected attention from the original orders, which were already biased in favour of the Adelaide River. It was neither the first nor the last time that Finniss misrepresented himself by his peculiar style of writing and speech-making.

The various accusations over the site showed the naivety of planning an ideal settlement in the mind's eye and then looking for somewhere to locate it. With the benefit of hindsight there was no place anywhere on the north coast of Australia adequate to meet the needs of the plan and the expectations of the land-order holders. The Adelaide River later turned out to have considerable potential for tropical agriculture but lacked a good site and a harbour for the capital. The next site chosen possessed an excellent harbour and high land for the capital, but its uneven hinterland was totally unsuited for the needs of a concentrated settlement.

Despite the biases of the inquiry, the commissioners found opportunity in their general conclusions to make passing reference to the leader's difficulties: the type of men, the lack of animal food, the sense of neglect arising from infrequent communication.[283] In preparations for the expedition Finniss had been pushed aside by Henry Ayers, who could not delegate on details and obsessively over-controlled everything he did.

The rejection of Finniss's choice of site meant that the Territory had been given a completely false start. 'I remember the time when attacks as noisy and as reiterated as those of which I have been the subject, were made against Colonel Light,' said Finniss:

> The authorities by whom Colonel Light was appointed, however, supported him in his decision, and the event has shown the wisdom of their course; and I feel no doubt that the opposite course persued by the Government in this instance, which has rendered useless nearly the whole of the expenditure, will ultimately, if persevered in, prove ruinous to the settlement.[284]

---

282 Finniss to Ayers 10/8/1864 (S.A.P.P. 89 of 1865, p. 6).

283 Northern Territory Commission. Report (S.A.P.P. 17 of 1866–1867, p. 3).

284 Northern Territory Commission. Proceedings, p. XXI (S.A.P.P. 17 of 1866–

Adding to Finniss's feeling that he had been set up was another charge. In September 1865, after exploring in the *Beatrice* down to the Victoria River, he had called in to Timor to get fresh supplies (to counter a possible threat of scurvy). Because of this deviation he was now found guilty on a charge of leaving his post 'without authority first obtained from the Government, and without sufficient reason'.[285]

Finniss knew only too well that the Royal Commission had been stacked against him. 'It is very pleasing and satisfactory,' he later wrote, 'to have charges brought against you that you may have the Supreme felicity of refuting them especially when your opponent appoints the judges who are to try the issue.'[286] To add insult to injury Hart hereafter piously maintained that the Commission had been set up especially to give Finniss a chance to clear his good name.[287]

The reverse side of Finniss' honesty was his self-righteousness. As soon as the report became public Finniss appealed for justice to the Governor and Executive Council, entreating them to hear him in person as 'the report was utterly and entirely at variance with the evidence'.[288] The government replied by politely enquiring whether he preferred to resign or to be dismissed.[289] He then petitioned the government for compensation for losing his honoured position in the civil service. That too was refused.[290] In September he carried his 'manifold grievances' directly to the House of Assembly in a long petition seeking to prove how the evidence did not fit the judgement.[291] The Assembly kept a stony silence.[292] Finally he took

---

1867).

285 Northern Territory Commission. Charges No. 6 and Report (S.A.P.P. 17 of 1866–1867, pp. 2 and 3).

286 Finniss Papers (S.L.S.A. Mortlock P.R.G. 527/6/7A & 7B).

287 *Register* 30/3/1868, p. 3 Hart's speech at Town Hall meeting.

288 Petition of B.T. Finniss No. 11 (S.A.P.P. 81 of 1866–1867, p. 2).

289 Boothby to Finniss 23/5/1866 (State Records Finniss Papers G.R.G. 35/643/45); Boothby to Finniss 25/5/1866 (*ibid.* 46).

290 Finniss to Blyth 16/6/1866 (State Records Finniss Papers G.R.G. 35/643/59); Richardson to Finniss 19/6/1866 (*ibid.* 58); Finniss to Richardson 17/7/1866 (*ibid.* 60); Richardson to Finniss 23/7/1866 (*ibid.* 61).

291 Petition of B.T. Finniss (S.A.P.P. 81 of 1866–1867).

292 S.A.P.D. 1866–1867 c. 453.

his grievances all the way to London and petitioned the Secretary of State for Colonies for redress and employment.[293] But the Duke of Buckingham was too much an English diplomat to burn his fingers on petty colonial squabbles.[294]

Such was Finniss's natural doggedness that in September 1866 he offered to go back to North Australia and lay out the lands on the Adelaide as a private contractor.[295] This broke the silence at last. He was ridiculed in parliament and the newspapers as a silly old man. The surveyor-general noted cuttingly: 'Mr B.T. Finniss's tenders … offer to do in 1867 for 3/11½ per acre, what cost him, but recently, £3 per acre to affect.'[296]

Finniss, however, did not stop there. In 1871 he went back to the Territory as agent for the British Australia Telegraph Company (an appointment supported by the government as a kind of compensation) during which he set up son Fred as junior clerk and the family representative in the Territory. Fred stayed on to become one of the original Old Territorians.[297]

Throughout the rest of his life Finniss lost no opportunity to argue his case in speeches, letters to the newspapers and public and private records. At times he even went near to lecturing his historians. Posterity, however, has seldom been kind or just to him, holding him almost wholly to blame for the troubled events that destroyed in little more than a year and a half the First Northern Territory Expedition.[298]

But this was only one half of the story. What then, of the others?

---

293 Daly to Carnarvon 19/3/1867 with enclosures (C.O. 13/121 Folio 122 to 128).

294 Buckingham to Daly 30/5/1867 (G.I.D. 17 of 1867).

295 Finniss to Blyth 29/9/1866 (State Records Finniss Papers G.R.G. 35/643/64).

296 Tenders for Northern Territory Surveys (S.A.P.P. 188 of 1866–1867, p. 2); 3/11½ means 3 shillings 11 pence h'penny.

297 B.A.T. Co. Correspondence sent by B.T. Finniss (S.L.S.A. Mortlock P.R.G. 527/17).

298 In 2003–2004 when the author advertised in the *South Australian Genealogist* for biographical information on the members of Goyder's expedition to Port Darwin he was overwhelmed with the number of responses. When he did the same in 2005 for the Finniss expedition to Adam Bay, he got not one response. At the Royal Geographical Society (Adelaide) in the 1950s the common view was that Finniss was totally to blame for the failure.

CHAPTER 3

THE INTERVENTION OF THE PARTNERS

'Oh! have you heard the news of late,
How we have tried to form a state,
And what is like to be the fate
Of the Northern Expedition'
Advertiser, 12 January 1865

The Other Partners

The disagreements within the government party and the failure of the ministers to support their chosen officer encouraged the land-order holders to add further confusion by demanding a say in choosing the site themselves. They did this despite the original understanding that the selection should be left to a public officer, carefully selected to act on his own good judgement. The first moves to interfere came as a direct consequence of Jefferson Stow's criticisms made on reaching Escape Cliffs and sent back by the return voyage of the *South Australian*. Within a week of his objections becoming public in Adelaide, an open meeting of subscribers, all clamouring for the right to restrict the independence of the leader to choose the site, was held in the Norfolk Arms Tavern, Rundle Street. This meeting of 10 January 1865 (held before the recall of Finniss) showed the dangers of giving the subscribers too much say in the matter; for as an alternative they demanded a detailed survey of the entire coast, which could have taken anything up to three or four years.

Unfortunately for the government an election was in the brewing, and the Opposition took an important part in the proceedings. One leading parliamentarian, Henry Bull Templar Strangways, produced a resolution requesting the governor not to allow the site to be fixed until all the coast had first been examined. Five spokesmen were then elected to take the resolution to the governor – three of whom turned out to be members of the opposition party.[299]

Governor Daly received the Norfolk Arms deputation graciously. No doubt he had been expecting them. 'I think you have acted exactly as you ought,' he said, and hastily explained that his advisers already of their own accord had decided to redirect Finniss to look further afield down the north-western side of the Arnhem Land Peninsula before fixing a site. Daly was at pains to emphasise that his advisers had made up their minds before the clamour raised by the Norfolk Arms meeting.[300] But when it suited them to say so, later ministries admitted this to be a lie.[301]

When news of the objection reached Adam Bay, Finniss, in a fit of doubt momentarily abdicated his autonomy in the matter. He wrote to Henry Ayers:

> … if the Government and the shareholders in the purchase of land – whose views must direct me, and whose interests are at stake – prefer the reports and judgment of their own particular agents to mine, I am relieved of future responsibility with regard to the selection of a suitable site.[302]

The agitation simmered down for the next six months until another, even more violent dispatch arrived from Stow, accusing Finniss among other sins of defying his instructions by pushing ahead with the town and country surveys at Escape Cliffs.[303] At the same time came news of widespread defections among the expedition. The alarmed government ministers went into recess to work out their course of action. For the first time some order holders were talking about having their money back. Another deputation, this time from the Northern Territory Company in Adelaide,

---

299 *Register* 11/1/1865, p. 3.

300 *Register* 19/1/1865, p. 3.

301 North Australian Company v. Blackmore. Brief on Trial in Supreme Court (State Records G.R.G. 1/20).

302 Finniss to Ayers 1/5/1865 (S.A.P.P. 15 of 1865–1866, p. 11).

303 *Register* 31/7/1865 leader, also p. 2 *seq.*

waited on the government.[304] Again the government moved to calm the rising discontent by holding out to subscribers more say in choosing the site. After several weeks of earnest discussion they decided to recall their own officer, Finniss, and replace him by the veteran explorer John McKinlay with orders to make a full year's careful exploration of places on the Arafura Sea.[305] This crucial decision was made by a government led by Francis Stacker Dutton on the eve of his being appointed agent general in London, where he would have to deal with English holders of land-orders face-to-face. The decision not only shelved the Northern Territory question most conveniently for a year, but also in effect yielded to the claims of the land-order holders to select their own site.

For months McKinlay had been awaiting a berth to Palmerston to take up the post of manager for the London company there. His appointment to the position had been known publicly as far back as February 1865 and followed requests sent from the London directors to the Adelaide directors asking them to suggest a suitable manager.[306] George Gibbes Mayo was appointed assistant manager, the land-orders were bundled up ready to be posted direct from London to Palmerston, and sheep were ordered from the Darling to provide food and to help settle the old argument of whether or not wool turned to hair in the steaming atmosphere of the tropics.[307] By April McKinlay and Mayo were ready to go, but months went by and no ship was available. When in August 1865 the South Australian government looked around for an explorer acceptable to the majority of land subscribers McKinlay was the obvious choice. He was waiting to leave, was local manager of the London company, had been recommended by the Adelaide company and could be relied on to protect the interests of holders of land-orders. He was also a most eminent explorer, who in 1861–1862 had made a famous journey to the Gulf of Carpentaria, and a grand South Australian. Paid for by the government, he left on 25 September 1865 accompanied by his own men and animals.[308] Several months

304 *Register* 26/10/1865, p. 2 report of N.T. Company.

305 *Register* 25/8/1865 leader.

306 *Register* 28/2/1865, p. 2.

307 *Register*13/4/1865, p. 2.

308 *Register* 25/9/1865, p. 3; 26/9/1865, p. 2 Shipping Intelligence.

later a second shipment of sheep and 40 experimental pigs followed in the *Ellen Lewis*.[309] The pigs and sheep were requisitioned by McKinlay after arriving at Escape Cliffs to further test the suitability of stock for the Territory.

The order of these events gives McKinlay a more important part in Northern Territory history than emphasised by earlier historians. His appointment showed how far the southern government had swung from the intention of making a trusted government officer solely responsible for the site, acting with the authority of previous explorers. It also gave his reports a great deal of importance, particularly with English holders of land-orders, who had no other way of gaining an unbiased picture of the country's prospects. What view of the Territory did he then send back to them?[310]

When the veteran explorer left Adelaide towards the end of September the times were unpropitious. Almost all the way westward to the Leeuwin, blustery spring winds pounded the sailing ship the *Ellen Lewis,* which the government had given him. Two days out and his horses were knee deep in water. His 203 experimental sheep and 20 goats, crammed in holds too small for them, died with depressing regularity. He finally headed into Adam Bay on Guy Fawkes day, 5 November, only to find that at the very end of the long dry season there was not a blade of green grass in sight with which to revive the surviving stock. By the end of the month only 72 miserable sheep and five goats were left.[311] But worse was to come. Before preparations were far under way the wet season closed in with its humid, unhealthy prologue; many of the party became temporarily half blinded with ophthalmia. This was followed in January by torrential, bogging rains.[312] It is doubtful if ever an expedition to these parts could have been better timed to give a visitor a more dismal impression.

Nevertheless, McKinlay launched his services in the Northern Territory with high confidence – and a blistering attack on Finniss's

---

309 *Register* 2/5/1866, p. 2, Shipping Intelligence; *Register* 9/5/1866 leader.

310 Jack Cross, 'McKinlay Explorer—Scotsman in Hell'. Paper presented to the Royal Geographical Society of Australasia Historical Division 20/5/1965.

311 McKinlay to Hart 29/11/1865 (S.A.P.P. 131 of 1865–1866, p. 1).

312 Clement Young's Official Journal (S.A.P.P. 80 of 1866–1867, pp. 7 and 8 *passim*).

settlement. 'To form any estimate of the state of matters, found on my arrival here,' he wrote to Adelaide, 'is beyond the power of my pen, and would require a personal inspection to be properly conveyed to one's senses.' This was dramatically effective for what it did not say, and those who had put down their money must have felt their assets getting suddenly lighter. Local improvements, he went on, were much overestimated at £200. The country lands were so low that 'not one individual land-holder out of every hundred could make a selection upon which he could erect his homestead, without the almost positive certainty of being washed off by the floods'.[313] Poor Finniss had the unhappy duty of accompanying these tidings back to Adelaide on the return trip of the *Ellen Lewis*.

McKinlay's instructions, which he had negotiated with the government, demanded a grand performance. Starting from the upper Adelaide River and with a generous complement of men and animals, he was to make broad inland sweeps across the Arnhem Land Peninsula, first to the mouth of the Liverpool, there to meet the *Beatrice* for supplies, then down to the Roper and finally back home by another route. If, after this effort his party had not been taken by floods, exhaustion or crocodiles, he could at his own discretion make another sweep in a western direction to the Victoria River.[314] And all the way he would take his herds of sheep, goats and horses with him in order to observe their response to the climate and vegetation. Those who later accused him of exploring like a Nabob, failed to appreciate the magnitude of the task he had set himself. He undertook to do too much before leaving South Australia and then was too conscious of his reputation to retreat when he found himself facing the obstructions of a Northern Territory wet season.

When the expedition into the country got under way with 15 men, McKinlay's miscalculations grew thick and fast. The veteran explorer's behaviour over the following wet season was so out of character that the Adelaide newspapers suggested that the 'wet' might have a 'deleterious' effect on the human brain. He condemned Finniss, got into a long dispute with his second in command, Edmunds, and finished up by branding Manton a coward and a maniac.

313 McKinlay to Hart 29/11/1865 (S.A.P.P. 131 of 1865–1866, p. 1).

314 Ayers to McKinlay 20/9/1865 (C.S.O.O.L. 762/1865 State Records G.R.G. 24/4/138).

His first major mistake was so to under-rate the severity of the monsoon that he delayed setting out for 70 days, by which time the rains had really set in. Edmunds tried to forewarn him often enough to make himself thoroughly unpopular – likewise Manton – but McKinlay was not prepared to risk such a well equipped expedition by leaving before the men and stock had completely recovered from the journey north. When they did set out on 14 January, the Adelaide River was a swollen flood and the lagoons along its bank terrible to negotiate. McKinlay took the easy course, going ahead inland by boat, while his men picked their way overland with the stock. This added nothing to his stature in the eyes of his party. The journey overland turned out to be a terrible experience. One of the party became lost and was eventually found hiding from the others, crazed and terrified, and fearing himself pursued by 'Malay savages'.[315]

Having completed the first stage of his plan – an inland exploration to the upper Adelaide – McKinlay could now embark on the second stage, which was to strike overland for the Liverpool River to meet the *Beatrice* for supplies, and so to approach it from its hinterland side. On 7 February he set out from the Adelaide in a general easterly direction over stony hills and boggy vales. Still the rains continued to fall. Each day the lowlands became harder to cross until eventually his party could bridge them no longer. They were marooned on a stony outcrop for six dismal weeks, tormented by insects and the humidity, and compelled to eat their wretched sheep and horses one by one.

But McKinlay refused to turn back. Edmunds (his second in command) was now convinced that the rains had crippled all chances to carry out the plan, that even if they made the Liverpool the *Beatrice* would almost certainly have gone. But his leader refused to admit the possibility of failure. In retrospect this seems his second major blunder. His first, to delay setting out, helped ruin the chances of success. His second almost cost the lives of himself and his men.

During a temporary lull in the rains at the end of March, the party managed to break free and off they set again bound for the

---

315 John McKinlay's Journal 14/1/1866 to 5/2/1866 (S.A.P.P. 82 of 1866–1867, pp. 1, 2, 3); R. Edmunds' Diary 14/1/1866 to 7/2/1866 (S.L.S.A. Mortlock D8043(L)).

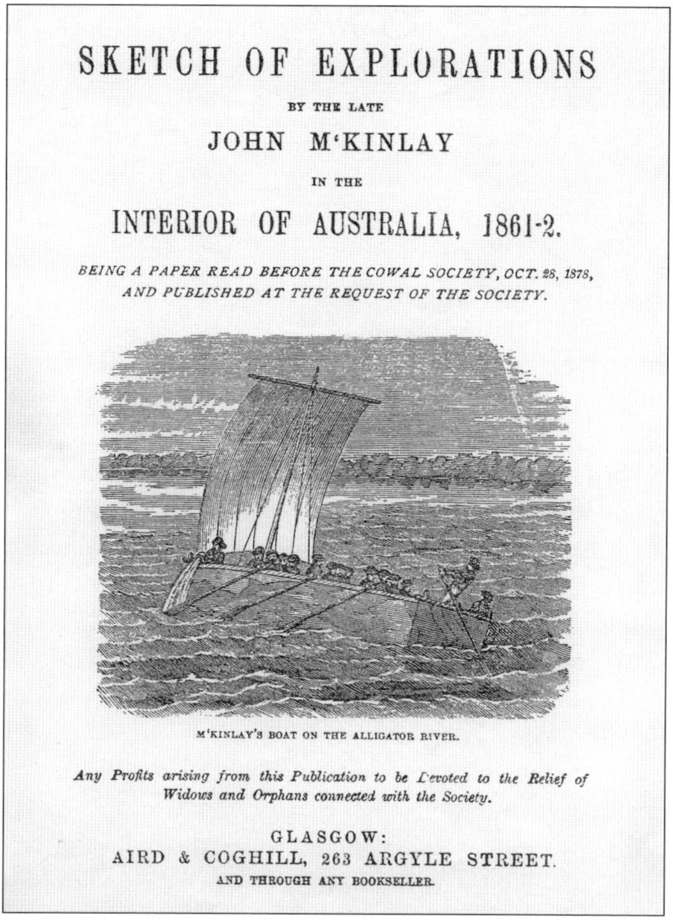

SKETCH OF EXPLORATIONS

BY THE LATE

JOHN M'KINLAY

IN THE

INTERIOR OF AUSTRALIA, 1861-2.

BEING A PAPER READ BEFORE THE COWAL SOCIETY, OCT. 28, 1878, AND PUBLISHED AT THE REQUEST OF THE SOCIETY.

M'KINLAY'S BOAT ON THE ALLIGATOR RIVER.

Any Profits arising from this Publication to be Devoted to the Relief of Widows and Orphans connected with the Society.

GLASGOW:
AIRD & COGHILL, 263 ARGYLE STREET.
AND THROUGH ANY BOOKSELLER.

McKinlay's dramatic retreat from the East Alligator River in a punt made of calico and jerked horse skins stretched around a frame of saplings, pursued by alligators and sharks. It did much to discredit the Northern Territory with land investors. (*Sketch of Explorations by the Late John McKinlay 1861–62*, Aird and Coghill, Glasgow, 1878)

Liverpool like rats in a maze, hedging their way around the edge of the coastal lowlands. By the end of May their strength had become so dissipated and prospects so dim that – according to Edmunds' version of the story – but for the intervention of his second-in-command, McKinlay would have disbanded the expedition and left each man, as in a routed army, to fend for himself. After becoming trapped in a sea of mud on the flood plain of the Mary River, they finally staggered onto the upper reaches of a large river (it turned out to be the East Alligator, over 70 miles short of their destination) where they slaughtered the surviving horses and constructed an outlandish punt of calico and jerked horse skins stretched around a wooden frame (inappropriately named the *Pioneer*), by means of which they gingerly navigated their way back to Escape Cliffs. Even in this last retreat fortune frowned on them. They were dogged down the river by hungry crocodiles and along the coast by sharks, which, savouring its aroma, anticipated making a meal of their punt.[316] They had been out six months, lost everything but their bare lives and carried out a fraction of the work. The costly adventure had, as the leader admitted, 'positively done nothing toward settling the point it was sent forth to set at rest'.[317]

All this made exciting reading in the colonial and English newspapers, but it gave the Territory a most notorious name. Worse still, Edmunds' jaundiced version of events attracted most attention. Driven by the need to return some sort of finding (and in between squabbles with the maniac Manton) he later undertook in two small boats a safe sea expedition down to the Daly River, which had been discovered by Finniss. But the best he could recommend was that Anson Bay, into which the river drained, had certain advantages, and that the West Alligator (which he had only skirted in his desperate retreat by punt) might conceivably have more and so prove a likely site.[318]

As for McKinlay, though he did think the inland of value for cattle, his journals gave the impression that here was a last miserable corner of God's earth. That was the story his reports sent back to the waiting ears of land investors in England.

The Great Debate

On 18 October 1866 the South Australian government decided on perhaps the bravest Northern Territory policy ever – and never let parliament forget it. The government led by the youngest chief minister the colony had known, James Penn Boucaut (whose father

316 John McKinlay's Journal 5/2/1866 to 29/6/1866 (S.A.P.P. 82 of 1866–1867, pp. 4 to 21); R. Edmunds' Diary 7/2/1866 to 5/7/1866 (S.L.S.A. Mortlock D8043 (L)).

317 John McKinlay's Journal 29/5/1866 (S.A.P.P. 82 of 1866–1867, pp. 19 and 20).

318 John McKinlay's Journal 27/7/1866 to 25/8/1866; McKinlay to Blyth 3/10/1866 (S.A.P.P. 82A of 1866–1867, pp. 4 to 9).

once worked for the East India Company) moved to abandon the Northern Territory settlement altogether.

This was contained in four resolutions: to withdraw the present survey party; not to replace it with another; discontinue surveys at once; and pay the purchase money back to those promised land.[319]

The debate and bitter inquisition the resolutions set off is one of the most far-reaching events in the Territory's history. Boucaut's government tried to confront parliament with a picture of gloomy realism. They had failed. There was no prospect of success, no suitable site and insufficient money left (less than a quarter remaining) to look further afield for another. The present locality at Escape Cliffs was worthless – even Manton and McKinlay must agree on that. But to refuse to hand up the 'promised land' would be to bring lasting dishonour on them all for deliberately committing a breach of contract.[320] It was a question, as one minister said, of getting out now by repaying 20 shillings in the pound instead of procrastinating only to pay 30 shillings later on.[321]

The debate took place at a time when the mood of easy optimism in South Australia was changing. A drought had set in in the pastoral areas. Also, owing to a bout of inter-factional fighting, parliament was passing through its third serious crisis since the colony gained self-government in 1857.

The Upper House begrudgingly accepted the decision to abandon the Northern Territory settlement with reparations. The Legislative Councillors' realism was helped by the Honourable Thomas Elder of the Northern Territory Company, who, as a member, cast veiled threats that 'the colony would suffer indelible disgrace' and 'would be ostracised' if it repudiated the contract.[322] But in the House of Assembly, guardian of the public purse, the members' behaviour proved not only unreasonable but inconsistently unreasonable.

Most in the Assembly confronted the move to abandon the

---

319 Minutes of Proceedings of the Legislative Council during the session 1866–1867, 18/10/1866; Votes and Proceedings of the House of Assembly during the session 1866–1867, 18/10/1866.

320 S.A.P.D. 1866–1867 c.674 *seq.*; S.A.P.D. 1866–1867 c.660 *seq.*

321 *ibid.* c. 671.

322 *ibid.* c. 670.

Northern Territory Plan with the idea that they somehow had been and were being tricked. Their suspicion was strengthened by the fact that Chief Secretary Arthur Blyth, who happened also to be a director of the Northern Territory Company, led off the debate. Throughout the proceedings members clung blindly to the promise (attributed to Hart, who luckily was out of the colony) that the newly added Territory could never become a burden on the South Australian taxpayer. Not even the colony's best lawyers could shake their faith. The Law Officers' considered opinion that the colony was legally and financially responsible for the failures was pushed aside, with suspicion being cast on the Law Officers. It was all a question, one member said, of how you *put* these matters to the lawyers.

The government's resolutions contained two consonant proposals. One was to disband the survey expedition; the other to abandon the plan of colonisation by refunding the full purchase money to all those who had bought land in advance. To have been consistently unreasonable the House of Assembly should have rejected both. But such was the members' anguish at seeing the land fund deflating, that a majority of them made up their minds to support only the first proposal. They ordered Escape Cliffs disbanded, where Manton was said to be wasting good money in idleness on land he himself acknowledged as worthless. The other proposal, to pay back the money, was treated by most members as an unthinkable insult.[323]

Even the Adelaide newspapers marvelled at the inconsistency which gave the politicians the worst of two worlds. All the money already sunk into Escape Cliffs would now be wasted, while the land fund was too exhausted to start out again in another place.

The Boucaut government withdrew from its bold plan, puzzled at just what parliament wanted it to do. Being puzzled, it did exactly as its predecessors had done. It devised a scheme to shelve the Northern Territory question.

First, the government went through the unusual routine of calling for private tenders to survey the lands, which it could hardly have accepted with the land fund in such a feeble condition. The

323 *ibid*. c. 710.

tactic gave it a good reason for doing nothing venturesome for the rest of the parliamentary session. Just how private contractors could have met the situation is hard to imagine. There was not even a site where the successful tenderer could go to lay out his 300,000 acres. When the conditions under which the tenderer would have to work were advertised they proved to be so demanding as to read like a deterrent. A tenderer had to find his own site somewhere between Port Darwin and Anson Bay good enough to pass general approval, besides binding himself to a £10,000 surety with a penalty of £10 for each day late in starting and £50 for each day late in finishing.[324] He clearly had to be many times more efficient than the government's own expeditions had been. As one observer put it:

> The advertisement assumes that individuals will come forward in the spirit of the enterprising American who offered in a moment of emergency to complete the Crimean war by contract.[325]

Nevertheless, 11 tenderers came forward as enterprising as the American, most of them about as unrealistic. Their offers ranged from eight pence (barely enough to pay the cost of getting there) to 52 pence for the survey of each acre. When all the bids were in, Surveyor-General George Goyder, not surprisingly, found it impossible to sort out the offers unless a common site was first fixed. Indeed the offer that most pleased him was on the Victoria River and outside the region advertised.[326]

Next, the government decided to send out yet another site-hunting expedition. On 9 January 1867, two days before the end of parliament and amid a rush of late business, it announced its intention of sending another explorer (later confirmed as Captain Francis Cadell, the River Murray steamer pioneer, newly returned from adventures in New Zealand having helped the government there launch the New Zealand navy during the Maori Wars) to make one last, conclusive investigation. This was probably no sudden decision. Three months earlier it was rumoured that Cadell

---

324 Survey of Land, Northern Territory (S.A.P.P. 128 of 1866–1867, pp. 1 to 4).

325 *Register* 16/11/1866 leader.

326 Goyder to the Secretary, Crown Lands and Immigration 12/12/1866 with enclosures (S.A.P.P. 188 of 1866–1867); sundry correspondence (S.A.P.P. 81 of 1868–1869).

had been approached for such a purpose. Cadell, like Finniss and McKinlay, was chosen first and foremost for being a famous South Australian pioneer. 'Captain Cadell,' said Commissioner of Crown Lands Lavington Glyde, 'was doubtless an excellent sailor, although it was questionable if he was a good explorer; and when he took pen in hand his ways were very remarkable.'[327] The appointment was set upon by the Opposition, out of political opportunism, as an irresponsible act and a disgraceful waste of time and money. But in May 1867, Boucaut's government collapsed, replaced by an Ayers government. When parliament reassembled in July, the same Opposition members found themselves in power and they showed themselves to be happy enough then that Captain Cadell was away exploring on the north coast. In fact, equally adept at delaying tactics as their predecessors, they used the explorer's absence to shelve the vexed Northern Territory question through the *entire* 1867 session, lasting five months in all. In view of the efforts made to move them, this was no mean feat.

Before following the adventures of Captain Cadell, the Boucaut government's one positive strategy, extracted like a small pearl during the 1866 Northern Territory debate, needs consideration. This strategy was to turn the clock back to the commonsense ideas of George Waterhouse and the unpretentious squatter, and was based on the observation that the only common attitude in parliament was a bitter recrimination against planned colonisation as the root cause of all their present difficulties. But the canny Waterhouse had already turned his back on investing in the Territory's pastoral industry. In 1869 he left for New Zealand where three years later he became premier and later again acting-governor; eventually he died a rich man.

In November 1866, the Boucaut government gazetted greatly liberalised pastoral regulations for the Territory. Blocks between 25 and 300 square miles could be taken up at a peppercorn rent for seven years and at 10 shillings a square mile for each of the next 18 years.[328] The newspapers even revived the old talk about McKinlay's and Stuart's routes becoming the chief avenues of colonisation. Here

327 S.A.P.D. 1866–1867 c.1449; 1868–1869 c.87.

328 *S.A. Government Gazette* 1/11/1866, pp. 1107 and 1108.

was the first effort to break free from the web of complications which had followed the adoption of planned settlement. Like all attempts to turn back the clock, it was wishful thinking. Since the days of Waterhouse and 1862 the north had suffered an extended dry, which, but for a respite in 1867, took hold of the interior between late 1863 and 1869 and made Stuart's more direct route across the continent not much better for colonisation than camel tracks over the Sahara. The second problem was the decision proclaimed by the Queensland government in September 1863 and confirmed in September 1864 to block the passage of stock from other colonies, along McKinlay's alternative route. South Australia's Pastoral Association had fought tenaciously to keep this 'best, if not the only practical route to the new settlement'[329] inside the bounds of South Australia, in 1862 pressing for the annexation of a territory with an eastern boundary continuous to that of South Australia by taking the existing boundary of South Australia straight north to the Gulf of Carpentaria. In London, Newcastle rewarded their efforts by leaving the prized strip temporarily part of Queensland, the government of which put it under quarantine restrictions, outlawing the entry of all foreign cattle and sheep. The rebuff only made the South Australians redouble their efforts, first by pleading then by persuading, and when these failed, by threatening to haul their unfriendly neighbours before the Colonial Office in London. But the Queenslanders stood fast, and no doubt remembering how the southerners had once claimed sole right because Stuart's was the only practical route to the upper Territory, bade them first to make use of what they already had. In response to all these set-backs, the Pastoral Association, disheartened by events, was wound up in November 1865.[330] The conditions were not yet right for pastoral colonisation, nor were they right until the end of the 1870s when the drought had long gone and a settlement was firmly established

329 Petition to the Honorable the House of Assembly, in Parliament assembled, from the Pastoral Association 14/6/1864 (S.A.P.P. 61 of 1864); Passage for Stock to Northern Territory (S.A.P.P. 111 of 1864).

330 *Register* 3/5/1864, p. 2; Petition to the Honorable the House of Assembly, in Parliament assembled, from the Pastoral Association 14/6/1864 (S.A.P.P. 61 of 1864); Ayers to Colonial Secretary in Queensland 10/7/1864 (S.A.P.P. 111 of 1864); Herbert to Ayers 9/9/1864 (S.A.P.P. 149 of 1864); *Register* 15/6/1864 leader; 25/11/1865, p. 3.

Arthur Blyth who advised Captain Cadell to proceed straight to the Liverpool River to forever settle the question of the site.
(*Australasian Sketcher* 18/4/1874, p. 12. Courtesy of the State Library of South Australia)

at Port Darwin. Even then, it was the Queensland pastoralist who pioneered the way.

Captain Cadell's investigation was prejudiced by his undisciplined scientific curiosity, which led him to waste valuable time, and the eventual suspicion of politicians and the press that he had been sent out to prove the suitability of a predetermined site.

Unlike other expeditions to the Territory, details of Cadell's appointment were largely kept hidden and leaked out in dribs and drabs. About two weeks after parliament prorogued, the Boucaut government announced that Captain Francis Cadell was about to leave on the schooner *Flinders* to investigate sites for a northern settlement near the Victoria River, just then attracting attention because of a letter from Augustus Gregory. Cadell considered the government schooner *Flinders* unsuitable, while South Australia's Chamber of Commerce wanted her kept on the south coast for port work. Then, on 20 February 1867 the Boucaut government announced it would hire in Sydney a suitable vessel, which turned out to be the *Eagle* owned by the Australian Steam Navigation Company used to bring the last of the Escape Cliffs people back. When Cadell left Adelaide six days later it was rumoured he had been given a free hand to look at all coastal sites from border to border. Only later in June did it emerge he had in fact been directed to prefer the Liverpool River.[331]

Before Cadell left Adelaide to form his expedition in Sydney (there being no suitable vessel in South Australia), Chief Secretary Arthur Blyth urged him to look for a site near the Liverpool River, provided it measured up to reasonable expectations. Looked at on a drawing-room map the Liverpool certainly had much to commend it: it was exactly central, high up in line with shipping routes through Torres Strait and safely inside the influence of the tropical rains. 'In a word,' wrote Cadell, 'Nature manifestly intended it as civilization's starting point'[332] – though no explorer, beginning with Captain Phillip Parker King, had ever before seen it in such a light.

Cadell's main instruction was clear: to set a hard course for the Liverpool River, study if its prospects were as good as they appeared on the map, and telegraph back the result quickly via Queensland's outport at Burketown. With this intention and a cheerful heart he set sail from Sydney on April Fool's Day, 1 April 1867, in command of a small fleet consisting of the steamship *Eagle* and the tender *Firefly* for what had now suddenly become the best placed river on the far north coast.[333]

Cadell's first encounter with civilisation's starting point was a memorable one. He and the doctor went ashore, only to be chased off by a group of Aborigines who as it turned out, were pursuing them for alcohol. The Aborigines then, wrote Francis Napier of the *Eagle*:

> commenced dancing, one fellow, the leader of the band, humming through a hollow branch about six feet long, another playing the bones, while a third went through the most comical movements and gestures, to the time of the band, quivering the thighs peculiar to the Australian

331 *Register* 25/1/1867 leader also p. 2; 6/2/1867, p. 2; 9/2/1867, p. 2; 1/6/1867 leader also p. 2.

332 Cadell to Ayers 7/1/1868 (S.A.P.P. 24 of 1868–1869, p. 1).

333 *Sydney Morning Herald* Shipping section 2/4/1867; 5/4/1867; 8/4/1867; *Empire* 12/6/1867.

natives, and always ending in a most extraordinary bound, in which he displayed great agility.[334]

On their first night ashore the party inadvertently sat down on the habitat of a crocodile, which at midnight made an appearance and stampeded the horses, two of which were never seen again. The next 15 days were spent in getting the horses back, setting up camp and chasing wild buffaloes for their meat, with disheartening results.[335]

The remaining two months ashore were devoted to three serious local expeditions along the coastal lowlands which stretched on both sides of the river. On the west side they were graciously shown round by a guide from the Gunavidji people called Calilly (or Corbilly), who because of the climate divested himself of the shirt and pants presented him but continued to wear a tall white hat. Everywhere Cadell found things to please him: a fine deep estuary, rich brown soil covered with open forest and feed four feet high, and moderately elevated land healthy for a capital.[336] By the end of August 1867 the explorer was back in Burketown, from where he sent – by telegraph – his enthusiastic report. He eventually wanted the actual surveys laid out down on the plain and reaching each way from the river, with the Blyth (which he discovered and diplomatically named after his political master) and King rivers as the two outer limits.[337] Though Cadell backed all his recommendations with careful reasoning, he never escaped the suspicion of having made them to please his masters in Adelaide.

Cadell now turned to considering exploration of a secondary importance – to see whether any other well-known sites measured up to his favoured Liverpool River. Already on the way back to Burketown he had taken a look at the Roper, where the *Eagle* suddenly ran aground on a sandbar on Maria Island and the *Firefly*

---

334 Francis Napier, *Notes of a Voyage from New South Wales to the North Coast of Australia,* privately printed Glasgow, 1876, p. 24. One of the earliest descriptions of Aboriginal dance and music on the north coast.

335 Cadell to Ayers 26/8/1867 (S.A.P.P. 178 of 1867, pp. 1 and 2).

336 Francis Cadell's Journal 23/5/1867 to 12/7/1867 (S.A.P.P. 24 of 1868–1869).

337 Cadell to Ayers 26/8/1867 (S.A.P.P. 178 of 1867 *passim*); Cadell to Ayers 18/2/1868 (S.A.P.P. 24 of 1868–1869, p. 2).

crashed into it and sank. Besides the sandbar problem, he found the area lacking in elevation for a main town.[338] Around the Victoria River he found a 'most wretched, rocky, barren, and waterless country, a perfect Tierra del Fuego'.[339] Adam Bay, which he then visited in October, pleased him more, except for its anchorage.[340] Here the party met Old Mira, who raced down to greet them dressed only in a felt hat and carrying a red flag. According to Francis Napier, not even a book or piece of paper had been disturbed as the Aborigines waited for their special visitors to return to the Escape Cliffs settlement.[341]

Cadell made all these coastal surveys with great care and thoroughness, thus completing the work begun by Matthew Flinders early in the century.

True explorer/adventurer that he was, Cadell, as the trip progressed, sent back detailed reports of his strange experiences whenever he could. Some of them seemed bizarre to his masters in Adelaide. On the Cobourg Peninsula he tried his hand at buffalo catching. On the Roper River he went after a solitary white man said by the Aborigines to be bearded to the waist and living with one of the tribes. When he failed to find the man, he left pieces of three-cornered calico behind, which the natives would soon discover and wear as 'fig-leaves', and on each garment he wrote a short inscription directing the lone man to cattle stations down in the Gulf. On the east Liverpool River he saw an Aboriginal woman 'formed more after the European model', and others on the west Liverpool without a nose. On the same river his party had a brief encounter with a hungry dingo so determined in its search for food that it tried to gnaw off one of the stockman's boots while he lay asleep with one leg protruding from the tent. His party met a family of Aborigines faithfully carrying around the bones of some departed friend. Cadell even paused in his journey to make a few cursory comments on the dawn of the Iron Age among the inhabitants. He came to the conclusion that 'iron meant to them war, wealth and

338 Cadell to Ayers 26/2/1868 (C.S.O.I.L. 298/1868).

339 Cadell to Ayers 7/1/1868 (S.A.P.P. 24 of 1868–1869, p. 1).

340 *ibid.*

341 *Register* 7/1/1868, p. 3; Francis Napier, *Notes of a Voyage from New South Wales*, p. 78.

Captain Francis Cadell, 'Doubtless an excellent sailor, although it was questionable if he was a good explorer; and when he took pen in hand his ways were very remarkable'. He also had a sinister side.
(*Town and Country Journal* 7/2/1880. Courtesy of the State Library of South Australia)

women'.[342]

None of this exotica was much appreciated in the south. The *Register* dubbed him Lord Nanboddo, the Great Traveller, and later even ranked him sarcastically with Marco Polo.[343] When Francis Cadell finally got back to Adelaide in February 1868 he had much overstayed his allotted time and the land fund had dried up to a 10th of its original size.[344] The citizens of South Australia – taxpayer, journalist and politician – were in no mood to appreciate him. When the happy adventurer wandered home he could hardly have anticipated the showers of abuse and ridicule rained upon him.

All the 12 months Cadell was away, resentment had been building up against what seemed a ludicrous state of affairs. There

342 Francis Cadell's Journal (S.A.P.P. 24 of 1868–1869, pp. 8 to 22 *passim*).

343 *Register* 17/10/1867 leader; 8/1/1868 leader.

344 S.A.P.D. 1868–1869 c.87, 88, 89.

on the north coast, no one quite knew where, was Captain Cadell out of reach and with money and time running out. Here in Adelaide were government ministers refusing point blank to talk about the Territory until the explorer had handed in all his reports. 'A ring-necked parrot or a magpie,' complained a leading member of the Opposition, 'might have done the country as good service as the Hon. Treasurer [and his] ... Captain Cadell! Captain Cadell!'[345] The explorer's name became synonymous with evasion during the entire 1867 parliamentary session. Even the government ministers, when it suited them, joined the stone throwing.

The directors of the North Australian Company in London were more careful in apportioning the blame. They saw clearly that the Cadell expedition was the climax to a long train of events starting with the Northern Territory debate of 1866, and the impossible, obstructive stand taken up by the House of Assembly. The McKinlay episode had shattered their faith in the new settlement; the Cadell episode absolutely convinced them that the time had come to pull out.

On 5 March 1867, soon after receiving news of the Northern Territory debate, the directors in London called together a formidable gathering of shareholders in the London Tavern, Bishopsgate Street. The intention was to gain public support for a complete retreat. There were good reasons for reading the gravest suspicion into the South Australian actions. Some of the colony's parliamentarians were advocating both the abandonment of surveys at Escape Cliffs and not paying back the money.Then, the dubious alternative of advertising for tenders to do cheaply what a well-equipped government party could not do at a large cost looked most reprehensible, as if the colony's government intended to lay out the lands along the first mud flat or ironstone ridge they could find. Already the London directors were certain that the agreement had been broken on one count: Clause 10, which implied that a large part of the land fund must go towards good government and development *after* the settlement was laid out. Then again, the government had abandoned Escape Cliffs with a finality frightening to read about. Most of the stores, paid for with the land money, were

345 S.A.P.D. 1868–1869 c.82.

recklessly destroyed or left behind. Those provisions surviving were auctioned at a disadvantageous price in Sydney and Adelaide.

The directors in London found no trouble in getting support, indeed they were hard put to keep their supporters from becoming too energetic. The chairman, Alexander Elder, played the part of chief pacifier, assuring the meeting that South Australians were honourable men not in the practice of repudiating agreements. Yet in case the colonials were tempted to repudiate the contract he let fly with a sufficient number of threats. He knew that a meeting of this kind carried much greater weight in London than in Adelaide. The majority of land-order holders were Englishmen. The colony borrowed from Englishmen for much of its development, and if there was one thing colonials hated it was having their mistakes aired in the 'home' newspapers.[346]

Intelligence of the London Tavern meeting, together with a formal demand for their money back, reached Adelaide when Cadell was somewhere on the north coast. Two thirds of all English holders of land-orders, it was claimed, had attached their written support. The government received the news in grim silence and refused to talk. Now the Adelaide company decided that the time had come to stand beside their English compatriots.[347] For three half-yearly meetings the directors in Adelaide had pleaded for patience,[348] but the point of being patient seemed to have vanished. In hoisting their banner Henry Ayers played a curious double role, first as chairman of directors moving the rank and file to action, then as leader of the government who tried to stave off the companies.

In November 1867 the two companies organised a combined assault on the South Australian government. This took the form of a deputation headed by George Anstey (who came from England to speak for the North Australian Company), Thomas Elder and Samuel Tomkinson (for the Adelaide company) and Maurice Salom, an individualistic Jew who represented certain independent holders of land-orders.

346 *Register* 13/4/1867 leader; 11/5/1867 leader; 23/11/1867, p. 2. Anstey's statement; correspondence with Northern Territory preliminary land-order holders (S.A.P.P. 175 of 1867).

347 *Register* 25/4/1867, p. 3.

348 *Register* 26/10/1865, p. 2; 26/4/1866, p. 3; 1/11/1866, p. 2.

Anstey (long-remembered in Adelaide for once fighting a duel with whips at ten paces with Captain Hart) was the main spokesman, and he forcibly described the embarrassing situation in which he and his fellow directors had found themselves. Since the details of the 1866 debate became public in London the shareholders were convinced 'the Colonials' were up to no good. Their suspicions were strengthened by the knowledge that colonials in London had coaxed them into the scheme and (with one exception) had always directed their company. All they now wanted was to get back their money and nothing, said Anstey, would dissuade or appease them. Chief Minister Ayers replied with like candour, describing how governments had been driven into their present policies by the attitude of the Lower House. Though his government recognised a contract, they could not and would not commit themselves until after Cadell returned.

The meeting broke up with Anstey, annoyed at the prospect of facing the impatient Englishmen with such a meagre reply, threatening to drag the question before the Imperial Parliament and to damage the sale of £800,000 of South Australian bonds shortly to be offered on the London Loan Market.[349] As events turned out, he was almost as good as his word.

The Second Northern Territory Expedition: 1868–1869

'Out spoke the hardy little wight
I'll go, so don't be nervous;
But 'tis not for your silver bright;
Tis for the public service'
Ballad to George Goyder, *Register*, 15 September 1868

In 1868 the Northern Territory problem became so confused that, out of desperation, something positive and daring was done.

The prime cause of this confusion was a Lower House election, held in April–May 1868, which sparked off a year of chronic party instability. For the first time the Territory became a large election issue, with voters given the opportunity to say whether they

349 *Register* 23/11/1867, pp. 2 and 3; *Advertiser* 23/11/1867, p. 3.

wanted it abandoned with reparations or whether they sided with the defiant stand taken by the old Assembly. As the campaign got under steam, it soon became clear that the electors knew nothing about the Northern Territory, except that as taxpayers they were not going to pay back any money. And they held to that view almost with fanaticism. Each candidate was cornered on the hustings to declare before all where he stood: for repayment, survey, or outright repudiation. If the candidate said that he stood for survey he was greeted with hearty cheers. More than three quarters of those destined to become ordinary members in the new Assembly pledged never to pay back the money. The rest, but two, dodged the issue by claiming that it was a subject on which only lawyers could decide.[350]

The five members of the Ayers ministry, fighting for re-election, had to take a more responsible approach. Midway through the campaign at an out-of-town dinner in Victor Harbor (safely 65 miles from Adelaide), they unveiled an ingenious plan to please everyone. It was described by the *Advertiser* as a 'post-prandial manifesto'. They proposed (they said) to break with the idea of concentrated settlement by allowing every person entitled to land to make his selection anywhere in the Territory provided he paid his *own* survey costs. This last provision was intended to please the taxpayer, for less than £10,000 remained in the land fund. For those who preferred land as ordered, they proposed to continue with the original scheme, while they would refund the purchase money to anyone preferring to give up his land-orders. This last proposal was well-received in England, not least by the harassed South Australian agent-general, Francis Dutton, who publicised it every chance he got.

As an additional compensation, the government proposed that the size of blocks for those preferring to select anywhere in the Territory would be increased from 160 to 320 acres, and for those wishing to stay with the original scheme the size would be increased to 240 acres providing they signed a supplementary contract ruling out the right to take the colony to court for failing to meet the conditions of the original Act. As a final bait, those land-order holders not wanting their money back would also have the right to buy 'additional sections' at a possible cheap rate.

350 Based on a survey of speeches by candidates, *Register* and *Advertiser* 3/3/1868 to 29/4/1868 *passim*.

Assuming about a third chose each course, survey costs would be kept to a minimum, the original scheme would not be ignominiously abandoned, and those threatening to take the colony to court would be staved off. The advertised blessings seemed too good to be true. A thoughtful critic, pointing out people's tendency all to rush to one side, believed that 90 per cent would take the money, leaving South Australia the great inconvenience and expense of setting up a few Robinson Crusoes on a deserted coast.[351]

As in Aesop's fable about the miller, his son and their ass, which was now quoted as a moral lesson, the intention to please all satisfied none in South Australia. Citizens had every reason to distrust foolproof plans – after all, these were the same Cabinet ministers (save one, Thomas Reynolds having replaced Hart) who in 1863 worked out a plan to settle the Territory at no one's cost or inconvenience.

Even before parliament assembled, the Adelaide press and municipal authorities stage managed an indignation meeting in the Adelaide Town Hall where about 250 citizens gathered to hear the ministry answer for their scheme, especially the part about paying back money. None of Ayers' ministers, astute men that they were, deigned to put in an appearance. In their absence those who attended turned on each other and the meeting degenerated into an autopsy over past mistakes, with Finniss (who blamed the bad system) and Hart (who blamed bad leadership) the chief combatants. Motions prepared by John Barrow of the *Advertiser* and moved by Richard Wells of the *Register,* were carried censuring successive governments for mishandling the Territory, with one Adelaide City councillor claiming that they were living in one of the worst-governed colonies in the world.[352]

Three days later the head of the government party in the Assembly, Thomas Reynolds, called a public meeting in White's Rooms, King William Street, on his own terms before a sympathetic audience to explain his policy of pleasing everyone.[353]

When parliament reassembled, the idea of refunding any

351 *Register* 12/3/1868 leader; 13/3/1868, p. 2; *Advertiser* 31/3/1868, p. 4; S.A.P.D. 1868–1869 c.169.

352 *Register* 30/3/1868, pp. 2 and 3.

353 *Register* 1/4/1868, p. 2.

money was rejected in the House of Assembly by 25 votes to seven, one of the most united votes for years. Instead, the government was instructed to proceed with surveys as soon as possible. In their decision members were comforted by lawyer and fellow parliamentarian H.B.T. Strangways (sometime known as The Tempter's Advocate because he opposed most things), who gave it as his expert opinion (other experts notwithstanding) that no time contract was involved. So certain was he of his opinion, he said that if the worse came to the worst, the surveys could be shelved for years until the slow-moving pastoralist opened up the country from the south.[354]

The thwarted ministers retired for a brief interval to reflect on whether they should resign; no they wouldn't, they decided, no doubt thinking the scheme was not worth that sacrifice. Instead they fell back on the old ruse of stalling for time, by advertising (yet again) for tenders to survey land, under the same disadvantages, with the site still undecided, and similar harsh penalties applied for late starting and finishing. At the same time, they pushed ahead with legislation to introduce concessions (such as enlarging the blocks from 160 to 240 acres) for those land-order holders prepared to sign a supplementary contract signing away their right to take the colony to court.[355]

In a dramatic last bid to influence the House, a spokesman for the land-order holders, leading banker, prominent member of the Chamber of Commerce and a founder of the Northern Territory Company, Samuel Tomkinson, obtained permission to appeal directly from the Bar of the House. The move was so novel that the speaker was sent delving into May's *Parliamentary Practices*. One newspaper honoured the event with a poem, which began 'One morn a Stranger at the gate, Of Wisdom stood disconsolate'.[356]

Tomkinson had been lobbying parliament on the subject for three years through a steady barrage of correspondence to the newspapers. His natural pessimism made him a natural prophet

---

354 S.A.P.D. 1868–1869 c.179 to 183; *Register* 21/8/1868 leader.

355 S.A.P.D. 1868–1869 c.237; Conditions of Tender for Survey of Northern Territory, 2/9/1868 (S.A.P.P. 83 of 1868–1869); Report on tenders by Surveyor-General (S.A.P.P. 100 of 1868–1869).

356 *Register* 1/9/1868, p. 2 for poem.

when it came to the Territory, which always seemed to be going down-hill as he foreboded. Having gained access to the House, Tomkinson took the initiative by attacking members with their own arguments, accusing them of being the real speculators, gamblers on a scheme of colonisation which had not paid off. The holders of land-orders, he claimed, could never be passed off as mere land jobbers until they received land with which to job. He accused members of seeking to sell lands in an infertile 'El Dorado 12 degrees from the Equator, swarming with alligators and infested with mosquitoes', and pointed to past failures as evidence.[357] No one troubled to answer him back, though one honourable member thought mismanagement had given the Territory such a bad name that settlers would no longer go there, and it would become a thorn in their sides for 20 years.[358]

This third major Northern Territory debate – after the ones in 1863 and 1866 – illustrates just why governments preferred not to raise the Northern Territory question in parliament if they could help it. It was, said Henry Kent Hughes in the House of Assembly, 'the apple thrown by the demon of discord into their midst'.[359] The debate started in August as a vote of censure against the ministry for their past inaction. This in turn precipitated another round of recriminations, often directed against Captain Hart and the original scheme of colonisation. It concluded a few months later with a privileges battle between the two Houses of Parliament, over the Legislative Council's right to further enlarge the size of the blocks as a compensation for the land-order holders having to wait.'[360]

In a memorable quotation H.B.T. Strangways described the Territory as 'the *bete noire* of the Ministry, that expression being French for white elephant'.[361]

By mid 1868 the Northern Territory question seemed no nearer solution than at the time of the 1866 debate. Indeed it was beset by worse difficulties. In parliament the colonial ministers were timid due to the warring of party factions. In England, the North

357 S.A.P.D. 1868–1869 c.292 to 296.

358 S.A.P.D. 1868–1869 c.298.

359 S.A.P.D. 1868–1869 c.24.

360 S.A.P.D. 1868–1869 c.787, c.819 to 822; c.878 and 879.

361 S.A.P.D. 1868–1869 c.29.

Samuel Tomkinson appeared before the Bar of the House on behalf of the land-order holders. His natural pessimism made him a prophet when it came to the Territory, which always seemed to be going downhill as he forewarned.
(George E. Loyau, *Representative Men of South Australia*, Howell, Adelaide, 1882, wood engraving by Jeffrey Bruer)

Australian Company shareholders were gathering their strength to wrest back their money by economic or legal force. So grim did the prospects appear that impatient voices were raised outside parliament for a new approach: for the factions, by a superlative effort, to bury their differences long enough to agree on a strong Northern Territory policy. No voice was more impatient or more influential than that of John Barrow (who had drawn up the motion for the Town Hall meeting in March) and his newspaper, the *Advertiser*.

With naive optimism editor Barrow believed that those entitled to land even now could be dissuaded from going to court if only the South Australian government would show some real action to demonstrate its sincere intentions to have the country settled. He held that the colony needed to send its best man, 'the Surveyor-

General himself', to do the work with a free hand and a well-equipped party.

> Mr Goyder is the only man in the colony who can and will (if allowed) survey the Northern Territory. And Mr Goyder will go. We take that for granted. Mr Goyder will go.[362]

Mr Goyder was not keen on going at all – his wife was unwell for one thing – and he officially made it plain that the statements in the *Advertiser* were false.[363] The idea of sending Goyder to save the day was not new. Twelve months earlier there had been talk of sending him. In 1865–1866 he had drawn the famous Goyder Line of rainfall, separating agricultural from pastoral lands in South Australia, based on thousands of miles of personal inspection on horseback. Following the success of the first Goyder Line the responsible minister later asked Goyder and Todd to draw a second Goyder Line for the Territory in 1884.[364]

Feared by many pastoralists, Goyder was the most hated, best respected, and the most dynamic public officer in the colony. And the more Barrow espoused the notion of sending him, the more convinced he was of its being a very good idea and the more zealous for it he became. He hounded the suggestion into the Lower House through his newspaper, at the same time flaying the Ayers government for its 'pusillanimous policy' of advertising for tenders.[365] In the Upper House, Barrow was able to use his considerable influence as a member. On the first day of normal business he broached the issue as a private member's motion.[366] He then would not let it rest, whipping it through debates, questions in the House, and newspaper propaganda.[367]

At first the Ayers government tried to stave off the so-called Goyder Agitation. Next, it asked Goyder himself if he would consider becoming a private tenderer – a strange request indeed

---

362 *Advertiser* 26/8/1868 leader.

363 S.A.P.D. 1868–1869 c.282.

364 'Rec. that line of demarcation be fixed between N.T. lands fit for Pastoral and those fit for Agricultural purpose'. (N.T.I.L. 807/1884).

365 *Advertiser* 25/8/1868 leader; 26/8/1868 leader.

366 S.A.P.D. 1868–1869 c.322.

367 S.A.P.D. 1868–1869 c.379 to 385.

to a senior public servant. He refused. Finally, they asked Goyder to draw up specifications for a government expedition, and submit them for Cabinet's perusal.

Typically in this period of political upheaval, the agitation to send Goyder only gained respectability through the machinations of a serious ministerial crisis – the fourth since gaining self-government in 1857. After finally ousting the Ayers ministry over the perennial land question of whether pastoral land should be resumed for farmers, the opposition party under Captain Hart, which came to power in September 1868, needed to convince everyone that its own programme was really not the same. This situation was not new in South Australian politics and most met it, as Hart did now, by scratching for side issues which could be bolstered into irreconcilable differences. He found just the right kind of issue in the Goyder Agitation. On the 6 October 1868, Hart boldly announced to parliament that Goyder would leave in just three weeks. He then proceeded to criticise the former government every chance he got for its past inaction.[368] When the terms under which Goyder had consented to go were made public, it became clear that he had driven a hard bargain. He had secured in general a free hand, especially in choosing the site, a large well-equipped expedition, and a bonus for himself and his men. Once Hart set the preparations rolling there was hardly any chance of turning back. Though Hart's ministry lasted only 19 days, and the next – an Ayers ministry again, 21 days before Henry Strangways took over the reins to steady the crisis – each found it most convenient to follow in the footsteps of the other.[369] Due to the twists of unstable government, Goyder was sent out by *three* ministries, each claiming the major share of the credit.

Barrow wrote in the *Advertiser* of 19 October 1868:

> It now seems to be pretty certain that the policy advocated in these columns with reference to the survey of the Northern Territory will be carried out. Whatever political crises may occur, and whatever ministry

368 S.A.P.D. 1868–1869 c.329, 519 to 522; 529 to 534.

369 Surveyor-General's Estimate of Northern Territory Survey (S.A.P.P. 101 of 1868–1869). This correspondence suggests that the Ayers Government was itself moving towards despatching Goyder and a government party.

John Barrow of the *Advertiser* advocated sending Goyder north to save the day. (*Australasian Sketcher* 5/10/1874, p. 108. Courtesy of the State Library of South Australia)

> may be at the helm of affairs, it is a foregone conclusion that Mr Goyder must go …
>
> He is a man of indefatigable energy and restless activity. He has also a reputation to lose. His professional character is involved in the success or failure of the undertaking; and no one who knows Goyder will doubt for a moment that if he engages to do the work, he will accomplish it to the satisfaction of the country.

Despite Barrow's assurances that the government would not back down, the newspaper man took no chances. He demanded Goyder should go immediately, even if, as with McKinlay, that meant arriving at the height of the wet season. But a combination of circumstances spared the party such a fate. As if its troubles were not enough, the Territory now became the centre of a privileges quarrel (one of many) between the two Houses of Parliament over compensating the preliminary purchasers of land for having to wait. In August 1868 – as foreshadowed in the Victor Harbor policy statement some months earlier – the Ayers government finally introduced a Bill to amend the Northern Territory Act which increased the size of blocks from 160 to 240 acres, provided land-order holders signed a new contract inside six months. The point of contention now was the right of the Upper House to further amend the size to 360 acres and the time allowed to nine months – which the speaker in the Assembly ruled to be a money matter beyond the Legislative Council's powers. The dispute was only settled in November, by resubmitting the amendment as a new bill through all stages of parliament, a move which made an early start unlikely.[370]

As did the question of finance … the second reason why an early start was unlikely. Only £10,000 was left and Goyder calculated the cost of the surveys alone at £25,000. Hart decided to meet the situation by passing legislation – the so-called *Northern Territory Loan Act, 1868* – so the government could raise a loan inside South Australia, with unsold lands in the Territory offered as security.[371] In this way, he used book-keeping to circumvent the various objections. His government could claim that the original promise not to spend taxpayers' money on the northern colony had in no way been broken. If members of the Assembly were dubious about this, they were too worn out to make an issue of it. The money-lenders, on the other hand, knew that ultimately the Treasury itself was their security. The method became the precedent for financing Territory settlement, allowing the cherished self-supporting principle to save face.

By the final weeks of 1868 the government-sponsored expedition was back in favour. The frustrated legislature had called on George Goyder to save it. The surveyor-general knew that, unlike Finniss, he could arrange the expedition on his own terms and in his own way.

The second survey expedition to the Northern Territory was so efficiently discharged as to be almost uneventful. The steps by which Goyder made an apparently formidable task appear easy illustrates just how well the diminutive surveyor-general (he was just over five foot tall) knew how to handle his South Australians. It also illustrates his penchant for order.

In the first place he kept the planning and the preparation of the

370 S.A.P.D. 1868–1869 c. 292; 375; 386; 787: S.A.P.A. 3 of 1868.

371 Goyder to Blackmore 5/10/1868 (S.A.P.P. 101 of 1868–1869, p. 2); S.A.P.D. 1868–1869 c.529; 805 and 806; 829 to 832; S.A.P.A. 4 of 1868.

expedition away from the clumsy hands of Cabinet, sparing himself the short-sightedness and bungling met by Finniss. He ordered the ministers hither and thither like livery servants – several politicians later wanted him removed for thus exceeding his station.

Goyder demanded full right to choose his own men, the botanist and doctor excepted. After that, he helped himself to a party of 137 men (the number varying from time to time), more than three times the original Finniss expedition, and ensured they were extremely well equipped. Each man was known directly or by reputation by the leader, carefully selected for his part and hardened to bush life. Fourteen had been in the Territory before. He also recruited men already bonded to each other – for example, at least six of the party from around the Reedbeds area west of Adelaide had extended, mainly family links to Goyder's colleague, the surveyor Richard Loveday the elder. A line of clear authority was organised from the leader down through six first-class surveyors and six second-class surveyors in charge of teams, to junior surveyors, chainmen and survey hands.[372] To bolster his authority, Goyder even asked to be appointed a special magistrate, but the Crown solicitor preferred discipline based on a master–servant bond.[373]

In fitting out Finniss's expedition, Ayers and Hart had been so 'cheese-paring' that the men finished up 'hunting for food like black fellows'. To prevent any repetition of this, Goyder selected his own stores and equipment, and caused a stir by passing over the normal contractors. He made provision, too, against the isolation which had sapped the heart out of Finniss's men. The Postmaster-General at Galle and the agents for the Royal Mail Steamer at Koepang and Batavia were officially asked to treat all mail from the survey party as urgent.[374] A small fast schooner was ordered by Goyder from Melbourne to scurry to the Indies and Adelaide for mail and supplies.[375] The Colonial Secretary at Ceylon was asked to broadcast

---

372 Goyder to Blackmore 5/10/1868 with enclosures (N.T.I.L. 1/1868).

373 Goyder to Blackmore 17/12/1868 (N.T.I.L. 15/1868); Instructions to Surveyor-General. Articles of Agreement with party. Crown Solicitor's Minute 21/12/1868 (N.T.I.L. 20/1868).

374 Cavenagh to Goyder 23/12/1868 (S.A.P.P. 175 of 1868–1869).

375 Goyder to Blackmore 14/12/1868; Goyder to Blackmore 15/12/1868 (N.T.I.L. 14/1868).

guarantees that South Australia would honour all debts incurred in the region.[376]

By Christmas 1868 the preparations were in hand, and the expedition's ship, the *Moonta*, lay resting at anchor in Light's Passage, Port Adelaide, awaiting fair seas. She was a 627-ton inter-colonial trader chosen by Goyder himself.[377]

There was no formality in the party's departure. On 16 December 1868, the men assembled in Adelaide's Survey Yard, and were told of their wages. At six in the evening of the 23rd they were called together again and given a mug and pannikin tea in a large store at Port Adelaide. At 7:20 a bell summoned them to the wharf, and as each filed up the gangway his name was marked off a roll. The only absentees were several having last-minute trouble with their bailiffs. At eight the vessel was towed out into the stream awaiting fair seas, where she stayed until the 27th when she set sail westward by way of Cape Leeuwin for the north coast.[378]

Several weeks before leaving Goyder had decided there was no site on the north coast that would meet all the expectations of the land-order holders, and so he had resolved to proceed straight to Port Darwin which, according to advice from the officers of the *Beatrice* and reports by earlier explorers, possessed at least a good harbour and high ground. He was also no doubt influenced by the government, which now (in the governor's words) wanted 'the establishment of a port of outlet for the Interior, and of communication with India'.[379]

On the way up, the men published five issues of their own newspaper, the *Moonta Herald and Northern Territory Gazette,* written in a boy's own style, (example: What officer on board is most like a sheep-bell? Answer: Mr Lambell). After an uneventful journey, punctuated by manly games such as boxing, shooting, quoits, as well as the occasional concert, they reached Port Darwin

---

376 Cavenagh to Goyder 23/12/1868 (S.A.P.P. 175 of 1868–1869).

377 Goyder to Blackmore 14/12/1868 (N.T.I.L. 13/1868); Elder Smith and Co. to Commissioner Crown Lands 30/11/1868; Elder Smith and Co. to Goyder 1/12/1868; Elder Smith and Co. to Goyder 8/12/1868 (S.G.I.L. 1621/1868).

378 *Register* 24/12/1868, p. 3; 5/1/1869, p. 4.

379 Fergusson to Mayor, Napier, Fitzgerald 20/5/1869 (enclosure in G.O.D. 22 of 1869); Goyder to Blackmore 5/10/1868 (N.T.I.L. 1/1868).

at three in the afternoon on the 5 February 1869. Most of the party expected it to be lush and green like the East Indies. 'We must confess to having been agreeably disappointed in our first impression of Port Darwin', wrote the editor of the post-arrival supplement of the men's newspaper.[380] But Goyder himself would not have agreed.

Goyder's next move, which led to his success, was to disarm all disagreement in Adelaide. As soon as he arrived he set about praising the site whenever he could, having previously taken care to exclude outsiders like Stow and Stuckey who might dispute his judgements. His first despatch, sent south inside a month of arriving, was almost unqualified in its praise: confidently predicting a rosy future for the region, generally lauding the large stock potential and specifically pointing out the valleys and slopes as suitable for agriculture. How such a fine country had so long been passed over, he could not understand. One wit called it '... announcing the miraculous conception of Port Darwin'.[381] His two further reports from the Territory praised in particular the situation of Fort Point in Darwin harbour, and though his enthusiasm for the climate and soil had mellowed a little, the reports still conveyed easy optimism.[382]

This news had the calculated effect in Adelaide, reviving discussion about bridging the continent to give the southerners a share in its wealth. Robert Dalrymple Ross, 'Assistant Commissary General', homeward bound for England, was induced to bring the old question of a trade in cavalry horses through North Australia to India before the Viceroy and the various Indian authorities.[383] A pastoral firm offered a fleet of camels to span the continent using Afghan cameleers by regular camel trains.[384] Others even dreamed of linking the two coasts with a transcontinental tramway or railway paid for by the American land-grant system, i.e. the builder of the railway or tramway would be paid not in money but with selected

---

380 *Moonta Herald and Northern Territory Gazette*, 24/2/1869 (Mitchell Library).

381 Goyder to Blackmore 2/3/1869 with enclosures (N.T.I.L. 9/1869); *Pasquin* 15/5/1869, p. 156.

382 Goyder to Blackmore 3/5/1869 with enclosures (N.T.I.L. 22/1869); Goyder to Blackmore 27/9/1869 (N.T.I.L. 57/1869).

383 Fergusson to Mayor 20/5/1869; Fergusson to Granville 21/5/1869; Bagot to Ross 22/5/1869 (S.A.P.P. 43 of 1869–1870).

384 S.A.P.D. 1869–1870 c.123.

land grants from either side of the line. The idea of a Great Central State was back in fashion, though there was more talk than action.

Meanwhile in London, the powerful North Australian Association raised its head again, through its secretary Edward Oppen. In order to set the Territory in motion, he proposed that the South Australian government should grant a million to a million-and-a-half acres of unsurveyed land to the North Australian Association in return for the Company bringing in 3000 to 5000 settlers within ten years.[385]

Remembering his South Australians on the Finniss expedition, Goyder next conducted the surveys on the principle that if they were put to work hard enough there would be neither time nor energy left for feuding. He spurred on each man and team with the promise they would all be home for Christmas 1869, reminding them the government had also promised bonuses for extraordinary effort. Each survey team would be given a fair month's work for a fair wage and all they managed to do above that was to be rewarded at a fixed rate per mile, a method of payment known as the Mileage Principle. Both of these incentives later became the cause of a bitter dispute between the men and their employers, but before then they managed an immense amount of work. On the first day of sustained effort, five fainted and had to be helped back to camp.[386] When the surveys got into full swing the best teams began work by candlelight in the morning and finished by candlelight at night, generally with a midday break. Insubordination was rare, except later directed against the doctor, Robert Peel, formerly of Adelaide Hospital, who was accused by the men of helping himself to the 'medical comforts'.[387]

Instead of arriving first as planned, the schooner bringing the party's iron tools and carrying the tiny river-steamer *Midge* arrived seven weeks after the *Moonta* on 27 March. But not even the want of tools could defeat Goyder's determination to keep the men busy. The delay, the only serious hitch in his arrangements, was caused when the schooner *Sea Ripple*, purchased and fitted out on his advice in Melbourne, turned out to be unseaworthy when it got to Port

385 Oppen to Blyth, plus memorandum 26/9/1869 (N.T.I.L. 75/1869).

386 Daly to Turton 23/2/1869 (S.L.S.A. Mortlock D6993(L)).

387 *Register* 14/3/1870, p. 3.

G.W. Goyder known as 'Little Energy'. He regularly drove himself to exhaustion. (George E. Loyau, *Representative Men of South Australia*, Howell, Adelaide, 1882, wood engraving by Jeffrey Bruer)

Adelaide, being condemned by the Board of Sea Captains because it had iron rather than copper bolts – and it had to be hurriedly replaced by the *Gulnare* (meaning pomegranate flower), under Captain Samuel White Sweet, especially purchased for £1700 for the occasion.[388] By the time the *Gulnare* arrived via the east coast route, Goyder and his men had explored the arms of Darwin harbour, set up a camp under Fort Hill on the north-east side and laid out a city across the tableland behind the hill.[389] Because this tableland joined the sea on three sides the intention to re-draw the medieval-style town of Adelaide had to be seriously modified. But Goyder's plan retained Adelaide's precise rectangular-shaped layout of streets and squares, while the spacious outer rim of parklands

388 Blackmore to Goyder 10/2/1869 (N.T.O.L. 35/1869).
389 Goyder to Blackmore 2/3/1869 (N.T.I.L. 9/1869).

Northern Territory Survey Expedition

as organised by Goyder on the eve of commencing the country surveys.

Base Camp Party
(Operating out of Fort Point)

George Woodruffe Goyder (Surveyor-General)
Robert Peel (Surgeon)
Joseph Brooks (Photographer and Draftsman)
John William Ogilvie Bennett (Senior Draftsman)
James Martin Lambell (Accountant and Postmaster)
Hugh Campbell McCallum (Storekeeper and Clerk)
William Webster Hoare (Assistant Surgeon)
David Donley (Cook)
William Barlow (Assistant Photographer)
Benjamin Wells (Carpenter)
Thomas Sayer (Blacksmith)
William John Gepp (Farrier and Blacksmith)
Robert Charles Beard (Assistant Storekeeper)
William Barrett Rowe (In charge of stock)
Robert Charles Burton (Overseer)
Edward Tuckwell (Staff)
William Frederick Henry Rowe (Staff)
Henry S. Hemming (Staff)
William Brelsford Hayes (Gardener)
James Burton (Coxwain)
James Robinson (General Hand)
Henry S. Bosworth (Cook)
George Price Deane (General Hand)
Donald McAulay (General Hand and Well Sinker)

The Woods-Mitchell Double Party
(To work from behind Palmerston)

Alfred Thomas Woods (First Class Surveyor)
Christopher Giles (Cadet)
Martin Burke (Survey Hand)
George Bayfield (Survey Hand)
Jeremiah Ryan (Survey Hand)
William Stanborough (Survey Hand)
David Johnston (Survey Hand)
Joseph Middlemore Thomas (Second Class Surveyor)
George Sydney Aldridge (Cadet)
Matthew Houston (Survey Hand)
Michael Keiley (Survey Hand)
William Houston (Survey Hand)
Thomas Sutherland Horn (Survey Hand)
Alfred Warren (Survey Hand)
Wilhelm Ludwig Homeyer (Camp Keeper)
Richard Hazard (Cook)
Alexander James Mitchell (First Class Surveyor)
Charles Newton Greene (Cadet)
Henry Cornish (Survey Hand)
Samuel Grosvenor (also Grosvenor Samuel) Walters (Survey Hand)
Richard Austin Horn (Survey Hand)
Robert Collard (Survey Hand)
Thomas Neate (Survey Hand)
Richard Randall Knuckey (Second Class Surveyor)
Charles William Lecky Sprigg (Cadet)
William Henry Edwards (Survey Hand)
William Guy (Survey Hand)

E. Martin Moyse (General Hand and Well Sinker)
Terence McIntyre (General Hand and Well Sinker)
Robert Price (Teamster)
Robert Hayball (Teamster)
Patrick Molloy (Teamster)
Peter Krüss (Teamster)
James Oborn (Teamster)
Charles J. Palmer (Teamster)
David Wilson (Teamster)
Michael Bennett (Teamster)
Charles Fry (Teamster)
North Smith (Cook)
Frederick Herman Heinrich Schultze (Botanist)
John Alfred Schultze (Assistant Botanist)
Arthur Hicks (Staff)
Michael Francis (Survey Hand)
Patrick (Paul Patrick Phelin) Kelly (Survey Hand)
John H. Ryan (Survey Hand)
Edwin Stow Berry (Draftsman)
Charles Spencely (Cook)

Base Camp Fort Point. Sketch by W.W. Hoare.
(Courtesy of the State Library of South Australia – B3239)

The Smith-Harvey Double Party
(To work from South Arm)

Arthur Henry Smith (First Class Surveyor)
Harrison Daniel Packard (Cadet)
James Henry Aldridge (Survey Hand)
George Richards (Survey Hand)
Thomas Loveday (Survey Hand)
Richard John Loveday (Survey Hand)
William Gunn (Survey Hand)
William Whitfield Mills (Second Class Surveyor)
David Landale Beetson (Cadet)
Thomas Cherry (Survey Hand)
George Hughes (Survey Hand)
Joseph Atkinson Ewart (Survey Hand)
John Lowther (Survey Hand)
Charles James Lines (Survey Hand)
Alexander Ringwood (Draftsman)
Adam Gaire (Cook)
William Harvey (First Class Surveyor)
Alexander McLeod McKay (Cadet)
Francis John Bennett (Survey Hand)
Robert W. Barrow (Survey Hand)
James Hereford Douglas (Survey Hand)
William Collett (Survey Hand)
Job Austin (Survey Hand)
Stephen King (Jnr) (Second Class Surveyor)
John Le Maistre Francis Roberts (Cadet)
Arthur Frederick Lines (Survey Hand)
John W. Smith (Survey Hand)
George Kersley (Survey Hand)
Donald Fraser (Survey Hand)
William Plaisted (Survey Hand)
Dennis Heir (Camp Keeper)
Alexander McKenzie (Cook)

The MacLachlan-McMinn Double Party
(To work from East Arm)

George Galbraith MacLachlan (First Class Surveyor)
Charles Frederick Wells (Cadet)
William George Holland (Survey Hand)
Edward Ryan (Survey Hand)
John London (Survey Hand)
Patrick Healey (Survey Hand)
Michael C. Ryan (Survey Hand)
Dominick Daniel Daly (Second Class Surveyor)
Thomas Bee (Cadet)
William Fisher (Survey Hand)
George A. Armstrong (Survey Hand)
Henry H. Irwin (Survey Hand)
John Gerald (Survey Hand)
Robert Rowland Stevenson (Survey Hand)
John G. Nottage (Camp Keeper)
Thomas Stevens (Cook)
Gilbert Rotherdale McMinn (First Class Surveyor)
John Sherlock Brooking (Cadet)
William Charles Musgrave (Survey Hand)
Cornelius Lowther (Survey Hand)
James MacPherson (Survey Hand)
Frank Wighton Hood (Survey Hand)
Walter Louis Samson (Survey Hand)
Edwin Mitchell Smith (Second Class Surveyor)
Philip Henry Burden (Cadet)
John Harrison Packard (Survey Hand)
Richard Hinton (Survey Hand)
Frederick M. Willson (Survey Hand)
William John Farrant (Survey Hand)
Heinrich Ralfs Krüss (Survey Hand)
Wentworth Marmaduke Hardy (Draftsman)
Charles Laycock (Cook)

Note: Walter Dalwood (Survey Hand) had already been invalided out and Alexander Kennedy (Staff) dismissed. Minor adjustments later made to this original organisation included: promotion of Deane and Hood to staff, Hayball and Warren changed places, William Frederick Rowe joined Knuckey's party. Seaman Michael Edward Fitch joined the surveys, as a replacement, at one stage working in Ross' party. Further changes were made from time to time as the surveying advanced.

(except on the land side) were curtailed into open esplanades between the allotments and the sea. When finished, the reserves and open areas covered considerably more land than the town acres themselves.[390]

With the *Gulnare* unloaded, the country surveys began in earnest. The logistics of Goyder's arrangements were impressive. He planned the country surveys around three parties each of 32 men, moving inland in a south to easterly direction from three starting points on Darwin harbour: from South Arm, East Arm and near base camp at Fort Point. He could thus make maximum use of the steamer *Midge* and the inland waterways. Each party of 32 men was further sub-divided into two teams of 16, which were again divided into work units of seven, the odd two men being either camp keepers, cooks or draftsmen. Each work unit, made up of surveyor, cadet and five hands with one hand being the chainman, was then allocated (as a general rule) 33 miles of surveying a month on standard pay, every extra mile surveyed to be rewarded with a bonus. For survey hands, the bonus was five shillings and one penny per extra mile per person. Behind the survey teams was back-up of about 40 teamsters, well-sinkers and various staff operating mainly from the base camp at Fort Point.[391]

The method produced enormous output. Soon the parties were surveying on average a total of 30,000 acres a week.[392] The system also produced errors: some land-holders were later angry to find themselves saddled with undersized blocks of land.[393]

By the end of August 1869 the surveys were virtually finished. In five months the men had laid out more land than usually done in temperate South Australia over a full year. The surveyed land spread over 660,000 acres of virgin bush, stretching 58 miles inland. It sliced up four overlapping tribal areas – the Woolna, Woolna–Larrakia, Larrakia and Warnunga – into geometrical 320 and 160 acre blocks

390 Goyder to Blackmore 27/9/1869 (N.T.I.L. 57/1869).

391 Goyder to Woods and Mitchell 29/4/1869 (N.T. Expedition Outletters, p. 46, State Records G.R.G. 35/11); Goyder to Smith and Harvey 30/4/1869 with Minutes dated 19/6/1869 (N.T. Expedition Outletters, p. 55 State Records G.R.G. 35/11); *Advertiser* 16/11/1869, p. 2, Northern Territory correspondent.

392 Northern Territory Survey Expedition 1868–1870. Monthly reports of field parties (State Records G.R.G. 35/8).

393 S.A.P.D. 1875 c.223 and 224.

(which would have pleased the seminal European thinker Plato, who considered geometrical forms a superior reality). The map of this land was embellished with future towns, roads and reserves and dotted with names from the other side of the world. 'The map precedes the territory', according to the post-modern proverb. The European had come to stay.[394]

In addition to the metropolis of Palmerston, Goyder laid out three country towns: Southport at the head of South Arm, Virginia near the Elizabeth River at the head of East Arm and Daly adjacent to Fred's Pass near the Adelaide River, each a miniature or modified replica of Adelaide. Goyder's last precaution was to keep an armed peace with the local inhabitants. Here he was so obviously successful that the governor, with the Colonial Office in view, asked him to write down his suggestions as a guide for future policy.[395]

Whereas Finniss tried to blunderbuss the Aborigines, and Manton tried to appease them, Goyder advocated a third strategy, which was a kind of apartheid. He had previously been made Protector of Aborigines to prevent any divisions on the subject.

Goyder believed that the Aborigines were naturally treacherous, bent on plunder and revenge, but also well-endowed with a primitive instinct for survival.[396] Because of this strong instinct for survival they would tend to avoid any conflict they might lose. The wily leader instructed his men to stay at all times in well-armed bands, which the indigenous people would respect and not molest,[397] and to keep sternly aloof from them, even when they wanted to trade by offering fish. If the 'natives' got too close at the base camp at Port Darwin, he would set off an old blank canon which made a lot of noise.

Goyder also believed that the exploitation of Aboriginal women and girls was the main cause of reprisals by the men. Referring to his policy of segregation based on race and sex, he later wrote: 'To this alone I attribute the immunity with which we were allowed to pass in every direction.'[398] The only opposition he encountered from

---

394 Goyder to Blackmore 27/9/1869 (N.T.I.L. 57/1869).

395 Goyder to Blackmore 27/9/1869 (S.A.P.P. 157 of 1869–1870, p. 3).

396 Goyder to Blackmore 27/9/1869, p. 13 (N.T.I.L. 57/1869).

397 Goyder to Blackmore 27/9/1869, pp. 1 to 14 (N.T.I.L. 57/1869).

398 Goyder to Blackmore 23/11/1869 (N.T.I.L. 68/1869).

the indigenous people were attempts to stop the surveys by burning out the countryside with their firesticks. This was an art at which they had been proficient for thousands of years.

The exception which seemed to prove the wisdom of the leader's precautions was the spearing of John Bennett, which took place at Fred's Pass near the Adelaide River on the 24 May 1869 leading to his death a few days later. Bennett was a young man of an idealistic turn of mind and gentle, studious ways. As soon as he got inland with a survey team he disobeyed instructions and formed a close friendship with the local Woolnas. He studied their language and allowed himself to be daubed in ceremonial paint. Then one day certain Woolnas speared Bennett in what appeared a ritual act and wounded Guy, a companion, whose wound never healed. This led some to believe that the Woolnas had put poison on the tips of their spears. According to Old Mira, who wept on hearing the news, the actual spearing was done by a man called 'Mepinge' of the Wodunga people at the head of the Adelaide River.

Goyder now showed considerable insight into the Aboriginal outlook, together with courage in restraining his men. In situations like this, Goyder's rationality is unmistakable. Judging this to be a reprisal for killings done by the first expedition under Finniss in which Bennett was a member (when ironically Bennett had opposed aggression against Aborigines), he wrote:

> I considered the attack upon Bennett and Guy the results of feelings of revenge on the part of those who had probably lost relatives in some previous contest with the whites, the more so as we were informed on arrival of the *Moonta*, by the blacks here, that those on the Adelaide, or near that locality, intended to kill two of our party.[399]

He would have known that at least two Aboriginal men were killed by Finniss's party at the upriver camp on the Adelaide River back in August 1864.

Goyder then refused point-blank the men's demands for some official act of retaliation.

---

399 Goyder to Blackmore 27/9/1869, pp. 4 to 14 (N.T.I.L. 57/1869) also S.A.P.P. 157 of 1869–1870. Quoted in *Ochre and Rust* by Philip Jones (Wakefield Press, Adelaide, 2007); Chapter Four, *Spearing Bennett*, is a detailed study of the events leading up to the spearing.

> To retaliate, therefore, even could we have identified the murderers, would have been to secure to our successors, less able to defend themselves, a debt of lives to be paid for our act of reprisal, unless we had annihilated the tribe, which was not to be thought of.[400]

But certain members of the expedition were outraged and not even Goyder could stop the unofficial reprisals. Knuckey, in whose party Bennett was working, wrote in his field book:

> Woods, Thomas, Mitchell rode off at once on horse-back well armed and Stanborough, Aldridge and Dick and Tom Horn and Davey Johnson went on foot well armed. Stanborough (soldier) armed with rifle and bayonet fixed twenty five (25).

Soon after, when the leader was out of sight, five innocent Larrakias were shot at Fannie Bay by two of Goyder's men in a sworn act of revenge. According to one report, the men first coaxed the Larrakias in range with offers of food and kindness.[401]

Though the surveyor-general shared the conventional white belief of European superiority, there is no denying him a genuine humanity. He was sensitive and imaginative enough to feel acutely for the indigenous peoples in their encounter with the invaders, and to let this influence his decisions:

> I had also to bear in mind that we were in what to them appeared unauthorised and unwarrantable occupation of their country, and where territorial rights are so strictly observed by the natives, that even a chief of one tribe will neither hunt upon nor remove anything from the territory of another without first obtaining permission, it is scarcely to be wondered at if when opportunity is allowed them, they should resent such acts by violence upon its perpetrators.[402]

When two of his men, Hardy and Greene, wantonly destroyed canoes moored on the beach, they felt the full force of Goyder's

---

400 *ibid.*

401 R.R. Knuckey's Field Book K 25/5/1869 (A.R. Miller to Cross, Survey Department, Darwin 3/1/1964); *Advertiser* 14/3/1870, pp. 2 and 3; *Register* 14/3/1870, p. 3; D.E. Kelsey's Manuscript on Northern Territory, p. 129 (S.L.S.A. Mortlock D3422(T)).

402 Goyder to Blackmore 27/9/1869, p. 12 (N.T.I.L. 57/1869).

fury for the 'malicious' and 'unjust' act.[403] In retrospect, Goyder's precautions might have done something to lessen the bloodshed that runs like an ugly artesian under Northern Territory history. Had lonely teamsters and prospectors heeded his advice only to work in groups, had administrators heeded his warning that abuse of Aboriginal women was a principal cause of reprisals, and had they attended to his suggestion that liaison officers were needed to see to the interests of the tribes,[404] many murders by both sides might have been avoided. But the Northern Territory colonisation got so out of hand that most of his advice was forgotten. In the 1880s and 1890s, in particular, inter-racial violence in the country became extreme, a period referred to by Aboriginal people as 'the killing times'.

The history of Goyder's well-ordered expedition closes on a brawling note, thanks to the inaction of the South Australian authorities. Throughout the arduous months Goyder had kept his party going with the expectation they would be home for Christmas and the promise of reward for extra efforts. In May 1869 he sent the *Gulnare* south to inform ministers that the surveys would be ready at latest by October, when the men would be available for removal home.[405] The schooner returned on 24 August with the unsatisfactory reply that the colony could not afford a vessel large enough to bring everyone back until the land was alienated and they could upload with settlers and supplies. Goyder himself, however, took up the option to go immediately by the *Gulnare* and to leave the expedition under the doctor, Robert Peel.[406]

The arrangement brought groans of disappointment from the men, who felt they had been let down. They considered themselves even more intolerably treated when Peel, acting on instructions from the government, ordered them to work, preparing the new metropolis of Palmerston, building log huts at the depot below Fort Hill and most onerous of all cutting a road up to the top of the

---

403 Note Book No. 38 Northern Territory By G.W. Goyder Surveyor General 1869, 1/8/1869 (S.A. State Records G.R.G. 35/256/12).

404 Goyder to Blackmore 23/11/1869 (N.T.I.L. 68/1869); Goyder to Blackmore 27/9/1869 (N.T.I.L. 57/1869).

405 Goyder to Blackmore 3/5/1869 (N.T.I.L. 22/1869).

406 Blackmore to Goyder 21/6/1869 (N.T.O.L. 65/1869); Blackmore to Goyder 21/6/1869 Draft letter (N.T.I.L. 22/1869).

tableland. As soon as Goyder, whom they feared and respected, was gone they turned their disappointment on the two most likely scapegoats: the Aborigines and the doctor. For a time even the local Larrakia people camped near the depot were forced to go into hiding after someone mysteriously opened fire on them,[407] while Dr Peel found himself harassed on all sides by threats of strikes. He wrote:

> It is very difficult under existing circumstances to know how to act; the majority of the men are so dissatisfied and disappointed at the non-arrival of a steamer, for it was expected they would have been in Adelaide at Christmas time. The men also consider that the agreement they signed was binding only up to the completion of the land survey.[408]

Christmas Day 1869 came, and the men ate their cheer thousands of miles from home. On New Year's Day a few men started 1870 by throwing missiles at the doctor's hut.

But even as they were complaining, relief was on the way. Three or four weeks after this episode, the *Kohinoor*, and later the *Gulnare*, hove in sight to take the men home, leaving about 40 who volunteered to remain as the nucleus of a permanent staff. The *Kohinoor*, in particular, was credited with bringing north a handful of the first private settlers. It left again on 6 February with 59 of Goyder's party, much the worse for toil, some looking ten years older, others 'as cracked and silly as March hares', in the words of a junior member.[409] And when they got home, not in a happy frame of mind, they suffered a second indignation: the intelligence that none of them were entitled to the bonus they expected. Before they set out, members of the expedition had been promised a £2000 cash bonus if they performed their task quickly and satisfactorily. Now the government told them that the sum had already been paid out through the Mileage Principle's incentive scheme. This meant that the non-surveying members were never entitled to extra money.[410] It is hard to say whether the mistake was first made by the workers

---

407 *Register* 14/3/1870, p. 3; Report from N.T. under date 27/12/1869.

408 Dr Robert Peel's Diary 28/12/1869 (State Records G.R.G. 35/307).

409 Daly to Harriet, 27/9/1869 (S.L.S.A. Mortlock D6993(L)).

410 Bonus to Northern Territory Survey Party (S.A.P.P. 201 of 1869–1870; S.A.P.P. 46 of 1870–1871; S.A.P.P. 89 of 1872).

or whether the South Australian government deliberately double-crossed them. Certainly no attempt was made to put the matter straight until after the work was done, and certainly, too, the men would never had exerted themselves so recklessly had the position been made clear at the start.

Stung by this second injustice, the men fought the government by deputations, through parliament and the press, but to no avail. The leader, George Goyder fared better, though even he must have doubted whether the sacrifice was worth making. He received the £3000 personal bonus promised him, but his health was permanently affected. During his absence in the Territory his wife Frances, who suffered from depression, was sent home to England to the shelter of her extended family. Soon after his return he learned that she had died in England from an overdose of laudanum, opium-based medicines being widely used at this time. He had to take leave in England to recover from nervous exhaustion.[411]

In parliament, a group of back-benchers sympathetic to pastoralists moved for Goyder's dismissal on the grounds that by his absence in the Territory he had proved himself 'not indispensable' to South Australia' s surveying.[412]

Restitution

> 'There is a day of reckoning still
> Linger it may, but come it will'
> Thomas Elder, Northern Territory Company[413]

Running more or less in parallel to moves culminating in the decision to send Goyder to save the day, were counter-moves in London aimed at brow-beating the colonials to pay back the money.

After the mistakes came the moves for restitution. Before Goyder set out to save the situation the Northern Territory companies had already determined to holler and fight until they recovered their money down to the last penny of interest. 'Wiser in their generation

411 For an excellent study of Goyder's expedition see Margaret Goyder Kerr, *The Surveyors: The Story of the Founding of Darwin*, Rigby, Adelaide, 1971.

412 S.A.P.D. 1869–1870 c.785 to 788.

413 S.A.P.D. 1867 c.287.

Thomas Elder of the Northern Territory Company.
'There is a day of reckoning still –
Linger it may, but come it will'
(George E. Loyau, *Representative Men of South Australia*,
Howell, Adelaide, 1882, wood engraving by Jeffrey Bruer)

than Shylock,' noted one journal philosophically, 'they are not to be cheated out of the blood.'[414]

They tried first one means of extortion, then another. Between December 1867 and December 1868 they concentrated on brow-beating the colonials by setting out to embarrass their efforts to borrow on the great London loan market. This tactic had been promised by George Anstey, who well knew how much the South Australians depended on loans for public works like railways. When the colonials refused to be intimidated, the complainants changed their attack and between 1870 and 1873 the North Australian

414 *Register* 20/11/1868, p. 2.

Company of London hauled them, like common defaulters, before the Courts of Law.

Most attempts to apply economic pressure were made through the venerable London *Times*, the so-called investor's Bible, and sought to create the impression that South Australians were bad risks as they were not always in the habit of honouring their obligations. First moves were made when the South Australians attempted to raise a loan in December 1867. The day before the loan opened, 'A Sufferer' wrote to *The Times* warning the lending public that the Australian colony now seeking its money had once before failed either to hand over the land paid for or hand the money back. The editor added a note in support of this view. The situation was just saved when the colony's agent-general in London, Francis Stacker Dutton, wrote a vigorous reply defending the good name of his government. The loan proved a moderate success and there was some tall talk in Adelaide about how the enemies-of-the-colony had been put in their place. But there were other loans.[415]

Between this and the next loan, some of these enemies turned their hostility on Dutton. 'I would not like to put in writing,' he reported, 'the language which has been used to me in my office on the same subject, by people coming to me insisting to have their money back'.[416]

Not that the friends of the colony were much more help to Dutton. His old advisers Elder, Anstey and Bagot actually led the attacks. His legal adviser, Charles Freshfield, a gentleman M.P. for Dover who had once let the former agent-general tempt him into the scheme threatened to drag the colony up for inquisition in the House of Commons.[417] Later still, Dutton's financial adviser, styling himself a 'Colonial Banker', a man reputed to have inside information, sent a letter to a leading newspaper hinting that the South Australians had already indulged in dishonest practices.[418]

415 Dutton to Reynolds 12/12/1867 with enclosures (S.A.P.P. 51 of 1868–1869, pp. 1 and 2).

416 Dutton to Reynolds 13/12/1867 (S.A.P.P. 51 of 1868–1869, p. 2).

417 Dutton to Reynolds 19/6/1868 with enclosures (S.A.P.P. 51 of 1868–1869, pp. 5 and 6).

418 A Colonial Banker to Editor of the *Australian and New Zealand Gazette* 15/10/1868 (S.A.P.P. 148 of 1869–1870, pp. 28 and 29); Dutton to Hughes 4/11/1868 (*ibid.* p. 27); Correspondence relative to letter signed by a colonial

In October 1868 South Australia had once again to ask for a loan on the London market. This time the immensely influential city editor of *The Times* took up the cause of the wronged land-order holders. In the 11 days between the South Australians first advertising their intention and accepting offers, he turned the venom of his journal on a colony normally too insignificant to deserve notice, criticising in turn its financial affairs, economic insecurity and political instability. According to one commentator, it was his tone of pompous condescension, as if Wakefield's pet colony had gone to the dogs at last, that colonists found hardest to bear.[419] As loan day drew nigh he focused on the ill-treatment of the Northern Territory investors, on 9 October warning anyone interested in the coming loan to 'bear in mind that the good faith of the Colony is not at present in the most unquestionable position',[420] following up next day with another derogatory observation. He resumed the attack on Monday 12 October,[421] then on Tuesday, the day the loan opened, turned up his trump card: the startling news that South Australia's assets had been frozen in London through an action taken in the Lord Mayor's Court.[422] All this time only the pro-colonial *Australian and New Zealand Gazette* tried to defend the South Australians. The colony's agent-general and his secretary had kept a judicious silence. 'What can I possibly write to the *Times*,' wrote the secretary, 'in refutation of what they say? – literally nothing.'[423]

The drastic move of freezing South Australia's assets in London had been made five days before, but publication was held over by *The Times* until the day the loan opened, convincing many South Australians that this was all a conspiracy. The writ was taken out by Alexander Elder for the North Australian Company on the plea that the colony in question was its debtor to the extent of nearly £20,000. As it was common knowledge that the Lord Mayor's Court could not permanently attach (or seize) the assets of overseas governments, the action was obviously taken to cause

banker (S.A.P.P. 148 of 1869–1870, pp. 14 to 17).

419 *Register* 24/11/1868 leader.

420 Newland to Blyth 9/10/1868 (S.A.P.P. 148 of 1869–1870, pp. 1 and 2).

421 *Register*24/12/1868 leader.

422 Dutton to Hughes 5/11/1868 (SA.P.P. 148 of 1869–1870, pp. 8 and 28).

423 Newland to Blyth 9/10/1868 (S.A.P.P. 148 of 1869–1870, p. 2).

Agent-General Francis Stacker Dutton. He prided himself on his ability to raise loans for South Australia in London and was riled by the North Australian Company's attempts to undermine the loans. (*Australasian Sketcher* 15/4/1873, p. 12. Courtesy of the State Library of South Australia)

embarrassment to the colonial government.

The disconcerted agent-general's friends were so few that he turned to the same Freshfield family that was threatening to haul South Australia before the House of Commons.[424] It took exactly two months before the writ was set aside and the colony could again raise its head like an honest citizen.[425] When news of the episode got to Adelaide it caused much resentment, more so as the writ bore the signature of an old colonist still deriving a princely income from the place. The *Advertiser* passed the episode off as a 'piece of miserable spite'.[426] The agent-general, who took pride in being an outstanding organiser of loans, sooled on by his government, publicly investigated

424 Dutton to Hughes 5/11/1868 with enclosures (S.A.P.P. 148 of 1869–1870, pp. 8 and 9).

425 Dutton to Hughes 21/12/1868 with enclosures (S.A.P.P. 148 of 1869–1870, p. 10).

426 *Advertiser* 1/12/1868, p. 2.

NORTH AUSTRALIAN COMPANY

(LIMITED).

Capital, £200,000, in 20,000 Shares of £10 each.
First issue, 10,000 Shares.

Deposit, 10*s. per Share on application, and a further sum of* £1 *per Share on allotment.*

Calls not to exceed £1 per Share, and not to be made at less intervals than three months. It is not intended to call up more than £5 per Share.

DIRECTORS.

Chairman—Sir RICHARD GRAVES McDONNELL, C.B., late Governor of South Australia.
G. A. ANSTEY, Esq., No. 14, Sussex Gardens, London.
C. S. BAGOT, Esq., Lincoln's Inn, London, and East Sheen, Chairman of the Kapunda Mining Company of South Australia.
A. L. ELDER, Esq., Director of the Imperial Bank (Limited).
JOHN BENJAMIN GRAHAM, Esq., Silwood House, Brighton, late Director of the Burra-Burra Mine.
EDMUND LEVI, Esq., Messrs. P. Levi and Co., of London and Adelaide.
Auditor—J. B. MONTEFIORE, Esq., Kensington Gardens Square, and late of Adelaide.
Bankers—The IMPERIAL BANK (Limited), London.
The NATIONAL BANK OF AUSTRALIA, North Australia.
Solicitors—Messrs. HUGHES, MASTERMAN, and HUGHES.
Brokers—Messrs. HUGGINS and ROWSELL, 1, Threadneedle Street.
Secretary (pro. tem.)—MR. ROBERT ANDERSON.
Temporary Offices—17, BUCKLERSBURY, LONDON.

ABRIDGED PROSPECTUS.

THE opening of the "Northern Territory" annexed to the Province of South Australia presents an advantageous opportunity for the Establishment of this Company. The operations of the Company will embrace the following, viz.:—

1. Purchasing, Leasing, and Selling Land.
2. Acting as Agents for Absentees and others; Purchasing, Selling, and Managing Property upon Commission; and transacting any other Agency Business.
3. Receiving Money in this Country on Deposit or Debenture, and investing the same in the Colony at increased rates of interest.
4. Making Advances on Mortgage of Real Estates, and on Government and other Securities.

As it is proposed to call up only £5 per Share, the remaining £5 per Share will afford an ample guarantee for Sums received upon Deposit and otherwise.

The Head Office will be in London, with Branches and Agencies in such places as the Directors may from time to time determine.

Advertisement for the North Australian Company (Limited).
(E.A. Oppen, *A Description Of the Northern Territory of South Australia,* Austin, Hertford, 1864. Courtesy of the State Library of South Australia)

the possibility of taking legal action against Elder and *The Times* for 'making false and utterly unfounded insinuations against the integrity of this colony'.[427]

As there was plenty of money available on the London market, the loan was readily filled, but Dutton reckoned the adverse criticisms cost South Australia, in less favourable terms offered by

427 Hughes to Dutton 6/1/1869; Dutton to Hughes 24/3/1869 with enclosure (S.A.P.P. 148 of 1869–1870, pp. 12 and 13); *South Australia and its first Two Agents-General*, Spottiswoode and Co, London 1876–1877, pp. 16 and 17.

the lending public, £12,000, while another put it down at £20,000.[428] Combined with the loss of goodwill, this was a high price to pay for debts of less than £20,000. 'How very small and narrow-sided our Legislature looks when viewed from this side,' observed a South Australian in England. 'They will not discuss the return of a few thousand pounds although they are thereby ruining the credit of the colony, by which more money would be lost than would pay the whole claims, to say nothing of injury to the reputation of South Australia.'[429]

But the colony's pride was at stake. As already described, the South Australian parliament counter-attacked by passing *An Act to amend 'The Northern Territory Act'*, increasing the size of the preliminary lots from 160 to 240 then 320 acres for any land-order holder willing to sign away all right to take legal proceedings against the colony.[430] The government said 320 acres actually made these purchasers gainers not losers for having to wait. At the instigation of the *Register*, purchasers were allowed only nine months in which to make their decision. After that the question was closed. If the Territory flourished, those who had refused the offer would spend the rest of their days regretting their inaction. But like a salesman who keeps extending his last offer, the government renewed the concession again and again. Each time a few stragglers, impressed by Goyder's achievements, entered the fold. Only in July 1872, four years after it was first mooted, was it closed. In the end about 91 per cent of those holding land-orders issued in Adelaide, and about 33 per cent of those holding orders issued in London, took the increased area.[431]

The South Australians' bribery did nothing to improve relations with the English company and order holders, who struck back by asking the Colonial Office to intervene.[432] But it did unsettle the Adelaide company and the local hangers-on. When the concessions were first offered, the Adelaide directors came together and, in cheerless and haughty tones, demanded nothing less than the full

428 Dutton to Hughes 4/11/1868 (S.A.P.P. 148 of 1869–1870, p. 27).

429 *Register* 24/11/1868, p. 2.

430 S.A.P.A. 3 of 1868.

431 S.A.P.A. 3 of 1871; Northern Territory Land Orders (S.A.P.P. 79 of 1873).

432 Freshfield to Granville 17/12/1869 (G.I.D. 1/1870).

money plus interest.[433] No sooner said, than they were embarrassed by the change of tide which attended Goyder's successes. For a few months the newspapers even revived old talk about the northern capital becoming a rich outlet for a horse and cattle trade with the East as well as the head of a cable and telegraph link with Europe. This caused a crisis within the company, with some wanting to stand fast and others wanting to accept the new terms. After several meetings held in camera, members decided to settle their differences by the drastic solution of annulling the company altogether.[434] On the last day of June 1869 its land-orders were sold by public auction for an average price of more than £54 each – before Goyder's expedition, they had been unsaleable at £10. Most of the purchasers were prominent land speculators and former shareholders of the Northern Territory Company. Thus the sale mainly redistributed ownership, concentrating it among people prepared to wait patiently on the off chance of reaping easy fortunes for themselves or their children. The auctioneer encouraged these hopes by stressing the wealth eventually made by the original land-holders at Port Phillip and Adelaide.[435] So the government had succeeded in quietening the belligerent beast, but only by knocking it on the head. The sad truth was that the company of local gentlemen organised to take the lead in the Territory's colonisation was gone forever. Two days later, on 2 July 1869, the Northern Territory Company was legally wound up.[436]

That left the London company to carry on alone the fight for restitution. When the directors of the North Australian Company received news that, undaunted by the directors' own economic and political pressure tactics, the small colony was actually trying to bribe land-order holders away from the courts, they determined that the time had come to take the matter to court. Unfortunately for South Australia, the frequent switches in course since the 1866 debate looked from London like deceitful attempts to avoid responsibility. As in Adelaide, individual shareholders looked to the local company to give a lead, which it soon provided with considerable energy. First

433 *Register* 20/11/1868, p. 2.

434 *Register* 19/6/1869 leader.

435 *Register* 1/7/1869, p. 2; *Advertiser* 1/7/1869, p. 2.

436 *Register* 3/7/1869, p. 3.

the Company issued the usual parley reiterating its claims:

> The scheme having notoriously failed, the Government should refund to the purchasers of preliminary land-orders the money paid, with interest from the date of payment.[437]

Then, in May 1870, with the moral support of several influential independents like the Freshfields, they took out a writ against the colony for breach of contract.[438] The quarrel had graduated to a new arena.

After March 1869, the date by which South Australia had undertaken to supply the land, the land-order holders' legal case was as strong as the colony's was weak. That fact did not deter the colonials from contesting the issue in every court up to the Privy Council. The case rested on a simple breach of contract plea, which the colony's own best law authorities conceded to be just. The only confusing element was that South Australia's government of 1863 and 1864 had never admitted binding itself to any two-sided contract. Thus the public and parliament were unprepared to accept a contract as true. When in 1863 Hart and Ayers sat over the blueprint for an improved model of colonisation, one of their cleverest refinements was to limit to a maximum of five years the period in which purchasers laying down their money prior to settlement could exercise their privileges. The problem that the condition cut both ways – that if order holders must select by March 1869, so must South Australia legally make the land available – was never considered, because no one anticipated any difficulty in getting it surveyed quickly.

The legal action dragged on from 1870 to 1873. With a disrespectful tilt at the language used by lawyers, the press divided it into two acts: the preliminary sparring, followed by the real fight.

In pre-trial sparring, the government rested its main defence on the *equity* of the case: that it was morally in the right, having been more sinned against than sinning. They argued that the original surveys started by Finniss at Escape Cliffs were called off expressly

437 Dutton to Hughes 26/2/1869 with enclosure (S.A.P.P. 148 of 1869–1870, pp. 11 and 12).

438 Blackmore v. North Australian Company, before Judicial Committee of the Privy Council (S.A.P.P. 50 of 1874, p. 4).

to satisfy the objections of the land-order holders themselves, so the plaintiffs were in fact parties to the delays. It was recalled how Stow and Stuckey, the Norfolk Arms deputation and most particularly McKinlay had clamoured in the name of the land-order holders to have the site altered. Furthermore, they argued, the plaintiffs had in fact gained and not lost by having to wait. The long search had enabled all conceivable sites on the north coast of the Territory to be investigated before Goyder eventually picked out Port Darwin as the best possible site for a settlement. As parties to the delays and gainers because of them, it was morally indefensible for land purchasers now to sue the colony on a technical breach of contract.[439]

The Company countered with strong objections to deciding the case on an equity basis. In May 1870, the dispute was referred to the courts and eventually allocated to a judge in chambers in the colony's Supreme Court, Mr Justice William Alfred Wearing (former legal adviser to the Northern Territory Company) who, after hearing argument for several months, ruled the equity arguments irrelevant. Stung, the government appealed to the colony's full Supreme Court (Justices Hanson, Gwynne, Wearing)[440] and later the Privy Council in London, both courts of which upheld the learned judge, the Privy Council observing that even had the equity plea been admissible, it would hardly have stood. The difficulty was to prove that those who once protested against the Escape Cliffs site in the name of the land-order holders were in strict law speaking for the same individuals now taking out the writ. It could even be argued that McKinlay was acting for the South Australian government, not the London company, when he let loose his criticisms.[441]

The outcomes of the actual trials were practically decided before they commenced. Without any equity arguments, the defence lawyers sounded very hollow indeed. By a good deal of hair-splitting they tried to prove that no contract was involved, only a statuary obligation (which the plaintiffs' attorney in the Privy Council later said meant the same thing), and that agreements between a

439 North Australian Company v. Blackmore. Brief on Trial in the Supreme Court, Equity Plea (State Records G.R.G. 1/20).

440 *ibid.* pp. 95 to 108; S.A. Law Reports 1871, pp. 149 to 156).

441 Blackmore v. North Australian Company, before Judicial Committee of the Privy Council (S.A.P.P. 50 of 1874, pp. 39 to 41).

In a memorable quote, H.B. Strangways described the Territory as 'the bete noire of the Ministry, that expression being French for White Elephant'.
(*Portonian* 10/2/1872, p. 106. Courtesy of the State Library of South Australia)

government and private parties were of a different and special order. The trial came up in the Supreme Court on 4 July 1871 before Mr Justice E. Castres Gwynne and a special jury. With a good deal of hauteur the judge ruled the matter 'a simple case … for breach of contract' (with time as the key), and the jury's verdict went with the company.[442] The *Advertiser* criticised the verdict, complaining that the colony had more than once been badly treated by the Supreme Court.[443] In August the government appealed to the full court wanting a re-trial on grounds of misdirection by the learned

442 *Register* 5/7/1871 pp. 2 and 3 Supreme Court proceedings.
443 *Advertiser* 6/7/1871 leader.

judge. This was refused.[444] Chief Justice Sir Richard Davies Hanson eventually handed down a written judgement of the full court to explain the contract at issue.[445] By now the disposition of the judges, so it appeared to some, had become contemptuous.

Still the South Australian government would not acknowledge defeat. They now demanded the right to take the matter (especially the equity argument and the time contract) to England and the Privy Council[446] – which, suggested one newspaper, was at least a just court. By now the judges were becoming embarrassed. The Chief Justice maintained that to trouble the highest court of the realm with such a straightforward case would make fools of the colony and the Supreme Court in particular.[447] But among the colonists there was a strong, popular desire to use the Privy Council for arguing the colony's moral innocence to British audiences.[448]

At last the Supreme Court agreed, though only because the government demanded it as a moral right and the plaintiffs did not oppose finalising the question in this way. In late 1873 the matter reached the Judicial Committee of the Privy Council in London, where the right of the Supreme Court to rule out the equity plea, the intrinsic worth of the equity arguments, and the nature of the contract itself were all aired and considered. Their Lordships had no difficulty in deciding that the case fell 'within the very narrow compass' of a contract, which, having been broken by the colonial government, made it liable for the usual penalties of returning the outlay with interest added. The last word had been said. After using up all the available courts of the realm, and taking three and a half years to do so, the case had to be settled.[449]

The cost was considerable. South Australia's government was ordered to pay back the capital, plus interest on the capital for 10 years. The Northern Territory was marked with a debt of £80,000

444 S.A. Law Reports 1871, p. 162.

445 S.A. Law Reports 1871, pp. 174 to 178.

446 North Australian Company v. Blackmore, Petition for leave to Appeal (State Records G.R.G. 1/20).

447 *Register* 25/9/1871, p. 3; *Advertiser* 25/9/1871, p. 2 Supreme Court proceedings.

448 *Register* 12/8/1871, p. 4 'The Month's News'.

449 Blackmore v. North Australian Company, before Judicial Committee of the Privy Council (S.A.P.P. 50 of 1874).

on its head, made up of repayment and court costs, even before it was properly got going.[450] Furthermore, the extended, dreary law suit gave the Territory's unfortunate beginnings a long public airing. In the struggle to maintain its innocence South Australia had contributed to increasing doubts about ever investing in the Territory. As *Adelaide Punch* put it:

> If you want remuneration,
> And don't work alone for glory,
> Avoid a close relation
> With the Northern Terr-itory.[451]

And when news of the Privy Council's decision came by telegraph to Adelaide, Samuel Tomkinson (who had once appeared before the bar of the House) celebrated the insult by arranging that the Town Hall bells of Adelaide be rung out for joy.[452]

---

450 S.A.P.D. 1873 c.1259. Northern Territory Loan Bill; S.A.P.A. 17 of 1873.

451 *Register* 25/3/1869, p. 3, 'Pickings from *Adelaide Punch*' 18/3/1869.

452 *Register* 17/11/1873, p. 4. He said he did so because the colony's reputation had been saved.

CHAPTER 4

A SECOND SOUTH AUSTRALIA

Complications

> 'The complications with the land-order holders, in which it found itself involved, deprived it of all inclination to make a fresh start.'
>
> *Register* 2 January 1873

In 1872 South Australia's governor Sir James Fergusson took the initiative and advised the Colonial Office in London to put the Territory under some other control. Fergusson had been a former Head of the India Office, had influential connections with the Colonial Office, and held a particular interest in the future of the Northern Territory. Using governor-talk he wrote:

> the propriety of the continued Government of such a settlement from the opposite extremity of the Continent must engage the early attention of Her Majesty's Government and that long before the difficulties attending it became apparent to the South Australian Government and Parliament.

To drive home the point he offered to go there himself to see what should be done.[453]

Though a site for the northern capital had been found, the system of colonisation which survived the process of finding it was practically unworkable. Like South Australia before it, the Territory began in confusion. The principle of separate development, the only condition under which the colony ever consented to act as coloniser, had broken down. The land companies supposed to give a positive lead were gone, as were the money raised to steer the new Territory over the first difficult years and the good reputation needed to attract settlers and capital from the world at large.

---

453 Fergusson to Kimberley 17/5/1872 (G.O.D. 38 of 1872).

Governor Sir James Fergusson. In 1872 he advised the Colonial Office to put the Territory under some other control.
(*Australasian Sketcher* 9/8/1873, p. 84. Courtesy of the State Library of South Australia)

On the other hand, the mechanism of a self-supporting system remained to complicate the chances of reform. The faithful inner circle who had bought their land in advance still owned the best land, and held a legally privileged position. The centre of settlement could not be shifted or modified, nor the land sold for next to nothing without repudiating the promises made to them in 1863 and reaffirmed many times in a bid to keep them from seeking legal redress. In short, the Northern Territory Plan had no back-up strategy in the event of its failure.

The progress of the Territory now faced a wall of vested interests. Any move to have it developed with South Australia's meagre resources was considered quite intolerable by most of the colony's taxpayers, while moves to try other methods of colonisation had first to contend with the legal rights of the land-order holders. For instance, in July 1871 Colonel William Feilding of the Emigrant and Colonists' Aid Corporation came to Australia from England and, with considerable help from B.T. Finniss, offered to take over the whole of the Territory, including all debts except debts on the overland telegraph. But the government was not free to accept the bold offer, even if it had wanted to. Feilding went his way to found a flourishing settlement for poor immigrants on the north island of New Zealand.[454]

At first, however – exactly as Governor Fergusson had predicted – the difficulties were not apparent to everyone. Following the false start, the true position only became plain when governments were called upon to launch the settlement as a second South Australia and to administer the elementary responsibilities of land and law and order.

The Indies Governor

The crucial role of first Government Resident at Port Darwin was given to a nautical man of wide experience: Captain William Bloomfield Douglas, R.N.R.[455] Douglas had been appointed Harbour Master at Port Adelaide in 1854, before which he had served in the Royal Navy as a coastguard officer and for a short time as master of the merchant ship *Bosphorus*, which brought him to Adelaide. Between 1842 and about 1845 he had helped Rajah Sir James Brooke, with whom he was distantly connected by marriage, set up a personal suzerainty over Sarawak, an achievement Douglas never forgot. His grandfather had been a pioneering archaeologist and associate of Turner, the artist, and his upper-class family included many eccentrics. Bloomfield Douglas was the first and last 'Governor' of the Northern Territory – a rank he held only in his own imagination despite untiring efforts to persuade everyone he met.[456]

For the aristocratic Douglas, the appointment was the fruition of a long, patient ambition going back to the days when the north of Australia was still part of New South Wales. He had first

454 Feilding to Blyth 18/7/1871 (S.A.P.P. 91 of 1871); Deering to Feilding 18/7/1871 (S.A.P.P. 91A of 1871); *Register* 2/6/1875, p. 4.

455 Cavenagh to Douglas 27/4/1870 with enclosures (S.A.P.P. 25 of 1870–1871).

456 *Register* 30/4/1870, pp. 3 and 5; Douglas to Young 5/9/1854 (C.S.O.I.L. 2986/1854). According to Tom Harrisson and his staff of the Sarawak Museum Douglas almost certainly over-stated his contribution to Brooke's retinue. Research Notes Hann to Cross, 19/4/1962. Research in progress on British Colonial governors by Stephanie Williams, London 31/10/2008. Though sometimes described in Australia as an aristocrat, Douglas technically was not a member of the aristocratic class. See current research by Stephanie Williams of London on British Empire administrators.

tried for the position in 1862, while the citizens of Adelaide were feting Stuart's return.[457] He had tried again in 1863 when South Australia decided at last to colonise the Territory.[458] Unsuccessful, but still hopeful of a small appointment, he helped Finniss fit out his expedition and generously shared his Sarawak experience on how to deal with the Malay pirates thought to frequent the north coast.[459] When news of Finniss's many troubles arrived, Douglas made it his duty to rush the dispatches from the port, a service not always much appreciated by the ministry.[460] At the same time, he took the precaution of writing letters of commiseration to Finniss.[461] When in 1869–1870 the residentship again came available, Douglas redoubled his efforts, turning his own considerable charm, and that of his wife and daughters, on the veteran politician John Hart. Hart acquiesced and Douglas got the job.

Hart noted in his diary: 'He requested me to use my influence to obtain for him the Gov. Residentship. Which I promised to do if it would be of use to him. What a fool the man is ...' adding he should stay in his present job.[462]

It is likely Douglas's weaknesses helped almost as much as his strengths in getting him the job over other strong applicants like Dr Millner (the acting Resident and a strong, stable human being) and explorer John McKinlay. There were people in Adelaide glad to see him go. He was an incongruous man: a compound of enthusiasm and weakness, intelligent, sensitive, depressive, pestering, well-bred to the point of being irritating and, above all, keen to work hard – so much so that the government in Adelaide had in the past loaded him up with the duties of harbour master and naval officer, collector of customs, inspector of distilleries, nautical surveyor, stipendiary magistrate and a host of other offices. At different times he was referred to in the Adelaide newspapers as 'Captain', 'Lieutenant',

---

457 Douglas to Waterhouse 19/12/1862 (C.S.O.I.L. 1266/1862).

458 Douglas to Hart 23/7/1863 (with C.S.O.I.L. 286/1864).

459 Douglas to Hart 1/3/1864 (C.S.O.I.L. 286/1864); *Advertiser* 18/4/1864 leader.

460 Captain John Hart's Diary 12/2/1865; 30/7/1865 (S.L.S.A. Mortlock P.R.G.218).

461 Douglas to Finniss 28/10/1864 (State Records Finniss Papers G.R.G.35/643/283).

462 Captain Hart's Diary 6/6/1869 (S.L.S.A. Mortlock P.R.G. 218).

and 'Major'. His eagerness and versatility made him a cheap proposition for the Northern Territory, and economy was thought the first need. Adding to his credibility were rumours (coming from people close to Douglas himself) that he had been head-hunted for the position of Harbour Master at Melbourne. He was also chosen for his boasted wide experience of settlements in the Indies, after which the new metropolis of Palmerston was expected to develop.

Unfortunately, this good public officer had a disastrous weakness in money matters, which destined him to a life forever on the move. On appointment, one of the first things he did was to apply for six months salary in advance to meet his debts.[463] He was also known to be prone to depression and occasional bouts of drinking. With his wife, seven children and an Irish maid, he hurriedly took his leave by the *Gulnare* on the night of the 28 April 1870, some doubts being raised as to whether he could go in view of his debts. He was farewelled at the Semaphore by ministers of the crown, civil servants and hopeful creditors, one of whom wrote in his diary, 'He never said a word about the £100 I lent him, I suppose now he looks upon it as a gift.'[464]

As soon as he reached Palmerston (a name with status much approved of by the new Government Resident) on 24 June 1870, Douglas began to act like a liberated man. He saw himself as an empire builder, an Indies-style governor with wide powers carving out for Queen and Empire a new European bastion among the coloured races of the tropics. He even applied, unsuccessfully, to the Lords Commissioners of the Admiralty for the rank of Honorary Commander as befitting his new position.[465]

'On arriving at Port Darwin Captain Douglas landed in great state,' recalled Elizabeth Sweet, who was aboard the *Gulnare*.[466] He was welcomed ashore by a guard of honour and a gun salute from a cacophony of weapons.

Douglas's first active step was to turn the resources of the

---

463 Douglas to Cavenagh 28/3/1870 (N.T.I.L. 24/1870)

464 Captain John Hart's Diary 28/4/1870 (S.L.S.A. Mortlock P.R.G.218).

465 Douglas to Derrington 9/2/1872 (N.T.I.L. 73/1872); Fergusson to Kimberley 24/4/1872 (G.O.D. 34 of 1872); Kimberley to Fergusson 18/7/1872 (G.I.D. 21 of 1872).

466 *Public Service Review* November 1907

settlement to building an imposing Residency. The foundation stone was laid by his daughter Harriet on 12 August. When finished it was surely the strangest government house in the world, combining the body of a far-eastern bungalow with a flat cement roof and a temporary flag staff. From the middle of the harbour, it looked like a battleship that had come to end its days on the edge of the tableland.[467] In Douglas's efforts to recreate the Raj he was assisted by his wife Ellen and adult daughters Harriet and Eleanor, who started a round of tea-parties, soirees, picnics and the occasional concert among the better class citizens, most of it at taxpayer expense. Douglas had brought with him a piano and a billiard table as a link to civilisation.

William Bloomfield Douglas, an incongruous man, a compound of enthusiasm and weakness, intelligent, sensitive, depressive, pestering and prone to occasional breakdowns.
(Courtesy of the State Library of South Australia – P.R.G. 280/1/14/337)

Events frustrated Douglas's lordly ambitions. In June 1870, while he was still en route to Port Darwin, South Australia's long defensive battle to prevent the undersea cable coming ashore in Queensland finally paid off. In that month the government received

467 Harriet W. Daly, *Digging, Squatting, and Pioneering Life in the Northern Territory of South Australia*, Sampson Low etc., London, 1887, Chapter XI.

a communication from the British Australia Telegraph Company, specialists in undersea cabling, undertaking to land the cable at Port Darwin, providing the government completed at its own cost a land-line from Palmerston to Port Augusta by January 1872. The victory was won at the last moment when in April Commander Noel Osborne, representing the British Australia Telegraph Company, visited Adelaide *before* Brisbane and was worked upon by Charles Todd, superintendent of telegraphs, and H.B.T. Strangways, attorney-general, to favour South Australia's grand plan over the more sensible scheme of the company itself paying for a land-line from Palmerston to Normanton, which was already connected by telegraph to Brisbane. The order of priorities for the Territory was immediately changed. Legislation drawn up in haste by Strangways was rushed through parliament in June. Charles Todd, who had become obsessive about the project, was given an almost free hand to supervise the immense engineering undertaking of a transcontinental line following loosely the tracks of Stuart to connect with the European cable coming down through Java.

Those who accused South Australians of lack of commitment to the Territory could never say the same of the way the colonists approached the construction of the overland telegraph. With an almost heroic vision, Todd planned the construction to be built simultaneously in three sections of five hundred or more miles each, using as a general rule 20 posts to the mile and across Australia incorporating a total of 12 repeater stations. The southern section extending north to near the South Australian border was entrusted to a private contractor and pastoralist, Edward Meade Bagot. The middle section to near Tennant Creek, considered the most difficult, was sub-divided into five stretches under proven government surveyors: Knuckey, McMinn, Mills, Woods and Harvey. All had earlier been with Goyder in the Territory. The northern section to Port Darwin, regarded as less challenging, was entrusted to private contractors Dalwood and Darwent.[468]

Douglas and his retinue knew very little about these plans until

468 Peter Taylor, *An End to Silence: The Building of the Overland Telegraph Line from Adelaide to Darwin*, Methuen Sydney, 1980, pp. 35 to 80. Mills took over from Beckwith as administrator of Section C when Beckwith became ill and eventually died.

two and a half months after their arrival when the *Omeo* appeared off Port Darwin with the northern contract party under William Dalwood. It came as a shock. In a second set of instructions brought by the *Bengal* which left over three weeks after the *Gulnare*, Douglas had been told to explore a route for the line via the Roper towards the Queensland border, from which he reasonably concluded that the company itself would build the line across to Burketown, thus freeing him for the proper business of colonisation. In fact he had already despatched Surveyor George Galbraith MacLachlan to explore the route toward Queensland.[469]

Douglas's first official duty on reaching Palmerston was to provide order holders with land for which they had paid their money six years before. The order of selection was first balloted for in the Land Office in Adelaide. The ceremony copied the original South Australian ballot 30 years earlier, even so that one of the original scrutineers, George Kingston, took part. A crowd of eager spectators gathered in Adelaide to watch the flouting of the colony's lottery laws.[470] As it turned out, luck seemed to favour those not deserving it. The London company, just then doing its best to libel the Territory, received four of the first six town choices and first, third and fourth selection of the country lands.[471]

While the ballot for the order of selection was conducted in Adelaide, the actual selection of land was supposed to take place in Palmerston so owners or their agents could see the blocks before selection. In May, seven land agents, with explorer McKinlay as their spokesman, hastened away to Port Darwin by the *Bengal* to select land for those they represented.[472] Some of the agents held land-orders themselves, but otherwise hardly a single block was chosen by subscribers themselves.

Douglas treated the agents as men of rank. They stumped across the surveyed country with the air of a picnic party, picking the eyes out of the country and keeping a weather eye open for gold (which according to legend existed on the north coast), never dreaming they were being shadowed by the Adelaide River Aborigines, who had

469 Further instructions to Douglas (S.A.P.P. 26 of 1870–1871, p. 2).

470 *Register* 11/5/1870, p. 5; 12/5/1870, p. 6.

471 *Register* 21/5/1870 Supplement, pp. 4 and 5.

472 *Register* 23/5/1870, p. 4 Shipping News.

taken it on their heads to kill them.[473] The actual selections were made on maps exhibited in new horse stables at Palmerston, the town allotments being chosen over four and a half days starting on 18 July and the country lands between 5 and 10 September. In all, 810 orders were represented.[474] By close of business, the best of the town sites (particularly the high sites at Palmerston) and the pick of the country lands (especially between the arms of Port Darwin and the Adelaide River) were taken up by land jobbers who would never dream of setting foot on a remote part of the world like North Australia. McKinlay, whose harsh words did more than any other to get the site transferred from Escape Cliffs, insisted on making his choice from Finniss's original surveys, and was much peeved when this was disallowed.[475] Strange to say, another critic of Finniss, Ebenezer Ward, who never went back to the Territory, also wanted to take up land on the Adelaide River.[476]

The agents included William Henry Gray, a land investor with the golden touch, who already owned much of the suburban lands west of Adelaide. He was so impressed by what he saw that he immediately set about buying up land-orders on the open market until he became the largest individual owner of land in the surveyed areas. Gray exemplified the speculative nature of the selection. Having acquired his land – his dream of wealth in the tropics – he refused to sell to local settlers despite considerable prodding. The last of his sections was sold by his estate, some time after 1960.[477]

Their work done, most of the agents returned to Adelaide. In a novel move Messrs McKinlay, Daly and Davis brought south with them three young Larrakia men who stayed several months before returning – the object being 'to civilize them; and that on their return to their country they may inform their tribes how numerous, powerful, yet kind the white races are …'[478]

---

473 *Register* 8/11/1870 Supplement, p. 3.

474 Douglas to Blyth 16/8/1870 (N.T.I.L. 87/1870); Douglas to Blyth 17/9/1870 with enclosure (N.T.I.L. 92/1870); Harriet W. Daly, *Digging, Squatting and Pioneering,* pp. 78 and 79.

475 Douglas to Blyth 16/8/1870 (N.T.I.L. 87/1870).

476 Ward to Blyth 28/6/1871 index only (N.T.I.L. 202/1871).

477 E. Hasenohr, *W.H. Gray A Pioneer Colonist of South Australia*, published by author, Adelaide, 1977.

478 McKinlay, Davis and Daly to Blyth 28/10/1870 (N.T.I.L. 104/1870); Ellis

On 15 September 1870 at Palmerston, Harriet Douglas performed the public ceremony of planting the first pole for the overland telegraph. Side by side with building the Residency and selecting the lands, this was the other main event in the life of the young colony. Her father grabbed the chance to praise his new empire, and his address was followed by the booming of three salutes – from Fort Hill, the *Omeo,* and the little *Gulnare.* The demonstration astonished the Larrakias, who wanted to know whether the Europeans were getting ready for a fight.[479]

Then began a strenuous tug-o-war between the Resident in Palmerston and his ministers in Adelaide over a question of priorities. The government had contracted to complete the telegraph work inside 18 months and subjugated all Territory matters to that fact. Douglas, on the other hand, feared that if the Territory was allowed to run down after the momentum given by Goyder's success it might never be started up again, so he set to work with grand schemes designed to turn the place into a separate colony like Queensland.

His two most ambitious plans were to establish tropical plantations and to import so-called 'coloured workers', neither of which was regarded as pressing in Adelaide.[480] 'I look with confidence to the success of the new Settlement,' he wrote in his first report, 'if the Sugar Cane, Cotton and other Tropical productions will thrive here, and provided Means are at once taken to ascertain whether Coolie labor can be obtained either from the neighbouring Colonies or elsewhere.'[481] While bringing Douglas to Port Darwin, the *Gulnare* had been forced to run to Brisbane for storm repairs, where, in return for being sworn in as a Queensland magistrate, Douglas had obtained free supplies of sugar cane and other plants from the Botanic Gardens.[482] Most of his many advisers in Brisbane

---

Edwards to Blyth 20/2/1871 (N.T.I.L. 23/1871).

479 *Register* 8/11/1870 Supplement, p. 3; Stapleton to — 16/9/1870 (S.L.S.A. Mortlock PRG 643).

480 The concept of 'coloured workers' or 'coolies' almost as a separate species, was central to much thinking at the time.

481 Douglas to Blyth 1/7/1870 (N.T.I.L. 81/1870).

482 *Queensland Express* 3/6/1870 (in the *Advertiser* 12/9/1870 Supplement, p. 4); *Brisbane Courier* 31/5/1870, p. 3; 2/6/1870, p. 2 Shipping.

thought the Territory's first need would be coloured labour, and Douglas could not resist telegraphing Adelaide for permission to go direct to the Dutch East Indies to recruit planters and coolies.[483] When the minister in charge refused to comply, Douglas continued his journey to Port Darwin.[484]

No sooner was he ashore, than Douglas was making plans to set up experimental gardens around Palmerston. He augmented the existing garden – situated below the tableland just east of the depot and holding plants found growing wild at Escape Cliffs – with tropical fruits and staples: tapioca, coffee, tea and spices. He then started experimental cane gardens, each of a thousand plants, at Doctor Peel's Gully and on the northern limits of the town surveys at Paper Bark Swamp. Each was soon flourishing luxuriantly.[485] 'I am very sanguine as to the success of the cultivation of the Sugar Cane in suitable localities,' he wrote hopefully in 1870.[486] 'Of the certainty of success in the cultivation of sugar I have not the slightest doubt, the experiments I have made have been rewarded beyond my most sanguine expectations,' he reported in 1871.[487] Meanwhile, in August 1870, the settlement's schooner, *Gulnare*, made first contact with the Dutch East Indies at Koepang, Timor and brought back, among other things, coconuts and paddy for testing on the swampy inland flats.[488] The coconuts were planted at Fannie Bay with the eager help of some Larrakia labourers who later dug them up and ate them as the need arose.[489]

About two months after his first plea, Douglas again sought permission to canvass for coolies among the neighbouring islands, and was ordered not to move out of his ground while the telegraph was being built.[490] Frustrated, he sought less direct ways of achieving his object. He began to pester the ministry for a regular shipping

483 Douglas to Blyth 1/7/1870 (N.T.I.L. 81/1870).

484 Blyth to Douglas 10/9/1870 (N.T.O.L. 178/1870).

485 Douglas to Blyth 1/7/1870 (N.T.I.L. 81/1870); Douglas to Blyth 16/8/1870 (N.T.I.L. 87/1870); Douglas to Blyth 17/9/1870 with enclosure C (N.T.I.L. 92/1870).

486 Douglas to Blyth 16/8/1870 (N.T.I.L. 87/1870).

487 Douglas to Blyth 2/6/1871 (S.A.P.P. 35 of 1871).

488 Douglas to Blyth 17/9/1870 with enclosure C (N.T.I.L. 92/1870).

489 Harriet W. Daly, *Digging, Squatting and Pioneering,* p. 72.

490 Blyth to Douglas 10/9/1870 (N.T.O.L. 178/1870).

service linking Port Darwin to Koepang and Batavia via which migrants could find their way,[491] and appointed the doctor, James Stokes Millner, to the lofty roles of immigration agent and quarantine officer.[492] During 1870, via the *Gulnare,* he obtained his first Malay servant from Koepang in Timor, a boy named Omah, and the next year added to his retinue four Malay boatmen and two stowaways, all of whom were urged to bring their friends and relations after them.[493] But the shipping service was shelved, and the few Malays who arrived by the occasional ship did not live up to expectation. It was a common joke for many years how Douglas took back from the Malays in court fines one week what he had paid them in wages the week before.[494] The Malays evidently took their rebukes in good part, for when South Australia's Commissioner of Crown Lands and immigration visited Koepang in 1873 he found they had sent home such glowing reports that he could have filled up the schooner with friends and relations bound for North Australia.[495]

Douglas soon decided that coolies from the Asian mainland might better suit the needs of his empire, telling the government that:

> It is, however, useless to depend on a supply from the islands in the Arafura Sea, or Java, or the Dutch East Indian Islands ... In some parts of British India, and the recognised trading ports in China, not the slightest difficulty will be experienced in obtaining coolies at from ls. to ls.3d. per diem.[496]

Thwarted over the shipping service, he then tried to obtain for his own use a faster ship with a crew committed to work anywhere in the regions of the north coast and the Indies islands.[497] He scorned

491 Douglas to Blyth 13/4/1871 (N.T.I.L. 67/1871); Douglas to Blyth 2/6/1871 (N.T.I.L. 130/1871).

492 Douglas to Blyth 2/6/1871 (N.T.I.L. 127/1871); Douglas to Blyth 2/6/1871 (N.T.I.L. 125/1871).

493 Douglas to Reynolds 10/7/1872 (N.T.I.L. 304/1872).

494 *Northern Territory Times and Gazette* 17/12/1875, p. 2 Barlow to Editor.

495 Report of the Commissioner of Crown Lands and Immigration of his Official visit to the Northern Territory (S.A.P.P. 55 of 1873, p. 3).

496 Douglas to Blyth 2/6/1871 (S.A.P.P. 35 of 1871).

497 Douglas to Blyth 22/10/1870 (N.T.I.L. 130/1870); Douglas to Blyth 2/6/1871

the *Gulnare*, as slow, unwieldy, costly, a 'dead weight on the funds' and 'a complete incubus on the Settlement'.[498] He wanted instead a navy ship, cheap, small and fitted with a six-pounder firepiece to keep the Macassan fishing proas at bay. The criticisms involved him in a quarrel with the *Gulnare*'s master, Captain Sweet (formerly of the South China Station, Hong Kong), and caused complications with the government in Adelaide, which considered her suitable enough for telegraph work. In October 1871, by a stroke of luck for Douglas, the *Gulnare* struck a reef on the Vernon Islands while over-loaded on its way with telegraph equipment to the Roper River. 'Douglas very pleased as he can now recommend Capt. Sweet's dismissal,' wrote Trooper Catchlove in his diary.[499] The *Bengal* being in port at the time was sent to help, and took off most of the cargo so that the *Gulnare* could get back to Port Darwin where, over the objection of her master, she was condemned in an inquiry led by Douglas, stripped for materials that could be useful for the overland telegraph, and left to deteriorate at Fort Hill. Between February 1869 and September 1871, the gallant *Gulnare* had made a total of five trips north to the Territory under Captain Sweet. The long-suffering South Australian government now became involved in a dispute with the ship's insurers. By the time a replacement – the cutter *Flying Cloud* under Captain Marsh – arrived in December 1872, Douglas's days were numbered.[500]

Behind all Douglas's schemes was the example of the nearby

(N.T.I.L. 130/1871); Douglas to Blyth 24/10/1871 with enclosure (N.T.I.L. 10/1872).

498 Douglas to Blyth 17/9/1870 (N.T.I.L. 92/1870); 22/10/1870 (N.T.I.L. 130/1870).

499 E.N.P. Catchlove Diary. 9/10/1871. (S.L.S.A. Mortlock P.R.G. 651/1). The loss of the *Gulnare* was a great set-back in Captain Sweet's career. For a time he did excellent work for Todd, sounding out the Roper River, before returning to Adelaide and setting himself up as a leading Australian photographer.

500 Sweet to Douglas 19/11/1871; Sweet to Townsend 27/11/1871 (N.T.I.L. 28/1872); Douglas to Blyth 24/10/1871 with enclosures (N.T.I.L. 12/1872); Douglas to Blyth 24/10/1871 with enclosures (N.T.I.L. 13/1872); Douglas to Reynolds 24/9/1872 (N.T.I.L. 371/1872). For study of the Douglas regime see: *Stable Guard and Fatigue – a History of Palmerston, Port Darwin 24 June to 24 December 1870 from the diary of Police Trooper Edward Napoleon Buonaparte Catchlove,* by Jeff Catchlove, 1970, courtesy of the author.

Dutch and British East Indies, a region he knew so well. He envisaged a colony of white sahibs and coloured workers, of white managers and obedient coolies. 'The fact is during the hot season,' he maintained, 'Europeans cannot labour in the middle of the day, thus the Government is paying the highest rate of wages, for merely a portion of a day's work and owing to the excessive heat that work not too energetically performed.'[501] In terms of hard cash, 'coloured people', he calculated, could do more work each day on half the pay and 50 per cent less rations.[502] He had no faith in the dozen or so European small settlers already in the Territory, some of whom had arrived in June 1870 by the *Bengal* (especially as they had come without food and had to rely on government handouts) – men like Christian Schmidt, Cossmann Kritzner and John Playford. These he castigated as lazy and useless, and waged a continual petty war with them. Their quarrels came to a head one week over the case of Schmidt the German storekeeper's 'perambulating piggery'. Schmidt's contribution to the progress of the settlement lay in the introduction from Timor of horehound (Schmid's Folly) for medical purposes, which overgrew the town[503] – and a herd of Timor swine, which played havoc with the experimental gardens. 'The Governor' or the 'G.R.', as Douglas was soon dubbed, eventually lost his temper and put himself at the head of an exciting pig hunt across the tableland followed by 20 or 30 enthusiastic Larrakia hunters brandishing their spears. The damage to what Schmidt called his 'running property' caused repercussions all the way to Adelaide.[504] He and the other white settlers demanded a public inquiry into the way they were being persecuted, and added the charge, usually raked up when there was someone to avenge, that Douglas was ill-treating the Aborigines.[505]

Douglas's many ideas for launching his kingdom during the first flush of settlement soon had his masters in the south dragging their feet for all their worth. Having resolved to give the telegraph absolute

501 Douglas to Blyth 16/8/1870 (N.T.I.L. 87/1870).

502 *ibid.*

503 *Northern Territory Times and Gazette* 25/3/1876, p. 2.

504 Schmid to Blyth 22/5/1871; Vosz to Ayers 14/2/1872 with enclosure (N.T.I.L. 213/1871).

505 Withers and Kritzner to Blyth 12/4/1871 (N.T.I.L. 90/1871).

priority, they knew that failure now to complete the line would make them a laughing stock, and their resolution strengthened even as the project encountered muddy waters. After planting the first pole at Palmerston, the contractors for the northern section, Darwent and Dalwood, set to work at a merry pace, covering over 200 miles before the monsoon hunted them down and stopped their operations. The shock of this setback threw the South Australian authorities into a frantic haste. The private contract of Darwent and Dalwood was declared null and void by the government overseer in Palmerston, William McMinn (for reasons known only to himself), and a large government expedition rushed north under R.C. Patterson to take up the work just in time to catch the next monsoon in 1871–1872. This party, too, became bogged. When it became clear they could not meet the deadline early in 1872, a party of reinforcements, under Charles Todd himself, scurried north to provide support. He set Captain Sweet, after he had lost his ship, to work surveying and navigating ships 100 miles up the Roper River so that it could be used as a supply point – a feat for which Sweet got no reward.[506] Adding to the panic, once the contract had been broken, the British Australia Telegraph Company threatened to revert to its original plan and run a line across to Normanton or Burketown to link with the Queensland system – a threat averted only when the BAT's own section of the cable between Port Darwin and Java suddenly broke in June.[507]

What the indigenous people made of all this frenzy will never be known. In 1871, Number 2 Depot, 79 miles from Palmerston, was attacked twice. Other responses were more difficult for the telegraph builders to understand. For example, at one stage they were visited by what seemed an official party of Aboriginal men, who at the conclusion of the visit marched off rhythmically 'slapping their buttocks as they went'.[508]

506 Correspondence re claim of S.W. Sweet (S.A.P.P. 32 of 1873).

507 *The Australian Encyclopaedia,* Aust. Geographic, N.S.W. 1996, p. 2322 *seq.*; Peter Taylor, *An End to Silence,* Methuen, Sydney, 1980 *passim*. For a more personal approach see Alice Thomson, *The Singing Line,* Vintage, London, 1999. PhD thesis on Sweet in progress by Karen Magee, University of Adelaide; British-Australian Telegraph (S.A.P.P. 156 of 1872 *passim*).

508 Early Experiences in the Northern Territory by S.W. Herbert 1870–1873, pp. 88, 109 (S.L.S.A. Mortlock D6995 (L)).

Meanwhile, the government in Adelaide was bending over backwards to prevent any activity starting in the Territory which might compete with construction of the overland telegraph. When in 1870 Lord Granville of the Colonial Office asked pointedly from London about 'additional measures for promoting immigration to the Colony' (he saw the Territory as a future separate colony), Cabinet replied, 'Recommend to His Excellency that nothing be proposed at present.'[509] When others, like Colonel Finniss, urged the introduction of an immediate Indies shipping service, the minister in charge ruled that 'as the settlement progresses & especially when the telegraph is completed this matter will necessarily be brought before the Govt'.[510] When 55 Adelaide capitalists asked for assistance to discover payable gold, Cabinet replied: 'As the discovery of a Gold field at this time would greatly interfere with the very important work at present in hand – it is considered undesirable to take any steps in that direction until the telegraph line is completed.'[511] In 1870 Dr Richard Schomburgk, the colony's foremost botanical scientist, urged the government to make an all-out effort to experiment with tropical agriculture.[512] But the responsible minister refused to appoint a scientist, recalled the botanist already there, delayed offering a sugar bonus, and habitually regarded the Resident's own brave efforts as glorified fruit and vegetable gardens.[513]

For two years Douglas found himself 'a mere storekeeper to the OT' (to quote his diary),[514] serving without honour a motley crowd of contractors, post-hole diggers and teamsters. South Australians, he sadly learned, were more interested in tying themselves by a tenuous cord to the Old World (that would give them first access to information from overseas and make Adelaide the centre for telegraphic communications), than in encouraging his minute kingdom.

509 Granville to Fergusson 9/2/1870 with Minutes (G.I.D. 5 of 1870).

510 Douglas to Blyth 13/4/1871 Minute 9, 7/7/1871 (N.T.I.L. 67/1871).

511 Morphett etc. to Blyth 23/7/1871, Cabinet Minute 1/8/1871 (N.T.I.L. 173/1871).

512 *Register* 26/4/1870, p. 5; 27/4/1870, p. 4; *Advertiser* 26/4/1870, p. 2.

513 S.A.P.D. 1870–1871 c. 459; Cavenagh to Douglas 27/4/1870 (S.A.P.P. 25 of 1870–1871, p. 2); Blyth to Douglas 10/9/1870 (N.T.O.L. 178/1870).

514 Captain W.B. Douglas's Diary, 2/5/1872 (Northern Territory Archives).

The telegraph line was completed only in August 1872, more than seven months late. Now the southern colonials could preen themselves in front of the world. Banquets were held in Adelaide, Sydney and London, and Charles Heavitree Todd was honoured by Queen Victoria for his contribution to the Empire. But no official celebration was authorised for Port Darwin, which annoyed Douglas very much.

The construction of the telegraph had cost £338,000 (or with repairs £480,000, four times the sum originally voted) for a population of only 82,000 adults. The lesson to the government was that they had overreached themselves in the grandiose scheme, and efforts were quickly made to cut spending to bedrock. Having once been shelved to make way for construction work, Northern Territory colonisation now looked set to be shelved again because of the debt incurred. Most of the final negotiations for the overland telegraph had been conducted outside parliament (there being a ministerial crisis) and many politicians, including Captain Hart and Ebenezer Ward, had been worried about the cost from the beginning. In fact, in June 1870 Hart as premier had argued against paying for all the direct route from Port Darwin to Port Augusta, but had been out-voted by parliament.[515]

During the telegraph's construction, the disappointed Resident had retaliated with wild, undignified sallies at the project that was overshadowing his ambitions.

In June 1871 he decided, under pressure, to send the *Gulnare* (which he had been keeping mainly for his personal use) to Adelaide with William McMinn and the dismissed contractors aboard, overriding an instruction by his minister that the *Gulnare* should be used during the dry season to take wire and poles around to the Roper River. After that episode, the minister put the *Gulnare* directly at the disposal of the new government construction party led by Robert Charles Patterson. Douglas also tried his best to prevent the construction teams using his equipment, particularly the small boat *Dolphin*, and complained bitterly about their 'discourtesy' in filching some of his staff, adding his fear that most other staff would

515 Overland Telegraph Receipts and Expenditure (S.A.P.P. 109 of 1876); S.A.P.D.c. 118 to 133. The precise cost is hard to calculate due to continuous re-poling.

eventually follow suit. By refusing to lend his boats while McMinn was away, he then successfully stopped all efforts by McMinn's second in command, Robert Charles Burton, to take wire by sea to Southport. When the minister in charge, Arthur Blyth, got news of Douglas's complaints he responded in strong language,[516] fuming that Douglas *knew* the Colony was committed to this great work and was racing against time:

> One would have thought that this was just the opportunity that any Officer who was not utterly blind to every consideration but his own fancied importance would have been thankful to take advantage of ... Mr Douglas however thinks this a fitting time to withdraw the little assistance which he was rendering to the party because for sooth one of his 'Staff' have been seduced from his service and it was necessary for him to indicate the position he occupied.[517]

After that the Adelaide ministers deliberately 'circumscribed his power of interference', a direction which meant giving Douglas much less power than he expected. His authority had now shrunk to supervising and over-supervising the lives of his European and Aboriginal subjects.[518]

Douglas did not give up his empire-building activities. In August–September 1872 he went to the Roper River Depot just when the telegraph construction teams were being disbanded. While Charles Todd had left orders that no horses and drays were to be lent to the men to get to newly found goldfields at Yam Creek, Douglas advertised the gold discoveries among the workers and instructed George Deane (in charge of government horses) to bring the government horses used in construction of the telegraph line overland in the company of a party led by Dillon Cox (one of the first overlanders) in order to provide construction workers with a safe direct passage on foot. 'My policy,' he wrote in his diary, 'is to

---

516 Blyth to Douglas 20/7/1871 (N.T.O.L. 387/1871); Blyth to Douglas 21/7/1871 (N.T.O.L. 404/1871); Douglas to Blyth 30/8/1871 with enclosures (N.T.I.L. 261/1871); Blyth to Douglas 3/11/1871 (N.T.O.L. 498/1871).

517 Douglas to Blyth 30/8/1871, Chief Secretary's Minute 16/10/1871 (N.T.I.L. 261/1871).

518 *ibid.*

encourage diggers proceeding to the diggings.' It was a policy that helped set off a rush.[519]

Douglas's desire to follow the style of an Indies governor was particularly seen in his attitude to the indigenous peoples. He sometimes called them the 'The Australians', in the sense of the *real* Australians. In contrast to other administrators, he saw the indigenous inhabitants as essential to colonisation as indeed they were in the Indies, as labourers, farmers and native policemen. But for many years, he thought, they would need to be under the supervision of white masters.[520]

Soon after he arrived in June 1870, together with his family he moved to establish formal links with what he called the 'kings' of the Larrakia tribe. These were the elders of the two main clan groups, the Nilungas and the Mirandas. There was a third – uninvited – clan, the Binmooks, whom Douglas (without really knowing) ruled of lesser rank.

Douglas's relations with the indigenous peoples remained the subject of many stories long after he left the Territory and returned to his main love, the Indies. At first relations with the Larrakia were generally cordial, probably because the local people saw the Europeans as visitors and traders who would eventually leave. To make relations easier, the local people happened to have very few possessions like pigs or gold that the Europeans might be tempted to take. Learning from his experience in the East, Douglas tried to distance the two camps to lessen the chances of cultural dissonance. Even so, there was conflict over the local people's tendency to take axes, billy-cans, food and the like whenever the opportunity arose. When a rumour started that the Big Gun – the Howitzer – would be turned on the Larrakias if they did not give back the axes, Narlunga, elder of the Larrakia, responded that they could not leave their home for fear of being attacked by the Adelaide River Woolnas who had been gradually encroaching on Larrakia lands.[521]

Another source of conflict was the burial custom of the Larrakia people. Not even the most tolerant Europeans accepted the practice

519 Captain W.B. Douglas's Diary, 23/9/1872 (Northern Territory Archives).

520 Douglas to Blyth 13/4/1871 with enclosures (N.T.I.L. 67/1871); Foelsche to Hamilton 10/4/1871 with enclosures (N.T.I.L. 87/1871).

521 Douglas to Blyth 16/8/1870 (N.T.I.L. 87/1870).

of burying bodies on a platform in a tree near European dwellings. Yet it was a practice profoundly significant to Aboriginal culture.[522]

As the visitors overstayed their welcome, resistance by the indigenous people began to grow and Captain Douglas's efforts to keep the peace became more problematic. A crisis came in April 1871 when an Aboriginal speared Charlie, a horse, which then had to be destroyed. In true Indies style, Douglas decided to take hostages until the tribe handed over the offender. First he instructed Captain Sweet to entice a number of Aboriginal men aboard the *Gulnare,* which they could only reach by canoe. In the panic which followed a sudden rush to grab them, the Aboriginal men jumped overboard in all directions and escaped. Douglas and his police force then marched to the Larrakia camp in full uniform and just took two hostages. These men were kept in leg irons on the *Gulnare* until the tribe after much debate handed over the horse-spearer, a young man called Binmook. Binmook's defence was that a settler had shot his dog, because as it later turned out the dog had killed some of his fowls. For his crime Binmook was given 12 strokes across his shoulders with a riding whip then released. After that, according to Douglas, the tribe showed no ill will and became co-operative. It is worth noting that the Larrakia people showed less hostility towards this sort of physical punishment than towards incarceration, which they apparently saw as a barbaric practice.[523]

On Christmas Day 1872 Douglas marshalled his Larrakia subjects together for an Aboriginal sports day to celebrate the Christian Christmas. They politely obliged because they thought otherwise the governor would 'growl'. There was much furious running, jumping and spear throwing at a white man-sized target, followed by the formal presentation of prizes including tomahawks, blankets, flour, tea and sugar. The event so pleased Douglas that he tried to repeat the celebration, without much success, a week later on New Year's Day.[524]

As time passed Larrakia women in particular took the lead in

---

522 *Northern Territory Times and Gazette* 13/2/1874, p. 2 J.N.W. to Editor.

523 Douglas to Blyth 13/4/1871 (N.T.I.L. 67/1871); Withers and Kritzner to Blyth 12/4/1871 (N.T.I.L. 90/1871); Douglas to Blyth 15/5/1871 (N.T.I.L. 114/1871); Douglas to Blyth 29/8/1871 (N.T.I.L. 245/1871).

524 *Observer* 19/7/1873, p. 11.

cross-cultural contacts. Aboriginal and European women shared a common interest in babies and children, and Larrakia women as the main traditional food gatherers were more accustomed to continuous toil. They soon became the washer-women and carriers of water and menial workers in exchange for 'tom-tom', a Pidgin word for food. That is, they became labourers in a capitalist system. In contrast, men would work intensively for one day and then rest for two or three or four. As a result of these contacts, within 10 years most Larrakias could speak English.

In true paternalistic style, Douglas was also trying to keep the peace between the local Larrakias and the neighbouring peoples from the Adelaide and Alligator Rivers.

Just two weeks before he arrived, more than a hundred Woolnas in war paint visited Port Darwin demanding food and white women from the Europeans. When they were unsuccessful, they attacked the Larrakias, killing a man named Orunga, and seriously wounding another, Neurlunga, and his woman companion. Douglas decided to visit the Woolnas to tell them not to ill treat the Larrakias and to explain the reasons why the Europeans had abandoned the Escape Cliffs site. He saw himself as a defender of the Larrakias, who were much less numerous than their neighbours. He had no faith in the white working class, least of all in the tropics, and hoped the Larrakias could become manual workers.[525] The response of the Woolnas was to shift into the Larrakia lands over the next few years, and this became the cause of much strife.

The nature of relationships between the Larrakias and Woolnas over the following years baffled the Europeans. Sometimes relations were cordial, and small groups of Woolnas would stay in the Larrakia camp. Sometimes there were mock battles using a light, blunted spear, young men on each side being urged on by the older women. Sometimes the Woolnas would attack the Larrakias in earnest, causing injury and the occasional death, so that the latter had to send their women, children and old men to the European houses for protection. Serious fights were held where whites could not witness them and casualties were hidden. In May 1876, for instance, Narlunga, a much-admired elder of the Larrakias,

525 Rough Journal of J.S. Millner 10/6/1870, 11/6/1870 (N.T.I.L. 80/1870); Douglas to Blyth 1/7/1870 (N.T.I.L. 81/1870).

was killed in a fight while others were wounded. The death was followed by great mourning. Secure in his Christian belief in life after death, Reverend Archibald Bogle (first clergyman in the Territory) referred to the 'helpless sorrow of these poor people'.[526]

Once or twice a year Woolnas would descend on the centre of the town in numbers begging for tobacco, alcohol and money, and offering their women at two shillings for young women and sixpence for older women, before being driven off by the Larrakias and the European police. Once, in April 1872, when Douglas caned a Larrakia boy for stealing, the indignant Larrakias threatened to bring in their dreaded enemy the Woolnas to drive the whitefellows out.

In early December 1872 a Woolna with Larrakia connections, named 'Scotchman' by the whites, tried to spear Douglas while he was on one of his tours of inspection accompanied by daughter Harriet (who acted as a kind of second-in-command) and a police trooper sweltering in full uniform. These ritual tours Douglas often combined with a spot of recreational shooting. Scotchman, dressed in war paint and bristling with spears, took up position in front of the Government Resident, barring his way. Ordered to go back to his people, Scotchman refused to move, then threw a spear which passed through 'the Governor's' coat between his arm and body and became embedded in his clothes. 'I then fired and missed the scoundrel,' wrote Douglas in his journal. Given Douglas's sympathetic attitudes, perhaps he aimed to miss – once before, following an armed skirmish, he rejoiced when he found no Aborigines had been hit. A second spear grazed Douglas's left arm and a third missile, a large stone, bruised his elbow. Between each attack Douglas retaliated with a shot from his revolver, so the confrontation took on the character of a duel.

Meanwhile, the trooper had moved to protect Douglas's daughter, who galloped off to get help. Soon Scotchman was joined by Aborigines (mainly Woolnas), appearing as if from nowhere. The Government Resident, with only two shots left in his revolver, was forced to make a dignified retreat.

Douglas blamed the Woolnas for this attack, but he suspected

---

526 Diary of A.J. Bogle 25/5/1876 (Mitchell Library).

the connivance of at least some Larrakias. On his previous day's tour of inspection, he had been threatened by about 30 Woolnas in war paint, who then spent the night in the Larrakia camp. Now Douglas was quick to show who was boss. The police immediately grabbed a Woolna as a hostage, while Scotchman was soon apprehended, summarily convicted, and set to work chained up by one leg as a lackey around the household of the Government Resident.[527]

Six years later, in 1879, Scotchman was speared to death by five Larrakia men. The attack on Douglas was mentioned in passing by Aboriginal elders as a factor, but mainly Scotchman was speared because in the interval he had killed three Larrakia people at different times. Generally the Europeans kept clear of such tribal killings, which occurred once or twice a year among the Larrakias. This time, however, the current Government Resident, Edward Price, insisted on arresting the five men and charging them with murder. The case failed. When the accused men were asked to face the bench, an elder of the tribe (an old, wizened man) deliberately turned his back and looked out the door to object to the meddling of the European law officers. The men were let off with a lecture telling them to abandon Mosaic Law in favour of Christianity.[528]

After the arrival of the *Flying Cloud* under Captain Marsh in December 1872, Douglas attempted to widen his field of influence among the Aborigines. Without authority, he had the *Flying Cloud* fitted out at great cost so it would be more comfortable for larger work. In March 1873 he was able to visit Melville Island, to try to make friends with the Tiwi people. Having gone inland without seeing any inhabitants and having shot one buffalo, the party returned to find their landing boat stoved in – whereupon the Tiwi attacked with great fury (a tactic they used on the Macassans) and had to be held off with gun-fire until the boat was patched. One reason given for the hostility (given by George Windsor Earl) was that in the past the Portuguese had raided the Tiwi Islands for slaves. After this episode Melville Island was declared out of

527 Douglas to Reynolds 3/1/1873, includes Douglas to Reynolds 18/12/1872 (N.T.I.L. 68/1873).

528 Morice to Price 22/1/1879 (G.R.I.L. A3299); Morice to Price 22/1/1879 (G.R.I.L. A3300); Morice to Price 23/1/1879 (G.R.I.L. A3301); *Northern Territory Times and Gazette* 25/1/1879, p. 2; 8/2/1879, p. 2 Police Court.

bounds, except for the occasional military expedition in search of wild 'English beef', left behind by the settlement at Fort Dundas in the 1820s.[529] It remained out of bounds until about 1895 when a man named Joe Cooper, backed by a band of Aboriginal and European buffalo shooters from the mainland, set himself up as 'King of Melville Island'.[530]

In April 1873 Douglas went on a ten-day cruise, taking in the Coburg Peninsula and its Iwaidja people, who were long used to contact with the outside world. On a previous visit he had been most impressed with these people because of the Malay influence, even finding that 'the women were modest enough to wear *Wooden figleaves*'.[531] This time he found one or two people drunk and many chewing seri and betel. What impressed him most was that the group addressed him as 'Commandant' in the Dutch style.

On the same April trip, accompanied by Dillon Cox, the first important settler who spoke Malay, he made contact with the masters (or *chicodahs*) of the Macassan fleet. This was at Blue Mud Bay near Port Essington (not the Blue Mud Bay on the Gulf of Carpentaria), where the Macassans were making their annual visit from the Port of Macassar in the South Celebes (now known as South Sulawesi) in search of trepang. Douglas wanted to engage in a *bichara* (negotiation) to induce them to use Port Darwin as a base for supplies and trade, thereby linking it in the network of local Indonesian commerce. And because the trepang was sent to China, he also hoped eventually to link into the great China trade.

Unlike most who reported on the Macassan fishers, Douglas was enthusiastic about what he saw. There were 25 proas plus numerous sampans operating from Port Essington to half-way down the west coast of the Gulf of Carpentaria, employing between one and two thousand men with great economic efficiency. On the shore of Cobourg Peninsula, he inspected a curing factory. He learnt that the Macassans, short of guns with which to defend themselves, were wary of Aborigines, especially the Tiwis of Melville Island.

---

529 *Chronicle* 22/3/1873, p. 6; Douglas to Reynolds 31/5/1873 (N.T.I.L. 127/1873); *Advertiser,* 18/3/1873, p. 2 Telegraphic News.

530 John Morris, *The Tiwi: From Isolation to Cultural Change*, NTU Press, Darwin, 2001, Chapter 5.

531 Captain W.B. Douglas's Diary, 7/11/1872. (Northern Territory Archives).

They employed (so they said) a few coastal dwellers in return for rations and tobacco – carefully avoiding mention of the main item of exchange offered by the Aborigines, which was sex. The whole enterprise was clearly the only flourishing trade link with Asia in the Territory.

In order to force the proas to visit Port Darwin – which he called the 'English settlement' – Douglas recommended the Macassan captains should each year first be required to call at the customs house in Palmerston to get a licence at a nominal fee of perhaps a pound, and return there for clearance before they left.[532]

Governor Anthony Musgrave reported to the Colonial Office on the strange way Captain Douglas was removed from office. (*Illustrated Adelaide Post* 6/8/1873, p. 1. Courtesy of the State Library of South Australia)

Douglas's positive attitude towards the Macassans was in contrast to moves made a decade or so later, when as a part of the trend to separate Australia from Asia, high customs duties collected at Bowen Strait followed by a complete ban drove them off the coast altogether. The expulsion of the Macassans was the first sign of an

532 Douglas to Reynolds 31/5/1873 (N.T.I.L. 127/1873). In contrast were local efforts to develop the trade. Next year Sinclair and others tried to start a trepang company themselves at Port Essington together with E.O. Robinson as supervisor using Aboriginal divers. But it failed. *Northern Territory Times and Gazette* 26/12/1874, p. 2.

Australian complex: the fear of people in boats, coming by sea from the north. There is no evidence that the Aborigines ever saw them in such a light. They feared instead people coming by land from the south.

The Indies Governor in Decline

All this time, Douglas's erratic behaviour was providing ammunition for those who had doubted his suitability for the job. His irregular orders for money charged to the South Australian government began to turn up in Adelaide and other colonial capitals as well. The minister responsible complained that as he could get no financial statement from the Government Resident, there was no way of answering the questions he was asked in parliament. Several times the Adelaide newspapers referred to the 'lack of dignity' in Northern Territory affairs. 'Capt. Douglas acting like a mad dog; all hands leaving the territory through him,' wrote the trooper Edward Napoleon Buonaparte Catchlove in his diary as early as 1871.[533]

Soon Douglas became a familiar sight venturing out on horseback for one of his 'picnics', generally in the direction of the gardens at Fannie Bay, with a bottle of whiskey stuffed in each holster at his side. The truth was he had failed to shrug off the old millstones around his neck: his weakness with money, proneness to depression and heavy drinking when troubles became unbearable. And at Palmerston he had his share of troubles and more as creditors pursued him and public finances became tangled. He was haunted by growing disillusionment, and by 1872 he was beginning to crack, referring in his journal almost daily to his numerous illnesses. On 18 June he described himself as very ill, 'vomiting', 'dreadful depression', 'comatose', 'suffering much in my head'. Two days later he took up arms to defend himself against his police force.

> The prevailing idea I had was that the Police had a warrant against me & altho Mr Foelsche in the morning had assured me such was not the case nothing would persuade me to the contrary. I closed my office, fancied every one was abusing me, even my own family & took arms to defend myself.[534]

533 E.N.P. Catchlove Diary, 20/3/1871. (S.L.S.A. Mortlock P.R.G. 165).

534 Captain W.B. Douglas's Diary, 18/6/1872, 20/6/1872 (Northern Territory

Between August and November, encouraged by his senior staff, he made an official visit to the Roper Depot to survey a town and port, taking the *Young Australian*, used in telegraph construction, as his base. His drinking and paranoia were so bad that Patterson, in charge of telegraph construction, pronounced him 'irretrievably gone'.[535] Suffering bouts of delirium tremens, he was later moved to the *Larrakeeyah*, a 'dry' former whale boat. 'As we have no medical comforts brandy wine, or anything of the sort I feel the depression very much,' he told his diary.[536]

A crisis came in February 1873 when news reached Adelaide that the Government Resident was mad and had been locked up. One day he had perched himself, gun in hand and very drunk, on the deck roof of his Residency, and threatened to shoot his police force, which he believed was coming to arrest him as a debtor. In the past Douglas had been particularly tough on heavy drinkers – who now joined the chorus of complaint.

Letters reached Adelaide at a time when Douglas, undergoing another bout of drunkenness, had been removed to the hulk of the *Gulnare* at Fort Point to dry out. A flurry of confidential telegrams went up and down the new line about the leader's condition, including rumours about his DTs. To Douglas's credit, his senior staff stuck by him, particularly the kindly doctor who prescribed: 'keep him at sea as much as possible'. Dr James Stokes Millner wanted to send Douglas on a dry voyage to Timor, but the minister in Adelaide would not release the *Flying Cloud*. The doctor also put Douglas under strict surveillance to prevent him trying to harm himself.[537]

As rumours were hawked around the streets of Adelaide, the minister in charge of the Territory, the Honourable Thomas Reynolds, announced he would have to leave for Palmerston on an important mission. Now rumours spread that Reynolds intended to sack Douglas in order to take his place.[538] 'Teapot Tommy'

Archives).

535 Private Diary of Robert C. Patterson while at the Roper River Depot 16/9/1872 (S.L.S.A. Mortlock D8103(L)).

536 Captain W.B. Douglas's Diary 23/10/1872 (Northern Territory Archives).

537 Thomas Reynolds: General report of Staff at Palmerston Minute 21 and enclosure D (N.T.I.L. 173/1873).

538 *ibid*, enclosure Z: Commissioner of Crown Lands and Immigration Minute

proceeded to Port Darwin by a roundabout way through the Indies so he could study the islanders' agriculture and assess their desire to emigrate. He met a situation which South Australians, emigrants themselves, had never anticipated: even though the islanders were short of living space – 'buzzing about like bees' – they felt no desire to move. Nevertheless, the minister believed he might convert the islanders to migration provided companies in the Territory could be enticed to start a natural population flow by introducing a few island dwellers and treating them well.[539]

In the Dutch East Indies Reynolds was treated as a very important person. He even got to stay in the governor-general's palace. In Batavia he met up with Price Cox, brother of the pioneering pastoralist Dillon Cox, who travelled with him to Port Darwin.[540]

Reynolds arrived at Port Darwin on 17 May like the hot, dry wind of retribution and declared himself amazed at what he must have already anticipated, the state of utter disorganisation before him. It was not to Douglas's advantage that Reynolds was a leading member of the Total Abstinence Alliance, nor that he had a reputation for good financial management. There was no record of the cost of public buildings or road work. Large sums of money had been spent without auditing; the Government Resident's household was living from the government store on credit[541] – it later cost the Audit Office in Adelaide much time and expense straightening out the accounts.[542]

The staff, too, were lax and disorganised. The store-keeper's quarter was doing an excellent business after being turned into a mining speculator's office, almost all the official staff had taken out

---

24/2/1873 and Cabinet Minute 25/2/1873; *Register* 11/8/1873, p. 5.

539 Report of the Commissioner of Crown Lands and Immigration of his Official Visit to the Northern Territory, 30/7/1873 (S.A.P.P. 55 of 1873, pp. 1 to 7 *passim*).

540 *Java Bode: nieuw-, handels-en advertentie-blad van Netherlandsch Indie* 16/4/1873 Research by Rini Hogewoning, Royal Institute of Linguistics and Anthropology, Leiden. Courtesy Dr Roger Wiseman.

541 Thomas Reynolds: General report of Staff at Palmerston 18/7/1873 Minutes 1, 2, 3, 8 and 18 (N.T.I.L. 173/1873).

542 Hitchin to De Mole 15/9/1875 with enclosures (N.T.I.L. 399/1875); Memo. Auditor-General 13/12/1875 (N.T.I.L. 578/1875 filed with 399/1875).

miners' rights, some were away on leave of absence at the reefs.[543] With the exception of the lavish (but structurally fragile) Residence, the telegraph station (with fowl houses abutting the main street) and the police station, there were actually fewer buildings than when Goyder left.[544] Reynolds was amazed to find Scotchman chained up by one leg, doing odd jobs around the Government Residency. The resistance fighter was released with uncommon legal speed. Reynolds advised in his report that a well-chosen person with the full powers of 'a true governor' would now be needed to solve the problems of the Territory.[545] The person he later recommended was himself.

Douglas was held to blame for the general disorder, but as critics noted the blame was as much due to the ministers in Adelaide. They had chosen the man in the first place, knowing him to be weak in money matters; the paltriness of the buildings was a consequence of their economies in favour of the telegraph; the Aboriginal prisoner (having earlier escaped) was chained because there was no gaol fit to keep Aborigines; and the laxity of the staff arose partly from divisions of authority. Douglas wrote to Reynolds that:

> The divisions of authority such as Customs, Telegraph, Police, Warden of the Gold-fields and to a certain extent in the Survey department has really placed me in a position of much embarrassment.[546]
>
> ... almost every difficulty here may be traced to the anomalous position I have occupied. I have been the head where it has suited the public or others to accord me that position but as a rule my authority has been so divided and refined that I scarcely knew where it commenced or ceased, or as to what I could, or could not do.[547]

The censure Douglas received from Reynolds was so severe

543 Thomas Reynolds: General report of Staff at Palmerston 18/7/1873 Minutes 7 and 11 (N.T.I.L. 173/1873).

544 *ibid.* Minute 10; Thomas Reynolds: report on government buildings at Palmerston 16/7/1873 (S.A.P.P. 120 of 1874); Report of the Commissioner of Crown Lands and Immigration of his Official Visit to the Northern Territory, 30/7/1872 (S.A.P.P. 55 of 1873, p. 10).

545 Report of the Commissioner of Crown Lands and Immigration of his Official Visit to the Northern Territory, 30/7/1872 (S.A.P.P. 55 of 1873, p. 9).

546 Douglas to Reynolds 2/6/1873, p. 7 (N.T.I.L. 134A/1873).

547 *ibid*, pp. 5 and 6.

that he resigned. 'I confess I am tired, and heart sick,' he wrote, 'and crave to be free for almost the first time in my life.'[548] He left 'Government House' and went to work on the reefs as a digger, at the same time beginning a long wrangle with the government over the financial compensation[549] – a question settled only in December 1875 when all the outstanding debts to the government had been hunted down and the former Resident was at last free to take what remained of his promised compensation.[550] In June 1873 he formed his own Douglas Goldmining Company, consisting of 12,000 shares at a pound each. His claim was situated at The Howley reef and christened 'The Bloomfield', to emphasise his connection with a family of British aristocrats associated with the Regent. He stayed there for about ten months, attended by two Malay servants,[551] while his wife and family left for Adelaide at government expense – and found themselves so short of cash there that Mrs Douglas had to beg the government ministers for money.[552]

In April 1874, having come south to improve his prospects, Douglas was engaged to bring in a trial shipment of Chinese coolies from Singapore for various mining companies. He never again returned to Adelaide. Having delivered his human cargo at Port Darwin, he went back to Singapore by the same steamer to take up a post as a magistrate there. His family followed from Port Adelaide soon after. Last public news of him in the Port Darwin newspaper came in 1879 when he was reprimanded for 'high handed conduct' at Klang in the Straits Settlements. He apparently dismissed one of the Tunkus for irregular finances![553] In 1876 he had been appointed Government Resident for Selangor. In 1882 his son-in-law Daniel Daly, whom he had rapidly promoted, was sacked for jobbery. In the same year Douglas himself was asked to resign.[554]

548 Douglas to Reynolds 4/6/1873 enclosures F and G (N.T.I.L. 173/1873).

549 Douglas to Reynolds 9/6/1873 enclosure I (N.T.I.L. 173/1873); Douglas to Reynolds 10/6/1873 enclosure J (N.T.I.L. 173/1873).

550 Hitchin to De Mole 15/9/1875 with enclosures (N.T.I.L. 399/1875); Memo. Auditor-General 13/12/1875 (N.T.I.L. 578/1875 filed with 399/1875).

551 Douglas Goldmining Co. Ltd. to Reynolds 17/7/1873 (N.T.I.L. 143/1873).

552 Ellen Douglas to Everard 4/2/1874 (N.T.I.L. 43/1874).

553 *Northern Territory Times and Gazette* 31/5/1879, p. 2.

554 Research Notes on Douglas in Malaya by J.M. Gullick, noted scholar on Malaya associated with the Royal Asiatic Society 6/12/1999.

If someone had to 'cast bricks' at Bloomfield Douglas, it should not have been Thomas Reynolds, the Honourable the Commissioner of Crown Lands. One of the most serious charges he levelled against the Resident was that he wilfully and corruptly sheltered the mining interests of his sons-in-law (Dominick Daniel Daly and J. Euston Squier) by advantageously granting them leases *after* being instructed from Adelaide that no more such gold leases were to be issued. He was indicted, too, for fitting them out at the government's expense with equipment and horses.[555] But Reynolds himself was no more fastidious when it came to his own vested interests and relations. In fact, one motive for going to the Territory was to set straight his considerable private investments, which had been mismanaged by his son. In June 1873 he instructed the Territory's officers to show no mercy toward debtors to the treasury. In direct contradiction to this, he then asked the government accountant to shelve accounts, amounting to £280, owed by his son's firm of mining agents, which was secretly facing insolvency. 'I suppose these amounts will have to be held over until the question of leases be decided by the Legislature,' he wrote in a memo. This was lease money entrusted to the firm by up-country mining concerns for eventual payment to the government. Reynold's son or his agent cashed £105 of this sum in Adelaide and the rest was swallowed up in the ensuing bankruptcy. Only during the following year, when the mining companies were hauled up for arrears, did they find that their agents had appropriated their money and were now unable to repay it. Then followed a hue and cry.[556]

Having removed Douglas, Minister Reynolds returned to Adelaide in July 1873–and resigned from the ministry as soon as he could find a good enough reason to do so. He announced that he had decided to forsake public life in South Australia and try his

555 Thomas Reynolds: General report of Staff at Palmerston, 18/7/1873 Minutes 19 and 20, and enclosures A and B (N.T.I.L. 173/1873); *Advertiser* 6/10/1873, p. 3 Reynolds to Editor 3/10/1873.

556 Bundey to Reynolds 13/8/1874 (N.T.O.L. 159/1874); Reynolds to Bundey telegram 15/10/1874 (N.T.I.L. 395/1874); Scott to Bundey 17/10/1874 (N.T.I.L. 476/1874); Reynolds to Bundey 18/10/1874 with enclosures (N.T.I.L. 480/1874); Bundey to Scott 15/1/1875 (N.T.O.L. 10/1875); Bundey to Reynolds 16/1/1875 (N.T.O.L. 42/1875); *Northern Territory Times and Gazette* 29/8/1874, p. 3 Police Court 21/8/1874.

fortune in the Northern Territory as its guiding light and founding father. Only later did other details leak out. According to Governor Anthony Musgrave in his regular dispatch to London, Reynolds had offered Douglas inducements to resign 'on some understanding about which there appears to be still a good deal of obscurity'.[557] Reynolds had then contacted his Cabinet colleagues in Adelaide seeking their approval to be appointed Government Resident himself. His colleagues refused on grounds that it was improper for a minister to remove one of his senior officers in order to take his job.

After what had happened to Douglas, the government found that no one of note wanted to become Government Resident. The job was hawked around and eventually offered to an almost unknown stipendiary magistrate who lived at Robe in the south-east corner of the colony, George Byng Scott – who later, in asking for special consideration, made much of the fact that he had been 'sought out' for the job.[558] The governor had a house in Robe and he may have influenced the choice. Reynolds was farewelled with a city banquet at which, taking the attitude of a Territorian, he made no secret of his hope that it would break away from the South Australians. Scott was farewelled by a minor celebration in the village of Robe. When both left together aboard the *Gothenburg* in October 1873, many people were amused at the curious relationship between the little governor and his big brother.[559]

Actually the arrangement proved not as strange as sometimes appeared. The Adelaide authorities had no need for a strong Resident now the telegraph linked them to Palmerston and certainly no desire for another Douglas, whose zeal tended to cause embarrassment. With Scott, rule by telegraph became an institution. The citizens of Palmerston turned out to greet him as a true governor. A leading citizen 'of swarthy complexion', dressed in gaudy pyjamas, a tropical helmet and attended by a boy holding an umbrella over his head, read him an address of welcome.[560] Scott replied appropriately in

557 Musgrave to Kimberley 12/8/1873 (G.O.D. 13 of 1873).

558 Everard to Scott 6/10/1873 (S.A.P.P. 123 of 1873).

559 *Advertiser* 6/10/1873, p. 2; *Register* 15/9/1873, p. 6.

560 George Byng Scott's Reminiscences of life in the Northern Territory during his term of office as Government Resident 1873 to 1876, p. 1 (S.L.S.A. D7478(L)). The leading citizen was barrister Villeneuve Smith.

a speech which emphasised his increased authority and powers.[561] Once the ceremony was over, however, he was hardly allowed to take up a pen without first receiving a telegram from the minister in Adelaide, the cost of which was carefully debited to the Northern Territory Account. One comic described the new situation in rhyme:

> Mother may I go down to swim?
> Oh, yes, you can, my daughter;
> But hang your clothes upon a limb,
> And don't go near the water.[562]

While the Government Resident had his hands tied, Thomas Reynolds employed his freedom to embarrass the South Australian administration, particularly by exposing it in the eastern colonies press – that is, 'in alien ground'.[563] The politicians and press in Adelaide thought this a most dishonourable stab in the back. When the question of Reynolds' and his son's debts came into the open they brought their former colleague to heel by putting him on a charge of wilful and corrupt perjury. It was now remembered that once before, back in 1862, he had been forced to resign as minister 'for abuse of office'.[564] The family's reputation was saved when, in February 1875, heading south to stir up the Northern Territory cause, Reynolds was drowned when the *Gothenburg* was wrecked on the Barrier Reef.[565]

Despite being tied by a long thin line to Adelaide, Scott and his wife Carolyn Ritchie, as first lady, worked tirelessly over the next two and a half years to bring order to Northern Territory affairs. His first move was to reconstruct the Residency, which he called 'a dilapidated barn', before it fell down. It was a kind of visual symbol for the empire-building activities of the former administration – even before Douglas left, the roof had begun to fall in. Designed and supervised by Douglas himself, it included a large stone central hall (where 'the Governor' had once hoped to meet his subjects) built

561 *Northern Territory Times and Gazette* 14/11/1873, p. 2.
562 *Northern Territory Times and Gazette* 11/12/1875, p. 2.
563 *Register* 10/7/1874, pp. 4 and 5; *Advertiser* 26/9/1874, pp. 2 and 3.
564 Bundey to Scott 30/10/1874 (N.T.O.L. 225/1874).
565 *Northern Territory Times and Gazette* 13/3/1875, p. 3; 24/4/1875, p. 3.

partly from cement meant for the Telegraph Station and was capped by a flat deck roof through which the rain came in the wet season. The hall was surrounded by six outer living rooms made of upright pugged poles set in the ground and constructed from mangrove trunks, which had been invaded by white ants, having been built over a termite's nest, while on the extreme outside stood bark-covered verandahs that gave the building a wretched appearance and needed continuous attention. The Adelaide government's reaction to Scott's complaints was to send a load of galvanised-iron sheets and wood, with which a second storey, a kind of shed, was built on top of the deck roof and with which most of the other rooms could be covered. When renovated, the building looked even odder than before.[566] The next Government Resident called it an 'unsightly shanty which was more like a cowshed than the Government Residence'. But for a year or two it was safer.[567]

Whereas Douglas modelled himself on the Indies governors, Scott was cautious and thoroughly South Australian in his approach. Within his restricted powers he tried to introduce the instruments of civilisation to the new settlement. He licked the rag-bag public service into shape. He built bridges and roads linking the main town to its hinterland. During his term the first district council was formed to clean up the town. A hospital was built near Peel's Well with the help of public subscriptions. The machinery for a newspaper, the *Northern Territory Times and Gazette*, came north with him on the *Gothenburg*. The first church was opened just as he arrived under the pioneering Methodist, Archibald Bogle, in a prefabricated public room 'for worship and reading', initially paid for by the Congregational Building Society. Scott even wrote a testimonial of support for a teacher, Henry Allport, whom he knew in Robe, who had been asked by the parents to start a school at Palmerston. But the Board of Education in Adelaide considered the place too remote and that there were not enough children.

George Byng Scott was later remembered as an 'able, dignified

566 Millner to Everard 12/9/1873 (N.T.I.L. 273/1873); Scott to Everard 5/11/1873 (N.T.I.L. 354/1873); Scott to Everard 10/1/1873 including Knight's Report 15/1/1873 (N.T.I.L. 60/1874); Knight's Report on Public Works 28/11/1874 (N.T.I.L. 511/1874).

567 Price to King 20/5/1879 (N.T.I.L. 261/1879).

and kindly man' and for the genial hospitality of the Scott family in their home – though Bogle complained that in his three years here the Resident had never once entered the church.[568]

Bit by bit Scott tried to turn Palmerston into an orderly provincial town, like Robe or Mount Gambier or Gawler. But there were always larger forces moving in the opposite direction. The failure of separate development had left South Australia with a raft of problems.

The 'Resulting Land Imbroglio'

> 'For a person to go to a new, wild country like that, where hundreds of millions of acres are lying waste, and find that he could not without indefinite delay, acquire the freehold or the use of land for cultivation or pastoral purposes, would be sufficient to drive him from the place in disgust.' *Advertiser* 13 June 1874

In pressing their claim to the Northern Territory, South Australians had emphasised the need for appropriate land laws in the Territory, especially as restless disorderly outsiders were about to move in across the borders. Yet for a full decade after the surveys were finally made by Goyder, the only farmers to get on the country lands were unauthorised squatters.[569]

What had gone wrong? If three key elements – concentration, preference, and an appeal to speculative motives – were expected to launch the new colony by its own internal energy, they now combined to produce a contrary effect. A generation earlier some of the critics of systematic colonisation in the Colonial Office had predicted that this could happen.

The first complication was the failure of the concentrated settlement. Even after all the hunting for a suitable capital, Port Darwin did not meet the need of a concentrated settlement – a moderately even environment over which settlers could move like a concentric wave from a central metropolis where the prized lands were held by a select band risking purchase prior to settlement.

---

568 *Northern Territory Times and Gazette* 27/2/1886, p. 2; Diary of A.J. Bogle 8/7/1876 (Mitchell Library).

569 *Northern Territory Times and Gazette* 17/8/1878 leader; McMinn to Price 15/5/1878 with Price's Minute (NT.I.L. 328/1878).

Government buildings at The Depot. The building materials – pugged-poles driven into the ground and bark roofing – were much enjoyed by termites. (Paul Foelsche, c. 1872)

An early photograph of government buildings at The Depot, Port Darwin. Tents were no longer used after about 1870.

Police station, Palmerston, 1871. 'Though a man may have lived forty years without having ever appeared in any Court, yet it is impossible for him to live in the Northern Territory for even a few months without becoming mixed up in some Court affair – libel, manslaughter, or something of the sort.'
(Paul Foelsche)

The Lock-up at Palmerston, 1871; much needed in a town where court activity was high.
(Paul Foelsche)

Gore's Store in Mitchell Street. For many years Palmerston looked much like a country town.
(Paul Foelsche, 1873)

More like a cowshed than a Government Residence, 1874.
(State Library of South Australia)

Billiamuk Gapal, brought to Australia in 1870 so he could return and tell his Larrakia people 'how numerous, powerful yet kind the white races are'.
(Paul Foelsche, 1890)

An Aboriginal burial platform; a practice with profound significance in Aboriginal culture, which others without a deep attachment to the land could not understand.
(Alfred Searcy, *By Flood and Field*, 1912)

Iwaidja at ceremony, Port Essington, 1877. The Iwaidja were admired by Captain Douglas because of the Malay influence.
(Paul Foelsche)

Government Offices, Palmerston, with Knight's Folly (also known as 'Mud Hut' and 'Mudville on the Sea') in the foreground – the first two-storey building in the Territory. (Paul Foelsche, 1887)

Commercial Hotel, Mitchell Street, 1874. The selling of alcohol became the Territory's most buoyant trade. (Paul Foelsche)

Wheal Margaret Mine, 1877.
(Paul Foelsche)

The Virginia mine, Stapleton, 1877. There was hope that gold would save the Territory.
(Paul Foelsche)

Anthill at Rum Jungle, 1887. Termites took on an almost mythical reputation.
(Paul Foelsche)

The exotic Baob tree, marked by explorer A.C. Gregory in 1855–1856.
(Paul Foelsche, 1891)

Glencoe cattle station, 1883 – the first station in the upper Territory.
(Paul Foelsche)

Daly River cattle station, 1887. An alternative model of colonisation.
(Paul Foelsche)

Two main streets and a Chinese quarter. Mitchell Street, 1885.
Pencil sketch emphasising detail by M. Fiveash.
(State Library of South Australia)

SS *Adelaide* at Roper Landing. Charles Todd's decision to supply construction of the Overland Telegraph from far up the Roper River was a stroke of genius. Thereafter the Roper River was seen as the superior site for the capital.
(Paul Foelsche, 1889)

Unloading supplies at Victoria River.
(Paul Foelsche)

Australia's link to Asia. Port Darwin jetty, 1880.
(Paul Foelsche)

The Depot, Port Darwin, 1873, with SS *Tararua* in the harbour – the steamship that brought the first clergyman. (Paul Foelsche)

The Depot, 1885, with Knight's eccentric palace in the foreground. (Paul Foelsche)

Stokes Hill. Hacking a road from the tableland down to the sea using picks, shovels, horses and carts became a major engineering exercise.
(Paul Foelsche)

The jetty at Southport at the southern extremity of Darwin Harbour. It was the headquarters for the lonely teamsters heading into the interior.
(Paul Foelsche, 1878)

Shackle Telegraph Station, Yam Creek, 1879. Stations like this were the tenuous link between Adelaide and Port Darwin.
(Paul Foelsche)

Alice Springs Telegraph Station, 1900. Because of the preoccupation with the north coast and Asia, Central Australia was left a lonely and isolated place until well into the twentieth century.
(Telecom Archives, Adelaide)

Town Hall, Palmerston. For decades the District Council was the 'leader of the opposition' against southern control.
(Paul Foelsche)

Henry Poett's coffee plantation at Rum Jungle. Poett hailed from Ceylon.
(Paul Foelsche, 1883)

Christening the first locomotive for the Palmerston–Pine Creek railway, 1887. The railway was seen as a first step in a South Australian dream to link Adelaide to Asia. (Paul Foelsche)

Picknicking, English style, at the new railway bridge over the Adelaide River. (Paul Foelsche, 1888)

Moo Tai Mue Chinese Temple at the bottom of Doctor's Gully, photograph c. 1900, structure possibly 1870s. (Courtesy of the State Library of Northern Territory, Peter Spillet Collection)

The Shou Lao statue, found at the top of Doctor's Gully in 1879 deep under the roots of a large banyan tree – a tree not indigenous to Australia. This was taken as evidence that Chinese had been there long before. (Courtesy of the Powerhouse Museum, Sydney)

Chinese gardens, Peel's Well, with the hospital in the background. The first recorded gardener there was Lim Ah Soey ('Jimmy' Soey) who came overland with Dillon Cox from Queensland. (Paul Foelsche, 1888)

Goyder's splendid countryside turned out on closer scrutiny to be patchy – as the agents found when they came to make their selections.[570] 'The land in the Northern Territory,' wrote Douglas from Palmerston, 'presents every variety, from the most barren stony rises to the richest alluvial undulating country.'[571] This unevenness meant that once the preliminary selectors had picked the eyes out of the surveyed lands only second-rate sections were left for the ordinary settlers. If they chose to come to the Territory at all, they would be driven to seek their livelihood further out, threatened by isolation (especially in the Wet season), insecurity and Aborigines. Here was one reason why the blueprint aimed at concentration eventually caused the opposite to happen, with the effect of deterring settlers altogether. In general, Port Darwin was not comparable to the evenly fertile plains surrounding early Adelaide.

In order to obtain money in advance for colonisation, land in the Territory was sold to preliminary purchasers, even before settlement took place, on the understanding that never again would it be offered so cheaply or at such advantage as in 1864. This idea of preference in favour of those who had bought land in advance proved the second major cause for the failure of the land system: the system's sheer inflexibility when the need came for sweeping changes. The original land laws hindered future attempts to attract settlers with the bait of cheap land, as the first Government Resident discovered when he wanted to reduce the price to three shillings an acre.[572] The idea of preference was linked too with the promise that the heart of settlement would not be shifted, even if better sites were later discovered. To transform Palmerston to a ghost town would have amounted to bad faith on the government's part. When the telegraph parties attracted attention to the Roper River as perhaps a superior site, no government dared go ahead developing it too enthusiastically for fear of offending the Adelaide speculators who had invested in land around Port Darwin. As these gentlemen had remained faithful while others had taken the colony to court, they demanded respect.

570 John McKinlay's Notebooks. (Records of John Wyles and Co. S.L.S.A. Mortlock BRG45).

571 Douglas to Blyth 2/6/1871 (S.A.P.P. 35 of 1871).

572 Douglas to Blyth 2/6/1871 (S.A.P.P. 35 of 1871).

A third reason for the miserable record of the land laws was that 'Absenteeism, so far as the Territory is concerned, is universal', as an observer wrote in 1871.[573] The speculative motive had somehow turned awry. The preliminary land purchasers, as it turned out, were not pioneer settlers but armchair speculators who wished to profit in comfort as the real pioneers added value to their property. Once absentee speculation passed a critical level it actually discouraged pioneers, and so brought about its own ruin with the ruin of everything else. Speculators began sitting round like an admiration society waiting for each other to move.

In 1872 Douglas complained to Reynolds that:

> The settlement of the Country by immigrants from the neighbouring Colonies, or South Australians visiting the Settlement, is absolutely prevented. Thus the whole monopoly of the land is vested in the hands of the Land-order holders who do not appear to have sufficient Enterprise to avail themselves of the advantages the country offers, whilst the existing regulations confirm such Monopoly.[574]

After failing to get land for himself and other Victorians in 1874, Robert Caldwell warned his countrymen:

> Settlement is ... absolutely proscribed unless indeed by purchasing from the original holders of land, who had a large tract parcelled out by persons for their own speculation, and who hold for fabulous prices.[575]

Where Douglas left off, Scott took up the complaint:

> the plan hitherto adopted is a rank failure; out of half a million acres selected not one solitary rood is fenced or even occupied.[576]

A year later, in 1875, he wrote:

> Already about half a Million Acres have been sold but not one rood of such land has been enclosed, cultivated or occupied – plainly showing

---

573 *Register* 13/2/1871 leader.

574 Douglas to Reynolds 7/5/1872 (N.T.I.L. 216/1872).

575 *Argus* 16/9/1875, p. 7; *Register* 21/9/1875, p. 6.

576 Scott to Everard 16/5/1874 (N.T.I.L. 190/1874).

> that it was merely a speculation by Capitalists who are waiting for the Country to rise in value by the pioneering and exertions of others.[577]

The system had choked itself. The price of land had not been sufficient to deter speculators. Indeed it is hard to imagine a system better suited to speculation.

And to mark the failures, the chief architect of the Northern Territory scheme in 1863, Captain John Hart, suddenly died of a stroke in 1873, aged 63.[578]

These failures landed South Australia in a delicate fix. The preliminary purchasers had taken up all the good land in and around Palmerston; the preliminary purchasers were all absentees; the South Australian authorities could not turn their efforts elsewhere for fear of dishonouring their obligation towards them, and the passing ministries were too timid to risk offending them with ruthless and daring reforms.

Once only in the 1870s, during the 1872 parliamentary session, was any government brave enough to try a full-scale liberation of the land laws. And that was mainly due to the personal, not altogether altruistic, efforts of the Honourable Thomas Reynolds who, as Commissioner of Crown Lands and immigration, assumed control of the Territory in March 1872.

Reynolds, it will be remembered, had ambitions of becoming the premier private citizen in the northern province. Before that, however, he resolved to free the entire land system without which no one could prosper there, large or small. The move immediately brought into the open the difficulties awaiting the Northern Territory land reformer. Members of parliament with vested interests set their face against any changes that might reduce the privileges of those who had bought their land in advance, while other politicians feared that if the new regulations were made too attractive they would entice farmers away from South Australia itself.

Reynolds, an old political fox, manoeuvred to divide the opposition by introducing 129 clauses and 23 schedules (the *Register*

577 Scott to Ward 15/9/1875 (N.T.I.L. 451/1875).

578 *Register* 29/1/1873 leader.

Thomas Reynolds set out to become the founding father and premier citizen of the Territory. He was tragically drowned with the wreck of the *Gothenburg* in February 1875.
(*Australasian Sketcher* 17/4/1875. Courtesy of the State Library of South Australia)

called it a Land Code) covering everything from pastoral leases to sea-slug rights, and dared his critics to reject or accept as they thought best.[579] He knew that above all else, most members wanted to see the Territory developing, and this required land laws at least as liberal as those in the neighbouring tropical colony of Queensland.

When it came to the *ownership* of land, the resulting 1872 Act was a compromise between competing points of view. The groups bent on protecting the rights of the preliminary land buyers gained two concessions. The minimum price of land was fixed at 7 shillings and 6 pence an acre, over twice the rate eventually paid by land-order holders taking the increased area, and all efforts by the Government Resident to have the price reduced were firmly rejected. Parliament also blocked moves by Reynolds to decentralise settlement. In clause six of the original Bill he proposed to give land-

579 *Register* 15/6/1872 leader; *Advertiser* 15/6/1872 leader.

order holders who had not yet chosen their land the right to make selections away from Port Darwin as a first step to decentralising settlement generally. The clause met such opposition from parties who feared an exodus to the fertile Roper River that Reynolds reluctantly had to strike it out altogether.

Groups fearing that the land laws might be used to tempt farmers away from South Australia were placated by final control being placed in the hands of people in Adelaide and by insisting on survey before selection. For the minimum price of 7 shillings and 6 pence an acre, settlers could take up land in three typically South Australian ways – especially as modelled in the *Strangways Act* of 1869 aimed at making primarily pastoral land in South Australia available to small farmers. They could buy already surveyed blocks of varying size by private contract, but only after the land had been advertised for four consecutive weeks in Adelaide and Palmerston. They could buy outright surveyed blocks of 1280 acres on credit, paying sixpence an acre deposit while they paid off the rest inside ten years – buying land on credit being a key feature of the *Strangways Act*. Again the routine depended on the government in Adelaide at every stage. The land had to be surveyed, a credit sale arranged, the opening date and particulars proclaimed in Adelaide and Palmerston, the selections received and placed in a box at the Land Office in Adelaide and Palmerston to be opened at noon of each work day. If more than one customer applied for the same section the winner was decided by lot.

The third typically South Australian way of acquiring land (which broke with survey before selection) was through a Special Survey of 10,000 unsurveyed acres. The procedure here was for a large company to choose an unsurveyed area that suited it, then make an application to the Commissioner of Crown Lands in Adelaide enclosing the cost of survey as deposit. If the commissioner approved, he would have the 10,000 acres surveyed and sold to the company at the cash price of 7 shillings and 6 pence an acre plus the cost of survey already paid as deposit.[580]

But the liberal part of the Act was the Plantation Clauses aimed at plantation owners in the region – and a fourth way of acquiring

580 S.A.P.A. 28 of 1872 *passim*.

land for agriculture. For those parliamentarians who looked to liberal land laws as a way of coaxing the Territory off their hands, there was a special provision for plantations, which Reynolds gained by referring to the ideas of the original colonisation scheme from the 1830s. He argued that:

> The product of the first lands sold in South Australia was applied to the importation of labour. Instead of adopting that old-fashioned principle the proposal was to place persons in a position to import labour for themselves for the cultivation of their land ... virtually giving the land away in order to induce immediate settlement.[581]

Under the terms of the provision concessions were to be given to selectors with *proven experience* and resources who at the time of application indicated they wanted the land specifically for tropical production, such as rice, sugar, tea, coffee, indigo, tobacco or cotton. If then they paid their rent of sixpence an acre, fenced the land, and worked it at such a rate that a fifth was under cultivation after two years and a half at the end of five years, the selection would become their freehold property without their having to pay the full purchase price. The minimum area for which the provision applied was half a square mile and the maximum two square miles.[582] The concession aimed at attracting experienced overseas plantation owners, especially from the north, rich enough to bring in their own equipment and coolies. Because there were no plantation owners in the south, it was acceptable to those who feared the loss of South Australia's own farmers, while the purchasers of land in advance could not complain about new landholders whose presence would increase the value of their own investments and in practice, being outside the Settled Districts, did not threaten their inner location. These Plantation Clauses were soon separately printed and distributed far and wide in Mauritius, East Indies, India and China.

The Northern Territory Land Act of 1872 became law on the 30 November. Reynolds soon migrated to the Territory to benefit from his achievement. But when he got there he was infuriated to find that his successors in government made no effort to implement most of

---

581 S.A.P.D. 1872 c. 1468.

582 S.A.P.A. 28 of 1872 part VII.

the Act and indeed seemed to be trying their best to ignore it. How much the delays were due to apathy and how much to corruption or some other cause is not known. One possible reason for the delays, continuing the train of complications that followed the failure of the system of colonisation, is that some ministers refused to move until the court case with the land-order holders was well and truly over, for fear the malcontents might gain some advantage. A few journalists suspected corruption: the withholding of the Act in order to throw settlers on the tender mercies of absentee speculators in Adelaide.[583] When Robert Caldwell, a Victorian, tried to obtain land at Fannie Bay for himself and other Victorians the commissioner in Adelaide, William Everard, ordered 'that the alienation of these lands must not be proceeded with and that he [the Resident] must await General instructions before dealing with any of the crown lands'.[584] On another occasion he ruled 'that the Land Regulations are practically in abeyance at present, in consequence of the policy of the Government not having been yet decided upon as regards putting land into the market'.[585] This, a year and a half after the 1872 Land Act was passed. Special Surveys were withheld, too, as the Adelaide capitalist and former politician William Henry Bean found when he wanted a large block on the Daly River.[586]

The passing of the 1872 Land Act had been given wide publicity, and successive governments' failure to apply it was the cause of much confusion. Some intending settlers were trapped into making the long journey for nothing. John Jessop, a Queenslander, set out to grow maize at Stapleton on the outskirts of the surveys. Assuming that he could secure his choice of land quickly, he laid out his plot, collected his wife, pitched his tent, and in 1874 prepared for operations. But no authority came and his money began to dwindle. Jessop collected his wife and went back to Queensland in disgust.[587]

583 *Northern Territory Times and Gazette* 24/4/1874 leader; 19/9/1874, p. 4 Reynolds to Editor.

584 Scott to Ward 24/8/1875 (N.T.I.L. 384/1875); *Register* 21/9/1875, p. 5.

585 Deering to Andrew 9/6/1874 (N.T.O.L. 100/1874).

586 Bean to Reynolds 9/7/1873 (N.T.I.L. 119/1873); Bean to Everard 14/8/1873 (N.T.I.L. 234/1873).

587 Scott to Ward 24/8/1875 (N.T.I.L. 384/1875); Jessop to Scott 3/4/1874 (G.R.I.L. A247); Jessop to Scott 10/9/1874 (G.R.I.L. A448); *Register* 20/10/1875, p. 5; *Northern Territory Times and Gazette* 17/12/1875, p. 2.

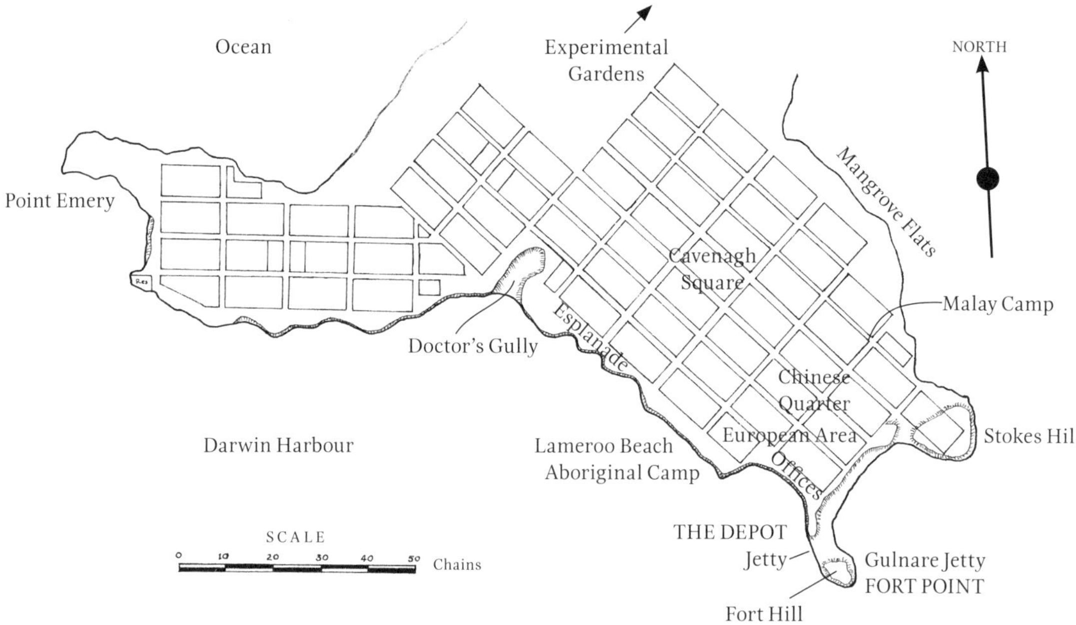

Palmerston in the 1870s – 'Two main streets and a Chinese Quarter'.
Base map Roland Schultz, 1963

In contrast, as evidence that it was the *sale* of land that was the sticking point, Northern Territory Pastoral Regulations were proclaimed in July 1871 under the original *Northern Territory Act (23 of 1863)*, and later changes were put under the *Northern Territory Land Act of 1872*. Pastoral Lease Number 1 was issued to Bagot, Tennant and Love in April 1872 for Undoolya eastside of Alice Springs. Leases could be taken out for up to 25 years for an area between 25 and 300 square miles at a peppercorn rent for the first seven years – *provided* (and this is an important qualification) that the land lay outside the so-called Settled Districts.[588]

Only in 1875 did Reynolds see his efforts rewarded and limited reforms on the sale of land introduced, and then only after Northern Territory affairs were made a separate ministerial portfolio, hived

588 Vern O'Brien, Manuscript of *Guide to Northern Territory Land Tenure*, plus Research Notes November 2002; O'Brien to Cross 15/11/2005; *S.A. Government Gazette*, pp. 1071 and 1072, 20/7/1871

off from the responsibilities of the Commissioner of Crown Lands. January 14 was a red-letter day in the life of the young settlement: the Territory had its first open land sale, in a tiny room too crowded to be healthy. Town blocks were sold to the value of £1037, most of them below average in quality, having been passed over by the preliminary purchasers. Many were bought by John Lewis of mining fame.[589] For Reynolds, the blessing came too late. A few weeks later he was drowned.

In an effort to free up land disposal, the Special Survey provision was reduced to 20 acres in 1876.[590] The Government Resident and his staff in Palmerston were never free to act quickly when opportunities for land sales presented themselves. Again and again Scott urged his minister to adopt the American Homestead system, where simply residing on a piece of land, cultivating and improving it became bases of ownership.[591] In 1878 the Resident estimated that a settler applying towards the end of the dry season (as was normal) might have to wait 18 months before he could make use of his land.[592] With Special Surveys the selection (on the appropriate form) had to be sent to Adelaide, advertised in the *Government Gazette* (where land speculators could inspect it), pass the scrutiny of bureaucrats and be then transported back again. If speculators challenged his choice, the intending settler might still be called upon to bid for it at a public auction.[593] Few people could afford to wait idly in this remote part of the world, which offered no alternative employment.

Then there was the cost of survey for small, isolated blocks. In 1878 the Territory's gold warden estimated 'the cost of surveying small isolated blocks under the 1876 change to the Special Survey provision would probably be five or six times the fixed price of land'.[594] This would put the total figure at between 45 shillings and 52 and 6 pence an acre, one of the highest prices for lonely virgin

589 *Northern Territory Times and Gazette* 16/1/1875, p. 2.

590 S.A.P.A. 48 of 1876 section 4.

591 Scott to Ward 15/9/1875 (N.T.I.L. 451/1875).

592 McMinn to Price 15/5/1878 enclosure Minute by Price 20/5/1878 (N.T.I.L. 328/1878).

593 S.A.P.A. 28 of 1872 sections 7 and 42.

594 Knight to Price 7/10/1878 (N.T.I.L. 612/1878); S.A.P.D. 1879 c. 1242; *Northern Territory Times and Gazette* 17/8/1878 leader.

bush anywhere in the world. 'The great stumbling block to … the genuine selector and farmer,' wrote the *Northern Territory Times and Gazette* in 1884 'is, "survey before selection", and we have no hesitation in saying, that this land law (which was never framed for a new colony) has done more to retard the progress of settlement and its productive industries, than any other cause.'[595]

The anomalies and injustices of the land system were advertised in the eastern colonies newspapers, probably because the news fed a belief that South Australians had always tried to keep other colonials out. Even so, all three Government Residents in the 1870s told of immigrants getting as far as Palmerston only to be discouraged by the complexities of the land law.[596] The would-be farmers returned home to warn others against repeating the mistake. The sad fact was that, for a whole decade after the first surveys were laid out by Goyder, the only farmers to get on the country land were those who squatted on their blocks without authority. The Chinese were adept at squatting, as were individuals like the enigmatic Manoel Gomez, who grew maize at Collett's Creek. These small gardens set in fertile spots flourished but squatting was not a secure livelihood for a farmer. It made for itinerant farming, with few opportunities to test the capacity of the same piece of land over successive seasons.

'Two Main Streets and a Chinese Quarter'

Every preliminary land purchaser was entitled to a half-acre block in the metropolis. The complications of absenteeism in the country were therefore faithfully reflected in Palmerston itself. In 1882, of 1019 city allotments only four were occupied by their owners; 99 per cent of owners of allotments were absentees.[597] There could be no greater hindrance to the prospect of a young capital than this.

In the infant days of Adelaide the preoccupation with land speculation (arising from concentrated settlement) had frustrated

595 *Northern Territory Times and Gazette* 18/10/1884 leader.

596 Douglas to Reynolds 7/5/1872 (N.T.I.L. 216/1872); Scott to Everard 16/5/1874 (N.T.I.L. 190/1874); McMinn to Price 15/5/1878 with Price's Minute 20/5/1878 (N.T.I.L. 328/1878).

597 W.J. Sowden, *The Northern Territory as it is*. Thomas and Co., Adelaide, 1882, p. 130; *Register* 22/2/1884 leader. The official figure of 1019 includes a small number of wharfage allotments besides a few others which do not appear on the final maps.

Colonel Light's vision and driven shopkeepers into narrow back streets. In Palmerston absentee speculation, more complete, stifled growth altogether. The main sections of the tableland east of Doctor's Gully fell into the hands of land jobbers who either refused to lease or sell, or held out for exorbitant prices. The rental in Cavenagh Street became 20 shillings per foot frontage a year with all buildings passing into the land owner's grasp after ten years' lease.[598] Here South Australia was hooked by a line of its own making. One of the reasons why owners held such inflated ideas was because publicity had taught them to believe in Palmerston as a future Singapore.

The landlord's stranglehold made the task of the small businessman setting up shop in Palmerston very hard indeed. One or two tried to evade the monopoly. The most noteworthy case was that of Adcock and Company, general merchants, who erected their store on a public reserve on the esplanade opposite the telegraph station and defied all efforts to shift them. This was resented by the other shopkeepers, who had paid high prices for their leases. In November 1872 the Government Resident appealed to Adelaide for help and the minister, after taking legal advice, sent back word 'to take summary proceedings'. Adcock refused to budge, quoting his lawyers and threatening to fence himself in. When matters became too serious he recanted, and begged for permission to stay temporarily. The minister in Adelaide, however, refused to relent and Adcock was charged with squatting on *public land* – whereupon the two local justices in Palmerston, in obvious sympathy, exonerated Adcock on the grounds that this was not public land, but the middle of a *public road*. Eventually he was convicted of squatting on a public road, and his store was pulled down round his ears. Adcock immediately appealed to the Local Court in Adelaide on the grounds that the land was not a public road at all – the two justices had been misdirected – but in fact *public land*.

Fortunately an accident intervened to settle matters. By some mischance the legal papers allegedly were lost somewhere between Port Darwin and Port Adelaide, and the parties grasped the opportunity to reach a settlement. Adcock, declaring himself a

598 *Northern Territory Times and Gazette* 2/9/1882, p. 2.

man of peace, shifted to Smith Street, and the minister, without his vital papers, was happy not to have to deal with the issue. But the example of Adcock remained as a warning to anyone foolish enough to try to evade the land monopolists of Palmerston.[599]

Nor did the District Council of Palmerston – proclaimed in June 1874 to clean up the town – fare much better. It held a preliminary meeting on 15 June attended by four members nominated by the government, the businessmen Joseph Skelton, Judah Moss (or Moss Judah) Solomon, Richard Wells and Robert Caldwell (in the chair), at which William Whitfield, the teacher, was chosen as clerk and instructed to prepare a valuation of properties. An election by ratepayers was held on 13 July, followed by the first general meeting on 27 July, at which Joshua Jones was elected chair and Robert Caldwell, William Barlow and Robert Fiveash took their seats as members.[600] The new council immediately set about clearing streets, repairing wells and erecting a pound for stray stock. One of its first tasks was to attack the horehound (Schmid's Folly), brought in from Timor now growing seven-foot high and blotting out the original vegetation. They set Larrakia labourers to work clearing vegetation.

Nine months later the council was broke – the Government Resident had to step in with grants in aid. As most of the ratepayers were out of reach in England and South Australia, their rates could not be extracted, except after three years of expensive court actions.

As a rabble-rouser the District Council of Palmerston was more successful. One of the objects in forming local government led mainly by local businessmen was to loosen the absentee-citizens' stranglehold on the town. After a ratepayer's dues fell three years in arrears, council had the legal right to start proceedings to sell up his land. At the council's request the names of non-payers were listed in the *South Australian Government Gazette*. They included many leading South Australians. The council complained that while locals gave value to the land, the absentee land-owners refused even to pay

599 Attorney-General's opinions on the illegal occupation of reserves at Port Darwin (N.T.I.L. 390/1872 also 396/1872); Douglas to Reynolds 6/1/1873 (N.T.I.L. 76/1873); Douglas to Reynolds 6/1/1873 (N.T.I.L. 110/1873); Boucaut and Bruce to Mann 21/7/1873 (A.G.I.L. 534/1873); *Register* 17/7/1873, p. 3 Local Court.

600 *S.A. Government Gazette* 11/6/1874 p. 1013; *Northern Territory Times and Gazette* 19/6/1874 leader; 17/7/1874, p. 3; 24/7/1874, p. 2; 1/8/ 1874, p. 2.

their rates. But when the time came the responsible minister, fearing an outcry, opposed taking legal action.[601]

As soon as it became clear that the government was not going to act, the local councillors began to turn on the government itself. Their favourite tactic was to lay claim to government lands piece by piece – and everything on them, including the Residency itself – on the grounds that they were outside the government reserves. This sent the ministers running to their law officers for advice. In September 1874 councillors threatened to pull the buildings down. They even claimed that the produce from the government gardens should be distributed democratically among the citizens. They also tried to stop Chinese being buried in the same cemetery as Christians.[602]

One farcical series of events concerned a well in Cavenagh Square that was built by the government in 1874, but handed over to the District Council soon after its formation. The Government Resident claimed back the well in October 1876, after a mare fell down it and councillors 'declined to interfere' – to which action by the government the council retaliated by taking away the bucket and chain. The Government Resident then tried to reassure the citizens by recommending to his minister that the well should be put under council control after all – but was later accused of secretly recommending the opposite. The minister in Adelaide (Ebenezer Ward, never one to tread lightly) issued a proclamation via the governor granting to the Palmerston Council control of Peel's Well and the OT Well on the beach, but conspicuously excluding the well in Cavenagh Square. Council led by the town clerk, responded with indignation. Even when a gloomy Dane named Thomson committed suicide and his body began to decompose at the bottom of the well, council and citizens did not give up their right to use it. In the end the climate and maintenance costs intervened and the quarrel over the well ran out of steam. But conflict between council

601 *Northern Territory Times and Gazette* 19/6/1874 leader; 17/7/1874, p. 3; 27/3/1875 leader also p. 3; *S.A. Government Gazette* 11/6/1874, p. 1013; 12/12/1878, p. 1747.

602 Whitfield to Scott 12/2/1875 (G.R.I.L. A676); Whitfield to Gott 27/5/1875 with additions (G.R.I.L. A878); Whitfield to Scott 10/6/1875 (G.R.I.L. A909); Ward to Scott 24/8/1875 (G.R.I.L. A1077); *Northern Territory Times and Gazette* 26/9/1874, p. 3.

and government went on long into the twentieth century.[603] And so Palmerston, hemmed in by absentee speculators, remained, in the famous words of the *The Times* of London, 'two main streets and a Chinese quarter'.[604]

The locking up of the town lands and the lack of development in general, shaped the town's social history at all levels. By any standards it was a strange place. As late as December 1884 George Bright wrote to the Resident that a 'small man' could hardly find a piece of land in the town areas on which to build a house.[605]

The response of the different ethnic groups to the locking up of the land was to congregate in enclaves or ghettos, surrounded by acres of unkempt space. Over the 1870s, each group came to terms with the absentee landowners in their own way. Most of the Europeans took up residence near Smith and Mitchell Streets in government or company houses – except for the itinerant Europeans, who dwelt in temporary bark or corrugated-iron huts and even tents. Between 300 and 500 Aborigines, depending on the season, lived at Lameroo Beach as they probably had done for centuries, unaware of a system of land ownership which would have seemed to them arrant nonsense. They chose Lameroo Beach because it had a regular supply of spring water and was one of the few places where they could beach their canoes. The Malay community, numbering about 30 males and one female, set up camp near Bennett Street as squatters. As prison proved no deterrent, the authorities eventually gave up trying to shift them.

Chinese people, who came by the hundreds in the second half of the 1870s, crowded together on single allotments, leased from some rich Chinese merchant, in or near Cavenagh Street, into which they crammed their shops, residences, fan-tan dens, brothels and livestock quarters. 'The first aim of the Chinese settler seems to be to possess swine, and the next to locate them in a fenced-off corner

603 Police to Price 21/8/1876 (G.R.I.L. A1656); Kelsey to Price 31/10/1876 (G.R.I.L. A1756); Kelsey to Price 8/5/1877 (G.R.I.L. A2062); Ward to Price 7/9/1877 (G.R.I.L. A2383); Kelsey to Price 20/8/1877 (G.R.I.L. A2272); Price to Ward 11/11/1876 (N.T.I.L. 485/1876); *S.A. Government Gazette* 19/4/877, p. 885; *Northern Territory Times and Gazette* 4/11/1876, p. 2; 17/3/1877, p. 2; 7/4/1877, pp. 2 and 3.

604 Extract from *The Times* re Northern Territory (N.T.I.L. 176/1886)

605 Bright to Parsons 6/12/1884 (N.T.I.L. 33/1885).

of his own house,'[606] wrote the *North Australian* in 1884. To save space, the Chinese used the absentee blocks opposite as a dumping ground for domestic waste. As the wind seldom blew from that direction, they were encouraged to restrict their settlements to the north-east quarter of the town – the vendors and their tenants in the vicinity of Cavenagh Street, and the itinerants further out between McMinn Street and Greene Terrace. 'I have induced the District Council to allot the Chinese a camp on the NE side of the town, on the Park Lands – As the wind seldom blows from that direction,' wrote Government Resident Price.[607] In 1880 the whole of the first Chinatown – its bamboo and grass huts, pigs, fowls, dogs and cats – disappeared in smoke while the Europeans rushed frantically around trying to save the place. The fire was caused when a sick man, Yee Hee, unstable on his legs, tried to cook over a naked flame inside his grass hut. Patiently, successive waves of immigrants rebuilt Chinatown much as it was before.[608]

Unable to move back or forward, Palmerston became a strange outpost of the British Empire, desperately isolated and without a supporting hinterland. Most of the white settlers worked either for the government or the telegraph company. As a mainly government town most of the officers were referred to by initials – the Government Resident being the 'G.R.'. Only a handful of people, like policeman Paul Foelsche, businessman Fred Finniss, businessman and politician Vaiben Louis Solomon, and public servant John George Knight, had any intention of staying on. They became the so-called Old Territorians. For the rest, it was a term of duty in the wilderness which might enhance promotion, or simply an adventure to remember.

Palmerston was also a town dominated by male attitudes and values. Among the Europeans the life-style tended to be aggressive, as one man tried to prove his prowess to another, and to impress his family down south. In July 1872 there were 16 white women (wives

606 *North Australian* 30/5/1884, p. 3.

607 Price to King 20/5/1879 (N.T.I.L. 261/1879).

608 Price to King 29/8/1879 (N.T.I.L. 419/1879); Price to King 20/5/1879 (N.T.I.L. 261/1879); Price to King 1/7/1880 (N.T.I.L. 375/1880); *Register* 26/7/1880, p. 6; *Northern Territory Times and Gazette* 3/5/1879, p. 2; 21/6/1879, p. 2; 24/4/1880, p. 2; 26/6/1880, p. 2.

and servants), 33 children, and 85 white men living in Palmerston; in November 1878, 35 women, 55 children and 110 men. While the disproportions were much greater in the country.[609] All this contrasted with the Wakefield axiom that there must be an equal balance of males and females for civilised existence.

Almost all the women in Palmerston were in domestic work, their only chance to contribute to public life being through charities often associated with the Anglican and Methodist churches. A small number established private businesses or found employment outside the home. With the opening of a hospital in 1874, Alice McGuire, who had learned many of her management skills in India, became the first matron. Anne Kelsey at one time ran a drapers shop. Sarah Bennett, Amelia Traversi, Ellen Ryan and others conducted pubs.[610] Some female pub-keepers doubled as Madams, and were held in awe by ordinary citizens. In general women are marginalised in the public records of the Northern Territory, but they are better represented in the private records, because of the women's habit of writing private letters. Few Chinese women came to Chinatown, mainly because the emperor forbade the emigration of women, in order to preserve the purity of Chinese civilisation. By 1881 there was one Chinese woman only, wife of a merchant, deeply polite, with small feet. A few years later there were more than thirty prostitutes in Chinatown, mainly Japanese, mainly from Hong Kong. Japanese prostitutes in traditional dress were part of the landscape at Palmerston until after the turn of the century. Some observers were struck by how lady-like they were, and one old-timer remembered the respect with which the Asians treated their prostitutes compared with the 'fallen women' attitudes of Europeans.[611]

Not surprisingly, none of these different groups were representative examples of their particular culture and race. Even the Aborigines were soon changed by forced dependence and

---

609 Douglas to Reynolds 10/7/1872 (N.T.I.L. 304/1872); Price to King 11/11/1878 (N.T.I.L. 613/1878); Barbara James, *No Man's Land: Women of the Northern Territory,* Collins, Sydney, 1989, *passim.*

610 *ibid.*

611 Research Notes David Sissons (Sissons to Cross), 1971, 1994; D.C.S. Sissons, Japanese in the Northern Territory 1884–1902 (S.L.S.A. Mortlock, D5691(T)).

cultural contacts. Because the population was small, interaction between the various groups was unavoidable. These interactions provided most of the domestic colour of Palmerston. And so the town of Palmerston, with the impressive name, but strangled by absentee owners, continued to struggle.

It is one of the ironies of Northern Territory history that, having been planned to short-circuit the years of pioneering barbarism, the instruments of civilisation, such as the school, the church, the mission and the rule of law, were very slow to get going. Only in 1880 was the area declared a school district and a permanent school built in Palmerston. Even then, preliminary land buyers (such as the Downer family) opposed the school being placed on the Esplanade (so as to catch the cool breezes and be near where the children actually lived) because that might block the outlook to the sea and reduce the value of their investments.[612]

Up to the 1880s the two leading advocates for the Christian cause were the Methodist Archibald James Bogle and the Anglican Edward William Price (especially after the death of his family on the *Gothenburg*). Both complained about the wildness of much Territory life. Two of their main duties were to fight the demon drink and to foster family life.

Bogle arrived with his wife Hilda on the *Tararua* on 17 August 1873. Before this, the Congregationalist Alfred Gore had conducted some services in the Residency and, after failing to raise enough money alone, had arranged with the Congregational Building Society to send north a prefabricated building to be used as a school and library during the week and a church on Sundays. But before the building arrived on the *Nerio* in August 1873 Gore broke down with fever and he had to leave the Territory. His son Dewhirst later became an outspoken defender of the indigenous peoples. Bogle bought the building for the Wesleyan Church and erected it on the corner of Knuckey and Mitchell Streets, where it was opened on Sunday, 2 November. Early in January William Whitfield started a school there. Bogle, an affable, unpretentious man worked tirelessly

---

612 Downer to King 2/12/1879 (N.T.I.L. 553/1879); Price to King 15/1/1880 (N.T.I.L. 52/1880); Price to King 30/4/1880 (N.T.I.L. 275/1880); Price to King 16/6/1880 (N.T.I.L. 370/1880); *S.A. Government Gazette* 2/9/1880, p. 866.

preaching at Palmerston, Southport and up and down the reefs, helping found a hospital at Palmerston and, with nothing but the pledge as a weapon, battling against drunkenness everywhere. Burdened by a growing sense of frustration, towards the end of his term he wrote:[613]

> Preached twice at Palmerston. I feel dreadfully discouraged with my work here. I have no fruit, & I feel that there is no sympathy in the congregation.[614]

Bogle departed in January 1877, and was replaced by Reverend John Dyer Langsford. Meanwhile, Edward Price, who was Government Resident, Anglican and 'acting lay reader', decided to start a permanent Church of England congregation in the Residency, having been promised £1500, or £300 per annum, by the Society for the Propagation of the Gospel. The move caused resentment because it split the Christian resources. By 1874, the Anglican congregation had been named (by persons unknown) Christ Church, which was seen by some as an attempt to pull rank over the Methodist and other denominations. Many South Australians had from the start abhorred the notion of an 'established church'.[615]

Price was appalled by the lack of a civil society, especially on the reefs:

> A few weeks hard work then an equal time of utter madness, drunk from morning till night lying about in filth and dirt till fever sets in and often ends it all and then the climate is blamed.[616]

In the early years most of the alcohol consumed was Holland schnapps imported from Timor in square black bottles and known locally as 'Square Face'.

Price also thought that many people came north as a last resort, to die. And indeed throughout the 19th century disproportionately

---

613 Research Notes by Arch Grant 18/7/1992; 11/8/1997; A. Grant, *Palmerston to Darwin: 75 years Service on the Frontier*, Dee Why N.S.W., Frontier, 1990, Chapters 1 to 7.

614 Diary of A.J. Bogle, 24/10/1875 (Mitchell Library).

615 *Northern Territory Times and Gazette* 10/2/1877, p. 2; 28/4/1877, p. 2; Bishop Philip Freier to Cross 22/11/2005.

616 Price to Blyth 14/5/1878 (N.T.I.L. 287/1878).

high numbers of Europeans in the Territory died with no known relatives. All this contrasted with Wakefield's emphasis on recruiting superior settlers, preferably energetic young married couples who had due respect for law and order. And, after the false start, nowhere was the reaction in parliament against the Northern Territory more apparent than on the long question of law and order.

Crisis in Law and Order

> 'The poor Northern Territory is made a wretched stalking-horse for the use of all members who want to attack their opponents in office.'
>
> *Northern Territory Times and Gazette* 29 August 1874

Another lever that colonial pressure groups had used to prise the Northern Territory from British authorities was the threat of lawlessness. But by 1870, when the permanent administration was set up at Port Darwin, the Territory had so fallen out of favour that South Australia's politicians would begrudge it only a half a system of legal protection – a sentiment soon strengthened by the costs of constructing the overland telegraph. The first Government Resident and his deputy were made special magistrates in charge of a Local Court with all the powers attending that position in South Australia.[617] A special magistrate, as a layman administering the law, was supposed to come cheap, and his jurisdiction was restricted to less serious offences such as assault and battery and petty larceny. The politicians made no provision for prosecuting major crimes against life and property beyond the impractical ones of bringing the South Australian Supreme Court periodically to Palmerston or shifting the accused, witnesses, and items of evidence lock, stock and barrel down to Adelaide.

No one had to wait long to see the defects of this arrangement. The first genuine settler in the Territory was a memorable character named Mathew Dillon Cox, who in 1872 overlanded cattle from Queensland, erected a rough homestead and set to work stocking a station on the Douglas Peninsula opposite Palmerston. While he was stocking, Cox was accused of wilful and corrupt perjury. He had sworn in the Local Court that a storekeeper named Chawner

617 Cavenagh to Douglas 27/4/1870 (S.A.P.P. 25 of 1870–1871).

(being dark skinned and so considered of lower intelligence) owed him money for cattle – whereupon Chawner, after a frantic search, turned up the receipt that proved his innocence. Cox, quick as a flash, pleaded loss of memory. (Chawner, an Afghan, had been the first hawker to cross the continent, selling to overland telegraph workers as he went, having set out from the settled areas of South Australia under the misapprehension that there was a road all the way to Port Darwin.)

Perjury was too grave a charge to be heard in a Local Court by a special magistrate, so in April 1873 the case was referred to the Supreme Court in Adelaide, and Cox and witnesses prepared to sail south on the *Gothenburg*. But then the minister, Thomas Reynolds, visited the Territory and controversially transferred the trial back to Palmerston. Cox was put on bail pending the setting up of machinery to try him. He begged to be tried, complaining the bail conditions prevented him going to Queensland to complete his stocking, so he would be ruined.[618] He succeeded in having the matter raised in the South Australian parliament, where the attorney-general responded that because he doubted if any jury would convict Cox on the evidence, he preferred not to spend money on sending a judge to Palmerston or bringing the accused and witnesses all the way to Adelaide – leaving Cox in limbo.[619] Nor did the key witness for the Crown, George Perrin, fare much better. He was instructed that he would be guilty of contempt of court if he left Port Darwin. So he stayed on, passing up one prospecting job after another and living on what savings he had left, having sold his business on being told to prepare to leave for Adelaide at short notice.[620] The impasse was only settled by events outside the law. In April 1874 as a result of another dispute over money, Cox was

618 Regina v. Cox depositions (A.G.I.L. 637/1873); Millner to Everard 29/8/1873 with enclosures (N.T.I.L. 248/1873); Memorial Catherine Cox to Everard 24/6/1874 (N.T.I.L. 315/1874); Administration of Justice in the Northern Territory, Cox v. Chawner (S.A.P.P. 140 of 1873); *Advertiser* 7/4/1873, p. 2 Telegraphic News; 8/4/1873, p. 2; 4/6/1873, p. 2 Telegraphic News; *Register* 7/4/1873, p. 5 Telegraphic News. The nature of the bail is open to dispute.

619 S.A.P.D. 1873 c. 1141.

620 Perrin to Scott 15/1/1874; Perrin to Reynolds 4/6/1873 Enclosures 2 letters to *Northern Territory Times and Gazette* dated 14/11/1873 and 19/12/1873 (N.T.I.L. 67/1874).

bashed at his station by his nephew Charles Bouchier (alias Boucher real name Butcher) and died a drawn-out death two weeks later. Bouchier, charged with manslaughter, demanded to go to Adelaide to plead his case. Instead he was smuggled aboard the *Contest* by its captain and passengers and off-loaded at Tien Tsin on the north-west coast of Australia. Last heard, he planned to head inland until the dust settled, then escape by ship back to the Dutch East Indies. So ended the matter of Cox, the first criminal case in Territory history.[621]

Because the invaders were mainly young males certain offences tended to dominate: drunkenness, disorderly behaviour, violence, sexual offences against Aboriginal women. Other problems came from cultural differences, like the Chinese preference for opium over alcohol.[622]

By 1873 the Territory was earning the name of being a lawless land. An influx of rough gold seekers had arrived from the south. These were the first wave of a permanent rowdy element in the Territory. The second wave came from Queensland a few years later with pastoral expansion. 'These low class whites,' sniffed the Resident's daughter, 'are a perfect curse to any settlement, and do more harm than the natives, both to life and property. Some of them, going still further down the social scale, herded with blackfellows, lived in their wurlies, and egged them on to steal and butcher the cattle ...'[623] Soon the wildest of the diggers were taking over the shepherded leases (leases sat on just to keep others out) by force and defying the police and wardens to shift them. A lawyer by name of 'Villainous Smith' (Villeneuve Smith), dressed in gaudy pyjamas, moved up and down the countryside inciting the rowdies to action and recruiting business at great profit to himself – for

621 *Northern Territory Times and Gazette* 24/4/1874, p. 2; 8/5/1874, p. 3; 5/6/1874, p. 2; Foelsche to Scott 8/5/1874 (G.R.I.L. A287); Cabinet decision 18/5/1874 (A.G.I.L. 853/1874); Bathurst to Sanderson 10/5/1874 (A.G.I.L. 289/1874); Bathurst to Sanderson 8/7/1874 (A.G.I.L. 440/1874); Bathurst to Sanderson 3/8/1874 (A.G.I.L. 487/1874); Sanderson to Bathurst 3/6/1874 (A.G.O.L. 666/1874); Sanderson to Bathurst 1/7/1874 (A.G.O.L. 691/1874); Sanderson to Bathurst 27/7/1874 (A.G.O.L. 715/1874).

622 W.R. (Bill) Wilson, *A Force Apart? A History of the Northern Territory Police Force*, Pecock Academic Press, Sydney-Hong Kong-London, 2001 *passim.*

623 Harriet W. Daly, *Digging, Squatting and Pioneering,* p. 308.

which the Resident later tried to get him struck off. His reputation was not enhanced by the rumour that he came from a French Creole background. Soon after his return to Adelaide he was imprisoned for defaming the wealthy Downer family.[624]

On the new gold diggings near Yam and Pine Creek this rough element of gold seekers kept the original owners at a distance with their firearms. According to Police Inspector Foelsche this was because the Wolwonga people were in the habit of following the miners for days on end everywhere they went in order to pick up scraps, which was interpreted by the miners as deliberately menacing behaviour. In December 1873, in response to many rumours, the warden on the reefs took steps to reassure the Government Resident that miners at Pine Creek were not about to take up arms against the Aborigines. Adding to the insecurity of the bush was the ability of Aborigines to communicate quickly with one another over great distances, which the whites attributed to mental telepathy and black magic.[625]

In October news was received from Burke (Burketown) that nine escaped ruffians, waiting trial for riot and assault, were heading for the Territory apparently believing they could find asylum there.[626] Alarmed by these developments, Attorney-General Charles Mann, a noted Adelaide lawyer, gravely warned parliament 'that things were in a most hopeless state of confusion and anarchy'[627]; unless something was done 'the whole settlement would have to protect themselves by lynch law and institutions of that kind which they saw in America in the early days of the diggings in California'.[628]

The fear that the new Territory would endanger South Australia's reputation for good order shocked successive governments into remonstrating with parliament for courts equipped to deal with serious crimes. Each time, ordinary politicians shut their eyes against the growing lawlessness, in the hope that it would somehow resolve itself. The year 1873 was noteworthy for three serious attempts to meet the situation, resulting in three outstanding failures.

---

624 Villeneuve Smith, see *Law Society Bulletin* Vol 8 No 10.

625 Foelsche to Scott 31/12/1873 (N.T.I.L. 57/1874); Frampton to Scott 11/12/1873 (G.R.I.L. A104).

626 S.A.P.D. 1873 c. 745.

627 S.A.P.D. 1873 c. 208.

628 S.A.P.D. 1873 c. 210.

Charles Mann warned that without full legal protection, the people in the Territory would have to protect themselves by lynch law as in California.
(George E. Loyau, *Representative Men of South Australia*, Howell, Adelaide, 1882, wood engraving by Jeffrey Bruer)

Following Reynolds' recommendations, made after visiting the north, the Blyth government decided in early August to appoint the commissioner of insolvency, Henry Downer, as a fourth judge of the Adelaide Supreme Court stationed at Palmerston on a salary of £1500 plus extras per year. He was also temporarily to act as the Government Resident. The move immediately met a hostile reception in both Houses, especially from Boucaut and Bray, with discussion side-tracked from questions of justice to an inquisition into the integrity of Henry Downer and all the wealthy Downer family. The matter proved so embarrassing both Downer and the government were pleased to see the subject dropped.[629]

A fortnight later, Attorney-General Mann came down with a weakened version of the original Bill, in which the fourth judge was to be replaced by a 'Limited Supreme Court' restricted only to the Territory and removable inside the first 12 months if both Houses of parliament petitioned for it. Mann added a warning that the

629 S.A.P.D. 1873 c. 91 to 98, 76, 77. Other references put the judge's salary at £1700; Correspondence re Mr. Downer (S.A.P.P 72 of 1873).

Territory was on the brink of anarchy.[630] But parliament's reception was no warmer than before. The Assembly made the court temporary, for 12 months only, unless redeemed in the meantime by Act of Parliament – by which time parliament would know if the Territory was going to survive.[631] The Legislative Council, offended by the cost, quashed the Bill by a common parliamentary device: 'that this Bill on this day six months be read a second time'.[632] Now the influential Adelaide *Register* began to join issue, accusing parliament of sanctioning lawlessness, jeopardising South Australia's name and proscribing the settlement of honest men.[633]

The temper of parliament was not improved by the appointment in 1873 of the brilliant J.G. Knight from Victoria (designer of Government House in Melbourne and the first to build a two-storey building in Palmerston) to the position of secretary to the Government Resident and general expert. A motion condemning 'the appointment of a stranger to South Australia' was defeated only by the government insisting on treating it as a vote of no confidence.[634]

As stories of lawlessness continued to flood in, the harassed government considered pleading with the Legislative Council to review its stand on the ground that the cost objection could be met by taxing the Territorians with miners' fees and customs duties and using the proceeds to establish the new court.[635] Instead, Mann came down with a third Bill: an even more diluted version of the original. He proposed to extend the authority of the Local Court already in existence and to introduce a so-called 'Local Court of Extraordinary Jurisdiction' under a special magistrate with at least seven years experience and with all the powers of a Supreme Court judge, except for felonies punishable by death.[636] The objection by parliament and the press now was that the 'emasculation' had gone to the point of absurdity: the pressing issue of dealing with capital

630 S.A.P.D. 1873 c. 207 to 211; *Advertiser* 27/8/1873 leader; *Register* 27/8/1873 leader; 9/9/1873 leader.

631 S.A.P.D. 1873 c. 272 and 273; *Register* 3/9/1873, p. 4.

632 Minutes of the Proceedings of the Legislative Council 23/9/1873 No. 6.

633 *Register* 24/9/1873, p. 4.

634 S.A.P.D. 1873 c.442 *seq.*

635 S.A.P.D. 1873 c. 580 to 582.

636 S.A.P.D. 1873 c. 701 and 702; 745 to 747; *Register* 10/10/1873 leader.

Henry Downer was considered for the combined position of judge and Government Resident in the Territory. The proposal met such opposition in parliament (especially from Boucaut and Bray) that both the government and the Downer family were pleased to see the matter dropped.
(George E. Loyau, *Representative Men of South Australia*, Howell, Adelaide, 1882, wood engraving by Jeffrey Bruer)

crimes remained unsolved, while an experienced magistrate to deal with the other extended powers would be hard to find and costly to keep. Barely a quorum turned out to give the Bill a cold hearing in the Lower House and the Upper House guillotined it with little debate.[637] At the end of a frustrating session, after proffering a Supreme Court judge and two watered-down versions (a limited Supreme Court and an extended Local Court), the attorney-general had to admit that: [638]

> in the present Temper of the Legislature especially of the Upper House, I am greatly afraid it would be almost impossible to pass the necessary measure.[639]

637 S.A.P.D. 1873 c. 998, 999; *Register* 15/10/1873, pp. 4 and 5; 12/11/1873, p. 4.
638 S.A.P.D. 1873 c. 1085.
639 Memo Admin of Justice in N.T. by Attorney-General Charles Mann 7/5/1874 (N.T.I.L. 144/1874).

Throughout 1874 law in the Northern Territory was left mainly to the Local Court and Providence. Between whites major crimes tended to be treated as minor offences and so within the bounds of the existing court. In August the citizens of Palmerston petitioned for either a permanent judge or a circuit court, claiming that in serious cases like robbery 'no information can be laid lest the parties should be *called to Adelaide*, as witnesses, and thus ruin their business prospects here'.[640]

At least one man was sent south to be tried in the correct way, an Irishman and alleged horse thief named Hanratty who, at great cost, was transported all the way to Adelaide in the thoughtful company of two troopers and the stolen horse. Once there he was acquitted on the grounds that he had merely *borrowed* the horse – without the owners' permission (the owners happened to be the police department). The much-travelled horse was then sold to Burton's circus.[641]

Early in 1875 the governor was left no choice but to send one of the three judges of the Supreme Court, Mr Justice William Alfred Wearing, on circuit to Palmerston. This was the practice in the north-west settlements of Western Australia, but in South Australia it involved a hard fight to get the funds from parliament.[642] Only Justice Wearing, and then only after much persuasion, was prepared to go. In February Wearing, surrounded by his aides and officers, conducted the Circuit Court in Palmerston's tiny court house. There were only three men awaiting trial: Ah Kim from Canton charged with an unnatural act; Henry Hazell, an English sailor committed for burglary; and Charles Christiansen a Norwegian (alias Johnson), for attempted murder with a revolver after a quarrel over eight tins of meat at Yam Creek. A fourth man, Hubeeb Abdoolah (alias Abdoolah the Arab), was at the last moment charged with theft

640 Robert Caldwell Memorial from residents at Palmerston N.T. praying for appointment of a Judge of the Supreme Court, or to visit in Circuit. Dated 20/8/1874 (C.S.O.I.L. 1618/1874); *Northern Territory Times and Gazette* 1/5/1874 leader.

641 Scott to Everard 10/4/1874 (N.T.I.L. 48/1874); *S.A. Government Gazette* 28/5/1874, p. 908; *Advertiser* 12/6/1874, p. 3 Supreme Court; *Register* 12/6/1874, p. 3 Supreme Court; *Northern Territory Times and Gazette* 13/2/1874, p. 2.

642 S.A.P.D. 1874 c. 1650 to 1652.

to make the numbers look larger. An Aborigine named Myranda, charged with killing a man named Narlunga, had escaped together with the chief witness for the Crown while being escorted from the court house to the gaol a few weeks earlier. Myranda's case illustrated some anomalies already appearing in Larrakia society. In a quarrel near Peel's Well, Narlunga had challenged Myranda in the traditional way with his spears, whereupon Myranda had counter-challenged with his newly acquired gun, and shot Narlunga dead – much to the consternation of the Larrakias as a whole. The gun had been given to the Larrakia people by Billy Harvey, one of Dillon Cox's men. After being caught between two cultures, Myranda found himself trapped between two systems of justice. Having escaped British law he was speared to death by relatives of the dead man.[643]

The fact that there were only three or four individuals awaiting trial was seized upon by some politicians and the press to justify the claim that this court was superfluous, but it rather proved how expert were the Territorians at settling disputes out of court. The only person convicted was Ah Kim who, given a life sentence 'for homosexuality', promptly escaped, which was easy enough from the Palmerston gaol. 'That Chinaman,' noted the *Advertiser* 'is a highly honoured individual.'[644]

Ah Kim himself would not have agreed.[645] An excellent cook and wood carver, he was considered by his admirers one of the most talented Chinese to come to the Territory. The police however, thought him a rogue and a thief.[646] In April 1874 he was charged before the police magistrate with stealing notes and cheques that had been mislaid by a bank manager. The evidence suggested he had either stolen them, or not returned after finding them where they fell from the manager's coat pocket (he took the police to the spot where he claimed to have found the package). While awaiting trial in the cramped cell he was accused of a homosexual

643 Scott to Bundey with enclosures 20/1/1875 (N.T.I.L. 137/1875); *Northern Territory Times and Gazette* 16/1/1875, p. 2; 13/2/1875, pp. 2 and 3 Circuit Court.

644 *Advertiser* 18/1/1875 leader.

645 *Northern Territory Times and Gazette* 13/2/1875, pp 2 and 3 Circuit Court.

646 *Northern Territory Times and Gazette* 28/8/1875 leader.

offence with another prisoner and remanded to appear before the Supreme Court whenever this would be possible. For nearly ten months he remained in gaol waiting to be tried. Finally in desperation he complained to the prison authorities and through the local newspaper: 'had a European been in my place, he would have been tried or discharged months ago, but I am only a poor d———l of a Chinaman.' The outburst earned him a conviction for insolence and insubordinate behaviour, the visiting justice to the gaol ruling that 'as he had been nine months confined in idleness it would now be necessary to give him two months imprisonment with hard labor'.[647] At last he was tried in the Circuit Court before Justice Wearing and a mixed race jury. After hearing the evidence the Chinese and Malays voted him innocent and the Europeans ruled him guilty. The judge, who needed to be out of the Territory aboard the *Gothenburg* in a few days, sent the jury back until they reached a decision. The white jurors prevailed, and Ah Kim was sentenced to solitary confinement for life. A few days later he broke gaol and added a fourth crime. For three months the hunt for Ah Kim was on, with police troopers searching assiduously while most of the district councillors, some local citizens and certain Chinese from Singapore did their best to hide him. Week after week he appeared like a will-o-the-wisp just ahead of the troopers. Then, just as he was preparing to flee the mainland in a well-stocked boat, he was discovered by two inexperienced water police, one of whom accidentally shot him through the head. 'Judicial murder', 'Jedburgh Justice', the local paper called it. Ah Kim became a martyr figure in the local agitation for effective law and order.[648]

While returning to Adelaide on the *Gothenburg*, Justice Wearing and his assistants were drowned when the vessel was wrecked on the Barrier Reef with the loss of 102 lives, fully one seventh of the Territory's European population and including many of its leading citizens. Even one of the men the court had come to try, Henry Hazell, acquitted and leaving the Territory quickly for his own good, was drowned alongside the learned judge and his retinue.

647 *Northern Territory Times and Gazette* 15/5/1875, pp. 1 and 2.

648 *Advertiser* 18/1/1875 leader; *Northern Territory Times and Gazette* 1/5/1874, p. 2; 8/5/1874, p. 2; 13/2/1875, pp. 2 and 3; 15/5/1875 p. 2; 28/8/1875 leader; Foelsche to Scott 29/6/1875 (N.T.I.L. 327/1875).

Wearing himself was the first to be swept overboard. According to evidence given by one of the survivors (Patrick Hogan), there was no panic. With British stoicism people formally said goodbye to one another as if departing for a brief time. Two of the Millner girls were later found clasped together in eternal embrace.[649] An hotelier, Ellen Ryan, cancelled her ticket at the last moment, and lived to become the leading woman in the Territory.

Thousands of citizens on both shores dug into their pockets to help the dependents of those who died. It was the largest fundraising effort so far in South Australia's history. A rhymester wrote:

> God save us from disaster –
> God shield us from a grief,
> Like that which smote the *Gothenburg*
> Wrecked on the Barrier Reef.[650]

Three survivors were honoured with gold medals made by Wendt the jeweller, for saving the lives of others.[651] Parliament voted a pension of £5500 to the dependents of Wearing and his court – and hastily debited it to the Northern Territory Account. Clement Sabine, associated with the Pastoral Association, acted as administrator of £4000 voted to Wearing's wife.[652]

Taking every advantage of the public sorrow, in September 1875 the Boucaut government came down with the fourth *Bill for the better Administration of Justice in the Northern Territory.* As in the last attempt, the Bill was designed to set up at a local Court of Extraordinary Jurisdiction by investing an experienced special magistrate with all the powers of a judge of the Supreme Court, except in cases of felonies punishable by death. It also, because of the difficulty in finding 12 unchallenged honest men, provided for juries of six. The reform met an unusually favourable reception in both Houses and was carried through all stages in a fortnight. The

---

649 Evidence to Enquiry, *Brisbane Courier* 19/3/1875, p. 3 quoting *Port Denison Times* 6/3/1875.

650 J.H. Lewis, *The Wreck of the Gothenburg*, Adelaide, 1875, p. 24.

651 Honoured by Governor Musgrave were John Cleland, James Fitzgerald, Robert Brazil.

652 S.A.P.D. 1875 c. 214 to 221; Sabine Papers (S.L.S.A. Mortlock P.R.G. 57/8).

Justice William Alfred Wearing, the first judge to serve in the Northern Territory by conducting a circuit court. He was drowned in the wreck of the *Gothenburg* on his return journey.
(*Australasian Sketcher* 17/4/1875, p. 8. Courtesy of the State Library of South Australia)

Legislative Council affected to welcome it as a vindication of its past refusals, but perhaps the honourable members were trying to justify their obstruction, which had led to the death of one of the colony's outstanding Supreme Court judges as well as two talented assistants, his associate L.J. Pelham, and J.J. Whitby, acting Crown prosecutor.[653]

The new court met at the end of the same year with Government Resident Scott as lay judge – according to Scott, he was first layman to assume Supreme Court duties in Australasia.[654] In contrast to what happened before, the court was so successful that the gaol suddenly proved too small. It had to be enlarged, sentences reduced and prisoners set to work outside for as long each day as possible. At the first sitting, Scott dealt with a motley crowd of Europeans, Chinese and Malays, including a Malay man-servant to the matron of the hospital named Emanuel Gaspar, who one night (he claimed)

653 S.A.P.D. 1875 c. 1251 and 1252; S.A.P.A. 15 of 1875.
654 Scott's Reminiscences p. 12 (S.L.S.A. D7478(L)).

inadvertently sleep-walked his way into his mistress's bed – at which she had grabbed him by the beard and banged his head on the ground until he yielded up his identity. He was speedily convicted.[655]

The limitations of the new court were immediately visible. William Thomas Johnston, master of the schooner *Florinda*, was charged with attempting to murder Mrs Ann Amelia Ramsay by sharing with her, without her knowing, the contents of a bottle laced with laudanum. He loved her, but could not marry her, so decided they would die together. As attempted murder was potentially a capital crime, Johnston was put on bail pending a decision on how to try him. Eventually he was tried at the court in Palmerston on the lesser charge of attempted suicide and acquitted, then sent to the Supreme Court in Adelaide to be tried again, this time for attempted murder – where at the trial (under pressure from the *Florinda*'s owners) the Crown withdrew the case.[656]

Law and Aborigines

The practice of summary justice fell particularly hard on the indigenous peoples, as illustrated by the Roper River killings of 1875. In June of that year Charlie Johnston, in charge of the Daly Waters telegraph station, was speared to death while mustering horses and bullocks near Leichhardt's Bar. Two companions, Daer and Rickarts, were wounded, the former dying from his wounds. The Europeans were shocked. Right up to the event the local Aborigines had ridden on the wagon and been friendly with these men. Johnston was also well-liked.

Soon two official parties, as well as several private expeditions, were fitted out 'to teach the natives a lesson'. 'The only things that have hitherto proved of any value in bringing the niggers to their senses,' urged the local newspaper, 'have been dogs and the revolvers; and we trust the party now gone out will not be afraid to use them.'[657]

---

655 *Advertiser* 15/3/1876 leader; *Northern Territory Times and Gazette* 25/12/1875, p. 2; 12/6/1875, p. 2; Scott to Ward 30/6/1875 (N.T.I.L. 280/1875).

656 Scott to Ward 13/12/1875 telegram (N.T.I.L. 576/1875); *Northern Territory Times and Gazette* 25/12/1875, p. 2; *Advertiser* 15/3/1876 leader.

657 *Northern Territory Times and Gazette* 17/7/1875 leader. The word 'nigger' seems to have been the most derogatory term used at the time to describe the

The two government parties, supposed eventually to link up, included a mainly police contingent under Corporal George Montagu and a telegraph group led by John Little, who was a relative of the dead man. The government cutter *Flying Cloud* was sent to the Roper to give assistance. When the government parties reached Leichhardt's Bar about a month after the murder, it soon became plain that private expeditions had already exacted a terrible revenge. At one stage Little's party came upon the remains of a native camp near Mount McMinn in which everything had been incinerated: the number of bodies found at the scene varied from two to many depending on who made the report. These atrocities were almost certainly committed by an expedition of nine men led by the overlanders Batten and De Lautour who were on their way back to Queensland – where William Batten himself was killed by Aborigines on the Coast Track two years later. The men left behind a letter boasting they had 'dispersed them thoroughly'.[658]

The death of C.H. Johnston, an example of a Boys Own style and representative of hundreds of similar illustrations in the British Empire in the nineteenth century, a genre that declined in the early decades of the twentieth century.
(*Pictorial Australian* August 1875, p. 8. Courtesy of the State Library of South Australia)

Aborigines, followed by 'savages', 'blacks'. More neutral terms were 'native', 'aborigine'.

658 *Northern Territory Times and Gazette* 18/9/1875, p. 2.

In Adelaide, the *Advertiser* reported that:

> Mr Little's party came upon the remains of one camp; where it was evident from the large quantity of human charred bones to be seen lying in a heap, that the natives had been surrounded, shot down, and their bodies afterwards burned.[659]

But the official party was not entirely innocent. In order to avenge their mates, the overland telegraph workers admitted to killing two men they happened to come upon at a lagoon along the river, for which the Government Resident later considered putting those involved on a charge of murder.

By the time it came to making arrests of Aboriginal men, they, with their extended families, had fled into the bush. In the end the combined government party decided to arrest a famous local guide from the Mara people named Ural (alias Bunganah Lowrie after Captain Lowrie of telegraph construction), who spoke fair English and had been kind enough to offer the *Flying Cloud* assistance in negotiating the river. He was arrested because when questioned he answered to the same name as one of the suspects – despite the fact that the alleged killer was over six foot tall and Ural was a much smaller man. According to Inspector Foelsche, Aborigines sometimes chose a name to please their hosts, or told the police what they thought they wanted to hear in order not to offend or embarrass them.[660]

Ural was brought to Port Darwin on the *Flying Cloud*, having been chained for days on the deck, flat on his back, in the blazing sun, arms and legs bound outstretched and a heavy chain across his throat. He was eventually discharged in the Police Court after Rickarts gave evidence that he had never seen him before. Before Daer died, he said he thought the assassins came 'chiefly from the Moles Hill blacks',[661] the much-feared Mangarrayi people. Ural was

---

659 *Advertiser* 24/12/1874, p. 6.

660 Neither Aborigines nor Westerners remotely seemed to understand the others' approach to law. Conversations with Lewis Yerloburka O'Brien, elder of the Kaurna people, 2002. See also Lewis Yerloburka O'Brien, *And the Clock Struck Thirteen,* Wakefield Press, Adelaide, 2007, for examples of differences and dislocations between the cultures.

661 Telegrams relating to organisation of party to apprehend murderer of Johnston 15/7/1875 (N.T.I.L. 300/1875); Little to Scott 29/8/1875 (N.T.I.L.

taken on foot back to his people by a trooper on horse-back, who used a stock-whip when the innocent man moved too slowly. He was then branded with a hot iron in case he came under notice again.[662]

The special magistrate himself complained how the limitations of his court encouraged a kind of lynch law.[663] The Adelaide *Advertiser* put the situation squarely:

> where protection is most required it is withheld. This is especially the case with respect to the natives, who are handed over to the tender mercies of the settlers, while the latter have no security but their rifles and revolvers ... The consequence of this state of things has been that the whites have taken the law into their own hands, and we now learn that the blacks are much quieter.[664]

The official South Australian attitude was to treat the indigenous inhabitants as British subjects in a society which would be concentrated, controlled and civilised. The Protector of Aborigines was instructed to be a liaison officer, learn the Aborigines' languages, study their customs, cure their diseases, teach them their rights as British subjects, protect their women, keep them clear of alcohol, distribute alms to the needy, encourage their industries, put medals of recognition on their chiefs and, most important of all, teach them the civilising power of hard work. He was also to set up reserves around their drinking and hunting places, similar to the reserves already existing in South Australia.[665] But the instructions did not give the Aboriginal people the one thing needful, treaty rights to their traditional land, which was the basis of their culture. Behind all these instructions issued to the Protector of Aborigines in 1870 was the admission that the plan to treat the indigenous citizens in

---

430/1875); Reports of Search party for Murderers of the late Mr Chas. Johnston 15/11/1875 (N.T.I.L. 589/1875); *Register* 15/9/1875, p. 4; 24/12/1875, p. 5; *Advertiser* 15/9/1875, p. 4; 24/12/1875 p. 6; *Northern Territory Times and Gazette* 25/12/1875, p. 2; 1/1/1876 leader; Little to Todd 29/8/1875, p. 2. (Papers of J.A.G. Little S.L.S.A. Mortlock P.R.G. 329).

662 *Quiz* 5/10/1889, p. 3. An early proprietor of *Quiz* was John Le Maistre Francis Roberts who had been involved in many Territory ventures.

663 Price to Blyth 19/2/1878 (N.T.I.L. 144/1878).

664 *Advertiser* 15/3/1876 leader.

665 Cavenagh to Douglas 27/4/1870 (S.A.P.P. 25 of 1870–1871, pp. 3 and 4).

a civilised way had not always worked well in South Australia after 1836. The Letters Patent setting up South Australia and instructions from the Colonial Office had supported Aboriginal land rights, but the *South Australian Constitution Act* and the profit motive had worked against it.

The plain truth was that everywhere in South Australia, north and south, the indigenous peoples were being gradually displaced from their own lands by various outsiders (European and other displaced Aborigines) – a point well made by a Kaurna song man of the Adelaide Plains as far back as 1844:

> *Wanti nindo ai ḳabba ḳabba? Ningḳoandi ḳuma yerta.*
> Where have you pushed me to? You belong to another country![666]

All this contrasted with the Macassan fishers who had visited the north coast for perhaps hundreds of years. Following the tendency of one group to look down upon another, they too saw the inhabitants of the land they called Maregè (or Marragie) as backward, living on the edge of the Malay civilised world. It was the home of mythical creatures, where the inhabitants were sometimes referred to as Orang Outang (bushmen or forest dwellers). But mercifully, unlike the Europeans, they felt no moral need to convert or to civilise the locals.

Successive South Australian governments had neither the will nor the strength to deal with the situation that developed away from Palmerston after the collapse of concentrated settlement. The Protector of Aborigines was seldom allowed to venture out of the town because he had other public duties, being generally the medical officer as well.[667] 'One thing should be borne in mind that Palmerston is not the whole of the N.T.,' warned a veteran cattleman gruffly, complaining that the bodies of the last affray were still lying unburied. 'With good and judicious management a great deal of trouble may be prevented. It all lays with the S.A. Govt. to cause or prevent many murders by both black and white

666 *Kaurna meyunna Kaurna yerta tampendi,* p. 22 (Graham Smith Peace Trust 2002). Could in addition refer to other Aboriginal groups being displaced by white settlement on to Kaurna lands.

667 Ellison to Scott 17/1/1874 (G.R.I.L. A362).

people'.[668] In general, the Aborigines of the north coast were used to contact with people from the outside world, and they were not prepared to give up their culture without a fight. Two events in particular led them to hit back.

The first was the 'bad deeds' done to Aboriginal women. The Aboriginal groups along the north coast made provision for sexual contacts with the outside world but always within strict business and moral codes, which carried with them reciprocal obligations.[669] The trouble came when some of the Europeans and a few Chinese and later some Malays abused their privileges by taking Aboriginal women away out of their tribal district. 'It is the taking away of the women that has been the cause of so many white men having been rubbed out,' wrote Alfred Searcy, customs officer and noted early author on the Territory.[670] Young women were particularly vulnerable.

> Dear Sir – Can you inform me which is the safest method to adopt to secure the services of a native woman. I noticed on a late visit to some of the mining townships that it is becoming the rule amongst a certain class of the community to adopt one of these native women and try to civilise her after their own idea of civilisation.

Thus wrote a correspondent to the local newspaper, and the editor replied:

> We have heard white men, who considered themselves civilised, deliberately make a boast of how they had scattered a camp of aborigines, singled out a woman and followed her until she has been compelled to climb a tree to escape being outraged.[671]

Sometimes then to be forced down at the point of a rifle.

The second provocation was the 'bad deeds' the strangers did to the land. Whatever the invaders might say about it being a dismal

---

668 Warland to Cockburn 19/4/1886, p. 4 (N.T.I.L. 452/1886).

669 For a careful study of contacts between Aborigines and Macassans see C.C. MacKnight, *The Voyage to Marege Macassan trepangers in northern Australia*, Melbourne University Press, Melbourne, 1976.

670 Alfred Searcy, *In Australian Tropics*, Kegan Paul Trench Trübner, London, 1907, p. 173.

671 *North Australian* 29/2/1884 leader and p. 3.

place, a last miserable corner of God's earth, the Territory was for the indigenous people not only the source of their sustenance, but the explanation and justification for their existence. Without the land, life became incomprehensible. Not surprisingly, when stock polluted their sacred water holes and miners honeycombed their sacred lands, they struck back with tough, resourceful responses and adaptations. By far the most common response was to burn the grass. They stampeded cattle, ambushed and speared lonely teamsters bringing stores, harassed and killed miners, learnt how to shape iron and glass tips to enhance the deadliness of their spears. They also learnt how to procure wire from the overland telegraph for tips of their spears, without getting a shock, by allegedly throwing waddies at the line. They blocked the path of overlanders. The response of the relatively few invaders, sometimes scattered over a wide area, was to resort to shock tactics. A noted overlander later recalled how:

> I let six stag-hounds go and away they went towards the rising moon. Then we heard a stampede like a mob of cattle breaking through scrub, then a native yelling for about five minutes, then all was quiet.
>
> About ten minutes later the stag-hounds came back to camp and were tied up again. They were covered with blood …
>
> In the morning I went out to where I heard the yelling … About 400 yards from the camp there was a native lying dead with his throat torn out … there was blood on their tracks for two or three hundred yards further afield.[672]

And so the intermittent war went on, with the scales gradually tilting towards those with superior technology. South Australian governments reacted with confusion. They were nonplussed by the hostility of the north-coast natives compared with those they knew, or thought they knew, in the settled areas of South Australia. In 1878 the South Australian government sent north three Aborigines from the Peake district to become trackers, native police and positive role models. Inspector Foelsche, who was a stickler for order, welcomed them as trackers but would not accept them as police.

---

672 Extract from the Reminiscences of Ralph Milner in the *Evening Star* NZ 24/8/1927, courtesy Russell Pugh, New Zealand. Full reminiscences, apparently written earlier, are now lost.

Government Resident Price claimed that unlike many other parts of Australia, the indigenous population seemed to increase in the face of invasion.[673]

Most of the local settlers, and many administrators, saw the conflict with the original owners as a battle for survival in an increasingly populous world over the world's most precious commodity – land. Their attitude was later summarised in a saying: 'The thing about land, is that God is not making any more of it any more'. The struggle over land was compounded by the view that hunter-gatherer economies were a wasteful use of a limited resource. The Europeans saw land as property – even property which you could destroy. There was little understanding of the profound spiritual significance the original occupiers saw in land. Nor did they understand the Aboriginal idea that like the air we breathe land is too important to be possessed.[674]

Towards the end of the 1870s notions of 'evolution' began to displace the old dream of Christianising and civilising the Aborigines. The immutable laws of history (so went the theory) favoured those with the superior technology for survival in a competitive, precarious, constantly changing universe. According to the laws of nature, the indigenous peoples were expected to resist. 'We are invading their country,' wrote the *Northern Territory Times*, 'and they have a perfect right to do – and it is but natural that they should – do their best to obstruct our passage through it.'[675]

With this approach Aborigines were defined rather by their relationship to other species, than by their relationship to God: 'Without any definite religion Government, or Laws,' explained the governor to the Colonial Office in London, 'they have deeply-rooted customs, and regard with the utmost jealousy any intrusion upon their haunts, the territorial limits of which are well understood.'[676]

Enhancing the notion that Aborigines were members of a dying race was the common observation that large numbers of indigenous people died from introduced diseases like influenza and measles.

673 Price to Blyth 8/3/1878 (N.T.I.L. 178 of 1878).

674 Conversations with Lewis Yerloburka O'Brien, elder of the Kaurna people, 2002.

675 *Northern Territory Times and Gazette* 27/11/1875, p. 3.

676 Fergusson to Granville 8/12/1869 (G.O.D. 59 of 1869).

But it was conveniently forgotten by many whites that Aborigines were superior to Europeans in their resistance to other diseases like food poisoning. The truth is that in the Territory, as in many colonial situations, disease often favoured the invaders over local peoples, because Europeans brought with them exotic diseases for which indigenous peoples had not yet built immunity, and so germs became more lethal than guns.

James Stokes Millner, the kindly doctor and a source of stability in early Palmerston. He was passed over for Government Resident and drowned with the wreck of the *Gothenburg* in 1875. (*Australasian Sketcher* 17/4/1875, p. 8. Courtesy of the State Library of South Australia)

Most officials of the South Australian government, however, took a strong stand to protect Aborigines against outside exploiters such as Macassan fishers trading in alcoholic spirits and pearling captains trying to recruit Aboriginal divers. In 1882 an agent for Barnums Circus, Robert A. Cunningham, a Californian musician and showman, arrived in the Territory from Singapore, seeking live Aborigines to exhibit in an American freak show as examples collected from the Antipodes of Primitive Man. To increase their drawing power, Barnum planned to exhibit them as 'bestial

Australian cannibals'. After much cajoling, Cunningham managed to obtain four local Larrakias. But Dr John Scott Wilson, acting as Protector of Aborigines, said he 'refused to let them go'. The persistent agent countered that Wilson could not prevent them, because they were British citizens exercising their free choice. This sent the Government Resident scurrying for advice from Adelaide law officers, who eventually ruled the Protector could not lawfully 'refuse to let them go'. Meanwhile, the Government Resident insisted that before leaving they must first confront the Protector as well as the head of police (Inspector Paul Foelsche), who dissuaded the Larrakias from leaving with horrendous tales about what might happen to them. On hearing these tales, all the alarmed Larrakias fled into the bush. Cunningham hastily headed south to Queensland where, apparently meeting little or no government interference, he obtained nine Aborigines from Hinchinbrook Island and Palm Island.

According to Roslyn Poignant, who wrote a book about the fate of these 'bestial Australian cannibals', the prejudice against indigenous peoples was just as bad in California as North Queensland. One of the so-called 'Captive Lives' taken by Cunningham from Palm Islands in 1883, a man dubbed 'Tambo', was found embalmed, apparently for exhibition, in a funeral basement in Cleveland, Ohio, in 1993.[677]

677 Wilson to Parsons 22/12/1882 with Minutes (N.T.I.L. 40/1883); Research Notes by Roslyn Poignant, curator of the exhibition 'Captive Lives', 1999; Roslyn Poignant, *Professional Savages, Captive Lives and Western Spectacle,* Yale University Press, New Haven, 2004.

CHAPTER 5

EXTREME SOLUTIONS

The Northern Territory settlement went on consuming like a 'Voracious White Pachyderm', to use the elaborate language of the day. By 1874 it was costing the significant amount of £30,000 a year to keep the elephant alive.[678] The policy of waiting for something to turn up was proving too expensive to continue.

Out of the need for revised policy came various attempts to relaunch the Territory, but always within the framework of the old system so as not to offend people with vested interests or to clash with South Australia's own growth as a colony.

On one point at least it was not hard for everyone to agree. The first obvious need was for people. The problem was how to attract people without having to offer them free land or a free passage, the first of which was unacceptable to the first purchasers, the other to South Australian taxpayers.

Over the 1870s three episodes gave hope they would trigger a flood of self-supporting immigrants and so revive separate development. The first was the discovery of gold at Yam Creek and Pine Creek in 1872. Next, the government tried an official policy of laissez-faire, opening the flood-gates of North Australia to South-East Asian migration and trade, and so incorporating the Territory in the sphere of the Indies. Of a different order were the government's attempts to make use of religious contacts, where economic motivation was seen as a proven failure. All involved extreme solutions.

---

678 Northern Territory Revenue and Expenditure to September 1877 (S.A.P.P. 10A of 1877). £30,000 was considered a very large sum of money at the time – calculated as five shillings for every adult person.

The Discovery of Lochac

> 'Nothing but gold can save the Northern Territory.'
> Captain Hart's Diary, 18 January 1866

In 1873 the respectable citizens of Adelaide lost the level-headedness for which they were in their own estimation noted. In spite of the warnings of their newspapers and government, and the sneers of their neighbours, they embarked on one of the strangest examples of mass hysteria and frenzied speculation in the history of any Australian colony.

In the bitter months which followed, thoughtful citizens diagnosed certain causes for their uncharacteristic behaviour. There was a surplus of money at the time, asking to be invested. And ever since gold rushes had made Victoria the premier colony in the early 1850s, South Australians had dreamed of doing the same. Already the colony's history was studded with gold discoveries, breathlessly compared with Bendigo and Ballarat, that fizzled out as mere 'surface signs'.

The idea that great mineral treasures lay hidden somewhere on the north coast had its roots far back in legend. When the Venetian traveller Marco Polo skirted the rim of South-East Asia in about 1290 on his return journey from China, he heard tales of the land of Lochac, a wild country, little visited by strangers, 1200 miles south-east of Java, where 'Gold is abundant to a degree scarcely credible'. This was the distance of the Australian coastline. In other ways too, Polo could have been hearing about North Australia. The inhabitants were said to be linguistically distinct, isolated, wild and set against all strangers – supposedly to conceal their great wealth.[679]

The land of Lochac was never entirely forgotten. Early New South Wales convicts dreamed about it in their misery, and a few brought upon themselves a terrible doom when they tried to find the gold beyond the Blue Mountains. No sooner had South Australia taken steps to acquire the Territory in 1863 than Bendigo diggers

679 Marco Polo, *The Book of Ser Marco Polo the Venetian concerning the Kingdoms and Marvels of the East,* trans. H. Yule, Third Edition, Murray, London, 1903. Book III, Chapter 7.

were pestering for the privilege to go there.[680] One old navigator even offered to point out the likely locality where the gold would be found.[681] Another secret correspondence told how a group of scurvy-stricken sailors foraging for water near the Roper had once found a creek 'flowing over immense blocks of quartz, thickly studded with gold.'[682] In 1872 the *Australian Town and Country Journal* in Sydney, after weighing up the evidence, concluded:

> It is, in our opinion a reasonable conclusion to draw that the Port Darwin Territory is part of the country described by Marco Polo under the name Lochac.[683]

The deduction made news in eastern colonies newspapers as well as the Adelaide *Register*.

Another source of the idea that the Great South Land was immensely auriferous came from early European navigators in the Indies in the 1500s, especially the Portuguese. The origins of the Portuguese tales are lost, but it is possible they were influenced by Chinese map makers who had sailed this quarter of the globe 70 or more years before the Portuguese. The preoccupation with gold was also possibly influenced by the Jesuit idea that God had planted El Dorados around the world to entice the spread of Christian civilisation.[684]

However, the stories were passed down. Centuries later three expeditions in search of gold set out from the settled areas of the Territory towards Blue Mud Bay on the western side of the Gulf of Carpentaria where, according to lore, rich deposits abounded. The first commenced in June 1874, when two eccentric gold-seekers, Permain and Borrodaile, set out alone with five Timor ponies in an easterly direction via Port Essington toward the Roper River. The men were never seen again. A search party led by John Lewis

---

680 Applications for Country on North Coast (S.A.P.P. 122 of 1863).

681 Pasco to Ayers 10/3/1864 (C.S.O.I.L. 372/1864).

682 *Chronicle* 6/2/1904, p. 33.

683 *Australian Town and Country Journal* 10/8/1872; *Register* 26/8/1872, p. 5; *Melbourne Daily Telegraph* 17/8/1872. Has misquoted the original source as the *Sydney Empire*.

684 *Advertiser* 25/3/1876, p. 10; see problematic text: Gavin Menzies, *1421 The Year China Discovered the World*, Bantam, London, 2002.

and later one led by Inspector Foelsche and Gilbert McMinn, a surveyor, failed to find any trace of them. The foolhardiness of this venture left doubts about the rumour that one or other of these men had once been African explorers. Stories about their fate circulated for years. According to evidence gathered by Inspector Foelsche from an East Alligator Aboriginal man, somewhere near Obiri or Tor Rock 'the natives speared the ponies first, ate them and then killed the two men cooked them on the fire and devoured them'.[685] The story needs supporting evidence given the tendency of some Aboriginal groups to demonise others further out. According to another Aboriginal grape-vine the explorers were robbed and then killed, but to the end refused to hand over their precious books (including the Bible) and papers. Whatever happened, no trace of them or their ponies was ever found.

A year later, 1 June 1875, a second party of five prospectors, according to the Government Resident 'hardy, experienced and resolute men', set out from the Union Reef. Their main interest was alluvial gold which was in short supply in the Territory. They were harassed all the way by Aborigines they thought were cannibals. The white men kept the Aborigines at bay with their guns. Two of the party were wounded, while the leader, Walker, was struck by a stone-headed spear and bled to death. He was buried on the beach at Blue Mud Bay. Near the Gulf the remaining men found what they mistakenly thought were the burnt remains of Permain's and Borrodaile's lost expedition. Four of the five horses lent by the Government Resident died. Always they were too much on the defensive to find the hidden gold.[686]

A third expedition influenced by the old stories chose a safer route, by sea. In September 1875 a well-equipped party of five men led by Joseph Lorence (possibly of Portuguese extraction) sailed around the coast in the schooner *Woolner* lent by the Government Resident. At Port Essington they picked up eight Iwaidja men under Jack Davis, a famous Aboriginal adventurer who had been

---

685 Foelsche to Lewis 5/6/1880 (S.L.S.A. Mortlock P.R.G. 247/2); Scott to Bundey 16/11/1874 (N.T.I.L. 427/1874); *Northern Territory Times and Gazette* 20/3/1875, p. 2.

686 *Northern Territory Times and Gazette* 27/11/1875, p. 3; *Advertiser* 1/1/1876, p. 11.

to China, who offered to take them to a place of gold, and show them the stone remains of an ancient settlement. This expedition too was a failure. The various Aboriginal guides, uncorrupted by money, could not tell the difference between stones and gold. And so the myth of hidden riches somewhere in the Territory continued unproven right down to Lasseter who, in 1930, claimed to have found a great reef of gold somewhere in Central Australia. He died trying to rediscover the site.[687]

Few people would have believed these legends whole-heartedly, but the fact that there *were* hints and rumours of gold in the Territory helps explain the ease with which citizens swallowed the incredible stories spread about in 1872 and 1873.

In 1870 specks of gold were found in the *Kohinoor's* ballast after it had been dumped at Port Adelaide.[688] The ballast consisted of stones picked up indiscriminately in Port Darwin harbour, and scores of excited people went down to view them. Hardly had the surprise subsided when stories came to hand that the men on the overland telegraph were finding minute traces of the metal everywhere, and that only by withholding rations could the workers be kept at the job at all. The most improbable rumour insisted that for 70 miles an ounce of gold was taken from every telegraph hole dug.

The next year, as a result of telegraph construction, an actual gold field was found, so good according to its discoverers that it promised to support a thousand miners at £4 to £6 each a week. The site, at first kept a close secret, lay 'about 150 miles down the line' from Port Darwin, beyond the Number 2 Depot. One of the discoverers was young Joseph Darwent, a nephew of the Darwent of the telegraph construction firm of Dalwood and Darwent. Other discoverers were Charles Slater and William Carter. Overjoyed by the prospect, Government Resident Douglas, proclaimed (as others were already thinking) that 'the presence of the precious Metal appears to be almost universal'.[689]

---

687 Scott to Ward 15/11/1875 (N.T.I.L. 588/1875); *Advertiser* 25/3/1876, p. 10; see entry on Lasseter in *Northern Territory Dictionary of Biography* Vol. One, editors Carment, Maynard, Powell, NTU Press, Darwin, 1990; *Lasseter's Diary*, Angus & Robertson, Sydney, Facsimile, 1986.

688 *Register* 27/4/1870, p. 5; Blyth to Douglas 3/9/1870 (N.T.O.L. 176/1870).

689 Douglas to Blyth 20/5/1871; Darwent to Douglas 17/5/1871 (N.T.I.L.

News of the discovery reached Adelaide in July 1871, when the recalled contractors returned with their telegraph party. Immediately a deputation, representing 55 Adelaide capitalists including Dalwood, Darwent and Stuart's patron John Chambers, waited on the government to urge that John Sibley Westcott, a Bendigo and Californian prospector then working in the colony, should be sent north to test if the stories were true.[690] The startled ministers, fearful that the telegraph work would be further disrupted, refused to help the deputation, tried to water down enquires coming from as far afield as New Zealand, but did take the precaution of appointing the chief surveyor in the Territory, George MacLachlan (Goyder's nephew), as gold warden governed by the laws already existing for the rest of South Australia.[691]

The appointment suited Douglas, who had no sympathy toward the overland telegraph. He immediately sent the new warden on an official gold-hunting expedition to the Pine Creek area where, sure enough, traces of gold were found in every test hole put down. (One of the party of gold-hunters, C. Gandy, was a nephew of Colonel Light's mistress.) After three weeks washing, MacLachlan and his men had found more than five ounces of gold. 'There is no doubt,' he reported accordingly, 'but there are large deposits of gold in this Territory.' The cautious Scot then warned against a rush of ill-equipped and ill-provisioned diggers to such a remote part of the world. Douglas, on the other hand, called on capitalists and diggers everywhere to turn their footsteps north toward this new and promising field.[692] In Adelaide, Governor Fergusson fell into line, writing to England that:

115/1871); Behrendt to Blyth 20/7/1871 (N.T.I.L. 175/1871); *Register* 21/5/1872, p. 12.

690 Morphett etc. to Blyth 23/7/1871 (N.T.I.L. 173/1871); *Northern Territory Times and Gazette* 17/5/1879, p. 3.

691 Blyth to Milne 14/7/1871 (N.T.O.L. 368/1871); Deering to Peterswald 20/7/1871 (N.T.O.L. 390/1871); Blyth to Douglas 20/7/1871 (N.T.O.L. 391/1871). The *Northern Territory Times* journalist Alonzo Brown later described Westcott as the father of Territory mining.

692 Douglas to Blyth 29/8/1871; MacLachlan to Douglas 21/8/1871 (S.A.P.P. 126 of 1871); for an overview of Northern Territory mining see Timothy G. Jones, *Pegging the Northern Territory: The History of mining in the Northern Territory, 1873–1946*, Northern Territory Government, Darwin, 1987.

> Although Mr Douglas may be too sanguine of the richness of the field, I have no doubt that a considerable number of persons will soon resort to the Northern Territory for the purpose of searching for gold, and once any immigration takes place the Settlement cannot fail to progress.[693]

The discoveries in themselves did not unsettle the careful South Australians. It took the ingenuity of the share rigger to achieve that. The 55 capitalists, after they had suffered a rebuff from the government, tried to form a prospecting company by public subscription, but Adelaide's citizens refused to join them. Next the entrepreneurs took to haggling with the government for pioneering concessions, particularly a guarantee that in the event of gold being found they could take out leases of 120 acres, provided each was more than five miles apart and capital at the rate of £450 for each lease was expended in searching or equipment.[694] Only after certain concessions were promised and certain leading capitalists (especially Edward Meade Bagot) had put their own money into the venture, did the public begin to invest and the Northern Territory Gold Prospecting Company Limited was launched. And only after that, following careful preparation, did John Sibley Westcott's prospecting party set out on the *Alexandra* on 7 February 1872 on one year's contract, ceremoniously farewelled by John Chambers and bearing a blue-silk, gold-fringed flag handsomely inscribed by Miss Priscilla Chambers: NO. 1 GOLD CLAIM, NORTHERN TERRITORY.[695]

As soon as the expedition reached Port Darwin, it struck inland toward Pine Creek, an area reported to be auriferous, the men laying out their tracks and putting up makeshift bridges as they went. At Yam Creek in July they discovered what appeared to be a rich quartz reef, which Westcott called the 'Priscilla'. This reef became the centre of much of the mining fever to follow. In early

693 Fergusson to Kimberley 11/10/1871 (G.O.D. 53 of 1871).

694 Coates to Reynolds 20/12/1872 (N.T.I.L. 395/1872); *Advertiser* 28/3/1873, p. 3.

695 *Register* 17/2/1872, p. 10; Members of the NT Gold Prospecting Company expedition who left by the *Alexandra* 7/2/1872 were: J.S. Westcott (leader), A.R. Hulbert (second in command), J.L. Noltenius (third in command), P. Valentine, P. Hyland, C. Tymn, H. Roberts, W. Boord, H. Hauschildt, M. Littlefield (cook).

1873 John Chambers and Captain George Newman (originally from Victoria), who had been selected as mining manager, supervised the construction of battery stampers in Melbourne and some months later the first rock was crushed and tested.[696]

Meanwhile, a second prospecting party made up of 15 men (with five horses and a wagon) had been organised in the former mining town of Kapunda and was sent out on the *Claymore* in June 1872 with provisions and equipment for five months. The leader, John Ford, wired on arrival to warn others against following until information about the gold was better established, but events soon overtook his caution.[697]

By July 1872 prospects for the Territory appeared better than at any stage since settlement began. The completion of the overland telegraph was now in sight, and the area's natural resources, it seemed, would compensate for choosing an inept system of colonisation. Then, eight days after the line was officially opened, a startling message was received in Adelaide:

> Port Darwin August 30, 8.5 p.m.
> An auriferous reef discovered near Yam Creek Telegraph Station has been traced a distance of about three miles (stop) Gold is visible to the naked eye for 150 yards (stop) Ten claims have already been pegged out (stop) Great excitement prevails amongst the prospectors (stop).[698]

It was the first of an avalanche of telegrams and reports that helped transform the cautious efforts of the pioneer prospectors into a gold mania, particularly in Adelaide. Gold manias were not new in the Australian colonies. What made this one complicated was that it then split into two parts. There was a rush of gold diggers mainly from Melbourne and a rage of gold speculation among capitalists in Adelaide.

The rush came first, set off partly by the activities of Victorian

696 *Register* 7/9/1872, p. 10; G.M. Newman, *The Northern Territory and its Gold-Fields*, *Advertiser* Adelaide, 1875.

697 *Register* 22/6/1872, p. 5; 10/8/1872, p. 11; *Kapunda Herald* 21/6/1872; Members of the Kapunda team who left by the *Claymore* 23/6/1872 were: John Ford, W.C. Pledge, J. Robertson, W. Kelley, F. Craig, J. Galloway, D. Radford, L.J. Hoskings, G. Gooch, W.G. Goodchild, F.B. Oldham, T.D. Hines, A. Buchanan, C. Crisp, T. Barrett.

698 *Register* 31/8/1872, p. 5 Telegraphic Despatches.

shipping agents. Even before the famous telegram, early in August the barque *Condor* was laid on in Melbourne to take telegraph equipment north. Finding the passenger list filling slowly, an enterprising agent called a public meeting to draw attention to the gold prospects of the Northern Territory, with such success that the *Condor* left with 120 excited diggers heading for a new El Dorado.[699] Melbourne storekeepers began selling soft felt digger hats labelled PORT DARWIN STYLE, while the local papers fanned the flames with extravagant news items, at the same time curiously accusing the South Australian government of inciting a rush in order to attract settlers.[700]

Early in September 1872 the steamship *Omeo* left Melbourne for Port Darwin. Its official task was to bring back the telegraph builders. It carried north 100 more diggers – who were so disappointed when they got there that many waited on the Government Resident for a free passage out.[701] When this was refused some threatened to plunder the local stores.[702] The diggers hailed from California, Chile, Cornwall, Mexico, New Zealand, Victoria and New South Wales. Most came without adequate provision for food and shelter, or horses to get to the reefs. They found little alluvial gold, which had been the mainstay of most Australian fields available for ordinary diggers. Trapped and resentful, they spent the wet season in shanties around the town. The dry season brought more miners and an outbreak of fever. Some men never left Port Darwin. They lay huddled in their humpies shaking with ague.[703] Others moved inland to the reefs, only to find their path crossed by different problems.

In Adelaide, the extravagant telegrams and news of the departures from Melbourne triggered a rush to establish gold companies to gain possession of the wealth before others did. By

699 Passenger Lists of Ships leaving Melbourne 5/8/1872; (Victorian State Archives); *Register* 22/8/1872, p. 5.

700 *Register* 4/10/1872, p. 5.

701 Passenger Lists of Ships leaving Melbourne 7/9/1872; Passenger Ships Outwards Register 7/9/1872 (Victorian State Archives); Harriet W. Daly, *Digging, Squatting, Pioneering,* pp. 140 to 145.

702 *Register* 22/10/1872, p. 5 Telegraphic Despatches; *Advertiser* 29/10/1872, p. 2 Telegraphic Despatches.

703 Harriet W. Daly, *Digging, Squatting, Pioneering,* Chapter XIV.

April–May 1873 a frantic speculation in gold shares broke out among common people unaccustomed to gambling on the stock market. By August there were nearly 60 registered companies jostling for the few available reefs. There was even a Jewish company financed by the local Jewish community in Adelaide that brought Vaibien Louis Solomon (later a famous Territorian) to the Territory. Crowds gathered at Port Adelaide to farewell a little armada of ships bound for the promised land, beginning on 20 April 1873 with the *Coorong* – initially hired by three companies (Kapunda Yam Creek, Telegraph Gold and Palmerston Gold) – followed by the *Linn Fern*, *Atlante*, *Gothenburg*, *Birchgrove*, and *Omeo*. The *Nerio* left in more guarded circumstances with a load of gun powder for blasting.

A key South Australian figure in the speculation was John Lewis, father of Essington Lewis later of Broken Hill mining fame, who had contacts with many leading Adelaide families and acted as their agent in the Territory, pegging out claims and making on-the-spot deals. At one stage he was agent for 16 of the 60 odd companies. He also occasionally contributed to confusion by sending telegrams to Adelaide in code to trap the unwary: 'buy' for 'sell', 'east' for 'west'. The new communications technology could be, he realised, used to put people off the scent.[704]

The speculation in gold drained money from general circulation in Adelaide, spreading it too thinly over too many companies for effective use. According to two detailed studies in the *Register* newspaper (attributed to Charles Mann, member for Burra), half a million pounds, or £6 for each adult person, was eventually sacrificed by the public, and the loss so affected the supply of cash that banks took advantage of the situation to raise the price of money. Yet hardly a single company was strong enough to pursue operations successfully. As a general guide, continued the *Register* survey, the experts in these matters in Victoria considered £20,000 a bare minimum to start reef-mining operations. The 12 largest companies averaged called-up capital of only £10,000 each, the remainder a little over £3000 each. Many of these smaller enterprises were simply swindles perpetrated by company promoters and

704 Diaries of John Lewis 1872 and 1873 *passim* (S.L.S.A. Mortlock P.R.G. 247/7/4); John Lewis, *Fought and Won*, Thomas & Co, Adelaide, 1922 Chapters X, XI, XII, *passim*.

Gold mining Territory style. Many captains parked their equipment on the beach and proceeded to live it up at company expense.
(*Portonian* 29/11/1873, p. 4. Courtesy of the State Library of South Australia)

brokers who trafficked in shares. In 21 of the 48 smaller companies the promoters grabbed half of the shareholders' money in bonuses.[705]

In the Northern Territory, the proliferation of gold companies 'before *one mine* was *tested*' (to quote the manager George Newman) led to fierce jostling for the available reefs.[706] Some claims were taken out on proven reefs at Yam Creek and Pine Creek, but others were in the middle of submerged swamps. Many mining captains dumped their equipment on the beach between Fort Hill and Point Emery, then went to live it up in the hotels at company expense. The consumption of alcohol soared. According to Newman one manager at the Howley mine had to be secured on a long chain during working hours so he could not reach his wine cask. Except by the pioneer parties gone before, little effort was made to test the so-called mines, and as the year wore on suspicion grew that it was not in the interests of the various companies to do so. 'I most decidedly give my opinion,' wrote the chief gold warden, referring to the stronger companies:

705 *Register* 19/4/1873 leader; 9/5/1874 leader.

706 G.M. Newman, *The Northern Territory and its Goldfields*, *Advertiser*, Adelaide, 1875, p. 8.

> that the Northern Territory swindles beat them out of the field. Claims have been taken up, telegrams reported, as shewing quantities of surface stone thick with Gold, and which claims in some instances had neither Quartz nor Gold – but are in the Wet season a swamp with a foot or so of water, in the dry a caked surface like brick, and a little true stone shewing on the surface. Stone has been sent to Adelaide, its approach telegraphed, and great expectations raised; the stone taken from the boxes; inspected by crowds, crushed with great result, and in some of these cases not a stone had come from the claim itself, but had either been borrowed or stolen.[707]

The most celebrated scam was the Morning Star Swindle, involving a mine near Brocks Creek. Discovered by 'two Queenslanders on horse-back, leading a packhorse' – one man was allegedly called Seale, the other Rabbich. It was floated in September 1873 after rich samples of gold were exhibited at the Palmerston Bank, and attracted leading South Australian investors, such as Thomas Reynolds, William Whitfield Mills and William McMinn, who said that he would not sell his own shares in the mine for £40,000. The mine was vouched for separately by mine managers Captains Paul and Newman, after a preliminary investigation. The company was wound up in June 1874 at a stormy meeting after it had been discovered that much of the lease was under water, the shaft had fallen in and the original mine had apparently been salted by Queensland prospectors, some of whom had disappeared.[708] The scam illustrated a famous definition of goldmining (blamed on Mark Twain): 'a hole in the ground owned by a liar'. A few months later one of the promoters was drowned with the wreck of the *Gothenburg*, giving considerable satisfaction to those investors who had lost their money and could not forgive.

One of the eccentrics of the mining boom was Captain William Carne Paul, who dressed immaculately in cool white clothes and

707 Conner to Scott 1/1/1874 (N.T.I.L. 59/1874, p. 5).

708 *Northern Territory Times and Gazette* 7/11/1873, p. 2; 14/11/1873, p. 2; 5/6/1874, p. 3; 12/6/1874 leader; 19/6/1874, p. 3; 26/6/1874 Carmichael to Editor; 3/7/1874, Newman to Editor; *Alfred Giles Reminiscences* pp. 19, 20 (S.L.S.A. Mortlock P.R.G. 1389/2); *S.W. Herbert, Early Experiences in the Northern Territory 1870–1873*, p. 177 (S.L.S.A. Mortlock D6995(L)).

a large pith helmet. Attended by his servant, he went around on horseback carrying a large white umbrella over his head.

Not all those involved in mining were scoundrels or eccentrics. Some were genuinely stunned by the wild state of the country and the want of transport. Repeated complaints, by way of apologies for doing nothing, were sent to Adelaide and deputations of anxious capitalists in Adelaide pestered the government for roads, bridges, jetties, a reef doctor, a gold warden, and, most of all, cheap Asian labour. In contrast few companies were set up in Victoria, at the time considered the experts on mining.

But that was not the end of the difficulties. In the jostling for reefs, the Adelaide capitalists and the diggers – mainly from Victoria, where there still existed a population of miners looking for the next El Dorado – clashed head-on over the miners' traditional right to 'jump' improperly worked claims.

The institution of jumping, which was well-known to the Victorians, provided that any digger holding a Miners Right could peg out a counter-claim on someone else's pegged area if the conditions of tenure were not being met. The obvious purpose was to keep the occupiers on their toes and to prevent absentee shepherding for ulterior or speculative ends. As most Adelaide companies occupied the reefs for no other reason, while many people not accustomed to speculating in shares had put their savings into these ventures and felt apprehensive for their money – agitation sprang up in South Australia for legislation against the Victorian interlopers.

The campaign against the jumpers was greatly helped by the muddling of the law-makers, resulting in two years of confusion. The rapid succession of mining laws were so badly drawn up and had to be revised so often that it was all too easy for interested parties in parliament to slant the legislation in their favour. 'So very badly drawn that it is almost impossible to put any intelligible construction on many of its provisions,' wrote Attorney-General Mann in 1873 of the latest piece of bad legislation.[709] Even today there is confusion about the meaning of some of the regulations.

Mining in the Australian colonies was based on two main

---

709 Minute by C.M. 25/9/1873 (N.T.I.L. 272/1873)

principles: the democratic Miners Right, useful in surface, mainly alluvial mining, and the Mining Lease for deep, mainly reef mines requiring considerable capital – generally taken out by companies. The question was where to put the emphasis. The Miners Right provided that any miner, no matter how poor, who had paid a small annual fee could peg out a small claim on Crown Lands providing no one got there first. If however a claim was not being worked it could be 'jumped'. The Mining Lease provided that lease-holders, having paid a much larger sum, could take out a much larger area for a number of years, provided they met the conditions. Otherwise, according to some interpretations, they too could be jumped by the many holding a Miners Right.

The first gold was discovered under a South Australian goldmining Act of 1870–1871, parts of which had been copied from Victorian legislation. There were confused references to the 'almost mystical concept' of the Miners Right and by implication all the judge-made laws and procedures which had grown up around the principle of the Miners Right in Victoria.[710] Adding to the confusion, new regulations loosely attached to this Act were gazetted in December 1871, which included special provisions for leases above the 26th parallel inserted to meet the demands of the so-called 'pioneering companies' – under which they then took out their leases. These special conditions provided for goldmining leases up to 40 acres. There were also liberal requirements for the employment of labour and the expenditure of capital, which were almost certainly *ultra vires*, i.e. beyond the powers allowed by the Act.[711]

In 1872 the South Australian government, guided by Thomas Reynolds, who saw gold as an excellent way to attract population, decided to incorporate this Act with suitable modifications into a consolidated Northern Territory Land Act so that intending settlers would have all the necessary land laws in one book. In making the modification, the emphasis was shifted to the Miners Right, because Reynolds believed it had worked well in attracting settlers to Victoria where it was never forgotten that mining had transformed

710 S.A.P.A. 26 of 1870–1871.

711 Regulations *S.A. Government Gazette* 21/12/1871, p. 1826 *seq.*

that colony in a few years. Despite the new emphasis on the Miners Right, the Mining Lease was kept for deep quartz mines. Those so-called 'pioneers' who had already received their lease under liberal provisions of the former Act were still to be treated liberally, even down to liberal extensions if they failed to meet the labour and capital conditions. But all subsequent leases were to be strictly enforced. As a result, new regulations were gazetted in December 1872 demanding strict expenditure on capital and labour, details of which were taken in part from the former Act – again almost certainly *ultra vires,* i.e. beyond the powers allowed by the Act. It was the first step leading to three years of utter confusion.[712]

For some strange reason (and contributing to the confusion), notification that the old Act had been repealed and replaced by another (the consolidated 1872 Land Act) was not sent north to Palmerston. Perhaps someone withheld it in order to protect the interests of some Adelaide speculators; or it was sent, then concealed by Captain Douglas in order to protect his family's and certain local interests.[713] As a result, between December 1872 and May 1873 decisions were made under laws already extinct, and the stage was set for chaos should anyone try to revoke them.

The first gold warden, Henry Dudley Melville, a diligent public servant, arrived in December 1872 and, not aware of the change, faithfully continued to make decisions under the repealed 1870–1871 Act. He set up his Warden's Court in a tent at Yam Creek with a low salary and wretched conditions and became the scapegoat for much of the confusion to follow. His main instruction was to grant 20-acre leases, with no conditions, on the payment of the first year's rent and other expenditures if he was satisfied the claim had prospects. He was ordered to act cautiously, which meant that in July he was able to refuse to approve a claim by Captain Douglas (ex-Government Resident) until it was properly investigated; reminding him that he had once blocked Melville's promotion in the customs department.

Melville's main problem, however, came because unknown to him the new 1872 Act expressly forbade granting the very leases

712 S.A.P.A. 28 of 1872 Part V; Regulations *S.A. Government Gazette* 26/12/1872, p. 1848 *seq.*

713 *Advertiser* 6/10/1873, p. 3 Reynolds to Editor; General Report of Staff at Palmerston 18/7/1873, General Minute 20, Enclosure B (N.T.I.L. 173/1873).

the old Act – under which he was still working – had encouraged. When this became known in the Territory in March and April, almost everyone turned on the gold warden in person and blamed him for the mistakes, including the politicians. There was a clamour to sack him. Even before the mistake was known, D'arcy Uhr (later secretary of the Northern Territory Prospecting Association) wrote: 'I wish to let you reign as long as you left me alone' (sic).[714] Melville described his nine months as warden as the most dangerous and difficult of his public career, after which no one ever wanted to promote him again.[715]

When news of the confusion eventually reached Adelaide in April 1873, parliament was in recess and the city was abuzz with the prospects of Northern Territory gold. The first news indicated that Victorians were jumping unworked claims on the grounds that the labour and capital clauses were not being met. Worse, individual jumpers were turning up having been issued with more than one Miners Right – a practice blamed on Douglas when Government Resident. A deputation waited on the acting Commissioner of Crown Lands (Wentworth Cavenagh), and the government, influenced by the public's involvement in share speculation, drafted a new set of stop-gap regulations which increased the maximum size of the claims and in practice swept away threat of forfeiture for companies or individuals not employing labour or working on the reefs.[716] Whatever the real intention, the new regulations were seen in the other colonies and by most people in the Territory as a blatant attempt to keep outsiders off the better fields.

A few months later parliament met and confirmed the government's action by passing a new gold-mining Act (the third used in under two years), the *Northern Territory Goldmining Act*, (18 of 1873), which removed the sacred and democratic Miners Right to jump improperly worked claims and made the more permanent Mining Lease the centre of the system. The Act set up an Absolute Tribunal, consisting of the Government Resident (George Scott), the stipendiary magistrate (Edward Price) and a new functionary,

714 Uhr to Melville 8/2/1873 (N.T.I.L. 260/1873).

715 Reminiscences of H.D. Melville Volume 4 (S.L.S.A. Mortlock D6976(1–5)(L)).

716 *Register* 22/4/1873, p. 6; *S.A. Government Gazette* 8/5/1873, p. 684 *seq.*

Samuel J. Way QC was called in to help resolve the mess into which gold legislation had fallen in the 1870s.
(George E. Loyau, *Representative Men of South Australia*, Howell, Adelaide, 1882, wood engraving by Jeffrey Bruer)

the chief warden (soon to be announced as Mountiford Longfield Conner), to adjudicate in title disputes. There was no right of appeal against this tribunal, which was directed by its terms of reference to rule in favour of the first of the contending occupiers.[717] This meant ruling in favour of the original holder against the would-be jumper. An angry Melbourne *Argus* correspondent wrote that the move 'had one guiding star, namely, to legislate for a few South Australians'.[718] The responsible minister, William Henry Bundey, replied:

> the great complaint was that the legislation of this colony had been for South Australians as against others. Now, he certainly thought that they who had borne the brunt should derive some benefit, and he thought *that* was hardly a subject upon which the House or the Government could be censured.[719]

In trying to resolve the confusion, Attorney-General Mann had obtained special legal opinion from Samuel Way, QC, one of the

717 S.A.P.A. 18 of 1873, Part II, III, IV; S.A.P.D. 1873 c.631 to 635.
718 *Register* 10/7/1874, p. 6.
719 S.A.P.D. 1874 c. 1088.

colony's foremost legal experts.[720] But the confusion would not be resolved – and more complications followed.

The legislative barriers protecting Adelaide companies were now firmly raised – all that remained was to break the news in the Territory. The new Act finalised and gazetted, the minister in charge sent a telegraph message to the gold wardens instructing them to put aside all title disputes as a Special Tribunal for this purpose would be set up in March. But he worded the telegram so strangely that it actually ordered the closing down of the Warden's Court altogether – to which the new chief warden, Conner, a former Victorian who disapproved of the legislation, replied by leaking the contents to the mining public. The government could hardly have contrived a worse way of introducing an unpopular piece of legislation. Enraged citizens in the Territory felt that they were being somehow robbed of their gold and that the arbitrary closing of a court of law deprived them of British justice. A public meeting was organised at Palmerston, during which one rabble-rouser, a lawyer called 'Smith' (Villeneuve Smith), talked of erecting barricades and repulsing the troopers as men had once done at Ballarat. The meeting was followed by others on the reefs, and the worried Resident warned his government about a 'considerable danger' of open violence.

When the full details of the 1873 Act became known in March 1874 by sea mail the uproar broke out again.[721] The two gold wardens, Mountiford Conner and Walter Frampton, complained that its effect would be to drive the good miners from the Territory, and the new chief warden, Conner, as a member of the Absolute Tribunal, continued to pass judgements in favour of the jumpers.[722] More embarrassing still, he published his reasons in the newspaper.[723]

720 Advice by S. Way (N.T.I.L. 52/1874). The various regulations were so confusing that there were (and still are) different legal opinions as to what they meant.

721 Closing of Wardens Court—correspondence (S.A.P.P. 121 of 1874); *Northern Territory Times and Gazette* 16/1/1874 leader and p. 3; 23/1/1874, pp. 2 and 3; 30/1/1874, pp. 2 and 3; 20/3/1874 leader; 27/3/1874, p. 2.

722 Scott to Everard 12/1/1874 (N.T.I.L. 10/1874); Scott to Everard 26/6/1874; 29/6/1874 (N.T.I.L. 180/1874); Bagot to Bundey 10/7/1874 with enclosures (N.T.I.L. 247/1874); Scott to Bundey 15/7/1874 (N.T.I.L. 263/1874).

723 Scott to Everard 22/6/1874 (N.T.I.L. 162/1874).

The effort to launch the Territory through the attraction of gold had stumbled from crisis to crisis – with three Acts and four sets of regulations in use in three years. The diggers were angry. They formed the Association of Mining Jumpers to defy the law and take over the reefs according to their own interpretations of justice. As the wardens appeared sympathetic and the police were few and silent, this required no special daring. Scott, the Government Resident, suspected a conspiracy between diggers, wardens and police, but could not prove it. 'I verily believe,' wrote the Resident, 'that if there had been a large population on the mines there would have been a riot.'[724]

Then the rains came. Everything changed in a few weeks. Gold speculation collapsed like a house of cards, saving the political situation. Speculators and diggers alike at last began to agree on one thing – and they turned on the wretched Territory with fury.

'That Insatiable Maelstrom'

> When this old hat was new,
> 'Tis more than six months since,
> We brokers daily grew
> As rich as any prince;
> But business now decays,
> And sales are small and few;
> 'Twas diff'rent in the days
> When this old hat was new.
> *Northern Territory Times and Gazette,* 5 January 1873

With the Wet season gold speculation collapsed. Companies everywhere were soon in liquidation, the dissenting gold wardens, Walter Frampton and Mountiford Conner, were eventually made to resign, and a stream of complaining diggers was leaving the country. According to Melville, Victorian and Queensland diggers were particularly bitter. The peak year of speculation had been 1873, and in November 1873 there were about 1750 immigrants,

724 Scott to Everard 11/3/1874 (N.T.I.L. 121/1874).

mostly European, in the Territory. By September 1875 the European population was down to 403.[725]

Having encouraged the outsider to leave, the Adelaide companies suddenly found that they had no interest in Lochac themselves. Thanks to unwanted company speculation, the dream of Thomas Reynolds and Captain Douglas to use the magnet of gold to attract settlers to the Territory had caused the opposite to happen.

In November 1873, five of the best prospectors to reach the Territory – Adam Johns, Phil Saunders, Sandy Grant, Tom McBride and Samuel Meaker – teamed up to develop the Union Reef, which eventually yielded (so it was said) over 4000 ounces, which tempted some desperate, hopeful diggers to try to jump their claim. But once the panic set in, not even discoveries like this could turn the ship around.[726]

Mining in the Territory became a low-key affair, punctuated by sporadic outbursts. Three of the stalwarts who helped carry the industry after the collapse were the brilliant Chinese merchant and miner Ping Que, who had made his reputation in the Ballarat area; the enigmatic Adam Johns (son of Isaac), chairman of the Northern Territory Mining Board; and the American John Sibly Westcott whose brother was a supreme court judge at Tallahassee in Florida. Westcott and Johns later died on the job in the Territory, but Ping Que returned to China just in time to leave his bones in his ancestral village.[727]

After the collapse, the genuine companies tried to combine resources, but they were always too short of capital to venture far from known territory. Almost all the mines were clumped in five areas within a few miles of the safety of the telegraph line: at Stapleton 38 miles from the meagre settlement of Southport and a mile and a half east of the line; Howley, 80 miles from Southport and five miles west; Yam Creek 90 miles, and four miles east;

725 Scott to Ward 25/9/1875 (N.T.I.L. 409/1875); *Register* 10/7/1874, pp. 5 and 6, Reynolds to Editor.

726 Timothy G. Jones, *Adam Johns Prospector, Miner and Explorer of the Northern Territory 1840–1896*, privately printed, Canberra, 2004.

727 Timothy G. Jones, *Ping Que – Mining Magnate of the Northern Territory 1835–1886*, privately printed, Canberra 2002.

The Union 122 miles, and five miles east; Pine Creek 128 miles (considered the limit of the goldmining country), almost on the line.[728] Each mining area was backed by a string of pubs.

The second Government Resident at Port Darwin, George Byng Scott, arrived just in time to see the tide running out and to suffer the slings and the arrows of disappointed inhabitants. The mining companies were accused of doing everything round the wrong way: providing a surplus of capital before obtaining labour, sending expensive machinery before having the means to transport it inland, so it was left rotting on the beach.[729] During Scott's administration from November 1873 to June 1876 the criticism was consistently proved correct.

In 1873 mining managers flocked to Port Darwin, ignoring the lack of transport and communications. There were no safe jetties, no roads, no bridges over the rivers and few teamsters. Between 1874 and 1876 Scott's greatest single contribution was to provide all these necessary links too late. At Palmerston he built two landing causeways where men had drowned trying to beach heavy mining equipment. He cleared part of the beach of rocks and constructed a road and sea-wall around Fort Hill. At Southport on the southern extremity of the harbour, he completed a jetty that became the headquarters for lonely teamsters going to the reefs. Best of all, over many months he caused a substantial road to be made which included seven bridges and reached all the way to the mines.[730] But before these amenities were completed, most of the miners had left.

Nowhere was the change of tide better illustrated than by the issue of Asian labour. On 23 December 1873 C.J. Coates, secretary and lobbyist for many Northern Territory companies (backed by

728 *Northern Territory Times and Gazette* 25/9/1896, p. 3; Timothy Jones, *Ping Que Mining Magnate of the Northern Territory*, privately printed, Canberra, 2002; C. Clement & P. Bridge, (eds) *Kimberley Scenes*, Hesperian, Victoria Park, 1991, p. 59; Chief Warden Plunkett First Report 5/2/1875 (N.T.I.L. 143/1875).

729 Conner to Scott; Frampton to Conner; Scott to Everard 2/6/1874 (N.T.I.L. 222/1874); Scott to Bundey 25/8/1874 (N.T.I.L. 366/1874); Plunkett to Scott 30/1/1875 (N.T.I.L. 143/1875); Scott to Ward 23/11/1875 (N.T.I.L. 593/1875); Knight to Scott 15/4/1876 (N.T.I.L. 208/1876); Price to Ward 15/5/1877 (N.T.I.L. 282/1877).

730 Knight to Scott 17/9/1875 (N.T.I.L. 450/1875); *Northern Territory Times and Gazette* 1/7/1876, p. 3 Scott's speech.

Edward Meade Bagot, leading investor, and John Lewis who had briefly returned to Adelaide) called a public meeting in his office in Register Chambers, Adelaide, to agitate for cheap imported labour to save the collapsing mining industry in the Territory – otherwise, claimed Coates, there would be a total failure. The proposal to import indentured labour was well-received by the meeting, the only debate being whether to employ Chinese, Malays or freed Negro slaves from America. The Chinese won out, and a delegation waited on William Everard, Commissioner of Crown Lands, on 5 January 1874 to ask him to obtain 200 Chinese coolies, experienced in mining, from the islands near China.[731]

The minister delayed taking action until April, a few weeks before parliament was due to meet, so that the move could be announced as a government initiative. On 2 April he sent a letter to Coates seeking guarantees to these questions: in the event of the government recruiting indentured labour, which companies wanted coolies? how many did each want? 'and whether they would subscribe to the agreement ordinarily entered into by employers of coolies as regards rations, wages, and return passages of the men to their own country'?[732]

As soon as he could, which was Monday 20 April, Coates called together a well-attended meeting of mining representatives in his office. Captain Douglas (briefly returned from the Territory) took a leading part in the discussions, lauding the magnificent quartz reefs and advocating Chinese coolies from Singapore because they were of superior quality. John Ford, one of the first Northern Territory prospectors from the Kapunda group, was invited to speak.

The companies wanted the government to employ the coolies to work on public works and then to subcontract the men to mining companies whenever the need arose. The government disagreed. It would only contract the Chinese if the companies first guaranteed to employ the workers on the mines and undertook to refund the government for the cost of obtaining them. The company representatives then went away to consult the shareholders.

---

731 *Register* 23/12/1873 leader; 24/12/1873, p. 4; 6/1/1874, p. 5; *Advertiser* 24/12/1873, p. 2; 6/1/1874.

732 Deering to Coates 2/4/1874; Deering to Coates 14/4/1874 (S.A.P.P. 65 of 1874).

Before this meeting took place Captain George Newman, manager of the original Northern Territory Gold Prospecting Company, had wired Bagot:

> This matter most important. On the proper selection of these men greatly depends the future of this country. If a large number of Chinese required, they should be culled from different districts in Victoria.

But Douglas as chief adviser had over-ruled the advice, for his own reasons.[733]

At a second meeting, held in Coates's office a week later, 13 companies pledged to take a total of 365 Asians despite Coates's previous advice to the minister that they had money enough for only 150.[734]

While the directors were still canvassing their shareholders, Coates, in consultation with the minister and Ned Bagot (who had risked more money on Territory gold than anyone else), on 22 April recommended that Captain Douglas should be appointed immediately as recruiting agent, so that he could leave next day by the outgoing mail for Singapore. Even before returning to South Australia Douglas had been angling for such a job, because he was looking for work back in the Indies. His appointment is proof of his persuasiveness. It caused much resentment in the Territory.

When Douglas reached Singapore four weeks later he found his task was not as easy as expected. He brought a contract with the government of South Australia that guaranteed each labourer two months pay in advance, a standard rate of eight shillings a week plus food, and a free passage home at the end of two years. Most of the Chinese, however, were suspicious of exploitation – which led Douglas later to advise that this first shipload must be treated well, otherwise the supply would dry up. Many of the willing were rejected because they suffered from disease or belonged to criminal gangs (some had been branded). Eventually 187 workers were coaxed to sign and organised under 11 head men – each of whom was to be paid a salary of £5 a month, and they maintained order

733 G.M. Newman, *The Northern Territory and its Goldfields,* p. 12.

734 Coates to Everard 21/4/1874; Coates to Everard 28/4/1874 (S.A.P.P. 65 of 1874); *Register* 21/4/1874, p. 6; 23/4/1874 leader; 28/4/1874, p. 6; *Advertiser* 21/4/1874, p. 3; 28/4/1874, p. 2.

by kicks and sticks. The contract allowed for 108 chests of opium, but no pigs: they flourished all too well in the Territory. An eastern trader, the steamer *Vidar*, was hired to convey the men to Port Darwin. Later it turned out that some had been shanghaied aboard because they owed money to Chinese merchants, who snaffled the men's advance payment of £40 with which they were supposed to establish themselves in the new country. It was also discovered that some of the men (perhaps a fifth) suffered from syphilis, which led Thomas Guy, the doctor accompanying Douglas, to believe healthy workers had been replaced by less healthy after the required medical examination.[735]

Meanwhile in Adelaide, on 13 July, the new and first minister for the Northern Territory, William Henry Bundey, met Coates to remind him of the deal – that the government as the primary contractor intended to subcontract the coolies to the companies; that the companies would be expected to refund the government the initial cost of procuring the labour (later estimated at £9 6s 6d per head); and that it would be a *sine qua non* for the companies to pay the agreed wage and provide adequate food and medical attention. Bundey, a practical lawyer, also emphasised that each company would be given the option to buy at cost from the government six months supply of the food, such as rice, that was brought with the coolies from Singapore. All this was reported to a meeting of directors in Coates's office on the 16 July at which there was no hint of the problems to come.[736]

By the time the *Vidar* reached Port Darwin on 5 August the speculation boom was rapidly cooling, and most of the mining companies that had promised to take the coolies were running low on money with which to pay them. As the Government Resident put it: 'The companies liquidating and not paying the coolies wages due to them.'[737] Many Chinese workers were underpaid, or not paid at all. Some were starved, employers consoling themselves that a Chinaman needed practically no food to live. Some were put in prison. Over the next two years about 30 died. Some took off to

735 Coates to Everard 22/4/1874 (S.A.P.P. 65 of 1874); Douglas to Scott 5/8/1874 (N.T.I.L. 364/1874); Douglas to Bundey 24/8/1874 (N.T.I.L. 424/1874).

736 *Register* 17/7/1874, p. 7; *Advertiser* 17/7/1874, p. 3.

737 Scott to Bundey/Everard 28/1/1875 (N.T.I.L. 135/1875).

do their own mining or grow their own vegetables. Many were sent back to Port Darwin. Almost half finished up working for the Government Resident at some stage on projects such as building a landing at Fort Point.

When the Chinese first arrived, 18 tents were set up in or near Cavenagh Square in what became known as the Coolie Camp. Many returned there to found Darwin's first permanent Chinatown. The Government Resident, George Byng Scott, after complaining that he had more coolies than he knew what to do with, wrote: 'These people clamoured for "Coolie Labor" and when they got it they take the benefit of three or four months work and six months rations and then cut the poor fellows adrift without a farthing and scarcely a rag to their backs. They also complain that they were not well fed.'[738]

In October 1875 Bundey's next important successor as minister, Ebenezer Ward, reported to parliament that one company only had met its contract, and £2600 was still owing by the mining companies. The venture in his view had failed.[739]

Despite all these difficulties, according to separate newspaper reports about a third of the Chinese eventually became excellent settlers as independent miners, merchants and gardeners. Indeed, their success against great odds caused some whites to fear that the Chinese were naturally adapted (such as by a mechanically more efficient body) to succeed in conditions where Europeans were a proven failure. 'They have been invaluable to my Department,' reported the Supervisor of Works in late 1874. When their contract expired at the end of two years only 21, most of them 'useless', chose to go home.[740]

Over the three years starting in 1874 the reaction against the wretched Territory was so strong, it seemed settlement could never survive. The place was branded an 'insatiable maelstrom', and it was said that people would rather put their money into Turkish bonds. Bagot, who expected £50,000 a year from his mining investments

---

738 *ibid.*

739 S.A.P.D. 1875 c.1406 Northern Territory Estimates. John Cox Bray stood in for a few weeks between Bundey and Ward.

740 Price to Ward 1/8/1876 (N.T.I.L. 288/1876); Knights report on public works 28/11/1874 (N.T.I.L. 511/1874).

Edward Meade Bagot lost a fortune on Northern Territory gold and never made up the loss. Ten years later he was found dead in mysterious circumstances at the bottom of a quarry at Yatala.
(*Pastoral Pioneers of South Australia* by R. Cockburn. Vol II, p. 24, 1927)

in the Territory, was forced to sell five pastoral stations to meet his debts. He never made up the loss, and died later at the foot of a cliff in mysterious circumstances. After 22 months three-quarters of the white population left.[741]

Most of the miners remaining had been carried there on a flood of golden promises, then left behind too poor or commercially compromised to leave. They were angry, broke and from many backgrounds. The domestic history of the expected pre-eminent colony became a round of personal feuding. 'Though a man

741 *Register* 9/5/1874 leader; *Northern Territory Times and Gazette* 19/8/1876 leader; Scott to Ward 25/9/1875 (N.T.I.L. 409/1875); *Register* 10/7/1874, pp. 5 and 6 Reynolds to Editor; George Byng Scott's Reminiscences of life in the Northern Territory during his term of office as Government Resident 1873 to 1876, p. 2 (S.L.S.A. D7478(L)).

may have lived forty years without having ever appeared in any Court,' wrote the editor of the *Northern Territory Times*, 'yet it is impossible for him to live in the Northern Territory for even a few months without becoming mixed up in some Court affair – libel, manslaughter, or something of the sort.'[742] Court records bear this out. Even when in June 1876 G.B. Scott thankfully took his leave of the place, one clique organised a feast to welcome the Government Resident's successor while another held a banquet to bid him farewell.[743] This fractiousness was enlivened by the free use of spirits, which became the only buoyant item of trade. The Government Resident (Scott) once petitioned for a mechanics institute so citizens could hold their indignation meetings in a loftier atmosphere than was provided by the five local pubs.[744] 'The consumption of ardent spirits,' he once explained, 'is truly awful and necessarily impairs the health and energies of the people, and many of them condemn the country and are dissatisfied with it when they should blame themselves.'[745]

In 1876 there was widespread destitution. Food became scarce and penniless miners begged for public work or a free passage out of the country. A few took to collecting rags and even bouilli (or Booyoolee) meat tins to extract the solder. When the Larrakias learned this craft, not even the town billy cans and quart pots were safe. By June prospects looked dismal indeed, and the local newspaper confessed 'that some action must speedily be taken by our rulers, or the Northern Territory must cease to exist'.[746]

'The Laissez-Faire' – Let the Market Decide

Following the failure to attract settlers with gold – over the mid-1870s the South Australian government turned to a new policy that came to be known as 'the Laissez-Faire'. The new policy began with the appointment of a new minister specifically responsible for

---

742 *Northern Territory Times and Gazette* 29/8/1874, p. 3.

743 *Northern Territory Times and Gazette* 1/7/1876, p. 2.

744 Scott to Everard 10/3/1874 (N.T.I.L. 112/1874).

745 Scott to Ward 15/6/1876 (N.T.I.L. 294/1876).

746 Scott to Everard 28/3/1876 (N.T.I.L. 138/1876); Scott to Everard 28/3/1876 (N.T.I.L. 137/1876); *Northern Territory Times and Gazette* 10/6/1876 leader and 12/8/1876, p. 1.

William Henry Bundey was the first minister in charge of a distinct Northern Territory portfolio. He launched the laissez-faire policy, throwing the north coast open to South-East Asian migration and trade and making it attract its own migrants and capital, or die a natural death.
(*Frearsons Weekly* 6/7/1878, p. 144. Courtesy of the State Library of South Australia)

the Northern Territory and was developed by following ministers. Between October 1874 and February 1877 three strategies were introduced aimed at re-launching the Territory as part of South-East Asia. These policies were to advertise the Territory's potential to the north; to open a free port; and to launch a regular shipping link to the East.

The confusion associated with the gold fever forced governments to set up a separate Northern Territory portfolio as a first step to straightening out the mess. In August 1873 the South Australian government under Arthur Blyth introduced legislation to create a sixth junior minister to take some of the lesser work off his seniors. Ten months later in July 1874 a self-educated lawyer (and later Supreme Court judge) named William Henry Bundey was appointed the government's sixth minister, in charge of the minor portfolios of Education and the Northern Territory.[747]

747 S.A.P.D. 1873 c.144, c.511; S.A.P.A. 5 of 1873; Minutes of Executive Council S.A. 2/7/1874.

Bundey inherited the backlog of neglect left by his predecessors. Since the Goyder survey, responsibility for the Territory had been palmed on to the Commissioner of Crown Lands, in whose office it had often been neglected. After taking his post, the new junior minister was directed by his seniors in Cabinet to revive the Territory using the principles of separate development by opening the settlement to influences from the Eastern Archipelago and by reducing its dependence on South Australia. In October 1874 Bundey took the first steps toward advertising the Territory's prospects in the overcrowded islands of Mauritius and Java. He offered on behalf of his government a £1000 bonus for the first hundred tons of sugar grown and manufactured in the Territory, had the liberal plantation clauses of the 1872 Land Act separately printed, and requested the British governor in Mauritius and the Dutch governor-general in Java to advertise the Territory's prospects in their respective domains.[748] The naivety of the approach was later apparent.

In June 1875 Ebenezer Ward became the new minister in charge of the Territory. In his hands the efforts to establish separate development reached fruition – indeed, they even became honoured with a title: the 'Laissez-Faire'. 'Let the market decide' was the catch-cry. It was now conveniently remembered that in 1863 the Ayers–Hart government had consented to colonise the Territory only on the understanding that it would be settled mainly from the islands and lands to the north.

Not for the last time would politicians, uncertain what to do next (or with no good ideas to inspire them), turn to the magic of the market to take the problem off their hands.

The new minister was the same Ebenezer Ward who in 1864 had been sent out of the Territory like a schoolboy in disgrace. It says a lot for the mobility of colonial society that having been a vandal, Ward was now called upon to try his hand at reconstruction. Between times, Ward had remained in South Australia and used his power as a journalist to tread the road to prominence. During his career he was associated with a string of country newspapers, became editor of Adelaide's *Daily Telegraph*, and founded two

748 De Mole to Boothby 26/10/1874 (N.T.O.L. 210/1874); Bundey to Scott 5/11/1874 (G.R.I.L. A585).

local newspapers, the *Northern Guardian* and the *Farmers Weekly Messenger*. In 1870 he entered the House of Assembly, where he established a reputation as an erratic and brilliant politician, and the best speaker in the House. But most of all, he built up a reputation as the farmers' defender and friend. He was particularly noted for his radical ideas about taking land from the squatters and selling it to poor farmers on easy credit. He represented a new parochial force in South Australian politics: the farmer or Cocky class (the so-called cockatoo farmers), who wanted their taxes spent on local roads and railways and schools, and who resented public expenditure on the Northern Territory. Ward had also become identified as the staunch advocate of the elder statesman (in the colonial sense of the elder), James Penn Boucaut, who now rewarded him with a junior portfolio. It was said that Boucaut gave Ward the job to keep him out of trouble.[749]

To head Ward in the right direction Boucaut sent him a note:

> Memo for the Minister of Agriculture & Education: It has occurred to me that the Government of South Australia ought now either to take some more active steps for the Northern Territory or else to give it up altogether. As it stands it is a continual drag upon the resources of this Province and no credit to its Government ...[750]

Ward took his job seriously. He brought to Cabinet a series of recommendations, the gist of which was to cut spending on the Territory to bedrock, fling open its doors and windows to the north, and make the country attract its own labour and capital or die a natural death.

When the third Government Resident (Edward Price) left Adelaide in June 1876 to take up his appointment, Ward secretly told him that he thought the odds were in favour of it dying a natural death.[751]

---

749 Minutes of Executive Council S.A. 3/6/1875; G. Searle and R. Ward, *Australian Dictionary of Biography* Melbourne University Press, Carlton, 1976, Vol. 6 pp. 351 and 352.

750 Memo For the Minister of Agriculture & Education: Boucaut to Ward 6/7/1875 (N.T.I.L. 292/1875).

751 *Register* 24/3/1883, p. 6 Price's speech; *Northern Territory Times and Gazette* 10/3/1883, p. 2.

With characteristic energy and equal lack of tact, Ward set about reducing staff and establishments to a minimum. Several official positions were combined, such as Government Resident and special magistrate, while others were abolished altogether. There was a general reduction in salaries. Those officers objecting were encouraged to go. Even the horses would have to live on 'bush hay' in the future. The retrenchment caused a head-on clash with the second Government Resident, George Scott, who telegraphed to Ward: 'I have faith in the country and respectfully recommend govt. to show faith also and not to reduce the staff to a minimum.'[752] It also encouraged Scott in his determination to get out of the tropics, especially since Ward kept accusing him of passive resistance, being incompetent, wasting money and appropriating specimens from the experimental garden for his own domestic purposes. In April 1876 Scott could bear it no longer. He wrote threatening to relieve himself of his post if the government would not do so for him, and soon he was replaced by a former stipendiary magistrate on leave from the Territory: Edward William Price, a lonely man who had lost his wife Minna and their five children earlier in the wreck of the *Gothenburg*, and was quite prepared to take up exile at a reduced wage beside the Timor and Arafura seas.[753]

About the same time as the need for economy was announced, the government (pursuing the Laissez-Faire policy) announced its decision to make Palmerston a free port. Behind the scenes, the ministers began to explore ways of linking the port to Batavia by means of a regular shipping service. Free trade was one of the most controversial aspects of separate development, especially with Adelaide merchants, because it put merchants in all other ports, being nearer, at an advantage. It was first introduced in 1864 as a prime pillar of independent development in order to encourage trade with Asia, but was given up when the gold potential made it appear that the Territory could yield South Australia some public

752 Ward to Scott 25/8/1875 (G.R.I.L. A1031); Scott to Ward 25/8/1875 (N.T.I.L. 383/1875); Ward to Scott 3/11/1875 (N.T.O.L. 321/1875); Ward to Scott 3/11/1875 (N.T.O.L. 323/1875); Scott to Ward 15/9/1875 (N.T.I.L. 451/1875); Scott to Ward 26/11/1875 (N.T.I.L. 602/1875); Scott to Ward 10/7/1875 (N.T.I.L. 296/1875).

753 Scott to Ward 24/4/1876 with enclosures (N.T.I.L. 215/1876).

Robert Dalrymple Ross, parliament's expert on the Empire. He believed that they had blundered disastrously by following the wrong example of colonisation, preferring the precedent set by Stamford Raffles in Singapore.
(*Pictorial Australian* March 1885, p. 56.
Courtesy of the State Library of South Australia)

revenue. Now it was reinstated in the hope that free trade might one day help make Port Darwin an entrepot centre like Singapore. 'The making of Port Darwin a free port would attract to the Northern Territory the very class we wanted there,' said Ward. 'If it became a commercial *entrepot* for the commerce of the islands, as Singapore had been in the past, the result would show that the policy was the best that could be carried out.'[754] Robert Dalrymple Ross, member for Wallaroo, strongly supported the measure. Governments had blundered disastrously, Ross argued, by following the wrong examples in colonisation. They had tried to make land disposal the main moving force in settlement. Instead they should have

754 S.A.P.A. 6 of 1864; S.A.P.D. 1875 c.201.

taken notice of the principles laid down by Sir Stamford Raffles for Singapore and made commerce and free trade the prime mover, with land disposal coming in due course. The result of their mistake was only too painful to behold.[755]

Ross, son of a West Indian plantation owner, had served as an imperial administrator in West Africa and Hong Kong, been aide-de-camp to Governor Daly, was son-in-law of pastoralist John Baker and was considered parliament's expert on the East Indies and empire matters in general. In imagining another Singapore on the southern extremity of the East Indies, Ross was echoing the ideas of his distant relative Alexander Dalrymple of the East India Company, who in the 18th century wanted a commercial centre in North Australia to counter-balance the increasing Dutch control of trade in the Indies Archipelago.

Meanwhile, in a series of newspaper articles published in England and copied in Australia, Lieutenant-Colonel George Palmer (one of the original colonisation commissioners in London responsible for founding South Australia in 1834) lectured the colonials on where they had gone wrong. In keeping with the idea of the great central colony or state, he wanted Port Darwin to be the entrée to Asia at the head of an overland railway reaching from north to south, with the project supported by the resources of a federation of Australian colonies. It was an idea well ahead of its time.[756]

In June 1876 Ebenezer Ward took charge of the country above the 26th parallel for a second term (replacing William Everard who had taken over for a short time), and the politicians' efforts to develop the country, and take it off their hands, advanced a stage further with a final strategy under the Laissez-Faire policy: the joining of Palmerston to Batavia by a regular shipping line.

The moves to join Port Darwin to the Dutch Indies coincided with efforts by the Dutch governor-general to link the East Indies to Australia. Previously shipping contact had been haphazard, as Dillon Cox and his relatives found when they wanted to move their enterprises from Batavia to Port Darwin.

---

755 S.A.P.D. 1875 c.345 to 348; 361.

756 *Northern Territory Times and Gazette* 28/10/1876 leader.

The first regular shipping service from Adelaide to the Territory had been introduced by William Bundey as a result of the gold mania. This was a service run every ten weeks by McMeckan, Blackwood and Co. of Melbourne that went along the east coast from Port Adelaide to Port Darwin. It started operating in November 1874 when the *Gothenburg*, which had already made several private trips north, left Port Adelaide. As the route was hazardous and fares high, there was some truth in the claim that the northern capital was harder to reach than old London.[757]

With the end of this first contract in sight, Ward called for alternative tenders to run between Port Adelaide and Port Darwin or alternatively Port Adelaide and Batavia calling at Port Darwin. But only one tenderer offered and his price was too high. Ward then asked the Queensland government to permit its new Torres Strait shipping line, running between Sydney, Brisbane and Batavia, to call in at Port Darwin, but the Queenslanders refused because it would cause delays.[758] While various possibilities were being considered, the agents for the famous Netherlands India Steam Navigation Company produced an offer to negotiate a service by private agreement, providing it was subsidised by the Dutch and South Australian governments.[759] In 1874 the same company, encouraged by a subsidy of £12,500 a year from the Netherlands–Indies government had made two trial runs – the *Jason* departing Batavia in May and the *Atjeh* ('a magnificent steamer') in July – aimed at circumnavigating Australia anticlockwise beginning at Fremantle and ending at Port Darwin. A third planned trial trip beginning at Port Darwin and ending at Fremantle never took place. But apart from Western Australia (and to some extent South Australia), the response from the various governments was disappointing. The dream of a service that would circumnavigate the continent and link Australia to the Indies was abandoned by the Netherlands India Steam Navigation Company, which now asked

757 Bundey to Scott 15/1/1875 with agreement enclosed (G.R.I.L. A713); *Advertiser* 25/3/1876, p. 11; *Northern Territory Times and Gazette* 17/6/1876 leader.

758 S.A.P.D. 1876 c.568 to 571.

759 S.A.P.D. 1876 c.569 to 570; Acraman Main and Co. to Ward 17/7/1875 with enclosures (N.T.I.L. 305/1875).

the South Australia government to help subsidise a route that would cover the eastern half only.[760]

Ward's response was favourable and so negotiations began. While the terms of the new contract were being worked out, the government approved a temporary service between Port Darwin and Java, that was largely the result of local initiative. In September 1876 a Dutch islander, *Egeron* of the Banda Steam Navigation Association, came to Port Darwin with an offer to run a regular monthly service to Sourabaya in Java, calling at intervening islands and acting as advertiser as it went. The offer was applauded by the Government Resident, local merchants and citizens alike, all of whom urged the minister in Adelaide to subsidise the vessel at least for six months until a major service could be started. The request was agreed to, pamphlets were prepared by the merchants, and the old screw steamer made four and a half shuffling trips, nearly always behind time, before the Government Resident terminated the service because on a previous run the captain had broken the contract by deviating to Singapore.[761]

The new agreement with the Netherlands company was signed and ratified, and in February 1877 the first steamer, the *General Pel* under Captain de Hart, made an inaugural run, reaching Port Darwin in March. The contract provided for five trips a year for five years from Batavia to Port Darwin and then via the east coast to Port Adelaide and back again. Governments in South Australia and Java supported the venture with subsidies of £1,666 13s 4d each per round trip.[762] As it turned out, the different reasons for their interest were not always compatible.

The Dutch colonial government saw the arrangement as

---

760 Correspondence relating to Northern Territory and Torres Straits Mail Service (S.A.P.P. 112 of 1874); Acraman Main and Co. to Ward 17/7/1875 (N.T.I.L. 305/1875); *Chronicle* 6/6/1874, p. 15; *Register* 17/8/1874, p. 4 Shipping Intelligence.

761 S.A.P.D. 1876 c.1341; *Northern Territory Times and Gazette* 30/9/1876, p. 2; Price to Ward 22/9/1876 (N.T.I.L. 388/1876); Price to Ward 26/9/1876 (N.T.I.L. 397/1876); Price to Ward 29/9/1876 with enclosures (N.T.I.L. 398/1876); Copy of Agreement made with owners of *Egeron* (N.T.I.L. 74/1877); Price to Ward 19/1/1877 (N.T.I.L. 52/1877); Price to Ward 12/3/1877 (N.T.I.L. 131/1877); Price to Ward 28/3/1877 (N.T.I.L. 146/1877).

762 S.A.P.D. 1876 c.568 to 571.

a way of fostering trade and commerce (but not emigration) between the two empires. For it, Port Darwin was the first and least important port; its eyes were set instead on Brisbane, Sydney, Melbourne and Adelaide. The South Australian government saw it as a ferrying service able to carry planters and their employees from the overpopulated Indies to the empty north coast of Australia. The prime concern was for people. 'With mail communication to the Eastern Archipelago,' said Ward, 'we might anticipate a vast increase of population calculated to settle successfully in the Territory.'[763] What impressed the South Australian politicians was the possibilities the arrangement opened up. For ten years the Dutch had been making Batavia the centre of a shipping network reaching to the major ports of South-East Asia. Along these routes via Batavia to the great southern continent population was now expected to flow.

Already a small Malay colony of about 30 nondescript fishermen had come down by the occasional ship to work mainly as domestic servants and local crewmen. Their presence in Palmerston, however, had been a mixed blessing, their camp near Bennett Street being one of the most fruitful sources of fights in the town. One reason for this was that they had only one woman between them and the self-proclaimed leader, 'Abdoolah the Arab', alias Hubeeb Abdoola, who really was a Turk, complained of how his countrymen connived to send him regularly to gaol in order to share the favours of Mrs Aboolah. His wife was later named as Miti Dowah, a Christian. From prison he even sent his friend Luie to catch out Miti practising as a prostitute out of Mrs Dillon Cox's house – difficult to prove. The fracas outside the house at midnight finished up in the police court. Hubeeb denied rumours that he had once tried to sell his Malay wife with her grateful cooperation to one of the Malay men for £22 9s 6d.[764]

Three laissez-faire schemes had now been introduced, aimed at attracting planters and capital from the neighbouring islands: advertising, a free port, and a regular shipping service. When they failed to attract much attention in places like Java and Mauritius, the

763 S.A.P.D. 1876 c.1751; 568 to 571.

764 *Northern Territory Times and Gazette* 26/9/1874, p. 3; 3/10/1874, p. 2; 11/12/1875, p. 2; Petition Hubeeb Abdoola 15/9/1876 (N.T.I.L. 437/1876).

The loss of the *Gothenburg* in 1875 became a symbol for Port Darwin's remoteness. (*Illustrated Adelaide News,* September 1875. Courtesy of the State Library of South Australia)

South Australian government decided to redouble its efforts – as it turned out, with *unintended consequence.*

In October 1877 the government was defeated and Neville Blyth (known as 'the reluctant politician') took charge of the Territory portfolio – the fifth politician to do so in three years. In a memorandum to Cabinet he proposed to increase the force of the advertising in the two overcrowded areas already being concentrated on. He also raised the possibility of approaching the British Emigration Agent at Hong Kong to see if family emigration could be arranged from China. The first proposal was accepted by Cabinet but, because of the risks involved, the second was deferred for further careful investigation.[765]

Blyth and his colleagues then set about improving the advertising by being more specific. They approached respectable mercantile firms in Java, Mauritius and the neighbouring island of Bourbon and asked them to act as their agents, providing them with publicity material pointing out the Territory's gold potential, the sugar potential, the proximity to the main ports of South-East Asia and the recent regular shipping service. They asked the agents

765 Memo by Blyth for the consideration of Cabinet 7/11/1877 (N.T.I.L. 565/1877).

to bring these advantages before the planters and capitalists, and waited.[766]

The publicity was given short shrift in Java, where those consulted denied there was any such thing as overpopulation on the island.[767] '… the Dutch Government,' observed Price, 'unfortunately do all they can to discourage emigration from the overpopulated island of Java'[768] (which practice did not stop the Dutch for many years after dumping destitute Europeans from Java on Port Darwin). But the forceful advertising created some excitement in Mauritius, where the publicity fell upon receptive ears, particularly those of the poor.

Since the government first advertised in 1874, efforts to attract settlers had been based on a wrong understanding of conditions in Mauritius and the neighbouring island of Bourbon. The French agent in Bourbon explained:

> But we have here two classes of inhabitants and planters: the *riche* and the poor.
>
> The first class want not to change and whatever may be the protection and advantages granted to them, they shall never consent to leave this country.
>
> The poor planters have no means to under-take an *establissment*, and even to pay passages and expenses …
>
> We then conclude that your plan cannot be realized nor here nor at Mauritius where things stand quite the same …[769]

For over 40 years the little island of Mauritius had been drifting toward a dangerous state of affairs in which the French-speaking plantocracy owned almost all the means of production and the Indian workers had become impoverished and crowded – by 1871 they were two thirds of the population. For most of the plantocracy, the naive invitation to come to the wild coast of North Australia to improve their fortunes must have seemed strange indeed. They

---

766 Suggested Correspondence to Commercial Firms 15/11/1877 with Minutes (N.T.I.L. 564/1877); Blyth to Lauratet and Le Roy 1/12/1877 (N.T.O.L. 373/1877).

767 Peet to Blyth 23/2/1878 (N.T.I.L. 203/1878).

768 Price to Ward 19/1/1877, (N.T.I.L. 52/1877).

769 Lauratet and Le Roy to Blyth 5/2/1878 (N.T.I.L. 210/1878).

enjoyed a sophisticated French provincial life-style, drank the finest wines and lived in beautiful chateaux. But the poor were a different matter. The English and French newspapers jumped to the conclusion that failing to get rich planters, the Australians would happily assist the passage of poor farmers and so they gave the proposals widespread publicity. The misconception was not unreasonable, for South Australians were known to assist immigrants to their southern shores and in their publicity they kept referring to their own generosity.[770]

In June 1876 the 'Father' of the Indian population in Mauritius (father in the sense of defender), Adolphe de Plevitz, arrived in Sydney with plans, even the necessary agreement form, for the communal migration to the Territory of about 2000 skilled Indians accustomed to working on plantations.

De Plevitz had already been commended by the Anti-Slavery Society in London for his defence of indentured Indian labourers in Mauritius. The acquisition of Mauritius by the British after the Napoleonic Wars had resulted in the eventual abolition of slave labour from West Africa in 1834 and its replacement a year later by indentured labour from India. But given the entrenched attitudes of the French-speaking planters, these indentured workers were treated little better than slaves. They were underpaid (by collective agreement between the planters), harassed by the police and imprisoned. Their rights to a return passage were removed. When they refused to renew their contracts – arbitrarily increased from three to five years – and preferred instead freedom and relative poverty, they were subjected to harsh pass laws.

De Plevitz had migrated from France via the Cape of Good Hope in 1858. He was descended from the petty nobility of Europe, and was idealistic, energetic and over-zealous. Soon he was defending individual Indians in court cases, as well as endlessly agitating in letters and petitions to officials and the press, culminating in a famous Royal Commission on the Indian question in 1872 and 1873.

Despite these considerable credentials, Ebenezer Ward refused to negotiate with de Plevitz, after he found that the plan involved paying the migrants' fares to the Territory. Ward, however, did

770 Ireland and Fraser to Blyth 22/1/1878 with enclosures (N.T.I.L. 121/1878); Ireland and Fraser to Blyth 4/2/1878 (N.T.I.L. 139/1878).

provide information about the laissez-faire plans, and de Plevitz went his way to encourage his next idealistic enterprise, the migration of Indians from Mauritius to Fiji.[771]

The same month that de Plevitz arrived in Sydney, another well-known Mauritian, Oscar Richard Coombes, having taken leave from the civil service, set out from Mauritius to Adelaide to arrange for the emigration of Indian sugar planters to the Northern Territory under the auspices of a company. When his request for assisted passages was refused, he returned to Mauritius the following year to launch the Mauritius Colonization Company under a board of directors in Mauritius and a manager in the Northern Territory. The basis of the scheme was a company like the South Australian Company; it proposed to give settlers the protection of size, combined with close communal living based on the principle of a 'Usine Centrale', a close settlement designed around a central place. The project failed to gain financial support in Mauritius from the government and private enterprise, though it attracted the interest of many potential emigrants. Eventually it died a natural death.

In June 1878 a third Mauritian, Eugene Aristride Bonnefin, paid his way to Melbourne in response to advertisements in Mauritian newspapers that £200 was available to report on the sugar potential of the Territory. Again the South Australian government (this time under J.P. Boucaut) refused to negotiate. He stayed on in Australia, and the Bonnefins became one of the pioneering Mauritian families in this country.[772]

Eventually, the *Register* censured successive South Australian governments for their methods of publicity which had given the poor people of Mauritius such unfounded hope. But the criticisms came only after the ministers themselves had admitted the whole scheme a failure.[773]

---

771 Plevitz to Ward 5/7/1876 with enclosures (N.T.I.L. 280/1876); Plevitz to Ward 12/7/1876 (N.T.I.L. 278A/1876); Plevitz to Ward 21/12/1876 with enclosures (N.T.I.L. 11/1877).

772 Coombes to Ward 19/9/1876 (N.T.I.L. 384/1876); Coombes to Ward 8/11/1877 (N.T.I.L. 1/1878); Coombes to Blyth 15/8/1878 with enclosure (N.T.I.L. 518/1878).

773 *Register* 13/6/1878, p. 11; S.A.P.D. 1878 c.4.

Dutch Response – and the Misadventures of Captain Cadell

Much more important than Mauritius, was how to attract planters and workers from nearby Java and the Dutch East Indies.

For two and a half centuries the Dutch had dominated the Indies Archipelago centred on Batavia in Java, beginning with the Dutch East Indies Company of 1602. Their main strategy had been to keep the Portuguese and British out. But by 1870 the Dutch governor-general had hopes of encouraging trade with the British Empire in New Holland, while at the same time discouraging emigration from the Indies to Australia.

Confronted by the South Australians' efforts to recruit population to the Territory, the first response of the government in Batavia was to adopt a wait-and-see policy. Then, from 1875, it began to apply strict restrictions on all Malays entering New Holland. One of the reasons for this response was the activities of the master pearlers who were operating out of North West Australia and Torres Strait.

The first pearlers on the coast near Nickol Bay in Western Australia had used Aboriginal skin-divers as harvesters, until 1870 when the Legislative Council there passed the first *Pearl Shell Fisheries Act* protecting Aboriginal divers against exploitation. The use of women and girl divers was forbidden because they were also used for sex, while all men were to be returned to their home tribe at the end of each season. The pearlers then turned to the neighbouring islands of Timor, Makar and Allor in the Dutch East Indies and tried to exploit the Malays in much the same way. In the 1870–1871 season Captain Francis Cadell, now become a master pearler, obtained a gang of Malay pearlers from Allor. Eight died from disease and six were killed by misadventure, and when Cadell returned the next year no Allores dared join him.[774]

In April 1872 the Minister of Colonies in The Hague wrote to the governor-general in Batavia warning him to resist attempts, already made or about to be made, to recruit Malay workers for

---

774 Director Internal Government, Batavia to governor-general, Netherlands East Indies 5/6/1872 No. 5869; Short Report concerning the situation in the Residency Timor, June-July 1872 No. 877 (Research Notes, Algemeen Rijksarchief). Courtesy of C.H.A. Plug, Second Secretary, Netherlands Embassy, Canberra, 8/3/1965.

places such as the Pacific Islands and Australia. He pointed out that the coolie trade was now seen in a less favourable light and that there was no overcrowding in the Indies Archipelago as a whole to justify emigration. 'The Netherlands cannot tolerate a slave trade in the Archipelago of the Indies. It also cannot permit under the recruitment of coolies a disguised slave trade to take place.'[775] In September 1872 the Council of the Netherlands Indies, an advisory body in Batavia assisting the governor-general, reviewed the emigration question carefully. It recommended that the situation required no special legislation; the existing ordinances were sufficient to protect Malay workers. The only evidence they had of recruitment of Malays was from the Timor Archipelago, and this region was difficult to police. The governor-general, not wishing to antagonise the Australians with trade prospects in view, concurred with his advisers, and a letter of reassurance was sent back to the minister in the Netherlands.[776]

Meanwhile, the Dutch consul-general for Australia, New Zealand and Tasmania, then on leave in Holland, pointed out that gold had been discovered near Port Darwin, that a company had been formed for the cultivation of sugar and that the South Australian government would try to acquire workers from the islands of the Arafura and Java Seas. He asked for instructions in the event of their doing so. He also warned the Netherlands India government to keep an eye on these settlements, especially as they were under Australian colonists, 'who take workers *against their own will* from the neighbouring islands, of which the latest information describes the saddest scenes'.[777] He also noted that the Government Resident at Port Darwin had already obtained a handful of indentured workers from Timor and had not returned them through lack of the means to do so.

Again the minister in the Hague expressed misgivings to the

775 Resolution of the Minister of Colonies to the governor-general of the Netherlands East Indies 17/4/1872 No. 6/581 (Research Notes, Algemeen Rijksarchief).

776 Advice of the Council of the Netherlands East Indies 20/9/1872 No. XXXIV; Governor-general, Netherlands East Indies to Minister of Colonies 25/10/1872 No. 1711/17 (Research Notes, Algemeen Rijksarchief).

777 Resolution Minister of External Affairs to governor-general, Netherlands East Indies 20/11/1872 No. 21/1807 (Research Notes, Algemeen Rijksarchief).

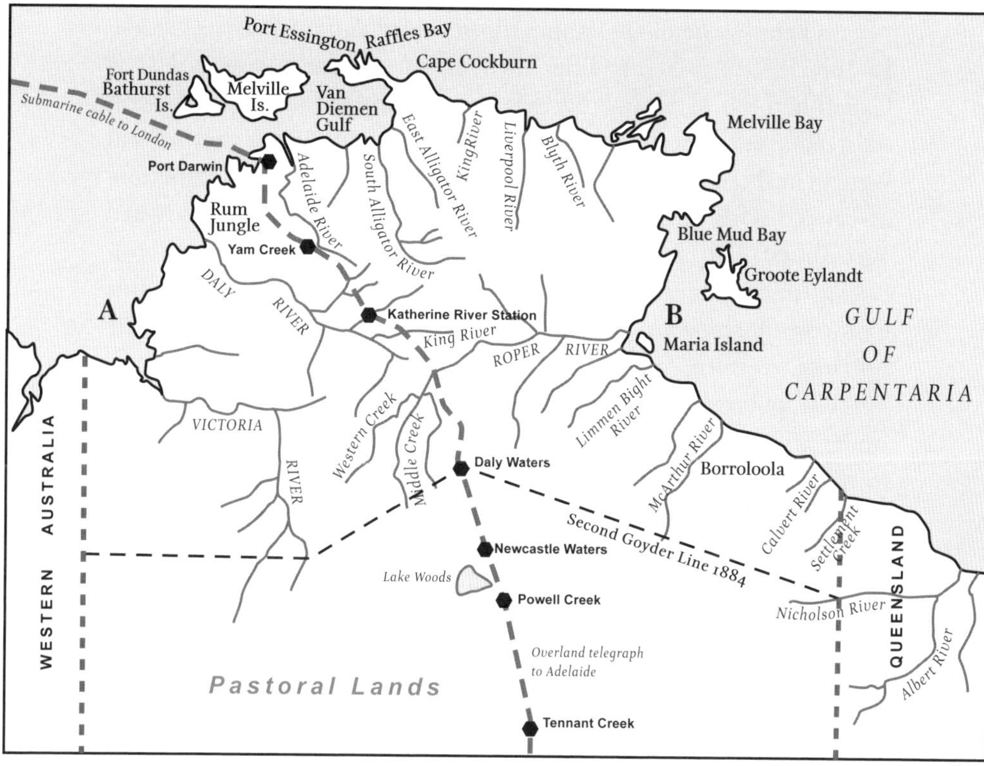

The Upper Territory – Arnhem Land was north of line between A and B.

governor-general in Batavia. The governor-general again consulted his advisers, who recommended that they continue to wait and see. The advisers thought that the South Australians would find difficulty in recruiting workers (the agricultural policy in the Indies discouraged it), but if they did succeed then the time would come to control the export of indentured labourers by regulation. The governor-general instructed the Resident at Timor to watch carefully the recruitment of Malays from his region.[778]

All these events had happened even before William Henry Bundey and Ebenezer Ward set out to revive the Territory by laying it open to settlement from the neighbouring islands. Soon after they did start this work, there was more trouble from freeloaders operating outside the law, in particular in Western Australia.

778 Advice of the Council of the Netherlands East Indies 28/2/1873 No. XIX (Research Notes, Algemeen Rijksarchief).

As before, one of the main culprits was Captain Francis Cadell. In July 1875 a police trooper in Western Australia reported that Cadell had left 17 Malay divers behind at Shark Bay (in north-west Australia) with food unfit for human consumption, so that several were ill and one had died, and that another master pearler sometime associated with Cadell, a dubious character named Charles Edward Broadhurst, had abandoned four others at the same place without paying their wages. Broadhurst hailed from the Dennison Plains Company formed in Melbourne in 1865 to pioneer grazing in the north of Western Australia.

The governor of Western Australia and his ministers, acting under instructions from the Colonial Office in London, decided to make examples of pearlers like Cadell and Broadhurst in a bid to curb the growing practice of taking divers from the islands then abandoning them without wages where and when their contract expired. '… a vigorous enforcement of the law,' wrote the colonial secretary, 'will serve to check such shameful proceedings for the future.' A magistrate from Greenough named Robert Fairbairn was sent north to conduct an investigation, which Cadell escaped by sailing to the Indies and leaving behind news that he intended to forsake Western Australian waters for good. The Western Australian government retaliated by selling up every piece of Cadell's property it could find and using the money to part pay the wages to the Malays so they could return to their homelands. It tried to do the same with Broadhurst (he appealed successfully to the Supreme Court) and began to look around for a fast ship that could run down the exploiters.[779]

Cadell, believing he would get less interference from the Queensland government, switched his activities to the Torres Strait where he was again accused of exploiting (even kidnapping) islander workers. At the same time, Cadell continued to recruit indigenous labour from the Northern Territory, particularly Port Essington, for his two work ships, the *Trois Amis* and *Gem*. In November 1877, Dewhirst Gore, Northern Territory storekeeper and Christian

779 Robinson to Carnarvon 7/8/1875 with enclosures (G.O.D.[W.A.] 94/1875); Robinson to Carnarvon 15/10/1875 (G.O.D. [W.A.] 115/1875); Despatches Concerning Malay Pearlers 1875–1877, Mainland to Eliot 27/7/1875 (S.L.S.A. Mortlock P.R.G. 145/2).

activist, took the unusual step of waiting on the premier of Queensland, John Douglas, who was then visiting Somerset, Cape York, to complain about Cadell's mistreatment of Port Essington Aborigines in Queensland waters – for which trouble he received a hostile response from the premier and was sacked by his employer. Somerset at the time was a base for pearling and a refuge port for shipping through Torres Strait. Gore took this action at Somerset after he had found the *Gem* packed with a crew-load of Port Essington Aborigines with whom he was acquainted. They pleaded with him to take them home or to ask the Government Resident or chief of police at Palmerston to arrange for their return, saying they were hungry and had been tricked into working for Cadell.[780]

Inspector Foelsche was ordered by Government Resident Price from Port Darwin to Port Essington to investigate, where he found the Aboriginal people very agitated. Back in October some of their number from the Bowen Strait area had been tricked into joining Cadell on the *Gem* on the understanding that it was just for a short time, and they had not returned. Then in March Cadell had come back for more, but none would join him – except some Alligator River people who then jumped overboard. In his report Foelsche advised that a Sub-protector should be placed at Port Essington and no indigenous person should be taken away without the express permission of the Government Resident or his officer. Both of these recommendations were later carried out.[781]

But the troubles with Captain Cadell were not over. In July and August 1878 a mutiny broke out in Torres Strait. First, a group of Aborigines led by Wandy-Wandy and Big Jack murdered one British, two Malay and one Chinese (all seamen) while they were away on a working party with Aborigines from Port Essington collecting wood and water for the *Gem* on Badu Island (now better known as Mulgrave Island, a name given by Captain Bligh) about 50 miles north-west of Cape York. Hearing of events ashore, the Aborigines on the *Gem* itself joined the fray. They waited until Cadell was away in a small boat then attacked and badly wounded

---

780 Gore to King 12/10/1878 with enclosures (N.T.I.L. 605/1878); Blyth to Price 14/8/1878 (G.R.I.L. A3060).

781 Foelsche to Lewis 29/7/1878 (Lewis Family Papers S.L.S.A. Mortlock P.R.G. 247/2).

the mate, Henry Brown, with a large knife as he came up from below deck. In the melee that followed, Brown shot four crew with his revolver before jumping overboard to escape the rage of the rest.[782] The Aborigines trashed the ship, took provisions, seized the long boat and sailed to Port Essington in high excitement with a complement of ten men and four women. Wandy-Wandy later became a political activist trying to drive the Europeans and Macassans out, before he was hanged in 1893 at a sacred meeting place where his own people would not miss it – and his body was left hanging there.[783]

Cadell, undaunted, now approached the South Australian ministers in Adelaide with a grand scheme to monopolise all pearling and trepang fishing along the entire Territory coast from Croker Island to the Queensland border. He hoped that his fame in South Australia for pioneering shipping on the Murray River in the 1850s, and his connections with leading Adelaide citizens would put him in good stead, and he went on to propose that the Macassan fishermen should gradually be pushed out because they exploited the Aboriginal people and contributed nothing to Northern Territory development. The government's response was cautious. They sought a report from the Government Resident on the Macassan trade, at the same time launching an inquiry in Adelaide into the complaints against Cadell. The Resident reported that despite various attempts, no European had successfully conducted pearling or trepang fishing on the Territory coast and that Cadell came there only to recruit Aboriginal workers.[784]

Meanwhile, the Boucaut government asked Cadell to gather further information in the East Indies about the Macassan trade.

At the end of September 1878 Cadell set sail from Torres Strait with a skeleton crew in his damaged schooner *Gem*, on a double mission. One was to repair the schooner at Kai Islands near New

782 *Argus* 30/8/1879, p. 9. Name of the mate inferred from evidence by James Lawson before Harbour Master, Melbourne; Cadell Papers p. 4 (S.L.S.A. Mortlock P.R.G. 145/1).

783 Foelsche to Lewis 24/7/1878; 25/7/1878; 16/8/1878; 9/10/1878; 31/1/1880; 5/6/1880 (Lewis Family Papers S.L.S.A. Mortlock P.R.G. 247/2); Press Cuttings Vol 4, p. 26 (S.A. State Records G.R.S.9).

784 Price to Blyth 2/7/1878 (N.T.I.L. 461/1878).

Guinea, and procure more workers on the way back, his supply of Aborigines having dried up. His second mission was to go to the port of Macassar in the South Celebes to prepare a report on the Macassan trade in an effort to persuade the South Australian government that it would be to their advantage to hand a monopoly over to himself. About Christmas time 1878 he sent an interesting but critical report from Macassar – writing that most of the trade was in the hands of three Chinese merchants, that 23 proas had sailed to Australia employing about 1000 men who were treated like slaves, and that a colony of Aborigines lived at Macassar as menial workers. These facts were vouched for by four other master pearlers at Macassar who complained bitterly that the Dutch government now demanded 200 guilders deposit on each Malay diver employed.[785]

It was the last anyone in Australia ever heard from Captain Francis Cadell. Together with his schooner *Gem* he disappeared without trace in the East Indies – murdered, it was suspected, at the hands of his own crew.

The details of Cadell's death remained a talking point in Adelaide newspapers for many years, mainly because his movements were so murky. For some reason the eventual trial of his alleged assailant was not widely publicised. In a letter to Cadell's brother in Madras, India, in 1880 (which was summarised in the newspapers) the government at Batavia reported that in March 1879, somewhere near the Kei or Kai Islands, Cadell had been shot six times in his bed by his servant, a Manila man (probably a Filipino) called Perman, who cried out, 'I have shot the Captain, because I have been in his service five years without receiving any wages,' after which Perman and the crew had taken valuables, including mysterious bags of Dutch dollars collected by Cadell at various islands, and scuttled the ship. This information produced more rumours in Adelaide – one of which held that Perman had been hunted down by the Dutch and hanged in front of the courthouse at Amboina (or Ambon) in the Spice Islands.

In fact Perman had been arrested by the Dutch authorities and kept in custody at Amboina for two years, before being handed over

785 Cadell to King 23/12/1878 (N.T.I.L. 83/1879); Roel, Craig, Mayne, Tischkey to King 23/12/1878 (N.T.I.L. 84/1879).

to the British at Singapore for trial. He was tried on 14 February 1882 before the chief justice in the Singapore Supreme Court and a special jury. The court heard the main facts of the case: how in March 1879 Perman, who had not been paid for five years, shot the captain six times with a revolver about nine o'clock one evening while Cadell was asleep in his bunk. According to crew members, Perman then bullied the crew into scuttling the ship somewhere near the Kai Islands. They took the long-boat and became lost for several days until they reached the Kai Islands where, dressed in Cadell's clothes, Perman represented himself as the ship's captain. He then obtained a passage on the *Ammat Aeydroes*, an Arab brig (with the long-boat of the *Gem* in tow), to Ambon where he gave evidence before a magistrate that his own ship, the *Gem*, had been wrecked at sea. But the magistrate, confronted by a Manila man dressed as an English captain, arrested him and began investigations, as a result of which he remained in custody for two years while the Dutch decided what to do with him. The court also heard how in the meantime a magistrate had conducted a full inquiry in the Kai Islands among the crew who, turning Queen's evidence, claimed that they had been intimidated into joining Perman. Some of these men were now transported to Singapore as witnesses for the prosecution. Though the main facts of the case were not in dispute, the trial soon ran into trouble: no copy of the ship's register could be produced in court, and there was a problem with jurisdiction: had Cadell been killed on the high seas or in territorial waters? Perman was acquitted: reading between the lines, the court had no desire to convict him.[786]

According to a later rumour, Cadell was killed on the orders of the Rajah of Allor, because of his mistreatment of Allorese workers – if true, a result not unacceptable to the Dutch government

The saga of Francis Cadell set off a long debate in Adelaide between his many supporters – led by Samuel Tomkinson who claimed he was a true British gentleman and a great South

786 First Government Secretary, Batavia, to R. Cadell 25/2/1880 (S.L.S.A. Mortlock P.R.G. 145/1); *The Straits Times/Singapore Daily Times* 15/2/1882 (Courtesy of British Library, London). For a recent overview of Cadell's life see: John Nicholson, *The Incomparable Captain Cadell*, A Sue Hines Book, Allen & Unwin, Sydney, 2004.

Australian and incapable of hurting anyone – and his fewer critics, who argued he was a regular ill-treater of coloured workers.

Cadell was not the only free-loader exploiting islander and Aboriginal labour and muddying the waters for those trying to attract migrants from the Indies Archipelago. In Torres Strait alone there were 100 pearling ships and as many on the north-west coast (more than 80 operating out of Cossack in 1873), scrounging for divers wherever they could be found. Cadell was, however, far and away the best documented. His activities after 1871 are worth emphasising because it fed a Dutch fear from the beginning that Malay emigration to Australia would lead to trouble.

Step by step, and in parallel to events outlined above, the Dutch put up the barriers.

About the same time as the accusations against Cadell and Broadhurst became public in Western Australia, news was received in the Australian colonies that the Netherlands India government had suddenly imposed harsh terms on foreigners seeking the service of Malays – so suddenly that the pearlers already in the area to recruit divers for the next season found themselves without the necessary security. The terms of the *Netherlands East Indies and Timor Act of 1875* required that outsiders employing native islanders in the pearl industry, or any other work, must first enter into a firm agreement in the presence of a Harbour Master about the nature of the work, the wages and the length of service. Strict penalties were prescribed for non-compliance. These requirements applied for the whole of the Dutch East Indies, but for the islands under the Residency of Timor additional stringent conditions were applied. For the Timor region nearest Australia prospective employers had first to deposit with the Government Resident at Koepang 200 guilders per head as a guarantee that each worker would be returned safely to his home village inside 13 months of signing, or the money handed over to the man himself or his relatives.[787] The restrictions were promulgated just when Ebenezer Ward, having taken office for the first time, was talking grandly about developing the Territory 'off everybody's hands' by opening the doors to the

787 Robinson to Carnarvon 28/8/1875 (G.O.D. [W.A.] 100/1875); Robinson to Carnarvon 17/11/1876 (G.O.D. [W.A.] 158/1876); Robinson to Carnarvon 23/2/1877 (G.O.D. [W.A.] 19/1877).

north. By the time he took charge for a second time and entered into a firm arrangement for a shipping service they were truly in force, and had even been reviewed in the Palmerston newspaper.[788]

And so the prediction of the first Government Resident's daughter – 'There is no doubt that one day we will see Malay villages, or Kampongs, all along these wild northern shores' – never eventuated.[789]

Plan Misfires

The response of the South Australian ministers was again to increase the force of the advertising and to extend it to the shores of the Asian mainland, until they over-reached themselves. In November 1877 Neville Blyth launched a campaign that made extravagant claims about the prospects of the Territory and South Australia's generosity. We have already seen how this kind of advertising misfired in Mauritius. Now it misfired in China.

The death knell sounded for the policies of laissez-faire during 1878. In that year the South Australian ministers under J.P. Boucaut and then William Morgan officially acknowledged their failure to attract plantation owners. The Lower House tried to reimpose customs duties (staved off by the Upper House until 1880)[790] and the Netherlands company tried to get out of its shipping contract on the grounds that it was not paying.[791] In that year also, the Chinese question got out of hand.

In 1877, 115 Chinese were recorded as living in the Territory, less than a fifth of the recorded European residents.[792] By March 1878, after just three shiploads had come, there were 604, approaching the size of the white population.[793] A month later the numbers stood at 1200, approaching twice the size.[794] A year on, in April 1879, there were 3406 Chinese, seven times the number of Europeans.[795]

788 *Northern Territory Times and Gazette* 14/10/1876, p. 2.
789 Harriet W. Daly, *Digging, Squatting, Pioneering*, p. 269
790 S.A.P.D. 1878 c.1424; S.A.P.A. 184 of 1880.
791 Blyth to Acraman Main 12/8/1878 (N.T.O.L. 217/1878).
792 Price to King 3/9/1880 (N.T.I.L. 473/1880).
793 Price to Blyth 20/3/1878 (N.T.I.L. 132/1878).
794 Price to Blyth 13/4/1878 (N.T.I.L. 225/1878).
795 Price to King 16/4/1879 (N.T.I.L. 183/1879).

By 1880 a further influx, mainly from Hong Kong, raised the numbers past the 4000 mark, and 1881 promised more.[796] It seemed that at last the Territory was becoming part of Asia. The supply of fresh vegetables increased enormously due to the efforts of Chinese gardeners. Almost every European who could afford it employed a Chinese cook. There were 400 million people still in China. The prediction of the Chinese cook seemed to be coming true: 'this place welly good, by and by, all China come – Emperor too!'[797]

The influx was partly the result of the open door policy and the publicity associated with it. As the repeated appeals failed to attract much attention except among the poor, governments became ever less cautious with their advertising. It was certainly not the result of any planned policy on the part of South Australia. On the contrary, with the examples of California and North Queensland before them, prominent South Australians had been cautioning each other for years against the trap into which they eventually fell.

According to the South Australian government, there were two general classes of Chinese immigrants, and the problem was how to attract one and not the other. Agricultural settlers and their families were desirable settlers, but not the itinerant gold seekers who since the forced opening of China in the Opium Wars of the 1840s and 1850s had been beachcombing the lands bordering the Pacific in search of wealth to send to poor relatives back home. These, it was alleged, were mere birds of passage who cost a country more than they contributed, sucked the land dry, propagated diseases like small-pox and syphilis, and being mainly males gave rise to grave moral problems.

But attracting families from China was not easy. From emperor down to local village, the emigration of women was discouraged in order to preserve the continuity of the family line, without which no one could gain access to most of the benefits of society, not even the emperor.

The difficulties were well illustrated by Neville Blyth's memorandum on family migration. In November 1877 he raised the possibility of attracting Chinese families for agriculture by

---

796 McMinn to King 30/12/1880 (N.T.I.L. 63/1881).

797 Knight to Price 26/7/1879 (N.T.I.L. 410/1879).

Chinese workers in the Territory were considered by some to have mechanically superior bodies to Europeans.
(*Pictorial Australian* April 1888. Courtesy of the State Library of South Australia)

offering them free grants of land when they reached Port Darwin. The question was deferred by Cabinet for further investigation.[798] It was then referred to a minor official of the Peking government, then visiting Sydney, who advised briefly that family migration was possible provided passage money was first paid.[799] It was also referred to the Government Resident for a full report. After consulting various local Chinese headmen, Price advised that the migration of families was only likely through Chinese capitalists taking up land and bringing their own agricultural workers. In an effort to attract these capitalists the Government Resident got in touch with the Harbour Master at Hong Kong, hoping that by working at this high official level he could prevent any wild publicity that might unloose a flood of itinerant visitors.[800]

What made the negotiations particularly hazardous was that the South Australian government had no legal right to exclude the itinerants if they did decide to come. Britain's existing treaties with China (encapsulated in the 1860 Peking Convention) guaranteed the easy entry of Chinese to the empire in return for the unequal concession of letting British traders exploit China itself. Also the British Empire was premised on a giant multi-racial society. It was not the imperial masters, but many local white colonial settlers that wanted to see a 'White Australia'. In 1876 the Queensland parliament had tried to restrict the entry of all Chinese, but the Colonial Office asked the Queen to disallow the legislation as offensive to a friendly power.

Meanwhile, powerful British, American and German shipping firms in Hong Kong were always on the lookout for places to which they could promote a rush of itinerant Chinese. These shipowners were outside the control of the governor of Hong Kong and had friends in the British parliament.[801]

The first large shiploads of human cargo to reach Port Darwin in March–April 1878 came because they had seen placards

---

798 Memo by Blyth for the consideration of Cabinet 7/11/1877 (N.T.I.L. 565/1877); Blyth to Price 17/11/1877 (N.T.O.L. 339/1877).

799 Correspondence with Henry Woolfe (N.T.I.L. 581/1877); Blyth to Woolfe 19/11/1877 (N.T.O.L. 344/1877).

800 Price to Blyth 19/12/1877 (N.T.I.L. 49/1878).

801 *Register* 30/4/1888 leader; *Nineteenth Century* April 1888.

on the wharfs of Hong Kong that promised work on a great transcontinental railway at £3 a week.[802] Many who could went back soon after arriving, disappointed and disillusioned, only to be followed by scores more with the same mistaken idea. The shipowners, rather than solid Chinese families, had answered South Australia's call about the attractions of the Northern Territory. The *Hong Kong Free Press* joined the throng and urged the beggars of China to head for Port Darwin to start a new life.[803] The promotion continued even into the 1880s when a terrible smallpox plague was ravaging China.

South Australia's officers on the north coast and taxpayers in the south were disturbed by the way Chinese kept coming even when the dry season made washing on the gold fields impossible. The choice then was either to put them to government work on rations or to run the risk of their wrecking the local stores. Over the dry season of 1878, £3900 was spent on relief to destitute Chinese.[804] Similar destitution followed in later years – a high price to pay for a laissez-faire policy supposed to lift the burden from the shoulders of the taxpayers. Neville Blyth hurriedly sent a telegram to the Harbour Master at Hong Kong denying rumours that work was available at 13 shillings a day. He followed up with a letter full of sober remarks about the possibilities of disappointment and destitution and stating with emphasis that the local Aborigines were 'treacherous and subtle'.[805] But as the governor of Hong Kong later revealed, all his attempts to control the rushes to Australia were undermined by the lobbying of ship-owners connected with the British parliament.[806]

The influx of nomadic Asians damaged South Australia's reputation for statesmanship, particularly in the Northern Territory and Queensland. Citizens of Palmerston held a public meeting during which some wanted to secede from southern control.[807] The

802 *Northern Territory Times and Gazette* 20/4/1878, p. 2.

803 *Northern Territory Times and Gazette* 27/4/1878 leader.

804 Price to King 13/12/1878 (N.T.I.L. 23/1879).

805 Blyth to Thomsett 14/3/1878 (N.T.O.L. 76/1878).

806 *Nineteenth Century* April 1888.

807 *Register* 28/1/1878, p. 5.

Brisbane newspapers kept referring to South Australia as the weak link in the family of Australian colonies. The government and its agencies were besieged by complaints about the Chinese. Civic leaders complained that they crowded in hovels, incubated diseases, turned their sick out to die, did not bury their dead respectably, and did not bury their dead at all –preferring to put dead bodies near or on the surface so they would soon decompose with the help of the hot sun and the bones could be taken back to China. The Chinese were also accused of smuggling out gold in the marrow bones and skulls of their dead comrades.

To add fuel to these prejudices the worst epidemic of fever since the gold rush of 1873 broke out in 1879. In the first few months of 1880 about ten per cent of the Chinese in the Territory died, and their bodies could be found strewn along the roads. Miners complained the Chinese would not find their own fields, but flocked like vultures in the wake of European prospectors. Officials despaired of getting them to take out miners' licences. 'We welly poor. We go to Gaol,' they would say.[808] The gaol contained only a few cells. The Government Resident complained that the visitors' strange custom of lighting camp fires on bridges threatened to destroy the whole transport system of a place where the bridges were made of wood and not stone.[809]

Fearing the Chinese would even take over the game of cricket, *Adelaide Punch* wrote (under a large cartoon):

> Ye Gentlemen of China, pray stop at home at ease,
> and let your wares alone be sent across the Southern Seas;
> For distance lends enchantment, and everyone agrees,
> though your teas are best when present, you are best as absentees.[810]

Over the dry season of 1879, the government was left no choice but to employ about 800 destitute Chinese on public works constructing a new experimental nursery at Fannie Bay, building

---

808 Knight to Price 18/5/1878 (N.T.I.L. 334/1878).

809 Possible explanations in a research note from Eric Rolls 26/4/1997 (author of *Sojourners,* 1992): most bridges in China were made of stone; they put little value on anything not connected with their clan; seem to have had a different perhaps less linear concept of consequences.

810 *Adelaide Punch* 7/12/1878

a road via the cemetery to Fannie Bay, and hacking out a road via Doctors Gully to Point Emery.[811]

Working in charge of a gang of Chinese navvies at the top of Doctors Gully, Edward Smerdon Strawbridge had a lucky break. According to Strawbridge, his men discovered a small Chinese statue, about four feet underground, firmly wedged in between the roots of a large banyan tree – a tree not indigenous to Australia. He put the statue in his pocket and with the help of his brother William, later surveyor-general, who was interested in art, sold it in Adelaide to a collector called Worsnop for five guineas. It was eventually identified as Shou Lao, ancient Taoist God of long-life. Over the years, it has been the subject of much interest as to how and when it got there, and taken as evidence that some Chinese had been there many years before. Once on loan to the South Australian Art Gallery, which refused to buy it, the statue was removed by the owners who feared in World War II that the Japanese would bomb the Art Gallery. Now it is an object of great curiosity in the Powerhouse Museum, Sydney.[812]

811 *Northern Territory Times and Gazette* 26/7/1879, p. 2, Price reply to memorial; Price to King 30/7/1879 (N.T.I.L. 395/1879).

812 John Wade, *Shou Lao: a Chinese Figurine excavated at Darwin in 1879* (Australian Society for Historical Archaeology June 1977); Drawings of the Shou Lao are still held by descendants of Edward Smerdon Strawbridge. Supporting information from Shirley Cameron Wilson, granddaughter of William Strawbridge, 2001.

CHAPTER 6

THE MORMON PATTERN

> 'The settlement of the Mormons in Utah will always remain as a proof that religious enthusiasm, and even religious charlatanry, may be used as the motive power of a colonizing enterprise, and that under such guidance energies may be evoked equal to overcoming the greatest natural obstacles, and enduring the greatest privations, until labour is rewarded by success.'
>
> *The Australasian* 22 April 1876

The 1800s was a period when there were large movements of people around the world in search of religious and political freedom. As well as the laissez-faire plans to rectify the Territory's fate following the false start, were strategies that sought to make use of religious contacts – none of which came from within the government ranks or legislature. Instead, money was voted to religious leaders or their agents who came forward with plans of their own. Like most attempts at religious migration, the motives were mixed.

In South Australia proper, the dream (some would say myth) of religious migration had been kept alive by the knowledge that in the 1830s and 1840s, 'Wakefield's colony' had attracted many non-conformists, like Methodists, who resented the restrictions placed on them in England. It was also kept alive by the historical idea perpetuated by South Australia's richest man, George Fife Angas, and his friends and relations, that the introduction of German Lutheran religious migrants mainly from Silesia had saved the infant South Australia when similarly tottering – indeed, one of his relatives by marriage, John Langdon Parsons, later offered to introduce Silesian Catholics to help do the same for the Territory.

But when it came to the special needs of the Northern Territory in the 1870s, it was the rise of the Mormons in Salt Lake Valley after

James Penn Boucaut, noted for his 'bold strokes of Bismarkism'. In 1866 he boldly moved to abandon the Northern Territory settlement. In 1876 he tried to save the Territory by seeking to introduce 40,000 religious refugees from Russia. (*Australasian Sketcher* 19/1/1878, p. 164. Courtesy of the State Library of South Australia)

1847 that seemed the best model because these people were migrants prepared to settle where most others would not.[813]

For a time communities meeting adversity in distant parts of the world almost, but never quite, became involved in the struggling colony.

Santals

The first opportunity to make use of religious contacts came from a discontent which had erupted in the Santal uprisings north-west of Calcutta in 1855–1856. The attempt to recruit Santals is worth emphasising because it demonstrated the difficulties of obtaining settlers from India – something which the government in South Australia did not anticipate.

The Santals were among the remnants of India's aboriginal

813 *Advertiser* 8/4/1876 leader.

population. In 1855 social and religious exploitation by Hindus and Muslims had become so unbearable and a desire for their ancient independence so great that they rose in aimless revolt against all in authority. A contemporary historian wrote:

> Armed chiefly with axes and poisoned arrows, large bodies of these half reclaimed savages carried fire and sword into scores of happy villages, attacked every outlying European bungalow, murdered with equal readiness English planters and railway-servants, native police officers, tradesmen, peasants, their wives and children ... A sudden frenzy, hatched by the arts of some Santhal chiefs burning for revenge on the swindling money-lenders and grasping law-officers of Bengal, a frenzy fostered by tales not wholly groundless of the cruelty, the unfairness, on the licentious habits of English railway-overseers, by other far wilder tales of a glorious Avatar now coming for the Santhal race.[814]

Instead, retribution came with the heavy tread of the Indian Imperial Army. The Santal homes were systematically laid waste. They had so neglected their own infertile lands that in 1856 many thousands died by degrees in the forests, too proud or afraid to beg for relief.

Through their inglorious rebellion, the Santals had inadvertently forced themselves under the eyes of the British authorities as well as humane people around the world. They found their champions in the humanity of Christian missionaries, particularly in the Baptist E.C. Johnson and the Lutheran Lars Olsen Skrefsrud.

Skrefsrud stands without doubt as one of the great pioneer missionaries of all time. He was born in 1840 in the hamlet of Skrefsrud, Norway, of a poor, pious mother and an alcoholic father. He was imprisoned at the age of 18, as a house-breaker and thief. Released four years later, he resolved to dedicate his life to the Christian Church, but no self-respecting seminary in Norway would have him on its campus. So he went to Berlin and threw himself upon the kindness of a big-hearted Danish engineer called Boerresen, who helped him gain entry to the Gossner Mission Seminary. In 1863 he went to India as a Gossner missionary, followed soon by Boerresen as co-worker. Then came the Schleswig-

814 L.J. Trotter, *British Empire in India*, Allan and Co., London, 1866, Volume One, p. 369.

Holstein War and the two Scandinavians fell out with the German mission. After a period of being down-and-out in Calcutta, the Norwegian turned to his life's work, a mission among the poor Santals in the arid parganas to the north-west. With the help of the Serampore Baptists, in 1874 he formed the independent Indian Home Mission to the Santals.[815]

For many years Skrefsrud's energies went into relieving the desperate misery of his adopted people. In an article reprinted in the *Northern Territory Times and Gazette*, he wrote:

> The Sonthals when we went first among them were in great distress, and moral condition was very low, because drunkenness and licentiousness are their besetting sins.
>
> These Sonthals live in great misery. Their condition is exceedingly deplorable. Hindoo Rajahs depress them; Hindoo moneylenders defraud them; Hindoo vendors cheat them; and at the same time their own chiefs taking advantage of their superstition, impose heavy fines and burdens upon them.[816]

Skrefsrud implored the Bengal government for agrarian reforms, but the civil service moved slowly. He set up communal mission estates in Benagaria, but these could only provide for a few. Dearest of all was his determination to find another home for his people, a New Santalistan on some virgin soil. Only in such a colony could he hope to relieve their distress, preserve the integrity of Santal culture and protect them as Christian converts.

In 1873–1874 Skrefsrud went to Europe on his first drive for support and funds. He made a great impression in England and Scotland where he was patronised by the Baptist Church, which held secret hopes of taking over his Lutheran mission when he retired or died. The plight of the Santals was topical thanks to a terrible famine over Bengal. At a Baptist May Meeting staged in London the missionary's words were dwelt upon, taken down in shorthand and distributed far and wide, including in other languages.

---

815 Research Notes, J. Gausdal of Arvoll, Oslo, Norway, Gausdal to Cross 1960. Gausdal is a leading biographer of Skrefsrud. His main work on the subject is: *Santalmisjonens Historie på Misjonsmarkem*, Santalmisjonens forlag, Oslo, 1937.

816 *Northern Territory Times and Gazette* 14/11/1874, p. 4.

While in London stirring up his cause, Skrefsrud met the pioneer South Australian and Baptist philanthropist who helped found the Royal Institute for the Blind, Charles Goode, there in charge of the English side of his merchant company. It was Goode's firm idea that the empty north of Australia would be an ideal country for Skrefsrud's Santals. He took the missionary to interview the South Australian agent-general, encouraged him to write to Adelaide and despatched his own covering note of commendation advising the government to pay the Norwegian's fare to Adelaide to negotiate. Skrefsrud's response was at first enthusiastic. He sent a letter to the South Australian government commending his beloved Santals and pointing out how their immigration would be a mutual advantage. He went on:

> Mr Boerresen and myself, besides gathering a large number of converts from amongst them, have been enabled to exercise no small influence over the people generally, and we are confident that they would readily follow our advice to emigrate to the Northern Territory of South Australia, if your Government should take up such a Scheme – the Chiefs and people having requested, nay implored us over and over again to emigrate somewhere with them.
>
> Should the Government of South Australia be disposed to entertain the project introduced in this letter, I should be happy myself to visit the seat of Government and afford further information, which may be called for; and I should be willing to visit the Northern Territory to select a location and expedite matters.[817]

When Skrefsrud's letter reached Adelaide six weeks later it came as the kind of windfall which politicians and the press had dreamed about. The minister in charge, William Henry Bundey, the first minister with a specific Northern Territory portfolio, showed particular interest in the idea of a nucleus settlement being funded to spring off further unassisted migrations;[818] and a letter was promptly sent back to Goode, thanking him for his trouble and assuring him that the Norwegian would be written to by the present mail.[819]

---

817 Skrefsrud to Dutton 16/4/1874 (C.C.L. I.L. 640/1874 filed with N.T.I.L. 155/1874).

818 Goode to Everard 11/4/1874 with Minutes (N.T.I.L. 155/1874).

819 Deering to Goode 17/6/1874 (N.T.O.L. 101/1874).

More than three whole months later, the government allocated £500 in the estimates to bring Skrefsrud to Adelaide and North Australia, where over the dry season of 1875 he could observe the country at first hand and make possible arrangements. The proposal met little opposition in parliament, and the veteran George Fife Angas, recalling how he had encouraged German religious migrants 35 years before, gave it qualified blessing. He thought the venture could be better organised.[820]

Four whole months after that, after a change of government, Ebenezer Ward sent a letter of acceptance to Skrefsrud, not directly but round about through the agent-general in London.[821] This reached London almost a year after the original request. As the Norwegian had long ago returned to India, the agent-general had then to make out another despatch and send the information halfway back again.[822] When at last it did arrive, the Norwegian missionary, deterred by delays and threats, and finding himself the centre of high politics, had turned his back forever on the subject of the Northern Territory.

Having addressed the South Australian government in April 1874, Skrefsrud had written to tell Boerresen of his plans. Boerresen, a cautious man, raised the question with representatives of the British civil service in India who thereby learned prematurely of negotiations that appeared calculated to bypass the imperial authority of the Indian government. But instead of reporting the colony of South Australia to the Colonial Office in London, the civil servants settled the matter quietly by threatening Boerresen and his friends that if they went ahead with the plan the Santal mission would come to 'nothing but harm'. Boerresen, in his turn, sent an urgent letter to Skrefsrud in Europe advising him to drop the scheme.[823] At the same time a high government official, a friend of the mission, wrote to England to inform Skrefsrud that 'Those Australians wished to turn the Santals into Sugar not into Christians

820 S.A.P.D. 1874 c.1644; 1747; 1748.

821 De Mole to Skrefsrud 28/1/1875 (N.T.O.L. 1875, p. 608).

822 Dutton to Skrefsrud 23/3/1875; Dutton to Bray 16/4/1875 with enclosures (N.T.I.L. 229/1875).

823 Research Notes, Olav Hodne of Gooch Bihar, India, Hodne to Cross 1964. Hodne is the main contemporary biographer of Skrefsrud.

the truth being they want Coolies to work there and grow sugar cane and such things'.[824] Skrefsrud was not the kind of man to back down on an offer already made, but the warnings were so serious that, even before he left for home, he wrote to a government official of the Santal Parganas advising that he had second thoughts about emigration to North Australia.[825]

The delays of the South Australian government added greatly to his difficulties. For month after month they did not even acknowledge his letter, so he had no way of ascertaining where he stood. Neither did South Australia formally approach the government of India, which seemed to confirm the suspicions Skrefsrud strove most to avoid, of trying to by-pass the correct authorities. Whatever chance the ministers in Adelaide had of procuring Santals was ruined by their failure to negotiate with the rulers in Calcutta or comprehend their recent cautious policy on emigration as advertised to the world in the *Indian Emigration Act of 1871.* This Act laid down strict rules for the manner in which the emigrants were to be engaged and employed, how they were to be paid, and the terms for their return to their homeland. Emigration was to restricted to three ports, Calcutta, Madras and Bombay and the governor-general in Calcutta had right of veto.

Only later, in 1879, did the South Australians follow the correct protocol, acknowledging 'that it would be useless for us to ask the Indian government to allow Indian immigration to the Northern Territory, unless we could satisfy the governor-general that legislation had been passed in accordance with the Indian Act'.[826] Only then did they discover how particular the rulers of India really were. The first set of South Australian laws framed to protect coolie migrants, and carefully copied from those in use for Indians in Mauritius and the West Indies, were refused the Queen's assent because the Viceroy detected 'deficiencies'. In the end in 1881 it was found easier to send a man (Major Fergusson, brother of the governor of Bombay) all the way to India to negotiate point by point

824 Allen to Boerresen 3/6/1874. Reported Statement. In possession of Olav Hodne, Gooch Bihar, India.

825 Skrefsrud to Hand 24/9/1874. In possession of Olav Hodne, Gooch Bihar, India.

826 S.A.P.D. 1879 c.1246 and 1247.

Bishop Francois Louis Bugnion of the Lords Church. He hoped that religious motivation would succeed where economic motivation was a proven failure. (*Illustrated Adelaide News* August 1876. Courtesy of the State Library of South Australia)

in person.[827] Even then, the best conditions he could obtain were beyond the colony's means to meet.

The caution was possibly influenced by the former governor Fergusson, now Governor of Bombay, who as far back as 1872 doubted South Australia's ability to manage the Territory.

The lesson from the Santal episode then was clear: that there was no point in seeking emigrants from India unless you first dealt face to face with the Indian government – or perhaps any other government in the Indies.

The strange, unexplained cooling of Skrefsrud's interest caused Goode back in London some embarrassment.[828] The missionary

827 S.A.P.D. 1882 c. 69 to 74.

828 Goode to Dutton 17/3/1875; Goode to Skrefsrud (extract) 4/12/1874 (N.T.I.L. 229/1875).

never acknowledged the South Australian invitation. Boerresen broadcast the news they had decided Australia was 'too far'.[829] Soon after, friends of the mission found a region inside India where Skrefsrud's vision could be fulfilled: far north in the wild hilly frontier of Assam, parts of which became available after the Bhutan Wars. The idea of migrating to Australia was forgotten. In 1881 a great trek, as great as the trek of the Boers, was made to the new Santal home.

Mennonites

No scheme involving religious contacts occupied more attention or was thought more promising than the idea of introducing Mennonite and Evangelical religious refugees from Russia. It became a kind of test case.

In the previous century Catherine the Great (herself of German background) had coaxed many of these German Mennonites to quit Prussia, where they were being persecuted for their pacifism, with bribes of free land and promises they would never again be called to bear arms. She wanted pious, thrifty people to colonise the rough virgin country near the Sea of Azoff as part of the southern consolidation of Russia, and she was not let down. Over three quarters of a century they built up an amazing agricultural empire, to the shelter of which came other religious communities. In the 1870s, however, Catherine's great grandson, Alexander II, decided to revoke the Mennonite privileges, particularly those which exempted them from military service. He fixed the deadline as the late spring of 1876, underestimating the strength of their convictions and the consequences of his decree. As their forebears had fled Prussia, many Mennonites at great personal sacrifice now prepared to leave Russia, taking also their skills and wealth. Communal leaders sent calls across the world asking sympathetic men to help find new homelands.

One agent to whom they appealed was Bishop Francois Louis Bugnion. He was a Swiss mystic, born near Lausanne in 1822, ordained a Lutheran pastor in 1845, and a fervent disciple of another mystic, Emanuel Swedenborg, son of a Lutheran minister. Early in

829 Research Notes, Olav Hodne of Gooch, Bihar, India, Hodne to Cross 1964.

his ministry Bugnion came to believe that his divine mission was to carry on the work of Swedenborg by forming a new religious community, the Church of the New Zion. Like Swedenborg, he believed the world of the Eastern Church the most promising field for his labours because it had strayed least from the primitive faith of the Saints. He became pastor to a Swiss and French colony at Shaba on the Dniester River near Akkerman in south-west Russia founded between 1823 and 1827, took apparently without right the title of Bishop, visited Petersburg and Moscow disseminating the doctrines of the New Church and made himself well known among the Mennonite and Evangelical colonies in Russia's deep south. He also earned, with good cause, the displeasure of the Russian Orthodox State Church, was almost sent to Siberia, and in 1857 fled abroad to save his ecclesiastical skin.[830]

These experiences stood him in good stead when later the religious sects began to feel the boot of Imperial Russian oppression. In 1869 he helped arrange a successful transmigration across the Atlantic to North America, for which the American authorities paid his expenses equivalent to £250. In 1873 he received an urgent letter from Christian Ganderr, an Evangelical communal leader at Shaba, describing the threatened withdrawal of privileges and appealing for help in finding a new homeland.

At the time Bugnion was in India, where the attractions of North Australia were claiming attention. He immediately set off for Sydney under the misapprehension that the Northern Territory was still part of New South Wales.[831] From Sydney in late October 1873 he wrote to Governor Anthony Musgrave in South Australia asking for £100 or a free passage to investigate the Territory's prospect for Russian refugees. He backed the request with a letter of personal recommendation from the influential Cowper Temple, the late Lord Palmerston's stepson (actually son).[832]

830 *Observer* 15/4/1876, p. 7. Research Note on L. Bugnion compiled by M. Kapran 1961 (State Archives of U.S.S.R., Moscow); M. Kapran was able to substantiate some of Bugnion's claims in his Memoirs. Ganderr was apparently sometimes called Handerr.

831 Bugnion to Way 7/2/1876 (N.T.I.L. 46/1877); *Northern Territory Times and Gazette* 20/3/1874, p. 3; Bugnion to Musgrave 24/10/1873 (C.S.O.I.L. 1693/1873).

832 Bugnion to Musgrave 24/10/1873 (C.S.O.I.L. 1693/1873).

Instead of inviting Bugnion to Adelaide at public cost, South Australian ministers sent him copies of the current land regulations under which he was led to understand the Russians could settle in the Territory. This action proved a deception because, as outlined in chapter four, the Act had never been applied, and this the ministers well knew.

Carrying the regulations with him, in March 1874 the saintly, erudite bishop, complete with biretta, cassock and staff, landed in the frontier town of Palmerston. Some thought him a Russian secret agent, others a fanatic, or simply demented. The local newspaper could only make of his complicated theology 'that he believes in everything that is good, and objects to everything that is evil'.[833] A few more thoughtful persons, notably the Government Resident and Paul Foelsche, the head of police, provided maps and assistance in investigating the land. For a month the bishop was a familiar sight traversing the landscape, every day growing more convinced that the hard-working Russians could succeed by settling along the river courses, especially the Adelaide River. Eventually, he notified his friends to sell out and prepare to come to their new home. But when he took steps to acquire the necessary land he discovered the truth: that it could not be alienated until new regulations were drafted. He also found that the cost was higher than comparable land in America. For two more months the bishop hung round Port Darwin anticipating the regulations. At last he despaired and wrote to the Russians with directions to alter course for America. Later he wrote:

> The strange way of dealing with me, two years ago, left no good impression upon my mind as to the policy *poursued then* by the South Australian Government.[834]

Two years passed, and in the Territory the gold bubble burst. What was needed to save the place, the newspapers said, was a bold stroke of Bismarkism – meaning a need for some exceptional action. Elsewhere the wealthy Mennonites and Evangelicals continued their exodus across the Atlantic.

---

833 *Northern Territory Times and Gazette* 20/3/1874, p. 3.

834 Bugnion to Way 7/2/1876, p. 6 (N.T.I.L. 46/1877); *Northern Territory Times and Gazette* 5/6/1874, p. 3.

From out of the depths of Bessarabia in south-west Russia the leader Christian Ganderr renewed his pleas. The problem was now more difficult and the deadline of the spring of 1876 very near. Many Mennonites and Evangelicals had since gone to Kansas, from where, greatly dissatisfied with the grasping company that had arranged their settlement, they warned the brethren against following.[835] This meant a prospect of migration from both directions to Australia.

This situation and a fortuitous train of circumstances gave Premier James Penn Boucaut, always a man of bold policies, a chance in 1876 to try his stroke of Bismarkism. In February his attorney-general, Samuel Way, rediscovered Bugnion in Sydney. Several prominent men vouched for Bugnion and his business sense. Again the question of Russian migration was broached. But the bishop this time was on his guard; he had every reason to distrust the South Australian politicians, and would only agree to go to Adelaide to negotiate if £50 was guaranteed for his costs.[836] The money was promised, and in March 1876 he made a flying visit.[837]

Bugnion saw the Russian colonists as a God-given opportunity at last to found the New Church. Sometimes he called them 'my flock', sometimes 'my sheep'. But neither the Russians nor the South Australian ministers saw Bugnion as more than a useful migration agent, a task he had already performed satisfactorily in North America. Boucaut put his government's attitude thus:

> I fully admit that we should not allow ourselves to be misled by anything or everything the Bishop might say; but where a man has great influence over a particular sect, and we have reason to avail ourselves of his influence and prejudices, it matters little as to his religious views so long as he succeeds in bringing people into the Territory. The idea of this Government was to give Bishop Bugnion credit for everything he said – saying they would not suspect him and harass him, and send spies to watch his acts throughout the world – but they would protect themselves by the second and fourth clauses in the agreement, which provided that he should bring the people in good health, that they

835 Bugnion to Way 7/2/1876 (N.T.I.L. 46/1877).

836 Bugnion to Way 7/2/1876 (N.T.I.L. 46/1877); S.A.P.D. 1876 c.194 and 195.

837 Bugnion to De Mole 21/2/1876 (N.T.I.L. 48/1876).

> should be artificers, and should have tools and provisions with them for six months...[838]

Boucaut arranged an agreement in which what he gave the migrants with one hand, he took back with the other. As soon as the settlers had proved themselves in good health and provisioned for six months they were to be refunded their passage money, which would then be taken off them again as they paid for the land. Boucaut also prided himself on his caution. Only George Goyder, the surveyor-general, who belonged to the Swedenborgians, was entrusted to do the bargaining with Bugnion. Goyder and B.T. Finniss were called upon to make separate reports on the country's suitability for white settlers. The migration could be terminated at any time. Boucaut even got in touch with Cowper Temple. The agent-general wired back: 'Temple reports most favourably Bishop Bugnion.'[839]

The agreement provisionally signed, and believing that its ratification would be a formality, Bishop Francois Louis Bugnion set off for Russia, via North America, as a migration agent in the pay of South Australia at the rate of £100 a month.[840]

Alas, he had not allowed for colonial politics. About this time Boucaut's ministry began to come unstuck. His commissioner of public works resigned. The chief justice died and his attorney-general stepped gleefully into the breach. Boucaut's chief secretary and treasurer, finding private business more profitable, announced their retirements. This left Boucaut with only one minister in his Cabinet, his protégé Ebenezer Ward. When he looked around (mainly among members of the Opposition parties) to form a new Cabinet he found that no candidate would 'sit in the same Government with a member whose presence was a disgrace to the colony' – meaning Ward. The elder statesman who had done so much to promote Ebenezer Ward, sadly had to demote him again, for which he earned the latter's bitter antagonism.[841] All this probably explains why Boucaut indulged his weakness for being too dramatic when the time eventually came to make the Bugnion

---

838 S.A.P.D. 1876 c.1969, changed back into first person.

839 Dutton to Blyth 18/4/1876 (S.A.P.P. 160 of 1876, p. 1).

840 Bugnion to Hawker 4/9/1876 (N.T.I.L. 406/1876).

841 S.A.P.D. 1876 c.4; *Advertiser* 18/5/1876 leader and p. 9.

agreement public. It was, as someone said, his way of detracting attention 'from the composition of a piebald ministry'.[842]

At a routine school celebration in the sleepy Adelaide Hills town of Nairne, Boucaut startled the public one April day with the intelligence that 40,000 religious immigrants, mainly Russian, would probably be settling in the Northern Territory of their colony. He could have had 100,000, he explained, but he knew the value of moderation.[843] Forty thousand were a lot of Russians. Any misgivings people had on that score were increased by the premier's somewhat hazy conceptions of ecclesiastical history. When he came to explain the details of his scheme, it became clear that Boucaut was uncertain just what a Mennonite was.[844] The public of the Australian colonies were not used to very large religious migrations (such as sometimes occurred in North America) and Boucaut's was an unfortunate way of gaining their confidence. Some feared a cunning plot by the Tsars to infiltrate into the colonies. Others suspected the bishop of being an 'enthusiast'[845] – a code word for fanatical dreamer or madman.

The news was received with jubilation in Palmerston. Boucaut had boldly tried to abandon the Territory in 1866; now with the same boldness he was going to revive it a decade later. When the new Government Resident, Edward Price, arrived in mid year he made himself popular by announcing to all the details of the plan.[846]

Boucaut's political enemies, Ebenezer Ward among them, were also quietly jubilant. The eccentric bishop was a sitting target for ridicule, and they went up and down the South Australian countryside sneering at the plan. At a public banquet to celebrate the opening of a rural Institute at Edithburg, Robert Dalrymple Ross, member for Wallaroo and a supporter of laissez-faire, brought the audience to their feet arguing that it was 'against the laws of nature' for white-skinned people from a cold climate to live in the tropics and by crying out against: 'the sufferings, the pitiable sufferings,

842 *The Methodist Journal* 14/4/1876.

843 *The Methodist Journal* 14/4/1876; *Register* 7/4/1876 leader.

844 *Register* 11/4/1876 leader.

845 *Advertiser* 11/4/1876, p. 7 Letters to Editor; *The Australasian* 22/4/1876, p. 534.

846 *Northern Territory Times and Gazette* 15/7/1876, p. 2; 16/9/1876, p. 3 Price's speech.

which would be entailed upon those unfortunate people. In fact, he believed it would be so great that a yell of execration would rise against the inhumanity of the statesmanship that countenanced such rashness and such folly' (followed by prolonged cheering).[847]

Parliament assembled and the piebald government lasted three days of debate. This landed its successors – and Ward in particular, because he again took charge of the Territory portfolio – in an awkward position: either they must eat their words or keep up the barrage. Faced by such a dilemma, the ministers tried to escape. They shelved the bishop and his 40,000 Russians until political events overseas removed their troubles for them. On 21 June 1876 they announced their decision not to proceed with Boucaut's grand plan. They would arrange, instead, for the bishop to bring a trial contingent of only two or three ship-loads.[848] This, the newspapers noted, was one way of knocking the scheme on the head because these people only moved in large communal groups.[849] Ward took no steps to notify Bugnion of the changes until three weeks had passed, and then only by slow sea mail when the telegraph was at hand.[850] Two months later Ward noted (hopefully) that negotiation with Bugnion was over.[851]

Meanwhile, the luckless bishop was sailing across the Pacific as an immigration agent in the pay of South Australia at the rate of over £3 a day. He reached San Francisco in May 1876 and there made tentative arrangements with Falkner, Bell and Company to carry migrants over the Pacific. Next he went to Nebraska, Kansas and Arkansas to whip up enthusiasm among the new Mennonite settlers. But his offers lost much of their fire, because no sanction was forthcoming from the South Australian legislature. In June he went to London. The colony's agent-general had nothing for him either. He went over to Geneva and cooled his heels by canvassing among his countrymen and making preliminary arrangements with Russian forward agents. Already in Bessarabia some families had sold their lands and were anxiously watching the deadline a

847 *Register* 22/4/1876 leader and p. 6.

848 S.A.P.D. 1876 c.181 and 182.

849 *Northern Territory Times and Gazette* 7/10/1876, p. 2.

850 Colton to Dutton 13/7/1876 (S.A.P.P. 160 of 1876, p. 1).

851 Ward to Hack 20/9/1876 (N.T.O.L. 410/1876).

few weeks away. Every week the Serbian War, in which Russia and Britain looked like participating on opposite sides, complicated matters. Meanwhile Bugnion's agent's allowance was running out, 'uselessly wasted in hotels,' as he said.[852] He begged Agent-General Francis Dutton for money, but as there was no intelligence, Dutton did not feel justified in granting it.[853] Finally, Bugnion borrowed money and set off to see his friends in south-west Russia. They were so agitated that he later dared not tell them the truth of the South Australian refusal, explaining it away as a postponement due to the Serbian War.[854]

Keenly embarrassed by the situation, Dutton wired Adelaide for instructions. He received notification a month later, misconstrued it to mean that Bugnion was to hasten back to Adelaide to work out a modified agreement, and informed him by telegraph to do so.[855] Ward's efforts to shelve the learned bishop and his Russians, wrote a commentator, 'like Muslim's curses had come home to roost'. In October 1876 Bugnion turned up in Adelaide much to the embarrassment of all.

Criticised by Opposition parties and the newspapers for bungling, Ward had now at least to make a show of negotiating with the bishop. The ensuing transactions, a far cry from those involving tens of thousands of self-supporting Russians, centred around a few ship loads of Bugnion's contacts in Mauritius, which he had visited after fleeing Russia in 1857. They were mainly Swedenborgians, poor people, living a hand to mouth existence, with no means or money to settle a new country. The tone of the meetings was never promising. The bishop was unsure of his hold over the Mauritian flock, having previously fallen out with them, and Ward, who preferred racehorses to bishops, was ill tempered and rude.[856]

852 Bugnion to Boucaut 6/5/1876; Bugnion to Boucaut 15/5/1876; Bugnion to Goyder 20/5/1876; Bugnion to Boucaut 22/5/1876; Bugnion to Everard 7/6/1876; Bugnion to Everard 8/6/1876; Bugnion to Hawker 27/6/1876; Bugnion to Hawker 1/7/1876 (S.A.P.P. 160 and 160A of 1876).

853 Bugnion to Ayers 9/8/1876 (N.T.I.L. 405/1876).

854 *Register* 11/10/1876, p. 5.

855 Dutton to Hawker (telegram) 4/8/1876 (S.A.P.P. 160 of 1876); Bugnion to Hawker 4/9/1876 (N.T.I.L. 406/1876); S.A.P.D. 1876 c.1965.

856 De Mole to Bugnion 13/10/1876 (N.T.O.L. 423/1876); Bugnion to Ayers 14/10/1876 with enclosure (N.T.I.L. 451/1876); De Mole to Bugnion

Inspector Paul Foelsche exhibited Germanic virtues; he was cerebral, disciplined, and authoritarian and he supported the idea of Mennonite migration. (Courtesy of the State Library of South Australia)

This last negotiation was memorable for the numerous titles Bugnion paraded: 'Right Rev Francois Louis Bugnion, permanent member of the Imperial Society of South Russia pro bono publico; honorary member of the E. Synod of Grousinia and Armenia; member Founder (Stifter) of the Rettungs Gesellschafe of Germany, Bishop of the Lords Church in Bourbon, Mauritius and India. 'I got,' he wrote, 'the official documents to substantiate every title.' In addition, Bugnion had experienced the laying on of hands 12 times.[857]

30/10/1876 (N.T.O.L. 435/1876); Bugnion to De Mole 31/10/1876 (N.T.I.L. 464/1876); Bugnion to Ward 2/11/1876 with enclosure (N.T.I.L. 474/1876); S.A.P.D. 1876 c.1963 to 1968.

857 *Register* 17/3/1877, p. 6; *Northern Territory Times and Gazette* 13/4/1878 leader; Research Notes supplied by Ken Reddig 27/2/1997 Provincial

At the end of 1876 the bishop with all his titles disappeared from the public gaze in Adelaide as mysteriously as he had first arrived.

The mishandling of the Mennonite affair was not easily forgotten. Many of these Mennonites migrated to Manitoba (annexed to Canada in 1870), where they proved themselves outstanding colonists. Within three years they had set up flourishing settlements carved from virgin land at the East Reserve and the West Reserve on either side of the Red River. In 1877 Lord Dufferin, governor-general of Canada, visited the settlements and applauded the Mennonites' steady capacity to succeed where others looking for worldly gain gave up. When Dufferin's report reached Adelaide in 1878 the *Register* branded South Australia's failure to take advantage of Mennonite migration 'an egregious blunder'.[858]

As before, South Australian methods of doing international business were unusual. Being a mere colony, its representatives had no right whatsoever to start negotiating with the citizens of a foreign power. For South Australian politicians this would have sounded a merely academic objection. They claimed the right, and there is no hint in the discussions of their ever having second thoughts, even when the foreign power was Russia, which was not on the most amiable of terms with Great Britain. There was a second irregularity. The Tsar had strictly forbidden outsiders to canvass emigration inside his empire, so the South Australians' agent was always liable to be arrested and sent to Siberia. Embarrassed by the prospect, the British Imperial Ambassador at Petersburg complained to the Colonial Office which remonstrated with Governor Musgrave in Adelaide.[859] Perhaps Boucaut best summed up the South Australian politicians' concern for such complaints when he asked how America would ever have been peopled if the Pilgrim Fathers and others had first sought the sanction of the English authorities.[860]

Archives, Manitoba; Research Notes by John Thiesen 8/7/1992 Bethel College Mennonite Archives, Kansas. Thiesen critical of Bugnion.

858 *Register* 23/1/1878, p. 4.

859 Carnarvon to Musgrave 4/8/1876; Loftus to Derby 18/7/1876 (G.I.D. 26 of 1876).

860 S.A.P.D. 1876 c.1968 to 1971.

Japanese

A third example of using religious contacts involved the strange case of Wilton Hack and his plans to set up a mission in Nagasaki and later at Hiroshima. Again the methods lacked sophistication, with the minister pursuing one policy in Adelaide and the immigration agent, a missionary named Wilton Hack, following a different track. The failure to make a distinction between the two has led historians to overstress the prospect of 1870s Japanese migration to the Northern Territory.[861]

Hack was of Quaker stock – 'born into the Society of Friends' – and an individualist. His self-proclaimed mission to procure Japanese migration was one side in his life-long desire to do something good for people in distress. In the drought year of 1867 he forsook the pastoral pursuits for which his father, Stephen Hack, a South Australian pioneer, had prepared him, to start out in Adelaide on a life of service 'in fields not tended by others'. He did pioneering social work among the prisoners of Yatala gaol, and later at Mount Remarkable in the lower Flinders Ranges attempted to start a village settlement for depressed workers run on communistic lines – being Hack's response to those people in Australia who at the time were heading for Paraguay to found a utopian society called New Australia. In Adelaide he married into the staunchly Baptist Stonehouse family, and so cemented a decade's loose and rather shaky alliance with the Baptist Church.[862] But Hack's Quaker roots never stayed far under the surface. He lived with the intense earnestness for social reform that has long distinguished the Society of Friends – and many Baptists too.

In 1873 Hack received an 'inward call' to preach practical Christianity to the people of Japan.[863] Following treaties forced on

---

861 J. Cross, *Wilton Hack and Japanese Immigration into North Australia* (Proceedings of the Royal Geographical Society of Australasia South Australian Branch Volume 61, 1959/60, pp. 55–59).

862 *Advertiser* 2/3/1923 p. 8; Wilton Hack, unpublished, *Sketch of My Life*, 1907 (S.L.S.A. Mortlock P.R.G. 456/35). For background information on the Quakers in South Australia see C. Stevenson, *The Millionth Snowflake – The History of Quakers in South Australia*, The Religious Society of Friends, Adelaide, 1987; also information from Herbert Stock, Adelaide Local Meeting, January 2006.

863 *Truth and Progress* November 1873; January 1874; October 1874; September

the country at gun-point by America and other Western powers in the 1850s, Japanese citizens were not legally allowed to become Christians until 1859. The number of Protestant missionaries rapidly increased from 28 to 47, Catholics having already burned their fingers in Japan. The same events had created a fierce anti-western reaction among many traditional Japanese.[864]

The idea of a lone, unsupported missionary venturing into a strange territory like Japan seemed midsummer madness to Wilton Hack's friends, but he would not be dissuaded. He sold most of his possessions and set sail with his family from Adelaide, accompanied by two ex-prisoners – forger Robert Baldry (alias Walter Travers), and embezzler Alfred Clode (with his wife) as mission workers. The party was aided financially by an aristocrat of independent means, William Wallace Legge, who was in gaol in Adelaide for killing his wife. Baldry, who had been imprisoned for life, was released on the understanding that he leave immediately for Japan.

Japan in the 1870s was a very insecure place indeed, owing to social upheavals attending on forced westernisation. There were rebellions in the south-east. Europeans in general, and Christian missionaries in particular, had to tread lightly. When Hack arrived at Nagasaki, the so-called 'European gateway to Japan', in January 1874 he could hardly have imagined the difficulties awaiting him. He found Nagasaki under constant threat of attack by Hizen insurgent rebels, with locals fleeing to the mountains. Different groups spoke numerous dialects, which made general mission work all but impossible. Other missionaries urged the new enthusiast to lie low until he had mastered the language and customs.[865] Few Westerners ventured out of their compounds without armed guards, fearing they might meet a samurai coming in the opposite direction with his sword.

But Hack would not be quiet. He circumvented the dialect barrier by purchasing a printing press, engaging a translator and with extraordinary energy distributing thousands of religious tracts in Japanese ideographic characters. He even grew so bold as to give them to Buddhist priests, Shintoist officials and, alas, the governor

---

1876.

864 Research Notes on Japanese Migration, D.C.S. Sissons, 1971/1972.

865 *Truth and Progress* June 1874.

of Saga himself. Hack set up his press in house 13 in Oura, the foreign quarter, overlooking the creek which formed the western boundary of the area reserved for foreigners, and was ably assisted by embezzler Clode, who had learned some printing skills working for the *Northern Argus* before going to gaol. For a brief period they also published an English-language newspaper called *The Rising Sun* in honour of the New Japan.

Leaving his mission at Nagasaki under the supervision of Clode, in June 1874 he took work as a teacher of English at 200 yen a month plus house at the government's English language school (in Japanese called the Eigo Gakko) in the city of Hiroshima 200 miles away, where he set up a second mission. There he employed a local Japanese orator called Hirota as preacher who attracted large crowds. The printing press at Nagasaki he claimed was the first mission press in Japan; the Church at Hiroshima he claimed to be the first away from the open ports.[866] In both Nagasaki and Hiroshima he built up small followings among the poor middle-class people feeling the pinch of industrial changes and attracted by his generosity and promises of social reform. After 12 months he had made 33 converts. Soon, however, his zeal brought him into trouble with the religious department of the Japanese government 'for disturbing the people in matters of religion'. In May 1875 he was dismissed from teaching and forced to retreat to Nagasaki, the financial support cut from underneath the mission. So, in the southern winter of 1876 Wilton Hack suddenly turned up in Adelaide appealing for funds to form a mission society. At a public lecture he prophesied that the Japanese people 'were on the highroad to greatness'. With the help of Charles Goode, the advocate for the Santal scheme, he had already toured England and the eastern Australian colonies. Though South Australian Baptists rallied to Hack's aid (George Fife Angas set the ball rolling with £100) it soon became clear that his success would not be great.[867]

While fundraising in Adelaide, encouraged by George Goyder (a tireless advocate for Territory colonisation) and publicity about the putative Mennonite settlers, Hack decided to approach the South

866 *Truth and Progress* May 1875; Wilton Hack, *Sketch of My Life*, 1907 (S.L.S.A. Mortlock P.R.G. 456/35); *Advertiser* 18/5/1876, p. 6 Frederick Searle to Editor.

867 *Truth and Progress* September 1876; *Advertiser* 27/7/1876, p. 3.

A Port Darwin "Jap."

A Japanese prostitute in Darwin. Old timers remembered the respect with which Asians treated their prostitutes compared with the Fallen Women approach in the West.
(Courtesy of the John Oxley Library, State Library of Queensland)

Australian ministers with a scheme to introduce a limited number of middle-class Japanese to North Australia.[868] It was probably no accident that the limited number later turned out to be about the size of his mission.

The proposal was well-received by Ebenezer Ward and the government that succeeded Boucaut's, though for different reasons than Hack might have wished. It coincided with negotiations for the Netherlands East India Company to link Port Darwin to Batavia and thence to all Asia. Ward consequently interpreted the idea of

868 Hack to Carr 29/7/1876 (N.T.I.L. 286/1876).

Japanese middle-class migration in the light of his own laissez-faire preferences for linking the Territory northwards and then advertising it among Asians and islanders rich enough to make the journey themselves as free settlers. In view of 'the proposed contract with the Netherlands India Steam Navg. Co.,' noted Ward, 'some good might be done by the dissemination of a Knowledge of the resources of the Northern Territory in Japan and neighbouring countries.'[869] A missionary about to return to Japan appealed to him as a conveniently cheap way of achieving this, particularly because Hack stressed that he had been employed by the Japanese government and had government contacts. So Hack was given a grant of £50 and a non-committal letter of introduction and sent off to probe the Tokyo government's attitude towards emigration, should anyone wish to leave.[870]

After Hack had gone, Ward made a statement to the House:

> The Government do not propose to introduce at the public expense either Japanese, Chinese, or heathens as immigrants to the Northern Territory; but they have taken steps to make known in Japan the resources of the Territory and its advantages as a field for emigration for the people of that country.[871]

Hack's subsequent activities raise a question of how far a government is responsible for the acts of an agent who apparently exceeds his instructions. Hack returned to Nagasaki early in 1877 to find his missions in chaos. His gaolbird helpers had gone, having first helped themselves to most of the money. Without the inspiration of his own practical Christianity his poor middle-class contacts were drifting away.[872] He reasserted his prestige among them by revealing how he had secured the promise of a new life in the rich, fertile land of North Australia. The effect of the news was like magic. Some began preparations to leave, and later wanted to brave the wrath of

---

869 Minute by Ward 4/8/1876 (with N.T.I.L. 286/1876).

870 Cabinet Minute 14/8/1876 (with N.T.I.L. 286/1876); De Mole to Hack 6/9/1876 (N.T.O.L. 406/1876); Ayers to Minister of Foreign Affairs in Tokio (sic) 19/9/1876 (C.S.O.L. 864/1876).

871 S.A.P.D. 1876, c.1106.

872 *Truth and Progress* August 1877. Clode and wife used the money to escape to Washington State, west coast America.

the authorities in order to follow him to Australia.[873] Hack drew up his personal scheme of colonisation, quite contrary to the ideas of Ward and the government, which in all probability he then showed to his followers. News of a colonial migration agent whipping up fervour without the consent of the Japanese authorities would have caused misgivings in London. But the London officials were apparently not informed about the negotiations.[874]

When he reached the capital Tokyo – styling himself 'Agent for the South Australian Government', and now seeking the approval of the correct authorities – the Satsuma rebels were threatening to overthrow the central government. These rebels yearned for the idyllic order of Old Japan and despised western missionaries. From the start the climate was bad for business. The basis for negotiation was not the existing South Australian land laws, framed to entice settlers under their own steam, but the principle of assisted immigration – the key element in Hack's own colonisation plan, which he had meanwhile translated into Japanese.[875]

His scheme required the government in Adelaide to provide free passages for a small migration of non-coolie Japanese leaving in about mid 1877. Having reached North Australia, the immigrants were to shut themselves away from other settlers in settlements under the control of village elders run on communal or communistic lines.[876] Hack did not explain his own role, but it seems that having led his followers to Canaan he would set himself up as a patriarch missionary propagating the precepts of practical Christianity away from the meddling of Japanese officials and the despair of poverty.

The men of the Japanese Foreign Office proved studiously polite, but cool. Hack grew annoyed when they somehow lost his cherished plan, which made him suspect they never looked at it.[877]

873 Hack to Ward 15/3/1877 (N.T.I.L. 260/1877).

874 Index 22,947/ Correspondence of British Consulate in Japan, Public Record Office, London. Officers of Public Record Office could trace no official notification from this index.

875 Hack to Minister of Foreign Affairs in Japan 16/2/1877; Hack to Minister of Foreign Affairs 16/2/1877; Hack to Minister of Foreign Affairs 26/2/1877; Ishibashi to Hack 26/2/1877; Ishibashi to Hack 27/2/1877; Hack to Ward 25/9/1877 (N.T.I.L. 489/1877).

876 Hack to Ward 26/10/1877 with enclosure (N.T.I.L. 508/1877).

877 Ishibashi to Hack 27/3/1877; Hack to Ishibashi 14/4/1877 (Held by the

The haggling via a series of letters that followed shows how Hack impatiently tried to pin the Japanese to a promise:

> Hack: Will you or will you not agree to this emigration?
> Japanese: Under the laws of our country no obstacle can be put in its way ...
> Hack: (Several days later) Will you put that down in writing?
> Japanese: (Pause of ten days) Under present circumstances we are not disposed to encourage the matter ...
> Hack: (Same day) Have you any objections to the plans proposed by me? Will you or will you not resist say 3 or 400 leaving at my government's expense?

Japanese: Yes. [878]

That was that. Hack was nettled. He bided his time until the eve of his departure, when he fired a parting shot:

> I deeply regret, that your department has regarded with so little favor the friendly overtures of the South Australian Government, and still hope, that in years to come a larger hearted sympathy may exist between your Empire and Australia.[879]

He later kept this blast from the notice of his South Australian ministers, though he made no secret of his fervent hope that the Tokyo government would be beaten up by the rebels.

Hack now had to set about cooling down his intending emigrants for fear their enthusiasm to defy their rulers led to trouble between Japan and South Australia. His religious and social idealism had suffered a severe setback. He returned to the safety of Nagasaki with his family in April 1877 so broke that the British consul there had to open a subscription among British nationals to get him out of the country. A modest sum was raised by passing around the hat. In thanking the donors, Hack said 'it made the future less gloomy in appearance'.[880] After asking the British consul

---

Japanese Ministry of Foreign Affairs).

878 Hack to Ward 15/3/1877 (N.T.I.L. 260/1877); *Register* 21/8/1877; Correspondence with Japanese Government (N.T.I.L. 489/1877).

879 Hack to Ishibashi 14/4/1877 (Held by the Japanese Ministry of Foreign Affairs).

880 H.S. Williams, *Foreigners in Mikadoland*, Turtle, Tokyo, 1963, pp. 182 and 183.

at Nagasaki, in a private capacity, to keep an eye on prospects, he abandoned Japan and returned to Australia in the southern winter of 1877 via Hong Kong on a 'coolie ship' crammed full of Chinese headed for the El Dorado of Cooktown in North Queensland.

The Adelaide *Register*, after an interview with the missionary, pointed to three reasons for the Japanese refusal. The presence of the Satsuma insurrection made emigration impolitic. The Japanese had their own colonisation plans aimed at spreading Nippon culture in the surrounding islands. The small artisan class, though depressed in the 1870s, were wanted to build up the New Japan.[881] All these were consistent with a standing Japanese policy against emigration acknowledged in the Adelaide newspapers even before Hack set out. In fact, already in 1872, in reaction to the recent exploitation of Japanese nationals in Hawaii, Guam and California, the government in Tokyo had passed Law 295, which forbade contract emigration exceeding more than one year.

The irony was that throughout this saga, Ebenezer Ward had been telling his countrymen how the men of his government, unlike other politicians he could name (referring to Boucaut), would never tolerate assisted immigration to the Northern Territory.

In October 1877 the government was defeated and Ward was never again admitted to a ministry, though he stayed on in parliament for many years as a fruitful source of scandals – mainly because of his consumption of alcohol 'taken for medicinal purposes'. Wilton Hack made a resolution never to go preaching again. His faith in Western religion severely shaken, he had to call Baptist friends to get himself out of debt. For a time he took up the more worldly life of a gold speculator. Later he became a socialist and a convert to Eastern mysticism.[882] When Hack died at Beverley, Western Australia, in 1923, he left instructions that his body should be cremated on the local common, which when carried out caused much local resentment.[883]

881 *Register* 21/8/1877, p. 5.

882 Wilton Hack, *Sketch of My Life,* 1907 (S.L.S.A. Mortlake P.R.G. 456/35); *Advertiser* 2/3/1923, p. 8; *The Beverley Times* 3/3/1923.

883 J. Barton Hack to J. Cross 23/2/1960; confirmed by Peg Kempton, Beverley Historical Society 21/12/2005.

In 1898 John Langdon Parsons, South Australia's consul to Japan, visited Tokyo and made a last desperate bid to entice Japanese capitalists with their own workers to take up land in the Territory. But in June 1898 the move was vetoed by the foreign minister in Tokyo because his government wanted to keep Japanese nationals at home to build the New Japan.[884]

So ended plans to bring in Japanese. After the Japanese victory over Russia in 1904–1905 a fear of their nation gradually took hold in Australia. Japan was seen as the leader in the global revolt against white domination. Historians like Roberts and Price later made much of how South Australia had once diced with actually inviting Japanese to settle in North Australia.885

An Alternative Israel

The dream of using religious contacts to develop North Australia was not quite over. In 1907 the Federal and South Australian governments were approached by an influential English Jew named Israel Zangwill about settling 50,000 Russian Jews in the Territory. But his request did not get far. Prime Minister Deakin opposed the idea of a state-within-a-state and Premier Price was too busy trying to off-load the Territory onto the Commonwealth. Zangwill's dream of finding an 'alternative Israel' received a setback in 1917 when, on the eve of General Allenby's taking the Holy Land from the Turks, the British Foreign Secretary Lord Balfour declared Britain's support for a Jewish homeland in Palestine – which promise it took 30 years to honour.

With the rise of the Nazis in the 1930s, the search for a Jewish refuge could not be delayed. In 1939 before the outbreak of war, the government of Western Australia moved to set up a large Jewish settlement, this time completely under Australian law, as a kind of alternative Israel, in the Kimberley near the Territory border. The two main actors in this scheme were Michael Patrick Durack, pastoralist and politician, and Isaac Nachman Steinberg of the

---

884 See article by D.C.S. Sissons, 'Japanese in the Northern Territory 1884–1902', *South Australiana,* Vol. 16, No. 1, March 1977.

885 Examples, see S.H. Roberts, *History of Australian Land Settlement,* Macmillan, Melbourne, 1924; A. Grenfell Price, *The History and Problems of the Northern Territory,* Acott, Adelaide, 1930.

Freeland League for Jewish Territorial Colonisation, who came all the way from Europe to visit the Kimberley and to negotiate. Behind the plan was the realisation that Jews were great travellers. There were Jews in China before Marco Polo and in India before the Portuguese. But the move, which just might have changed the course of world history, was later vetoed by the Commonwealth government – partly because the hope of 'an alternative Israel' met a hostile reaction from Zionists in Melbourne.[886]

886 Research information from Steve Howell, State Library of Western Australia 27/11/2006, especially the paper by Bill Hornadge, *The Israel of Oz,* 1999; Steinberg to Durack (State Library of Western Australia 4588A/JS 9/2); *Gadfly* 20/2/1907; *The West Australian,* 19/3/1938, p. 3; 9/7/1938, p. 21; 22/9/1938, p. 21; 17/6/1939, p. 25; 1/7/1939, p. 7; 8/7/1939, p. 5; 12/7/1939, p. 16; 15/7/1939, p. 7; 9/8/1939, p. 16; 30/8/1939, p. 14; 14/9/1939, p. 6, 11/11/1939, p. 14.

CHAPTER 7

COMING OF THE GAUCHOS

'These ... gauchos lead a strange life, bullocks and blacks, bad flour and too frequently bad everything else.'

Diary of William Nation, 20 October 1872.

Other Colonisers: Different Stories

With the gradual passing of the 1880s, South Australia's control over the Territory became much less certain. There was a change in strategy from controlled (in fact too controlled) methods of colonisation concentrating on the north coast to almost the opposite further inland, with the effect that much of the Territory became a rough, vigorous, chaotic pioneering society with many of the characteristics that Edward Gibbon Wakefield and his high-minded reformer friends would have regarded as barbarous. Much of the change came via the remote outback of north-west Queensland.

By the 1880s it was clear to most South Australians that the dream of a self-supporting colony that was concentrated, controlled and civilised, as well as a bridge to Asia, could not be revived. What was needed was some method of settlement which circumvented the land monopolists of Palmerston. And about the same time newspapers in both the upper Territory and North Queensland began to put forward the idea of the two regions combining to form a new northern colony.

Why had the plan for a self-supporting and concentrated settlement facing Asia failed? Or to reverse the question: Why did the failure of closer settlement succeed in preserving so much of the traditional landscape and culture intact, with the result that today we still have places like the reserved region of Kakadu and the languages and cultures of the Yolngu of Arnhem Land?

The most often quoted reason for the failure heard towards the end of South Australia's reign – originating particularly from John Langdon Parsons and Herbert Angas Parsons, both politicians with

John Langdon Parsons, later minister in charge of the Northern Territory and Government Resident. He and his son argued that the first five years ruined the Territory.
(*Frearsons Monthly Illustrated Adelaide News* April 1884, p. 52. Courtesy of the State Library of South Australia)

a deep interest in the Territory – was that 'the first five years ruined the Territory'. This explanation referred back to the arguments over a site, the litigation with the land-order holders and the frequent changes of government.

The problems of the first five years however, were not the only ones. Much of the scheme was anachronistic, being at least 30 years too late. Nowhere was this better seen than on the issue of Asian immigration. The Territory was settled on the assumption that there would be an unlimited supply of cheap labour near at hand: Indonesians, Malays, Indians, Chinese, Mauritians, even freed Negro slaves, and so on. George Windsor Earl, adviser to the government in 1864, had promised that the supply of labour would be 'inexhaustible'. By the 1870s the situation has changed. A world reaction had set in against the hasty exportation of coolies to other lands because of their mistreatment. All the major governments in the East – Japan, China, India and the Dutch East Indies – moved to discourage emigration to the Northern Territory, or for that matter Australia in general. In Australia's migration story, it is a point not often made. But for this resistance by these outside governments, Australia would probably now be a more Eurasian society than it is.

Then in 1880 the South Australian House of Assembly took the first steps to restrict the immigration of Chinese to the Northern Territory. The so-called White Australia Policy was on the way. The moves were seen as a threat by older South Australians interested in the northern province. Not 20 years earlier they had taken it over on the assumption that the north-west coast was as much part of Asia as Australia. B.T. Finniss wrote to the *Register* arguing that such restrictions 'would be absolutely fatal to the progress of that colony, which must of necessity be largely occupied by Asiatics'. He believed Chinese to be the best prospect, because they were physically superior to all other races.[887] When in 1880 the ministers in Adelaide asked J.G. Knight, perhaps the Territory's most brilliant official, to suggest strategies to develop the region, he wrote that 'the territory must, in the main, become an Asiatic settlement'.[888] In the House of Assembly, Lavington Glyde (who had introduced the original legislation to launch the Territory in 1863) expressed his disdain for restrictions on Chinese with a poem:

> The high-priced, clumsy, lazy whites
> Were no match for this saffron chap,
> And they now deplored that when he snored
> They had raised him from his nap.
> They raved and tore and wept and swore
> To drive him home again;
> But never an inch would the Pagan flinch,
> For it paid him to remain.
>
> 'Tis wrong, I know, to smile at woe,
> But it's rather a joke to see
> The civilized white put in such a fright
> By the barbarous Chinee![889]

887 *Register* 28/7/1881 Supplement, p. 3 Finniss to Editor 23/7/1881.

888 Knight's Report on the Requirements of the Northern Territory 10/1/1880 (N.T.I.L. 87/1880).

889 S.A.P.D. 1880 c. 592. I have omitted the side comment.

A Different Way of Looking at Asia.
After Japan's victory over Russia in 1904–1905, Japan was seen as a leader in the world revolt against 'White Domination' – and a fear of Japan took hold in Australia.
(Drawn by Frank S. Koch for *Gadfly* 8/5/1907 p. 1206.
Courtesy of State Library of South Australia)

The less populist Upper House, under Henry Ayers, vetoed the anti-Chinese legislation twice before giving way to a compromise poll tax on Chinese in 1881.[890]

The moves to restrict their entry came as a direct result of an inter-colonial conference called by Henry Parkes, premier of New South Wales, in 1880 and again in 1881. The main public pressures for restrictions came from the colony of Queensland and Working Men's Associations around Australia, such as the Port Adelaide Working Men's Association. A new class was entering politics, the working class, even less interested in the future of the Territory than were the 'Cocky class' of the early 1870s.

White Australia was part of a worldwide movement that

---

890 S.A.P.A. 213 of 1881 *An act to regulate and restrict Chinese Immigration.*

emerged toward the end of the 19th century, built in part on a fear that Western civilisation might be overwhelmed by the 'coloured races', combined with a conviction that only 'white culture' could achieve liberal reforms like the basic wage and universal suffrage. The Territory was again a generation too late. Whereas the Northern Territory still required cheap labour and pioneering conditions, the rest of Australia in the 1890s was moving toward equal opportunity and trade union rights. [891]

Another reason for the failure was a mismatch between the plan of colonisation and geographic reality. The planners of 1863 and 1864 misunderstood the geography of the far north coast because they saw it as part of the southern perimeter of the Indies Archipelago and much like Java. In fact, it was a Wet–Dry tropic, bound by the pendulum of the monsoon, moving back and forth between the Himalayas to the far north-west and the Australian desert to the south. The upper Territory has been described by meteorologists as a desert where it rains hard for a few months a year. When the environment turned out to be more difficult than anticipated, the colonisers turned on each other with accusations of ineptitude, corruption and lack of will – recriminations that eventually did much to discredit the Territory.

A good example of the failure to understand the geography was the attempts in the 1880s by a succession of enthusiasts with limited capital to experiment with tropical agriculture. These endeavours were based on the northern hemisphere idea of finding the one great staple – be it sugar, cotton or maize – that would launch and sustain the Territory. There was a burst of new hope and new excitement. For a time it seemed that the idea put forward by Richard Schomburgk, the colony's foremost botanical scientist, that South Australians should make an all-out attempt to test the north for tropical agriculture, was being enacted in earnest.

In 1880 William Morgan's government introduced a Sugar Plantation Bill, sparking a brief agricultural boom in the Territory.

---

891 Marilyn Lake and Henry Reynolds, *Drawing the Global Colour Line,* Melbourne University Press, 2008, *passim*. The idea of a worldwide white culture is a good example of 'an imagined community', invented partly in response to a feeling that the era of European domination might be coming to an end.

Dr Richard Schomburgk, distinguished scientist, driven out of Germany because of his involvement in the 1848 revolutions. He advocated an all-out effort to test the Territory for tropical agriculture. (George E. Loyau, *Representative Men of South Australia*, Howell, Adelaide, 1882, wood engraving by Jeffrey Bruer)

The Bill started out simply to sanction a deal with William Owston of Spence and Owston, one of the first sugar planters in Fiji, who in 1879 approached the South Australian government with an offer to pioneer sugar growing in the Territory. The Legislative Council widened the Bill to include other growers, and the resulting Act provided for generous land grants in fee simple (ownership without limitation) to successful applicants, if after six years they had spent 10 shillings per acre calculated on all the land selected and then produced a quantity of commercial sugar (or some other approved crop) equal in value to 10 shillings per acre.[892]

Having selected land on the Daly River, Owston failed to anticipate the difficulties and in 1883 the Palmerston Plantation Company was wound up, after producing no sugar. The publicity associated with passing the Act, however, attracted a rush of

892 S.A.P.D. 1880 c 1681, 1682; S.A.P.A. 194 of 1880; S.A.P.P. 179 of 1881.

applicants seeking to take advantage of the generous provisions. Unfortunately, the Morgan government decided to reward only South Australian applicants, most of whom (as with the original land-order holders and, after that, the gold boom) turned out to be speculators waiting to benefit from the exertions of others. The rush of applicants in turn tempted some growers in the Territory (often as squatters) to try other tropical crops. Henry Poett, formerly of Sri Lanka, tried coffee at Rum Jungle, for instance, and the pastoral firm of Fisher and Lyons established an indiarubber plantation at Beatrice Hill.

Of the companies that selected land under the 1880 Act only the Pioneering Sugar Company, which chose land at Delissaville on the Douglas Peninsula, showed any promise. It became the test case for investors wanting to invest in tropical agriculture. The company started well in 1881, employing 16 Europeans and 45 Chinese, with its management inspired by the promise of a grant of 10,000 acres at the end of six years. But in 1882 after disputes with the company secretary G.T. Bean, who needed quick returns for impatient Adelaide shareholders, manager Benjamin De Lissa resigned from the so-called 'De Lissa Company' and took the chief engineer with him to grow sugar in Borneo. By 1884 the Pioneering Sugar Company in the Territory had spent £20,000 on machinery, buildings and a jetty in return for seven tons of sugar crushed in 1883 and five tons in 1884 and was wound up in 1885.[893]

A few small farmers who had been pushed aside in 1880 by Adelaide speculators showed promise, the most noteworthy being Otto Brandt, who took up land under the 1872 Land Act at Shoal Bay eight miles from Palmerston. By 1890 he had crushed 100 tons of sugar in total and after a heroic battle against termites, rats and climate, with little help from government, he gave up in 1891. Only Chinese gardeners in select spots (practising what was called 'petit agriculture') mastered agriculture in the Territory – and they were soon encouraged to leave because of the rising tide of anti-Chinese feeling.[894]

893 *Register* 9/12/1880 Supplement, p. 1; *Advertiser* 9/12/1880, p. 5; 24/9/1886, p. 7; *Northern Territory Times and Gazette* 1/1/1881, p. 2.

894 *Register* 10/10/1884, p. 6; 24/9/1886, p. 5; *Northern Territory Times and Gazette* 28/11/1890, p. 2.

In 1882 the South Australian government sent Professor Ralph Tate, foundation professor of natural science at Adelaide University, north to *prove* the potential of the region. In his report Tate was one of the first to emphasise that the tropics of North Australia were quite different from the tropics of the Indies. When he concluded that the potential for agriculture was much over-rated he was attacked from many directions: 'the guesses of science,' said the minister, 'are not worthy of any more credence than the guesses of superstition'.[895]

Running in parallel to attempts to promote agriculture on land were efforts to develop the pearling industry in Port Darwin harbour. These began with the arrival from Singapore via Koepang of the *Sree Pas Sair* (formerly owned by the Rajah of Pas Sair) under Captain Chippendale in February 1884, using eight Malay skindivers, followed soon by 23 boats from Thursday Island with the first of many Japanese divers, including some equipped with deep-diving gear. A local North Australian Pearlshell Company formed the previous year in Palmerston was revived. But by 1887 the beds had been worked out and the fleet was gone.[896]

The so-called 'Great Depression of the 1890s' hit South Australia in 1884, six or seven years before the rest of Australia, and brought a premature end to experiments with tropical agriculture on the north coast. The window of opportunity beginning in the 1860s – more than two decades of reasonable prosperity in South Australia – was drawing to a close.[897] After about 1885 development near Port Darwin went into a slow rambling decline and remained so until after the Federal government took control in 1911.

Ralph Milner and the Southern Route

By far the most important reason for the changes after 1880 was the advent of the cattle industry further inland, which provided

895 Professor Tate's Report on Northern Territory 27/6/1882 (S.A.P.P. 63 of 1882); *Register* 22/7/1882, p. 6 Tate to Editor; S.A.P.D. 1882 c.941.

896 *Northern Territory Times and Gazette* 16/2/1884 leader; 23/2/1884, p. 2; *Register* 5/6/18845 Supplement, p. 2.

897 Douglas Pike, postgraduate seminar, Department of History, University of Adelaide 1956. The author was given the job of testing the hypothesis by working through 1880s newspapers.

John Baker, one-time associate of John Chambers.
He argued vigorously that pastoral settlement must come before agriculture.
(State Library of South Australia)

an alternative model for the development of the Territory and which survived in the end by using Aboriginal workers on pittance wages. Because pastoral development did not fit well in their theory Wakefield and the systematic colonisers had always underestimated it as a colonisation strategy. They saw it as an *uncivilised* method of colonisation.

Writing the early history of the Territory's pastoral industry is a nightmare for historians. The events were chaotic. One overlander more or less followed the tracks of the other, then spread out into new grazing lands, only to abandon them if he thought he could find better. Most of the information is based on oral tradition, much of it contradictory after repeated retellings.

In general, the stock were overlanded into the Territory from two directions, the northern outstations of South Australia and via the Gulf Country in Queensland.

The pastoral industry began in Central Australia in 1872 – a region since 1865 officially known as Alexandra Land, named at the request of John McDouall Stuart. But the stations in the centre went largely unreported, partly because of South Australians' preoccupation with the tropical north facing Asia but also, because it took the form of an 'inexpensive infiltration' from south to north – just as George Waterhouse had predicted when he applied for the Territory on behalf of the South Australian government back in 1862, and confirming the conjecture of the same year by the Duke of Newcastle, secretary of state for colonies, that the country up to the Tropic of Capricorn was a natural extension of South Australia. The inexpensive infiltration northwards was hastened by the construction of the overland telegraph. Thus in 1872 Edward Meade Bagot, contractor for the southern section of the line, took up Undoolya station near Alice Springs in the MacDonnell Ranges, which was stocked by his son Ned by 1874. The first cattle from Alice Springs to Port Darwin left Undoolya on 24 June 1875: 75 head driven north for the butcher Abbott by the drover Tom (also known as Tim) Nelson, who came all the way from Palmerston to collect them.[898]

Also in 1872, Joseph Gilbert, brother-in-law to Dr W.J. Browne (later founder of Springvale Station), took up Owen Springs in the MacDonnell Ranges, which was stocked by his son William Gilbert by 1875. In remote areas like this, well-established southern pastoralists tended to combine forces. Bagot and Gilbert worked together before going their own ways. These pioneers were followed by Parke and Walker at Henbury; Grant and Stokes at Idracowra and Glen Helen; and Gilmour, Hendry and Melrose at Mount Burrell, all of whom managed to stock their leases in the 1880s.[899]

In contrast, the development of the pastoral industry in the northern half of the Territory was given great prominence by the press and politicians – in fact, following the precedents set by

898 *Northern Territory Times and Gazette* 10/7/1875, p. 3; 27/11/1875, p. 3 Giles to Editor; Alfred Giles, *The First Pastoral Settlement in the Northern Territory* (unpublished), p. 32 (S.L.S.A. Mortlock P.R.G. 1389/2).

899 M.C. Hartwig, *The Progress of White Settlement in the Alice Springs District and its effects upon the Aboriginal Inhabitants, 1860–1894*, Ph.D. Thesis University of Adelaide, 1965, Chapter 4, *passim*.

explorers like Leichhardt, Stuart, Burke and Wills and McKinlay the reports tended to take on an epic proportion.

The first epic overland journey of stock from the far north stations of South Australia to the upper Territory was made between 1870 and 1872 by the Milner brothers, whose experiences demonstrated that the southern route was impassable in a dry season and would always be difficult, especially north of the MacDonnell Ranges.

In late 1863 Ralph and John Milner set out from Adelaide with a large mob of sheep headed via Coopers Creek toward the Gulf of Carpentaria. In January they had reached Clare, the northernmost point of the settled areas, where Ralph Milner married Phoebe Durling, his late cousin's widow, before both headed into the wilderness. By March they had reached Mount Chambers. The party now consisted of five men, one woman, two bullock drays, one cart, 13 horses and 1500 sheep.[900]

They were not alone in making such a venture. In the 1860s other leading South Australian pastoralists sent mobs north – John Baker's drovers, for instance, set out under drovers like William Stettiford Johns for the Gulf of Carpentaria in July 1865.[901] But all these enterprises were frustrated by the protracted drought that took hold of the centre after November 1863 and continued with one interlude until 1869.

For six years the Milners were held up near Coopers Creek, where they waited year after year for the drought to lift. In an effort to find a way through, Ralph Milner made exploring trips from his base at Coopers Creek across Sturt's Stony Desert and as far, he claimed, as the Herbert River. His party established an outstation at Kopperamanna on the Cooper River from where they sent wool and sheep south, the wool sometimes carried by Afghan cameleers with their camel trains.

Kopperamanna was also a mission station that the Moravian Brethren in Melbourne had been asked to establish in order to save the souls of the natives there as a special thanks for their kindness to John King, the camel man and only survivor from the Burke

900 *Register* 2/4/1864, p. 2 correspondent from Mt Chambers.
901 D. Johns to H. Johns 30/10/1865 (copy with author).

and Wills expedition. But the thanks met resistance, and in 1867 the missionaries had to take refuge at Milner's Station until police were sent to protect them. The following year the mission at Kopperamanna was abandoned.

In April 1868 as the drought deepened, the Milners moved to Killalpaninna close to another mission on the Cooper, the Lutheran Mission, which was staffed by missionaries from the Hermannsburg Mission Society in Germany. The Milners built shelters about two miles away at the other end of the lake, from where they presented the Lutherans with 61 sheep. Already in January they had sent horses south to rescue these missionaries who had run into difficulties while bringing their wives north to support them. In May 1868 Phoebe Milner died of heat exhaustion at Killalpaninna, gently nursed by the German women at the mission. With little to lose, Ralph Milner decided to make another attempt to cross the continent.[902]

The new expedition set out from Port Augusta in September 1870 with the intention of following the telegraph builders as far north as possible, then using the explorer Stuart's journal to negotiate the rest. When fully assembled, the party consisted of Ralph Milner, leader and owner, his brother John Milner, second in command, Kyrke, Ashwin, Thompson, Brown, Lamb, Pybus, Wooding, and two Aborigines from north of Peake known as Fannie and Charlie. There were 4300 sheep, 160 horses, 150 goats and 17 working bullocks dragging two spring drays, two bullock drays and one large wagon. The strategy was to send an advance party ahead each day to explore a track and find water before moving the stock on from the last camp.

Their great trek across the continent was made in a series of starts and stops. By mid November 1870 they had reached Finniss Springs. The first hold-up came in February 1871 at the dry Finke River which, on the very night they made camp, came down a

902 *Kirchen—u.—Missionblatt fuer die Lutherische Kirche Australiens* 11/5/1868, 1/6/1868; L. Grope, 1989–90, 'In the Wake of Burke and Wills', in *Yearbook of the Lutheran Church of Australia*, ed. K.J. Schmidt; H. Kneebone, & C. Rathjen, October 1996, 'Men with a Mission', *Journal of Friends of Lutheran Archives*, ed. Joyce Graetz; E.H. Proeve, *A Scattered Homeless Flock, Mission among the Dieri*, Point Pass, South Australia, 1945.

banker, about a quarter of a mile wide, and they had to wait five weeks before they could swim the sheep across in single file. From April they had to rest two months in the MacDonnell Ranges because the ewes were lambing and the stock fatigued. They built an out-bush station with huts, stockyards and other pastoral amenities. From here the brothers sent a letter south via the telegraph builders, conspicuously addressed 'Orana Springs' and dated 10 April 1871:

> We have had plenty of feed and water all the way as yet. It is a good stock country as far as we have got. All our stock are looking well, and we have not had any loss. We are busy with our sheep lambing, which will detain us about six weeks, and then we shall go on to Port Darwin.[903]

But Port Darwin was further than they thought. Once they left the safety of the MacDonnell Ranges and neared the northern-most base of telegraph construction at Bonney Creek, their good luck began to change. About half their sheep, now increased to a flock of 8000, died from eating the beautiful, poisonous wall-flower plant. In one night alone, near the ominous Devil's Marbles north of Tennant Creek, 1500 sheep and goats were found dead.

On 30 August at Attack Creek, John Milner was clubbed to death by an apparently friendly Aboriginal man while he was resting in the shade of a tree. The Aborigine (who was then shot) had been with the party for some time and Milner was an easy-going, affable man and one of the few who did not keep all Aborigines at arm's length. According to one interpretation, the murder was committed because the Aboriginal man resented Milner's friendship with Fannie, a beautiful young woman who generated a lot of jealousy among the men. Whatever the reason, for years after, the death of John Milner (like the death of Bennett earlier) was cited by those who believed that Aborigines treated kindness by people outside their group as weakness, because (so it was said) they lacked any firm concept of a universal humanity based in a universal God.[904]

---

903 *Register* 17/6/1871 p. 12 Letter from R & J Millner (sic), Orana Springs, MacDonnell Ranges 10/4/1871.

904 This accusation of a lack of humanity would certainly not apply to a person like the Aboriginal elder Mira. There is some disagreement as to how

On 12 December, a day of total eclipse of the sun, the overlanders met an advance party of the overland telegraph construction coming from the north. By Christmas Day 1871, they reached the Roper River, still 500 miles short of their destination. Then came their third, longest and most frustrating hold-up. The wet season closed in with loud thunder, and rain poured until only the tops of the trees were visible. For four months the party was trapped at the Red Lily Lagoon, a tributary of the Roper, under siege from hordes of insects. They built a large stockade on high ground, where the sheep battled to keep the coarse grass at bay. A few miles distant, Patterson's telegraph builders were in a similar plight, facing slow starvation.

Ralph Milner never made it through to the north coast with his large herd. He sold 1000 sheep for 25 shillings a head plus 50 horses and two teams of bullocks to 'Hungry Patterson' and the beleaguered telegraph construction party, then made a second sale of the remaining thousand-odd sheep to Patterson at the end of the wet. According to Charles Todd, this chance meeting between the overlanders and the telegraph builders helped save the telegraph enterprise from complete collapse.

With a rump party of three of his men and two Aborigines, 100 horses and two spring drays, Milner left the Roper in April and reached Port Darwin in June 1872. Because he had a broken arm, Milner was brought across from Southport ahead of the others, arriving on 13 June. As soon as the arm was put in splints, he headed back to bring his party on. It had been the first wheeled expedition to cross the continent, and had proceeded under the misapprehension that its participants were entitled to a reward. Milner was told in Palmerston that the question of a reward had been quashed while they were on their way across. He eventually appealed all the way to South Australia's parliament, but without success.

Fannie and Charlie took fright on seeing the Port Darwin Larrakias because they were different and some were uncircumcised,

---

long the man who killed John Milner had been in camp. John Deckert of Westprint Heritage Maps (Nhill) has completed extensive field research on the exact location of Milner's grave.

and walked back in another epic journey across the continent to their own people.[905]

Curiously, Milner may not have been the first to try to reach Port Darwin with a wheeled expedition. In March 1871 an advance party of the northern section of the telegraph builders came across dray marks and cattle tracks heading more or less north at Yam Creek, then at Mount Cunningham and again on the Katherine River. They also saw local Aborigines with blankets and a billy-can. About the same time someone found untended horses on the Adelaide River. Theories abounded that these were the remains of a party said to have left Newcastle 18 months earlier, or of Mr Cameron's party, believed to have set out from Queensland about two years before. Yet another theory was that the tracks had been left by Ludwig Leichhardt's lost expedition. Captain Douglas despatched a party under surveyor George MacLachlan to investigate, but the mystery of the tracks was never solved.[906]

Having reached Palmerston, Milner hung around for six months unsure what to do next. With the horse trade with India in mind, he considered starting a stock station on the Douglas Peninsula opposite Palmerston, making a tour of inspection during which he disappeared for a while. But the lease had already been promised to another famous overlander, Mathew Dillon Cox. According to one of Milner's drovers, Milner was passed over because he was not a Government House man and did not fit the proper standards of White Australia.

Demonstrating his indecision, Milner made two exits from the Territory. He left in January 1873 by the ill-fated *Springbok*, which was almost wrecked in the Gulf of Carpentaria because of drunkenness among the captain, crew and many of the departing miners, busy drowning their sorrows. When the *Springbok* reached

905 For more information on the Milner expedition see: Ralph Milner's Reminiscences, *Evening Star* (N.Z.) 24/8/1927; E. Kyrke, description of Milner's expedition *Advertiser* 14/7/1873, p. 3; Elizabeth Milner and Russell Pugh Research Notes (N.Z.); Diary of R.C. Patterson 25/12/1871, 26/12/1871 (S.L.S.A. Mortlock 8103(L)); Captain W.B. Douglas's Diary 13/6/1872 (Northern Territory Archives); *Northern Argus* 2/12/1870, p. 3; Petition to the Honourable the House of Assembly (Held by Russell Pugh, New Zealand).

906 Douglas to Blyth 12/3/1871 (N.T.I.L. 83/1871); *Advertiser* 10/7/1871, p. 3; *Register* 10/7/1871, p. 5.

Charles Heavitree Todd, the driving force behind construction of the overland telegraph – by world standards an immense engineering achievement and an aid to pastoral expansion.
(*Australasian Sketcher* 12/7/1873, p. 72. Courtesy of the State Library of South Australia)

Somerset, Milner changed his mind and caught a telegraph-construction ship back to the Roper, where he mustered some of his lost horses. Next he crossed to the mining districts, taking out a lease on the Lady Alice at Fountain Head where he had a brief encounter with the Morning Star swindlers. He finally left the Territory on the *Gothenburg* in November 1873.[907]

In the wake of the Milners, Alfred Giles drove 5000 sheep north from South Australia at least twice to supply telegraph stations between Charlotte Waters and Yam Creek, while early in August 1873 Fred Campbell reached Southport with 120 light horses (most

907 A.C. Ashwin, *Gold to Grass: The reminiscences of Arthur C. Ashwin, 1850–1930,* Book II, Hesperian Press, Victoria Park, Western Australia, 2002; Milner's departure on the *Gothenburg* November 1873 is a deduction.

too light for local needs) from Elder's station at Blanchewater in northern South Australia.

But already the southern route was losing ground in favour of the route from Queensland, pioneered by Dillon Cox together with his drover, Wentworth D'arcy Uhr. This alternative path proved by far the most successful. Even former South Australian pastoralists such as Charles Brown Fisher, who helped found Glencoe Station in the 1880s, preferred it.[908]

Dillon Cox and the Queensland Side

Cox and Uhr were representatives of a new breed of colonist in the Territory. Their prime interest was large stock. They did not believe sheep were suited to the tropics. They had learned their bush skills in eastern Australia. They were courageous, rough and enterprising, and not always straight in their dealings. Their story is worth telling because it is symbolic of a wholly different, rough culture of colonisation, marked by strenuous individual toil and loss of official government control.

Mathew Dillon Thomas Cox was the first genuine settler in the Territory. Born in 1829, he came to Australia in 1850 as one of the restless masses of Irish Protestants who, never feeling quite at home, left to become administrators, soldiers and entrepreneurs throughout the British Empire. It was a time when Australia and Asia were often lumped together. His great uncle had been the first to build a road across the Blue Mountains and some of his distant cousins were wealthy pastoralists in New South Wales. His father served as an army officer in South America, South Africa and Mauritius. His wife, Catherine Mary Bathurst, whom he married in 1861, was born in the Presidency of Bombay and was connected to a family of imperial administrators. Cox himself first came to notice as a horse dealer based mainly in the district of Fitzroy, Melbourne, and trading with most Australian colonial capitals. He became widely involved in the pastoral industry, especially in Queensland and New South Wales.

Because Australia offered too limited an opportunity for his

908 Alfred Giles, *The First Pastoral Settlement in Northern Territory*, p. 7 *seq.* (S.L.S.A. Mortlock P.R.G. 1389/2); *Observer* 9/8/1873, p. 3; See *Argus* 2/12/1873, p. 6 Shipping.

ambitions, in September 1861 Cox (with his business partner Bill Younger) moved to Batavia to become a dealer and stable manager in the huge Indies trade in cavalry horses, taking with him 78 horses, 21 tons of hay and 1400 bushels of bran. In gaining entry to the Dutch East Indies he was sponsored by Peet and Co., a leading shipping agent in Batavia. He was accompanied on the ship by his nephew, William Justin Beauchamp Cameron, who in 1860, aged 15, had been sent from Ireland to join Cox in Australia. Cox's wife joined him in Batavia in 1863.

Cox, who liked to surround himself with protégés, gathered around him a clan of them in Batavia. Cameron learned to speak Dutch and Malay and became manager in a large merchant company, Hunter and Houghton. They brought out three of Cameron's brothers and two sisters, as well as another of Cox's nephews, Charles Butcher (who for status used the Irish spelling 'Bouchier'), son of Colonel Butcher of the Royal Marines. As a family they were hot-tempered, which led to disputes that sometimes spilt into the courts.[909]

On one occasion Cox (according to family sources) saved his nephew Beauchamp Cameron from execution after Cameron, in a fit of rage, hanged a Malay man for failing to carry out his orders. And Dillon Cox used his influence to get the younger man's punishment reduced to a prison sentence, for which the Cameron family owed him a life-long debt. As we shall see, the hold over Cameron was only removed when Dillon Cox died.[910]

But Cox could not stay in one place for long. Keen to expand beyond just dealing in horses, in June 1870 he submitted to the governor-general of the Dutch East Indies a scheme to establish a stud farm in Timor to produce an improved breed of horses for the East Indies, which lacked cavalry horses suitable for

---

909 For information on Dillon Cox, Family Research Notes: Barry Cox, Melbourne 1994–2003; Family Research Notes: Bert Forsyth, Canberra 1992; *Argus* 20/7/1861, p. 4 Shipping; Permit for Foreigners to Live in the Netherlands Indies 10/5/1862 (Arsip Nasional Republik Indonesia); Margaret Reeves, *A Strange Bird on the Lagoon,* Boolarong Publications, Brisbane, 1985 *passim*.

910 Bathurst to Mann 10/5/1874 (Attorney-General I.L. 189/1874); Bathurst to Mann 3/8/1874 (Attorney-General I.L. 487/1874). So far I am unable to get corroborative evidence from Indonesia.

local conditions. He proposed to cross 35 sandalwood stallions, bred in the Indies from Arab stock, with 1000 mares sired of a cross between Australian and English breeds in order to obtain 'tractability, courage, vigour and increased size'. In return, the Indies Government would provide 36 square miles of land cleared of wild animals, pay him a thousand guilders for each breeding horse imported and undertake to buy all the suitable offspring – calculated at 3760 stallions after 10 foalings. The governor-general sought the advice of his chief veterinary surgeon (horses) and his military advisers in the Department of War, all of whom recommended against the proposal. The former preferred to breed from the best local stock, while the latter thought the Dutch army should control its own source of cavalry horses.[911]

Cox always felt that he had been discriminated against because of the rivalry between the Dutch and the English. He decided to transfer his stud breeding ambitions from Timor to Central and North Queensland, which was then a focus of pastoral expansion. In April 1871 he set sail in his private schooner, *Kathleen*, a former Netherlands Indies Navy gun boat (a Kruisboot) built of teak in the Java naval yard. But at Koepang, where he called for provisions, he happened to cross paths with an official of the Northern Territory government, Hugh Campbell MacCallum, who was in Timor in the tender *Larrakeyah* delivering the mail and obtaining supplies. MacCallum persuaded Cox to redirect his enterprise to Port Darwin. With typical enthusiasm Cox obtained a quick passage on the *Marié Elizabeth*, which was taking telegraph wire to Port Darwin, where he arrived on 8 May 1871. His schooner followed 20 months later.[912]

So began the saga of the first genuine settler in the Northern Territory.

Cox was well received by Captain Douglas, the Government Resident, who saw him as an East Indies man like himself, and

911 The Petition of M.D.T. Cox, dated Batavia 15 June 1870, 'pertaining to proposals to establish a Stud Farm on the Island of Timor with the aim to improve the breed of horses being used by the Army of the Dutch-Indies'. Resolution 28 of 1871 29/6/1871 with various enclosures (Arsip Nasional Republik Indonesia).

912 Douglas to Blyth 2/6/1871 (N.T.I.L. 126/1871); *Register* 8/1/1873, p. 5 Telegraphic News.

who lent him horses – including his favourite horse 'Bowerlee' – and equipment to inspect the countryside. (About the same time, Douglas's half brother was developing pastoral interests in Queensland, but there is no evidence that the two members of the Douglas family ever met.) After a month's search, Cox chose a pastoral lease on the Douglas Peninsula across the harbour from Palmerston. He and other locals gradually began to re-name the area the Cox Peninsula. In size and location it suited exactly the needs of his horse stud. Next he made the long sea journey on the *Gulnare* to the Land Office in Adelaide to finalise his claim. While in Adelaide during July 1871, he wrote a letter to the *Register* severely criticising what he called the government's 'hobby-horsical' system of colonisation, which was quite unsuited to the conditions of the Territory, because it concentrated on centralisation and speculation rather than rewarding the actual settlers who developed the land. As an alternative, he advocated granting full ownership of the land to the occupiers, according to a formula of 100 acres for each 100 large stock on the property and pro rata for sheep. He negotiated with the government to liberalise the pastoral leases in the Territory, with the results gazetted on 20 July 1871. The new regulations gave the Government Resident power to approve leases, with a duplicate then sent to the surveyor-general in Adelaide. Because they were outside the preliminary surveys, the South Australian government could be more liberal and experimental with pastoral lands.[913]

With a guarantee from the government in hand, Dillon Cox set off through the eastern colonies to Rockhampton (at the time the main port for the expanding cattle industry), where in November and December he gathered together horses and cattle and looked around for drovers. According to information from the *Peak Downs Telegram* preserved by Cox's wife's family, he bought BY brand horses from Messrs Kelman. He also purchased the right to use the BY brand, which was well known in Eastern markets. Kelmans owned stations at Springsure (including Meteor Downs) and were related to Alexander Busby, who founded the famous BY horse

913 Cox to Douglas 15/5/1871, 17/5/1871; Douglas to Blyth 26/5/1871 (N.T.I.L 119/1871); *Register* 15/7/1871 news item, p. 4, and letter from Cox to Editor 13/7/1871, p. 5; *S.A. Government Gazette* 20/7/1871, pp. 1071, 1072.

stud at the frontier district of Cassilis in New South Wales. Cox also bought cattle from Collaroy station, another pioneering station with headquarters near Cassilis.[914]

The man Dillon Cox chose to lead the expedition overland was Wentworth D'arcy Uhr, who knew the Gulf Country well. Uhr was son of the sergeant-at-arms to the Legislative Assembly in Brisbane and had been named after a family friend, D'arcy Wentworth – the highway robber from the upper class sent by his family to Botany Bay to keep him out of trouble. Uhr had first come to notice as a police sub-inspector at Burketown, where he gained a reputation for tracking down outlaws and for his punitive expeditions against the Aborigines, as illustrated in the *Port Denison Times*:

> A sad day for Burke Town,
> One of danger and disgrace,
> Uhr and five white troopers
> Have started for this place.
> They'll ride up here some morning,
> Their sabres clinking loud,
> Bringing despair and terror
> To all the rowdy crowd.[915]

Burketown at the time was considered the wildest settlement in Australia, a homing place for ruffians escaping from the law down south. Some of these ruffians took Aboriginal 'wives' and later became drovers and labourers in the North Territory cattle industry.[916]

By the early 1870s Uhr had good reasons for wanting to move on. In 1869 he left the police force after acrimonious disputes with his superiors. Following his resignation the feud continued, and they arrested him 16 times. At Normanton in 1871 he was acquitted in controversial circumstances of a charge of tracking down and shooting an Aborigine who had killed one of the squatter MacIntyre's men. Uhr in turn had been vigorously tracked down

---

914 Papers of W.L. Forsyth, son of Catherine Mary Bathurst, Family Research Notes: Bert Forsyth, Canberra, 1992.

915 *Port Denison Times* 18/4/1868 courtesy of Frank Uhr.

916 Family Research Notes on Wentworth D'arcy Uhr: Frank Uhr, Brisbane 1993–2003.

by the local police, leading to his arrest. The pioneering cattleman Alfred Giles once wrote: 'D'arcy Uhr was one of Queensland's best and undaunted bushmen and was in his element when confronted by flood or drought, dense scrub and hostile savages'.[917] 'Savages' was the kind of word used by Uhr himself.

The Cox expedition set out from Rockhampton in February 1872 along the Peak Downs track, intent on following Leichhardt's route of 1845 through the Gulf Country to Leichhardt's Bar on the Roper more than a thousand miles away. The expedition in turn was followed by two parties of gold prospectors, one European and the other Chinese. In a later book, Cox's brother-in-law Edward Wilkinson Bathurst claimed to have surveyed the route for them, but this is unproven.[918]

Near Normanton, Uhr temporarily left the expedition and on 2 May 1872 married Jane Esther Hayes, (with whom he already had a child) at the local post office. Jane soon yearned for a more settled life, and the marriage lasted only about five years.

The real plunge into the wilderness began on 25 May when the men left Burketown with eight weeks' supplies. The party now consisted of seven men: Uhr as expert drover; Cox as owner; William Harvey, who stayed on to help set up Cox's station; James Barry, a small man; James Broderick, who later died at Glencoe; and two Chinese, Ah Chew, the cook, and Lim Ah Soey (known as Jimmy Soey), who later became the first recorded Chinese gardener at Peels Well, Doctors Gully. The mob consisted of 163 cattle, mainly breeders, most of which Cox hoped to sell to local butchers, plus 125 horses including four stud entires to make a start on the breeding programme, 50 of the horses being unbroken.

The party picked their way through the boggy lowlands in a zig-zag route, with arguments between Uhr and Cox whether they should go further inland or down along the coast. Luckily it was not a Big Wet year, so they could get through. 'Cox, Uhr and the others that came through appear to have gone in and out in all directions,'

917 *Brisbane Courier* 12/10/1871, p. 3; 13/10/1871, p. 3; Alfred Giles, *The First Pastoral Settlement in the Northern Territory* p. 6 (S.L.S.A. Mortlock P.R.G. 1389/2).

918 Edward W. Bathurst, *Men I have met*, Marchant & Co, Sydney, 1906, pp. 10 and 11.

wrote Knuckey of the overland telegraph.[919] Cox and Barry even went exploring down the McArthur River after being told by an Aboriginal man from a friendly tribe that mysterious white men lived there. Because they took 15 weeks travelling from Burketown to reach the Roper, rumours spread in the Gulf stations that Cox's party had perished.

The Aborigines were morally bound to oppose anyone, black or white, passing over their sacred land without permission – particularly if it was a large group. Uhr organised the party as a miniature expeditionary force. First his men should offer presents – axes and fish hooks – to the local people to let the cattle pass. If that failed, they were ready to shoot their way through. This truly looks like an invasion.[920] Each member carried on his saddle a Westley-Richards carbine and a revolver, while at the helm Uhr toted a high-powered Martini rifle, an advanced piece of military technology capable of killing the enemy before they came within spear range. The members were taught military practices: how to fire in rotation and 'Form a Square' – in which infantry took a square formation, with each soldier facing out so as to cover all directions, with supplies and the wounded in the middle. The technique had been used with great success against French cavalry at Waterloo, and later adapted for use against tribesmen in Africa.[921]

Three pitched battles took place: somewhere near the border about a hundred miles from Burketown; somewhere between the Robinson and McArthur rivers at Calico Creek; and, in the major battle, at Wickham River, where in the middle of the day the European party was rushed by more than a hundred Aboriginal men. Many Aborigines were shot before the survivors were forced to surrender their spears, which were then broken up.[922]

In memory of Cox and his venture, Wickham River was later re-named the Cox River.

---

919 *Northern Territory Times and Gazette* 12/9/1874, p. 3.

920 Example: James Miller, *Koori: A Will to Win*, Chapter 2, Angus and Robertson, Sydney, 1985.

921 Research Notes on Forming a Square supplied by Michael Ball, 26/7/1999 National Army Museum, Chelsea, London.

922 *Brisbane Courier* 16/9/1874, p. 3; 27/10/1874, p. 3.

The arguments between Cox and Uhr demonstrated the weakness of having two leaders – owner and expert drover contracted to get the stock through – in the same expedition. In the last month of the journey Cox set out ahead of Uhr's party so he could get to the Roper River Landing first. Having arrived there on 7 September 1872, he demanded of Patterson, who was in charge of telegraph construction, that Uhr should be taken to court. Uhr turned up soon after and refused to hand over the cattle because of an argument over whether the contract ended at the Roper, as Uhr thought it did, or Port Darwin. A bitter court battle followed – the first case of note in Territory history. Cox charged that about five weeks earlier Uhr in a fight had rushed his 'master' and pulled out some of Cox's beard, for which he should forfeit all his wages and the existing contract should be terminated. The case was heard before Captain Douglas (flanked by Patterson and MacLachlan) who happened to be on an official visit to the Roper Depot prior to it being closed down. Douglas negotiated an out-of-court settlement in which Uhr was paid off at the rate of £3 a week for services to date plus a month's provisions – after which, making use of mutual protection, Uhr accompanied the main party on to the diggings.[923]

The journey from Roper Depot to Yam Creek coincided with the end of telegraph construction and the party took on the character of a caravan, being joined by a mob of government horses under George Deane, as well as telegraph construction workers heading for the diggings.

On 17 October 1872 Cox, with 35 horses, reached Yam Creek ahead of the others on his way through to finalise his lease in Palmerston, which he took out 10 days later – 180 square miles for 25 years. About three weeks after that the main party arrived in Yam Creek with the cattle in good condition, after which Cox's party (in particular Billy Harvey) took the remainder of the cattle on to the north coast of the continent. Two years later Uhr, who had returned by land to Queensland, was ready to drove another mob overland, this time from Bowen Downs to Port Darwin with

923 Diary of R.C. Patterson 13/9/1872 (S.L.S.A. Mortlock D8103(L)); *Brisbane Courier* 24/2/1872, p. 5; 18/10/1872, p. 2; *Advertiser* 10/10/1872, p. 2 Telegraphic News; 12/11/1872, p 2; Information Before Capt. Douglas 18/9/1872 (N.T.I.L, 374/1872).

William Hay. He became the first overlander to do the trip both ways, and the first to do two trips.

As soon as he reached the diggings in November 1872, Uhr began to peg out claims with frenetic energy, even jumping reefs that had already been pegged, such as Lewis's and Daly's claims at Pine Creek. This caused resentment among the prospectors and companies who had arrived first. According to Lewis, when quartz gold was found by the prospector Paul McGrath on Uhr's Pine Creek claim, the experienced Captain Westcott, acting on a tip-off from McGrath, tricked Uhr into giving up the claim before he could realise its true value. Westcott then made an alleged fortune for himself and Adelaide capitalists. An alternative version of events popular in oral tradition is quite different. It holds that Uhr mined 1000 ounces of gold at Pine Creek – the first payable gold in the Territory – and with his fortune returned to Queensland prepared to buy cattle for yet another overland expedition.[924] This version was possibly put about by Uhr himself, who was described by the gold warden as 'nothing but a Queensland Blower – and not possessed of a shilling', to which accusation Uhr took considerable objection.[925]

Meanwhile, Dillon Cox had been disposing of his stock. By now the mining boom had been going for some time and there was strong demand for cattle and horses. Instead of stocking up his lease Cox sold most of his cattle and some of his horses for an immediate profit, selling beef to the local butchers, for instance, for a shilling a pound. With great energy he then set about building his station – near Cox's Hill on the Cox Peninsula – which included a six-room homestead, outbuildings, stock yards and fences. He named the place 'Bowerlee' after Captain Douglas's horse. It was also called the Peninsula Station. Someone else described it as a camp.

---

924 Diary of John Lewis 17/10/1872 to 17/2/1873 (S.L.S.A. Mortlock Library P.R.G. 247/7/4); Research Notes by Frank Uhr. Example of the oral tradition: at the time of writing there is a monument at Pine Creek erected in the 1960s honouring Uhr as the *true* discoverer of gold in the area. See also *The North Australian Monthly* March 1957. See also Bert Bolton, *Stories of the Outback*, Brolga, Victoria,2008, p. 133 *seq*. There is also some dispute as to where Uhr finally left the expedition.

925 Uhr to Melville 8/2/1873 (N.T.I.L. 260/1873). Though disputed, there is not much doubt that the warden made the statement.

It is typical of Cox's enterprise that while on the Roper waiting for Uhr to arrive, he asked permission to muster the wild cattle left behind on the Coburg Peninsula from the former Port Essington settlement. His request was shelved by the government, partly because others wanted the cattle too, and partly because there was doubt about the legal standing of the area, which had been leased to Captain Francis Cadell in 1868 and for a time declared stocked because of the wild cattle roaming there.[926]

Cox also joined with three mining companies, as well as individuals like George Cooper, in laying on the *Coorong* at Port Adelaide to bring north equipment and passengers – including his wife Catherine Mary, and his nephew Beauchamp Cameron. On 1 December 1872, they had arrived in Adelaide from Batavia accompanied by a Mr Houghton, a leading East Indies merchant banker, who waited on the Commissioner of Crown Lands, Thomas Reynolds, for a briefing about trading prospects between the Territory and the Indies. Houghton reported that Eastern planters were keen to go to the Territory.

Beauchamp Cameron had been a leading businessman in Batavia. While waiting in Adelaide he joined forces with William Whitfield Mills, discoverer of Alice Springs, with the goal of investing in mining and pastoral lands. Later the partners applied for a pastoral lease on both sides of the Mary River. Their request was refused.[927]

When the *Coorong* reached Port Darwin on 18 May 1873, the passengers celebrated their safe arrival by throwing a concert in aid of the hospital. Two hundred people crowded into Chawner's store, then most of the crew deserted and headed for the mines.[928]

Meanwhile on the north coast, Cox's station building activities were meeting resistance from the Larrakia people. In November he was in court for selling a horse for £45 to Becker and partner, but on delivery switching it over for an inferior one: £20 to plaintiff plus court costs.[929] A few months later he was in court again:

926 Cox to Douglas 23/9/1872 (N.T.I.L, 372/1872).

927 Pastoral Lease 170 of 1873 (Commonwealth Archives, Darwin).

928 Chronicle 31/5/1873, p. 6; 19/4/1873, p. 10.

929 *Northern Territory Times and Gazette* 21/11/1873, p. 2; 7/11/1873, p. 2 Local Court.

Police Court Palmerston 5 March 1874

Cox v Cameron
Absence from service
Plea: not guilty
Fined £2 plus £3.7.0 costs, or 7 days imprisonment.

Cox v Cameron and Harvey
Assault
Withdrawn

Cameron v Cox
Assault
Withdrawn[930]

G.F.B. Cameron was his nephew and W. Harvey his leading hand.

With the station ready, Cox now turned to bringing a second mob of breeding horses overland to meet the lease requirements and so he might start his horse stud for Eastern markets. By now he even had hopes of starting a sugar and coconut plantation at his station as well.

Then events began to go wrong. As an additional source of income he set his schooner *Kathleen* to work transhipping mining equipment from Port Darwin to Southport. In June 1873 the vessel capsized in a storm on the way to Southport because it was top heavy with mining machinery. Four lives were lost. The schooner was not insured.[931] In April 1873 he was charged with perjury for falsely swearing in court that Chawner owed him money for cattle, but released on an undertaking that he would be available when needed, pending the setting up of some court machinery to try him. This prevented him from returning south to bring over the horses for the Indian remount trade. In the end it was decided that his brother Price Wynne Cox, who had recently arrived from England via Batavia, should return south on the *Gothenburg* to drive the second mob overland. Price Cox was a man of means whose ambition was to join the squattocracy in Australia. Before leaving England he sold his Fusee Watch Chain Works at Christchurch,

930 *Northern Territory Times and Gazette* 6/3/1874, p. 3 Police Court.
931 Board of Enquiry Report 23/8/1873 (N.T.I.L. 306/1873).

Hampshire, and his father's house there, which he had inherited some time earlier. His wife, Mary Williams, was described as 'a lady with property'.[932]

After being held up in Batavia by a lack of shipping, Price Cox reached Port Darwin on the 17 May 1873 on the government cutter *Flying Cloud* in the company of Commissioner of Crown Lands Reynolds. His wife and four children aboard the *Jason* followed 14 months later via a circuitous route: Batavia to Fremantle to Adelaide to Port Darwin.

Because Price Cox had no bush experience, it was proposed that his nephew Beauchamp Cameron, who owed Dillon Cox for saving his life in Batavia and was an excellent bushman, should accompany Price on the overland trip. Cameron's diary contained a set of instructions and a map showing how to get from Burketown to the Roper River Depot – based, no doubt, on information from Dillon Cox.

Then misfortune struck. When Price Cox's party was in the Gulf Country on the Leichhardt River on its way back, Dillon Cox died suddenly on 4 May 1874 aged 44 years, after a fight over a business deal with his nephew Charles Bouchier at Bowerlee Station. It was a rough industry. Another nephew, George Francis Blundell (Frank) Cameron, took over the management.[933]

In 1874 the Gulf Track was proving very dangerous indeed. The second party of overlanders to attempt it (after Cox and Uhr) was led by George De Lautour, who belonged to the North Queensland establishment and was accused of adding the 'De' when it suited him to do so. Other members in the party were William Nation, Leonard Elvy (alias other names) and a boy called Butcher, servant to the leader. Elvy's claim to fame (perhaps mythical) was that as stockman at Bowen Downs he gave evidence against the bushranger Henry Readford (alias Collins) who in 1870 lifted a large mob of cattle and took them all the way to South Australia. The trial was held at Roma in February 1873, but the jury was so impressed by Readford's daring that he was acquitted – at which

932 Ernest Whitfield, *The Youl Family,* privately published, 1907, pp. 51–55.

933 Margaret Reeves, *A Strange Bird on the Lagoon,* pp. 164 to 166; *Northern Territory Times and Gazette* 8/5/1874, p. 3; Memorial Catherine Mary Cox to Everard 24/6/1874 (N.T.I.L. 315/1874).

point Elvy decided it was time to move on. Later Readford went to the Territory where he became famous, particularly after his exploits were used by author Rolf Boldrewood as one of the models for Captain Starlight in the novel *Robbery Under Arms.*[934]

Nation was a moderately prominent South Australian who had moved to Queensland. At various stages he had been aide-de-camp to the acting governor in Adelaide, chief clerk to the Colonial Secretary's Office and later Protector of Aborigines on the Murray. Nation recorded details of the trip in his diary. The party started out from William Hann's Maryvale Station, near Townsville, on 1 September 1873, intending to pick up cattle on the Flinders River. Nation continually refers to the harsh country they crossed and the primitive lives of the pioneering squatters he met on the way. Probably reflecting a South Australian prejudice, he called these pioneering squatters 'gauchos' after their wild counterparts in South America. On the Flinders, Lautour managed to buy 105 cattle from MacIntyre's Dalgonally Station and on 8 October they set out for the Territory. Elvy and Nation took charge of the 21 horses and Lautour and the boy the hundred-odd cattle. According to Nation, Lautour proved a 'spiteful' leader – a 'dingo', a 'blower' – in the way he treated his men. And he was not much better with those he met. When at Jacks Lagoon some young Aboriginal women became attracted to the youthful Alf Butcher, Lautour shot their dog and scared them off by threatening that the much-dreaded Queensland Native Mounted Police were coming at sundown. On 8 March 1874 the disagreements became so bad that the party broke up. To celebrate, Lautour named the spot Settlement Creek.

Nation and Elvy were told to leave the camp and struck out for the Roper rather than returning to Normanton. At first they made good pace, but soon the flooded terrain slowed them to a few miles a day. Then Nation's health broke down near the Limmen Bight River (he was an old man) and the meagre rations given them

934 It is hard to prove Elvy's 'claim to fame' one way or the other because from time to time he changed his name; for information on the model for Captain Starlight see essays by Rolf Boldrewood, 1904, 'How I wrote Robbery Under Arms', in Alan Brissenden, (ed.) *Rolf Boldrewood 1826–1915*, with Introduction, Queensland University Press, Brisbane, 1979, pp. 491 to 498. Frank McCarthy, *The Man who was Starlight*, Allen & Unwin, Sydney, 1987.

by Lautour ran out. On 15 May Leonard Elvy set out alone for the Daly Waters telegraph station to get help, reaching the spot 10 days later. A search party under R.R. Knuckey (of the telegraph construction party) was despatched but by the time it found Nation's camp he was dead. 'He had evidently felt his end approaching,' wrote Knuckey in his report, 'and had packed everything carefully and then covered himself up with his blankets and lain down to die.'[935]

Nation left behind a touching letter to Government Resident Scott (with whom he had earlier gone to California) wishing him well in this world and the next. The last entry in the diary found beside his body read:

> Thursday 1 June
> A bitter cold wind cutting me to the marrow. I feel general torpor. Great trouble to move in my bed. The last hour fast approaching. Legs as cold as ice. Cannot get warm. Great effort to get to the water. Could just get back. Only two quarts left. Will last me to the end. Prayed to God and Jesus for release. I shall now close this. Tomorrow I shall not be able to rise. W.N.[936]

Having named a range and a creek in honour of Nation, Knuckey proceeded on a new mercy mission to rescue Lautour's stock which had earlier become stranded.

A day or two after Elvy had reached Daly Waters with news of Nation's difficulties, the other half of the party which had split up, comprising George Lautour and his boy, had arrived at the same place by a different route, weak and desperately short of food having left their cattle behind on the McArthur River. Lautour returned with the party searching for Nation, after which Knuckey and his men proceeded to the McArthur to help Lautour locate his cattle, which were later brought on with the generous assistance of two telegraph workers, Bob Brown and Harry Suttor, as drovers.[937]

---

935 *Advertiser* 16/7/1874, p. 4.

936 Diary of William Nation (courtesy of James Cook University Library, Queensland).

937 *Advertiser* 16/7/1874, p. 4; *Northern Territory Times and Gazette* 10/7/1874, p. 3; 5/12/1874, p. 3; 16/1/1875, p. 2; 20/3/1875, p. 3; 3/4/1875, p. 3; 19/2/1876, p. 2. Batten took over from Suttor.

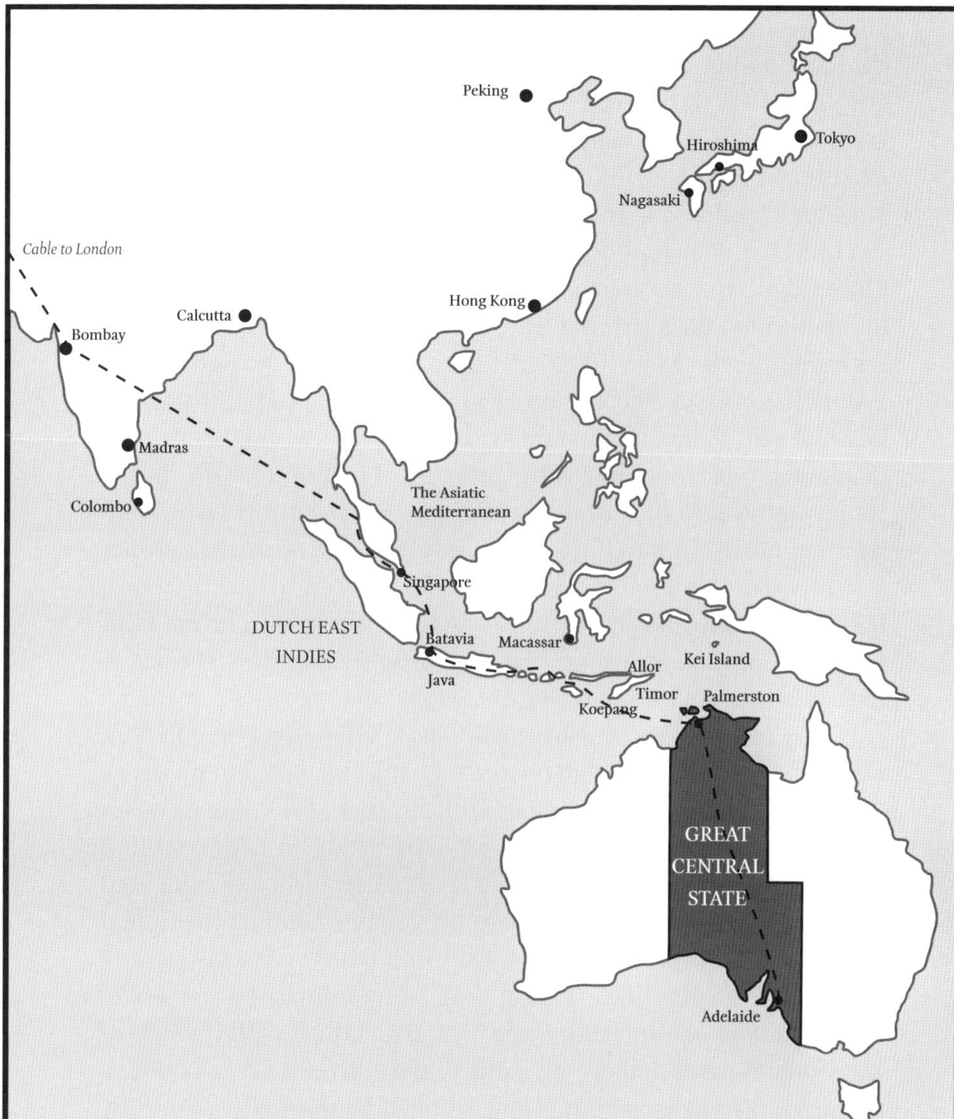

The Great Central State and the Unlimited Asian Market

The third known party to attempt the coast track was that of Price Cox, Dillon Cox's brother. After setting sail from Port Darwin, Price Cox and Beauchamp Cameron had left the *Gothenburg* southward bound on 1 July 1873 at Newcastle to arrange the purchase and delivery of BY brand horses originally bred at Busby's stud at Cassilis. In September 1873, Cox passed through Robert Gray's famous station at Hughenden. 'In September,' wrote Gray, 'a Mr Cox passed through from NSW with a fine load of breeding mares for Port Darwin, the intention being, I believe, to produce horses for the India market'.[938]

But Cameron had other plans: he wanted to buy a station in Queensland and get married. He would have already known that his application for a pastoral lease with William Whitfield Mills on both sides of the Mary River had been refused. He moved on at a distance from Cox keeping an eye out for good land and stock to buy and sell. When in September the great Palmer gold rush near Cooktown broke out, he saw the prospect of realising his dreams by supplying meat to the hundreds of ill-provisioned miners who were flocking north. In an effort to retain his services, Cox then struck a deal with Cameron in which, working from a joint account, both would buy and jointly muster half-wild cattle from the Gulf Country outstations. Young Cameron would take the cattle across to the Palmer goldfields during the wet season.

They met on 20 November near Gibson's station on the Flinders, where Cameron managed to obtain 532 cattle. He noted in his diary: 'Cox seems to be having trouble with his men. NO management. His horses are very thin and tired.' According to Cameron, the pair abandoned the deal because Cox's horses were too exhausted to help muster the cattle. 'We have broken our contract by mutual agreement,' he wrote. 'OF THIS I AM VERY GLAD.' As a last gesture of goodwill to his uncle Dillon Cox, Cameron first went off to Normanton to get stores for Price Cox, then set off with the help of his drover Burnell to move his cattle to the Palmer gold rush, where hundreds of miners were starving, trapped by the wet season.[939] By now he would have known that his uncle Dillon Cox was dead – and released from his debt to him for saving his life in Batavia,

938 Robert Gray, *Reminiscences of India and Nth Queensland*, Constable, London, 1913, p. 197; Passenger Lists for Newcastle (Newcastle City Council Archives).

939 Margaret Reeves, *Strange Bird on the Lagoon*, including W.J.B. Cameron Journal, pp. 164–172; Additional Family Research Notes by Pat Bonham, Iluka, NSW, 1994.

Beauchamp Cameron went his own way and did not return. He later justified his decision not to accompany Price Cox across the Territory as a 'premonition'.

The rains started on 26 November 1873 and before proceeding further Price Cox rested his horses on the Leichhardt River for the next seven months waiting for the wet to clear. It turned out to be one of the wettest years on record.

The party now consisted of seven men, led by Joseph Williams from Peak Downs, an expert drover. His contract was to bring horses over from Queensland at £5 per week. Others were Duncan McPhee, George Reid, John J. Aitkins, Harry Bligh Waller, Charlie Miller (cook) and Price Cox as owner. Again the presence in the same party of the owner and contract drover led to disagreements.

About 15 July 1874 the expedition set out for the Roper River Depot, not realising it had already been abandoned. The trip proved a disaster.

According to Joseph Williams, the party's main mistake (probably due to the insistence of Price Cox) was to spend too much time rounding up the straying horses. As a result the men's food ran out. They were forced to live entirely on horse flesh, which led to diarrhoea and slowly sapped their strength. They had brought no salt, so they had to kill horses for meat every day. After a desperate struggle to get the remaining horses through the thick scrub on the lowlands, and after being lost for four weeks, they eventually reached the Limmen Bight River, which they mistook for the Roper. By now they were all very weak. There followed a chapter of accidents:

> *26 September:* Charlie Miller, the cook (who it was reported had made the crossing before and thought he knew the way), left for the Roper on foot – he was not a horse rider. Next day they saw him again, but he would not return. Two of the men asked to be paid off. They were refused.
>
> *27 September:* Cox, Reid, Aitkins and Waller (as pilot) went ahead to get supplies from the Roper Depot, which they thought was 25 miles away. They eventually found the depot abandoned. It was six days journey away.
>
> *30 September:* Williams and McPhee, who had stayed behind

on the Limmen Bight River with the horses, were attacked by Aborigines in a daylight raid and most of their equipment taken. At night the Aborigines returned to kill them, but their spears got tangled in the tents and bedding used as a shield. McPhee was wounded in the neck by a heavy blow from a 'nullah-a-nullah' aimed at his skull.

5 October: Cox having now been gone for nine days, Williams and McPhee decided to leave for the Roper Depot. Previous to this, they had taken the saddle horses across the river for a quick start and fixed messages on the bells of the bell-horses they left behind. Finding the Roper Depot deserted and no sign of Cox, they set out for Katherine Telegraph Station.

10 October: Williams and McPhee came upon Lautour's tracks, which they followed. On 17 October they caught up with Lautour's camp at Abraham's Billabong, about 70 miles from Katherine. Lautour (having retrieved his abandoned mob from the McArthur River) was driving his remaining 87 cattle on the last leg towards Port Darwin.

18 October: Lautour, taking Williams with him, turned back in search of Cox with provisions and fresh horses, leaving his cattle moving on in charge of drovers Browne and Batten, accompanied by McPhee. They found Cox at Hart's Range north of the Roper. Cox, having returned to Limmen Bight River to find his mob scattered and his men and equipment gone, had abandoned the expedition and was proceeding with the remainder of his party to Port Darwin.[940]

As soon as news of the failure reached Palmerston, competitors such as Sam Reynolds, one-time friend of Charles Bouchier, began gathering like vultures waiting to take advantage of the pioneering work done at Bowerlee Station.

Price Cox, with his wife Mary and their four children, then decided to head south by the next available ship. Joining them were

940 *Northern Territory Times and Gazette* 31/10/1874 leader; 12/12/1874, pp. 2 and 3; *Advertiser* 26/12/1874, p. 3; Johnston to Little 24/10/1874 (G.R.I.L. A525). According to the *Maitland Mercury* 23/10/1937, the Fairhall brothers also brought some stock from Newcastle to Port Darwin by ship in early 1874.

Frank Cameron, who had been managing Bowerlee since Dillon's death, as well as the head drover Joseph Williams.

But the Cox family did not give up. At a family conference they decided that Catherine Cox, Dillon's wife, would stay on to look after Bowerlee while Price Cox, Frank Cameron, who had been managing the station, and Joseph Williams the drover would sail south by the *Gothenburg* immediately to buy and overland more horses in a last desperate bid to restock Bowerlee Station.[941] Lautour, who had reached Port Darwin on 19 November 1874 and intended to return overland to Normanton, was asked on his way back to look for Cox's horses left behind at the Limmen Bight River. A notice was placed in the newspaper, under the full name George De Lautour, offering a £200 reward for information leading to the conviction of any person or persons caught interfering with Cox's horses roaming free somewhere in the thousand-mile stretch between Katherine and the Flinders River in Queensland.[942]

The third overland expedition by the Cox family never took place. Price Cox (plus his wife Mary and four children, who planned to stay for a while with relatives in Sydney), Frank Cameron and Joseph Williams were all drowned in February 1875 when the *Gothenburg* became wrecked. Lost, too, were all the family papers and his father's medals which Price Cox was bringing to Australia for the Cox dynasty in New South Wales.

About the same time, Billy Harvey, who had helped Dillon Cox set up Bowerlee Station, died alone from a fever in a Port Darwin pub.[943]

The irony of the tragedy was that back in June, Mrs Dillon Cox had petitioned for extra time to stock Bowerlee. On 30 December 1874 the Blyth government had proclaimed new regulations clearing the way for this to happen. Soon after the *Gothenburg* sank, a letter arrived for the Government Resident from the minister in Adelaide,

---

941 Catherine Mary Cox to son Pryce Whynne Dillon Cox 17/2/1893 (Held by Barry Cox, Melbourne).

942 *Northern Territory Times and Gazette* 6/2/1875, p. 2 Public Notices. The nature of the deal between De Lautour and the Cox family is unclear.

943 *S.A. Government Gazette* 11/11/1875, p. 2087; *Northern Territory Times and Gazette* 6/3/1875 leader and p. 3.

John Cox Bray: 'I presume the application can be granted.'[944]

The great dream of starting a horse stud on Cox's Peninsula for the British and Dutch East Indies had died.

With no prospect of now meeting the lease requirements, Catherine Mary Cox (Dillon's wife) left the Territory on the *Claude Hamilton* in July 1875 for Melbourne, where two years later she had to place her two young children in a destitute home. On 11 July 1877 the rights to Dillon and Price Cox's stock still wandering free in the Territory were sold to a wild Irishman named John McGrath, who spent the next few years defending his roaming property by threatening to shoot (and actually shooting) any stock with Cox's brand found in the possession of others, whether legally obtained or not.[945] For many years after, the progeny of Cox's thoroughbred horses, roaming wild in the vast interior, were much sought after by stockmen. At one stage the horse catchers Jack (Brumby) Clarke and Dick Moore set up a camp at the Calvert River to trap Cox's horses.

From the point of view of the cattle industry, the sacrifices of these three pioneering parties of overlanders were not in vain. It was soon recognised that many of the difficulties had been caused by following a path on the lowlands too near to the coast. The Blyth government considered despatching a survey party back overland with Lautour to map a safer route, but instead the Government Resident asked him to prepare a newspaper article titled 'Travelling Directions for Future Overlanders' intended for various publications in Queensland.

Later again Lautour became a strong advocate for a marked tree-line stretching from where the telegraph crossed the Elsey, down the Roper to the Roper Crossing, then across to the Nicholson. This, he said, would lead to a natural gravitation from inland Queensland to Port Darwin. He first took up the matter with Thomas Reynolds, the minister, and later Dr Browne in London. Because it involved Queenslanders, nothing was done by the government in Adelaide.[946]

944 Memorial from Catherine Mary Cox to Everard 24/6/1874 (N.T.I.L.315/1874); Bray to Scott 30/3/1875 (G.R.I.L. A829).

945 *Northern Territory Times and Gazette* 21/7/1877, p. 2 Public Notices.

946 *Northern Territory Times and Gazette* 16/1/1875, p. 2; Queensland to Port Darwin 5/1/1875 (G.R.I.L. A628); *Observer* 31/7/1880, p. 185 De Lautour to Editor 10/5/1880.

And what eventually became of George De Lautour? Having reached Port Darwin, Lautour yarded his cattle at Knuckey's Lagoon 12 miles out, from where he sold the beasts for meat at more than £20 a head. In May 1875 – after being accused of contracting to sell stock to one butcher called Colgan but selling them to another called Abbott, for which Colgan took him to court and was awarded damages of £100 – Lautour made a hasty exit ('skedaddled' said the newspaper) from the Territory back overland toward Queensland, reaching Normanton in December of the same year with a 'large mob of horses'. He almost certainly managed to round up some of Cox's lost horses on the way back. He was therefore the second overlander known to have made the trip both ways.[947] Next year he set up yards and paddocks at the Four Archers near the Limmen Bight River in the hope of catching more of Cox's horses.[948]

For years after, Lautour was derided and scorned by D'arcy Uhr for committing the unforgivable bush sin of abandoning his men – especially as Lautour considered Nation and Elvy not good bushmen.

All this chaotic activity was typical of the hit or miss approach of the new pastoral industry that replaced systematic colonisation.

De Lautour last appears in the Territory in 1881, but this was not the end of his saga. He became involved in the brutal Kanaka trade, settling in the New Hebrides (now Vanuatu) where he was notorious for his hostile attitude to the local people. He had a notice pinned to a tree –

NOTICE

Dogs and Niggers are Forbidden to enter inside the Portals of these Gates.

Any Dogs or Niggers found therein will suffer the Penalty of Death.

By order of George de Lautour,
British Resident.

– and drove the message home by placing a human skull on top of each gate post, under which was nailed a St Andrew's cross made

947 *Northern Territory Times and Gazette* 19/2/1876, p. 2 quoting *Cleveland Bay Express*. First to complete the return trip was D'arcy Uhr.

948 *Brisbane Courier* 30/11/1876, p. 3 courtesy of Tony Roberts.

from two human thigh bones.[949] He was killed by natives in 1890, and so was his innocent son, Willi – 'sins of the father …' According to the famous anthropologist, Tom Harrisson, who went to the New Hebrides as a young man, a punitive naval expedition was then despatched and the local people shot down one by one. As with many remote pioneers, Lautour had lived with no limits, either in respect of his own survival or his treatment of others.[950]

Despite the difficulties of the pioneering pastoralists, the cattle industry in the Territory did not die. Indeed in 1877 a pastoral land boom broke out and by 1881 the Government Resident reported that 'nearly three fourths of the whole territory had been taken up'.[951] That is more than three times the area of the British Isles. The boom was mainly speculative (with many speculators simply pointing to a spot on the map), fuelled in part by low rents and surplus money, but it set off an uncoordinated movement of overlanders driving their stock before them in search of the new plains of promise. With one exception, all the mobs were driven overland from Queensland, at first along the Gulf Track pioneered by Cox and Uhr and later along the tableland route further inland.

Two pioneering stations in particular stand out because they were the first to import large numbers of stock to the upper Northern Territory. Springvale Station near Katherine was established in June 1879 at the instigation of Dr W.J. Browne, a leading South Australian pastoralist who had retired to England. Browne was among the pastoralists who had urged the South Australian government to acquire the Territory in the first place. Unlike his counterparts in Queensland who tended to begin their stations with make-shift camps, he did everything on a grandiose scale. In 1869, hearing of Goyder's likely success, he had asked for a million acres of leasehold land in blocks of 100,000 acres for pastoral and agricultural purposes

949 Douglas Rannie, *My Adventures Among South Sea Cannibals*, Seeley, Service & Co., London, 1912, pp. 145–155; Jane Black, *North Queensland Pioneers*, C.W.A. Townsville, 1931, p. 74; Research information Gerry Egan, Cambridge, England; also Jacqueline Marshall, Centre for South Pacific Studies, University of New South Wales.

950 Tom Harrisson, *Savage Civilisation*, Victor Gollancz, London, 1937, pp. 226–227. I was reminded of this observation about remote pioneers by Dr Roger Wiseman.

951 Price to Parsons 28/9/1881 (N.T.I.L. 585/1881).

(especially cotton growing), with the right to buy 20,000 acres later on. But the government considered the scheme 'too indefinite'.[952] He took up pastoral leases in the Katherine area in 1876 and two years later launched probably the most ambitious and complex pioneering drove in Australian history, engaging Alfred Giles to overland 12,000 sheep from the upper Flinders Ranges to Katherine – Browne wanted to send 30,000, but Giles talked him out of it. In a linked expedition, Alfred's brother Arthur Giles was put in charge of 3000 cattle driven in mobs of 500 from the upper Darling. The surveyor Alfred Woods was sent ahead as leader to lay out the route. Browne called it 'the most wonderful journey with sheep ever performed'.[953]

He combined his pastoral operations with various other large schemes. When the Italian patriots Achille Fazzari and Menotti Garibaldi (son of the great Giuseppe) wanted to start an Italian settlement in New Guinea, Browne urged they should be approached to switch their sights to the Northern Territory. When nothing came of this, Browne proposed an association of 500 selected English persons (plus servants) who would choose their land from 10,000 square miles set aside on the Victoria River. He wrote an open letter 'To my Fellow-Colonists of South Australia' criticising their method of colonising the Territory. 'At present,' he wrote, 'every man amongst you is taxed to keep it useless'.[954]

Meanwhile, under the supervision of Alfred Giles the station at Springvale was built of solid stone based on South Australian station designs as if to last forever – unlike the rough make-shift structures used by Queenslanders until the country proved itself.

At first the pastoralists would only employ Aboriginal workers recruited from outside the area because they tended to side with the Europeans and were seen by the local Aborigines as outsiders like the white men. In November 1880, while Springvale Station was still being built, local Aborigines showed their resentment against the intruders by killing two indigenous employees from Alice Springs and Pine Creek.

---

952 Browne to Cavenagh 28/5/1869 with Cabinet Minute (N.T.I.L. 16/1869).

953 W.J. Browne to A. Giles 30/10/1879 (Seven Letters 1879 to 1887 S.L.S.A. Mortlock P.R.G. 1389/3); Research notes Vern O'Brien 26/5/2006.

954 Browne to Blyth 5/5/1879; King to Browne 6/9/1879; *Observer* 27/9/1879, p. 20; also in S.A.P.P. 128 of 1879, p. 1; *Advertiser* 1/12/1879, p. 10.

Browne wanted to test the overland route from South Australia pioneered by the Milners, as well as the suitability of the tropics for large-scale wool growing. The sheep did not thrive. Early in the dry season of 1880 the first load of wool arrived at Southport, but there was never much more. In an effort to diversify, Browne and his manager started stations further south at Delamere and at Newcastle Waters where they concentrated on large stock. The latter was first stocked with 2000 heifers and a few bulls brought overland from Queensland by D'arcy Uhr and Fred Morck; during the expedition Uhr, in what became a famous case, was arrested near the Roper River for cattle stealing. It appears that Uhr had been given permission by the pastoralist C.B. Fisher's manager to pick up for a fee stray stock left behind by Fisher's drovers, but when it came to handing them over he had kept some unbranded calves for himself. The chief witness for the Crown was Henry Mant, Uhr's head drover who had fallen out with him. On 19 March 1884 Uhr was acquitted in the Palmerston Police Court, although the magistrate said that the charge against him had not been 'frivolous'. For Uhr this was not the end of the matter. Because of the suddenness of the arrest and because at the time he was separated from his partner Morck by floods, he had been forced to abandon his herd of 970 cattle, 570 of which were never retrieved. Breathing fire, he pursued Fisher's manager Hildebrand Stevens for compensation all the way to the Supreme Court in Adelaide, where he was awarded £2000 for loss of stock and £1000 for loss of reputation. The bush had its own code after all.[955]

In 1881 George Goyder estimated that Browne had already lost about £50,000, a large sum of money at the time when wages were often less than £1 a week. Confronted by continual losses, Browne in 1887 walked out of the Territory as dramatically as he had first come. The 'grand plan' approach had failed again.[956]

---

955 *Northern Territory Times and Gazette* 15/3/1884 leader; 22/3/1884, p. 3 Police Court; 27/12/1884, p. 3 Police Court; *Register* 1/4/1885, p. 7; 2/4/1885, p. 7, Supreme Court Proceedings.

956 For general information about the history of Springvale station see: Browne to Parsons 29/12/1880, Minute by Goyder 6/1/1881 (N.T.I.L. 707/1880); W.J. Browne to A. Giles 24/3/1886, 23/8/1887 (Seven Letters to Alfred Giles 1879–1887 S.L.S.A. Mortlock P.R.G. 1389/3); Alfred Giles, *The First Pastoral Settlement in the Northern Territory* (unpublished); Alfred Giles Springvale

The other important pioneering station was Glencoe near Yam Creek, established in June 1879 for the pastoral firm of Travers and Gibson of Queensland with 1200 cattle overlanded along the Gulf Track from Aramac Creek by Nat (Bluey) Buchanan, a famous Queensland pioneer and drover. The manager, Gordon McKean, came around by steamship six months earlier to prepare for the party's arrival and chose a site near Fountain Head on the junction of Yam Creek and the Margaret River, where stray stock were known to hang about. By the time the mob arrived, he was so well prepared that 31 head were on their way to market within a few weeks. Prior to this, much of the groundwork had been done by Albert Sergison, Travers's agent and explorer in the Territory. Sergison had accompanied a government expedition to investigate the land along the Katherine River, and in 1877 led a private expedition financed by Travers to explore the Victoria River country. He published his findings (again with Travers's help) in a pamphlet advertising the pastoral potential to the world. Both Travers and Sergison had dreams of selling cattle to Java and Singapore as well as local markets, and of selling horses to Calcutta and Madras. At first Glencoe was more like a bush camp, which enabled it to start functioning just before Springvale. Responding to the make-shift arrangement, the local 'Alligator people' soon burned it down in an effort to defend their land.

Travers's venture into the Territory ended in personal tragedy. On the trip across, at the Limmen Bight River, a nephew acting as cook in the party (and a likely future manager) was beheaded by an Aborigine who crept up behind him while he was making damper. His almost severed head fell into the cooking pan. The camp was raided and food and equipment taken. A year later the teamster John Barry met a similar fate when he apparently fell asleep while his mate McKenzie was away looking for a ford to cross the horses. McKenzie returned to find Barry's skull crushed, two spears in his neck and all the stores and equipment gone. For years, the Limmen Bight River Mara people and the Garrwa people were feared as expert raiders of overlanders passing through their sacred land.

Station Diary 8/7/1870–16/7/1871 (S.L.S.A. Mortlock P.R.G. 1389/1); Peter Forrest, *Springvale's Story: and Early Years of the Katherine,* Murranji, Darwin, 1985.

Such events were soon repeated in many places in the Territory, and the Europeans later took a terrible revenge. For instance, in the 1880s the brumby hunter Dick Moore reportedly shot 'bush Aborigines' on sight. Eventually the Aboriginal people managed to kill him with an axe in 1894.

Soon Travers sold Glencoe station to the firm of Fisher and Lyons of Melbourne, for whom Buchanan overlanded a second mob of 20,000 head to Glencoe in 1880. It was the first of many large mobs of cattle to come from Queensland. Many of the first stock died in the years to come, or had to be shifted elsewhere.[957] With time Glencoe homestead turned out to be one of the most pleasant places north of the Daly, situated on the banks of the Margaret River and surrounded by green lagoons and permanent springs. But for all its beauty it did not prove an ideal station.

Over the next five years Glencoe was followed by a string of new stations, pioneered mainly by Queensland pastoralists, along a cattle belt reaching from the Herbert (later Georgina) River on the Queensland border, through the Gulf Country and the Barkly Tableland, then across to the Victoria River country and on to the Kimberley (pioneered by the Duracks) in Western Australia. Stations such as Alexandria Downs, Elsey, Victoria River Downs, Wave Hill, Ord River, and so on. By trial and error it was found that the best cattle country lay further inland than Glencoe or Springvale and far distant from Port Darwin. When it came to markets, most of the cattle had to be driven inland for long distances in a south-easterly or southern direction away from the coast facing Asia and along famous stock routes to places like Camooweal, Cloncurry and Longreach in Queensland, or the railhead at Hergott Springs (now Marree) in South Australia, or Bourke on the Darling in New South Wales. Later the Western Australian government opened the Canning Stock Route from the Kimberley south-west through

957 For information on Glencoe see: Travers and Sergison to Blyth 17/4/1878 with pamphlet (N.T.I.L. 232/1878); G. Buchanan, *Packhorse & Waterhole*, Angus & Robertson, Sydney, 1933, facsimile edition 1984 Hesperian Press, Perth, *passim*; *Northern Territory Times and Gazette* 4/8/1877, p. 2; 13/4/1878, p. 2; 21/12/1878, p. 2; 26/4/1879, p. 2; 27/9/1879, p. 2; 27/12/1879, p. 4; 2/4/1881, p. 2; 6/8/1881, p. 2; 10/12/1881, p. 2; Price to Parsons 30/6/1883 (S.A.P.P. 53A of 1883–1884).

the Great Sandy Desert to the railhead at Wiluna, but due to the harshness of the country it was never a great success.

The gradual victory of the Queensland route over that from the south did not pass unnoticed. In 1878 the *Brisbane Courier* wrote:

> We have always been of the opinion that this Northern Territory would only become colonized by the expansion of settlement in Queensland. The history of Australia teaches us that there is the greatest difficulty in establishing a new settlement in an isolated position, but that old-established and prosperous communities will constantly expand by growing outwards.[958]

Supporting that view, in 1878 Gresley Lukin, the proprietor of the *Brisbane Courier* and *Queenslander* newpapers, despatched the explorer Ernest Favenc from Blackall to Port Darwin to investigate a possible railway route between Queensland and the Territory, paid for by private enterprise which would eventually tie Queensland and the Northern Territory together and so correct what he considered a grave mistake made in the 1860s when the Territory was grabbed by a colony on the opposite side of the continent.[959]

One effect of this rapid expansion by pastoralists over the Queensland border into and across the Territory was that the South Australian government lost control of the relations between the invaders and the indigenous peoples, particularly in the 1880s and 1890s. The contrast is striking between South Australia's lofty rhetoric at the outset – talk of a concentrated civilised settlement, talk of entrée to Asia – and what eventually happened in the pastoral lands. The generalised violence first showed up in the Gulf Country as pastoralists spread out from the Gulf Track and moved westwards. There are many reasons why the Gulf Country in particular became one of the most dangerous places in Australia. It was seen by both the Queensland and South Australian governments as 'border country' and low on their list for providing police protection. Many of the Europeans (like Black Jack Maori

---

958 *Brisbane Courier* 18/4/1878

959 Ernest Favenc, *The History of Australian Exploration 1788–1888,* Turner and Henderson, Sydney, 1888, pp. 274–276; James Anderson and Peter Monteath, *Ernest Favenc and the Exploration of the Northern Territory,* (Flinders University Monograph, 2007).

Reid) were violent characters running away from civilisation down south, while the Aboriginal groups were numerous and were required, often on pain of death, to defend their sacred land to the last. It is a great irony that people of this so-called 'conquered race', working as stockmen on rations and a pittance of a wage, later turned around and saved the pastoral industry in the North.[960] But that is another story.

Two Territories

The Palmerston press sometimes wrote about the two Territories. 'One half the world does not know how the other half lives,' wrote the *Northern Territory Times and Gazette* in 1878.[961]

The cattlemen brought with them an older and different experience of Australia compared with that of the 'naïve newcomers' from South Australia. The pastoral expansion from Queensland across the Territory to the Kimberley was the last phase of a squatting movement that had started north and west of Sydney 60 years before. During this period a distinct outback culture had developed in response to the hazards of the Australian inland.

It was not uncommon for South Australian government officers to complain about the chaotic methods of the early pastoralists, who were moving from place to place, often failing to meet their rents, almost outside the influence of the law. Yet their methods suited exactly the unequal patchwork of the Northern Territory landscape. With this approach the Wakefieldian dream of establishing instruments of civilisation, like the school, the chapel and the rule of law at the very frontiers of colonisation, was out of the question, as indeed it had been in outback South Australia.

Whereas the South Australian planners tried to deal with the Aboriginal inhabitants as British subjects within the framework of British law, the pastoralists had long come to the conclusion that this did not work. The debacle at Escape Cliffs over conflicts with the Aborigines was quoted time and again to prove that such a policy made colonisation impossible. Repeatedly South Australian governments were blamed for their high-minded liberal attitudes

---

960 Tony Roberts, *Frontier Justice A History of the Gulf Country to 1900*, University of Queensland Press, St Lucia, Queensland, 2005 *passim*.

961 *Northern Territory Times and Gazette* 24/8/1878 leader.

Despite the original plan to treat the Aborigines in a civilised way, it was the 'Queensland Method' that prevailed in pastoral areas. (From A.J. Vogan, *The Black Police*, London 1890. Courtesy of the National Library, Canberra)

which, it was said, led to double standards and caused atrocities rather than prevented them. In contrast, most pastoralists advocated what was called 'the Queensland method' of managing the Aborigines. This method was to leave them alone, but the moment they speared a white man or killed cattle, to deal them such a stroke of retribution outside the law they would never dare do it again. The strategy had only limited success. For one reason, 'natives and cattle' competed for the same resources, so that whatever their fear, Aborigines just had to fight. There was also conflict over burning the bush – each year for thousands of years the Aborigines burnt the grasslands to hunt for animals, a practice seen by pastoralists as wantonly destroying feed for cattle. Alfred Giles, who stayed on to become one of the Territory's most important cattlemen, wrote from Springvale Station:

> lately we have stocked the Newcastle Waters Station with cattle & that Mr McPhee the manager writes me that owing to the cattle being located on all the large waters and all small and backwaters drying up, the blacks are forced in amongst the cattle and although they have not yet speared cattle they three times threatened to do so unless the cattle are removed, and Mr McPhee adds that unless something is done for

> them by the Government they will undoubtedly spear both cattle and stockmen and the only remedy will be the rifle.[962]

According to the historian Robert Foster, beginning with pastoral regulations proclaimed in 1851, pastoral leases in South Australia did not extinguish the right of Aborigines to hunt and practise their ceremonies on leasehold land; on the contrary the legal right to hunt and gather food was guaranteed. But the situation was less clear in Queensland.[963]

Finally, whereas the South Australian planners of 1863 wanted to tie the north coast to the Indies Archipelago and Asia, the pastoral industry looked inwards to the so-called 'Inland' for inspiration. Hart, Ayers, Finniss and later Douglas had all planned their colonisation on the assumption that the far north coast was on the southern perimeter of a great natural region reaching all the way to Asia and sharing different degrees of the same tropical climate. Then with the advent of 'White Australia' towards the end of the 1800s the whole geographic concept was gradually transformed and North Australia became the so-called 'frontline against Asia'. Whether the north coast could have been settled by Asians, or religious migrants living a little above subsistence level, will always remain a conjecture, because events elsewhere in Australia and Asia overtook cheap immigration. It was a common view at the time that nowhere in the world would new colonies succeed unless people were plonked down and made to fight for survival.

When the north coast became the boundary against Asia, the numerous ancient contacts between South-East Asia and North Australia were conveniently forgotten. As an example of such contacts, even the feral cats were said to be of Asian origin. One of the casualties of this change in outlook was the failure to complete the promised north-south railway line – as the link to Asia.

---

962 Alfred Giles to Protector of Aborigines 26/5/1884 (G.R.I.L. A6900).

963 Robert Foster, *The Origin of the Protection of Aboriginal Rights in South Australian Pastoral Leases,* 13/11/1997 (History Department monograph, University of Adelaide).

CHAPTER 8

CONCEDING DEFEAT

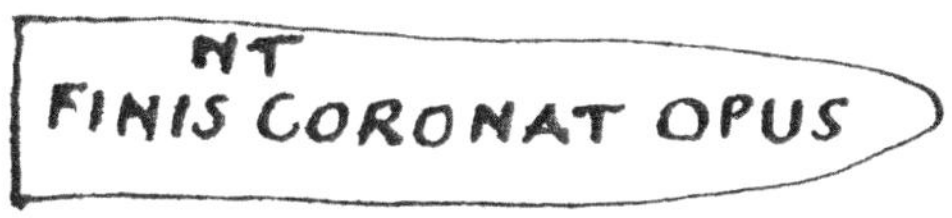
NT
FINIS CORONAT OPUS

Diary of R. Edmunds 1/5/1865 (State Library of South Australia – D8043(L))

'The end crowns the work.' The bold motto used at the launch of the Finniss expedition came back to haunt everyone. The end was defeat.

Running in parallel with the growth of the cattle industry, the other major event of the 1880s was the first move to construct a transcontinental railway from Port Darwin to Adelaide. The construction had two primary goals. The first was to tie South Australia and the Territory together, even if the worst should happen and later it was placed under some other control – such as Queensland. The second aim was to keep open South Australia's access to the so-called Unlimited Asian Market – at some time in the future. There was talk of some kind of an overland rail link even before Stuart's epic journey in 1862. Always, the problem was how to pay for it, whether by raising government loans or by the American land grant system. In 1862 the *Port Augusta and Northern Railway Act* authorised a land grant of two square miles, selected from either side, for every mile constructed by a private capitalist to an agreed point north of Port Augusta.[964] But no entrepreneur took it up. The 'land-grant railway' was raised in parliament again in 1872, and again the next year, but no progress was made on the railway because of disagreements on how it should best be financed. The idea of giving so much land to one capitalist was not popular in a colony where many citizens still clung to the founders' belief in the moral superiority of small business. Meanwhile a railway paid for from government loans was pushed through to Oodnadatta,

964 S.A.P.A. 28 of 1862 *An Act to encourage the formation of Railways northwards from Port Augusta.*

bit by bit, to meet local needs. Much of the transport north of Oodnadatta was then done by Afghans and their camel trains – again illustrating the links with Asia at this time. Later as part of a rising tide against Asians, and despite their great contribution to the inland, efforts were made to freeze Afghans out of work altogether.

In 1883 the South Australian parliament passed an Act that enabled work to start on a railway linking Palmerston and Pine Creek about 150 miles to the south. The legislation was steered by minister in charge of the Northern Territory, John Langdon Parsons – later Government Resident of the Northern Territory and later again agent-general to Japan – and was well supported in both houses. The only concern was whether the voracious giant termites, which had now acquired mythical status, would eat the jarrah sleepers as quickly as they were laid down. Costs would be met both by government loans (charged against the Territory account) followed by sales of land along the line.[965] In other words, parliament combined two systems of paying for the project: government loans and income from the sale of land opened up by the line. The sale of land was not to be concentrated on one person. Construction began in 1887 and was completed when it reached Pine Creek in 1889. As in California, this was achieved mainly by the use of cheap Chinese labour, including the first of the noted Ah Toy family. The venture seemed to mark the end of an era, for the Great Depression of the 1890s hit South Australia early; and already there was a reaction throughout Australia against using what the *North Australian* newspaper called 'slave labour' to help pay for large construction projects.[966]

Before raising a loan for the railway the South Australian government had petitioned the Colonial Office in London to make possession of the Territory 'absolute and irrevocable', replacing the Letters Patent. But the request was firmly rejected.[967] The Colonial Office had not abandoned entirely the idea of a separate colony facing Asia possibly along the entire north coast, and in fact for

965 S.A.P.A. 284 of 1883 *An Act to provide for the formation of a Line of Railway from Palmerston to Pine Creek*; S.A.P.D. 1883 c. 815 to 825.

966 *North Australian* 1/10/1886 leader.

967 Jervois to Kimberley 19/7/1882 with enclosures; Derby to Robinson 6/1/1883 (S.A.P.P. 113 of 1883–1884).

The Larrakia at Port Darwin, a society organised on the principle that everyone must have a place. A way of life further threatened by the policies of White Australia. (Photograph by Paul Foelsche, c. 1876. Courtesy South Australian Museum)

many years north Queensland, the upper Territory and the Kimberley tended to be linked together with stock and men moving backwards and forwards between each area.

For the next 20 years, until the Territory was ceded to the new Federal Government in 1911, the completion of the transcontinental railway became the fundamental preoccupation of successive South Australian governments. Having put so much energy into the Territory they did not want to lose contact with such a promising land in the end.

A period of moderate prosperity that began in the 1860s was over in South Australia by the mid to late 1880s. With the change of tide, the ambivalence increased between those who believed the Territory would make South Australia great and those who reckoned it was beyond the colony's means to manage.

In 1895 the Kingston government set up a Royal Commission to decide what should be done. In general it reported favourably on the prosects of the Territory.[968]

968 Report of the Northern Territory Commission (S.A.P.P. 19 of 1895). For the first book refuting a very optimistic view of the Territory see: B.R. Davidson,

With the federation of the Australian colonies in 1901, the future of the Northern Territory became a national issue – and the cause of crisis in South Australia. The question of whether the Territory should be transferred to the new Commonwealth dominated the first decade in South Australia after Federation. Territorians wanted it transferred to the Commonwealth, South Australians kept changing their minds, while people in the more populous states like New South Wales and Victoria disliked the idea of having to pay for the Territory's upkeep. While Queensland which had missed out all along particularly opposed South Australia gaining some advantage.

The steps by which it was eventually transferred in January 1911 were also full of controversy. Firstly, in April 1901, soon after Federation, South Australia's premier, Frederick William Holder, offered the Northern Territory to the Commonwealth without first consulting the state parliament.[969] Holder had come to the conclusion that if the Commonwealth would not allow South Australia to develop the Territory with non-Europeans, then the Commonwealth should pay for it. And, a second controversy when the Northern Territory was transferred in 1911, it was done without putting the question to the South Australian people – this despite the clear requirement of Section 123 in the Federal Constitution that no state could be substantially reduced in area without 'the approval of the majority of electors'. As late as the 1950s representatives of prominent families associated with the Royal Geographical Society in Adelaide were talking as if the transfer was all a piece of skulduggery perpetuated by politicians without vision looking for a quick hand-out from the new Federal Government.[970]

In December 1905 the House of Assembly in South Australia passed a resolution to transfer the Territory to the Commonwealth, and in February 1906 Labor Premier Tom Price, (who wanted the money to relieve debt and for welfare) offered it for £3,400,000, provided the Federal Government started building a transcontinental railway within 12 months similar to the east-west railway – the construction of which commenced in

The Northern Myth, Melbourne University Press, Melbourne, 1972.

969 Transfer of Northern Territory to Commonwealth (S.A.P.P. 27 of 1901).

970 Discussions the author had with members of the R.G.S. 1956.

1912 and was a main condition under which Western Australia had joined the Federation. South Australia's hopeful plan was to keep some control over the Territory while getting the rest of the federation to pay for it. Eventually both sides were forced to compromise. The Commonwealth, led mainly by Alfred Deakin, paid South Australia £3,931,086 to cover all previous costs on the Territory including loans, plus £2,239,462 for the southern section of the transcontinental line from Stirling near Port Augusta to Oodnadatta. It undertook to complete the transcontinental line, but only on the understanding that no time limit was set, and along a route of its own choosing. Deakin even entertained the idea of the track veering off into Queensland or New South Wales. The deal was solemnly sealed with the South Australia's *Northern Territory Surrender Act 1907* and the Commonwealth's *Northern Territory Acceptance Act 1910*, and at the beginning of 1911 the Territory was transferred.

As part of the deal, the South Australian parliament officially withdrew its legal opposition to the east-west railway passing through its land on a route to be decided by the Commonwealth – and this probably explains why the financial compensation was so generous. Negotiations over the east-west and the south-north lines began more or less in parallel.[971]

The large compensation paid allowed the vaunted self-supporting system – the only condition under which the South Australian government ever consented to act as colonisers – to retain some vestige of dignity. To mark the transfer the unpopular name Palmerston was changed to Darwin.

As 'surrender day' drew near, the second thoughts increased. There was increasing anger in Adelaide over ignoring Section 123 of the Constitution; but because no one had the will, or would put up the money to challenge the matter in the High Court, nothing was

971 S.A.P.D. 1905c. 1002 to 1004; S.A.P.A. 946 of 1907/1908 *An act to Surrender the Northern Territory of the State of South Australia to the Commonwealth of Australia and for other purposes*; Commonwealth Act 20 of 1910 *An act to provide for the Acceptance of the Northern Territory under the Authority of the Commonwealth and for the carrying out of the Agreement for the Surrender and Acceptance*; P.A. Howell, *South Australia and Federation*, Wakefield Press, Adelaide, 2002, Chapter 3.

done. Many people believed that the loss of the vast north would make South Australia a minor state like Tasmania. The *Advertiser* regretted they had not settled the matter at Federation by choosing a new name for South Australia which combined the north and the south. Others (like Travers Borrow of the Finniss family) argued that South Australia had no right to surrender the Territory at all because under the Letters Patent it had never been fully acquired. Only the British government had the legal right to cede the land and the British government was not asked.[972] Two late lobby groups were formed to oppose the transfer. One was the Great Central State League associated with the *Register* newspaper – a state which would hold the far-flung former colonies reaching over a large continent together and prevent too much concentration along the eastern seabord. The other lobby group was the Land Grant Railway League associated with Simpson Newland and J.L. Parsons. Both men believed that if only a transcontinental railway were built, the value of the Northern Territory would become obvious. In 1906, Simpson Newland went to London and helped raise funds for a land-grant railway (called the National Construction Co. Ltd) with J.T. Moate as director. But the Labor government of Tom Price still would not be swayed. As late as 1910, efforts were made by the public to repeal the so-called 'Transfer Act'.[973] The era of the 'Northern Territory of South Australia' was at an end.

Still with their belief in South Australia as 'a special colony' (they preferred 'province') unshaken – at the end of the same year as the transfer South Australians celebrated their first 75 years of achievement with self congratulation. They had contributed to the so-called 'New British Empire' referring to Wakefield's reforms. The *Register* wrote about:

972 K.T. Borrow, *The Northern Territory of South Australia and Federation*. R.G.S.A. S.A. branch Proceedings LVII, pp. 15 to 24; *The Northern Territory of Australia, North Australia and Alexandra Land (1882 to 1900)*. The Australian Law Journal 28 (22 July 1954), pp. 148 to 151. Additional Notes to the author 1972.

973 Simpson Newland, *Memoirs,* Preece, Adelaide 1926; P.F. Donovan, *A Land Full of Possibilities,* University of Queensland Press, St Lucia, 1981, Chapter 10.

> the greatness of the achievements of South Australia in the relatively brief period of three-quarters of a century.[974]

And the *Advertiser* wrote:

> It inaugurated a new era... It included a new departure in the applied science of colonisation.[975]

In the end the attempt to set up a second South Australia on North-West Arnhem Land as a bridge to Asia (and using the home colony's unique experience in systematic colonisation) failed comprehensively – and having failed, it left a legacy of complications that made it difficult for successive governments to be flexible and try other experiments.

As predicted, South Australia became a minor state like Tasmania. The state was still hemmed in between the dry north and the sea which stretched all the way to Antarctica. The north coast became the front-line against Asia, isolated from the rest of Australia by thousands of miles and cut off from its near neighbours to the north. The idea of a deliberately planned multi-racial society was abandoned. Among those who suffered most because of the new Commonwealth emphasis on White Australia were the original inhabitants who had been there for tens of thousands of years. Within 20 years of taking over the Territory the Commonwealth government began the assimilation policy of *forcing them* to be Europeans, based on the mistaken idea that you can change cultures almost overnight. Had 'Arnheim's Land' – to give it an old name – been under the control of the Dutch who ruled the nearby Indies, the story might have been different.

Except for extensions in the late 1920s down to Birdum and up to Alice Springs, decade after decade passed and the promised transcontinental railway was not built. It came to be known as the Never-Never railway line. Out of desperation, in 1962, the premier of South Australia, Thomas Playford, took the Federal government to the High Court to get the line built. The appeal failed.[976] Only in

974 *Register* 28/12/1911 leader.

975 *Register* 28/12/1911 leader.

976 The State of South Australia & Anor V The Commonwealth of Australia (1962) 108 CLR 130.

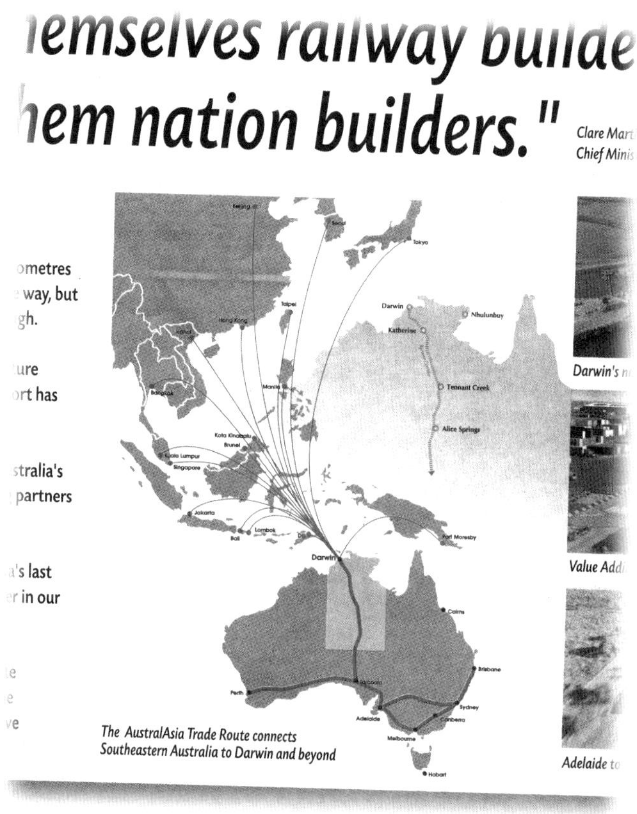

Map in the *Australian* newspaper, 15 January 2003, to mark the completion of the railway from Adelaide to Darwin.
Belated realisation of a nineteenth-century South Australian dream.

the 21st century was the joining of the north and south ends revived (to quote Prime Minister John Howard) as a 'nation building' project for the new millennium – at a time when attitudes toward Asia and non-European migration were changing again.

South Australia continued, on and off, to run most of the education system in the Territory up to the end of 1973. The completion of the transcontinental railway was thus the last belated event linked to the South Australian era.

EPILOGUE

In retrospect what makes this episode in Australian history memorable is the application of a certain grand style based in part on a belief in progress and liberal optimism – what today critics would probably call 'classical modern discourse' – to perhaps the most resistant environment in Australia.

Small unpredicted inputs can often lead to large unintended consequences. What the systematic colonisers could not anticipate was a multitude of intervening variables. History it seems plays many tricks on those whose approach to planning is too single-minded to adapt to the vagaries of change – those who try to steer history on a straight course with a firm hand. A weakness of the Northern Territory Plan had been that it lacked a back-up system, no escape strategy in the event of failure.

Only now is there some prospect of the Northern Territory realising the original dream of entering the Great Asian Market.

DOCUMENTATION: ABBREVIATIONS

One of the effects of the so-called 'history wars' (where historians were criticised for not relying on documentation enough), is that historians have become very careful in documenting their research, especially archival research. Reflecting this trend, documentation has been given a prominent position in this book.

N.T.I.L.	In-letters or in-correspondence of the government department controlling the Northern Territory of South Australia (most being catalogued as GRSI, State Records SA.)
N.T.O.L.	Out-letters of the government department controlling the Northern Territory
G.R.I.L.	In-letters of the Government Resident
G.R.O.L.	Out-letters of the Government Resident
G.O.D.	Out-despatches of the Governor of South Australia
G.I.D.	In-despatches of the Governor
S.G.I.L.	In-letters of the Surveyor-General's Department
S.G.O.L.	Out-letters of the Surveyor-General's Department
C.S.O.I.L.	Chief Secretary's in-letters
C.S.O.O.L.	Chief Secretary's out-letters
C.C.L.I.L.	Commissioner of Crown Land's in-letters
C.C.L.O.L.	Commissioner of Crown Land's out-letters
Attorney-General I.L.	Attorney-General's in-letters
S.A.P.D.	Debates of the South Australian parliament
S.A.P.A.	Acts of the South Australian parliament

S.A.P.P.	South Australian parliamentary papers
H.P.D.	Hansard's parliamentary debates (United Kingdom)
S.A. Government Gazette	Government Gazette of South Australia
C.O.	Colonial Office papers
P.R.G.	Private record group at the State Library of South Australia, Mortlock Collection
G.R.G.	Government record group at the State Records of South Australia
B.R.G.	Business record group at the State Library of South Australia, Mortlock Collection
Research Notes	Notes sent to the author by researchers
Copyright	Where copyright is involved every effort has been made to trace the holder of the copyright

AUTHOR'S NOTE

This book is the result of 40 years of detailed archival research concentrating on the period 1860 to 1911 and using, where possible, only primary or contemporary sources. Not until the first draft had been written did I seek out and study general secondary sources. In the primary research I worked line by line through well over half-a-million pages of documents. The approach proved useful because general indexes rarely cover all the information in a text and, in the 19th century, discursive styles tended to be expansive with numerous side comments and additions, at times on a different subject.

The first stage began with five years of full-time postgraduate research. For this initial period acknowledgment is due to:

1. Douglas Pike of the University of Adelaide, under whom I started my apprenticeship in history writing, who had an encyclopaedic knowledge of early South Australian history, and suggested many contacts and leads. He advised me, in a world over-supplied with books, to focus my career on constructing 'one thorough history'. He also advocated an archival method of history research, working from the original records and avoiding secondary sources for as long as possible before studying in detail all known research by others. He also believed that Australian history can never be told in isolation from the rest of the world – a good example of 'the rest of the world' being the attempt in the 1870s to make use of religious contacts in India, Russia and Japan.
2. Gerald Fischer (Head of the State Archives department of the State Library of South Australia) and his staff, who made it

possible for me to construct much of the first draft in the State Archives surrounded by (and thus able to cross-study directly) original newspapers, public records and private records. Because the three categories are now stored in different places this kind of direct cross-referencing is no longer possible.

3. Members of the Royal Geographical Society, that unique institution in South Australia. I first made contact with the RGS in the early 1950s as a young student when it was patronised by many of South Australia's leading pioneering families and was a unique source of oral history anecdotes and leads about the Territory extending back as far as the 1860s. Few of these people are now alive and the RGS has become a very different place, but their help deserves recognition. It was also a place where the relative merits of respective ancestors were continually being debated – for instance in regard to the Territory, the supporters of McKinlay versus the supporters of Edmunds, or the defenders of Finniss (who seemed to be the main scapegoat) against his critics.

Over the last 28 years, I have systematically examined the sources a second time (plus any new material) and rewritten much of the text. For this final period acknowledgment is due to:

1. The South Australian College of Advanced Education, which released me for four months to work on the text as part of its contribution to the State's 150 celebrations – Premier John Bannon having asked each tertiary institution to contribute.
2. Nick Walker from what was then the South Australian Government's Wakefield Press gave useful advice about presentation and arranged for the first draft to be read in the Northern Territory.
3. Professors Alan Powell and David Carment, Ms Robyn Maynard from the Northern Territory University and Ms Helen Wilson from the Northern Territory History Unit, to whom the early manuscript was sent and who suggested useful improvements, particularly in updating the text.
4. Staff of the Aboriginal Studies and Teacher Education Centre of the South Australian College of Advanced Education who

suggested some strategies for dealing with documents relating to Aborigines.

5. The University of South Australia, which released me for several months to prepare the final version. The University also gave me access to Beverley Barnes, publications consultant and editor, Sydney, to provide an interim report on presentation.
6. Professor Wilf Prest from the University of Adelaide and Bob Reece from Murdoch University for their continual encouragement.
7. Particular thanks for Philip Jones from the South Australian Museum for permission to use photographs from the book *The Policeman's Eye*, Philip Jones, 2005. I also wish to acknowledge Philip Jones for his careful work as a proof-reader.

But I must emphasise that no one acknowledged above should be held in any way responsible for the eventual contents.

Over the last 14 years in particular, I have received help from the following organisations and people in Darwin: the Northern Territory Archives Service; Museum & Art Gallery of the Northern Territory; Northern Territory Library and Information Services; individuals like Peter Spillett and Vern O'Brien (especially for his knowledge of pastoral legislation and his help with maps); and Barbara James for her work on women in the Territory and discussions about the title of the book. June Tomlinson and the Genealogical Society of the Northern Territory did excellent work providing certain biographical information.

In gathering information for the book I have relied on newspaper sources extensively. A column-by-column examination of the daily newspapers, the *South Australian Register* and the *South Australian Advertiser*, from 1858 to 1890 was conducted noting in detail all references to the Northern Territory. A detailed examination was also made of the *Northern Territory Times and Gazette* as well as the *Northern Australian and Northern Territory Government Gazette* from their inception to the same year. The detailed reading was then followed by selected reading of all the above up to 1912. Other newspapers consulted for specific events included: *Argus* (Melbourne); *Age* (Melbourne); *Brisbane Courier*; *Sydney Morning Herald*; *Australasian Post*; *Northern Argus*; *Kapunda*

Herald and Northern Intelligencer; *Methodist Journal*; *Truth and Progress*; *Quiz*; *Quip*; *Gadfly; Adelaide Punch.*

A second comprehensive source of information was incoming and outgoing correspondence of the various government departments controlling the Territory. As the indexes proved unreliable a docket-by-docket search was made twice over – first before writing the text and then after initial drafts of the text were completed. The Governor's Despatches, the Surveyor-General Department records and the Chief Secretary Office correspondence were also widely consulted. Most of these records are held by the State Records of South Australia with some in the Australian National Archives, Canberra.

A third main source of information was numerous private records now held mainly in the Mortlock Library of the State Library of South Australia and several other Australian libraries, such as the Mitchell Library (State Library of NSW).

In the early stages I was helped by a powerful oral tradition in South Australia about the Northern Territory, from which I gained leads and anecdotes. Prior to World Wars I and II many old Territorians returned to Adelaide to retire who then passed on their stories to their children and grandchildren. We now live in different times and very little of this oral history survives.

One of the advantages of a longitudinal study was that specific queries could be sent to individuals and organisations which sometimes took months and even years to resolve. In this regard the regular exchange of information over many years with Barry Cox, Frank Uhr, Tony Roberts, Vern O'Brien and Bert Forsyth on aspects of the pastoral industry in the Territory proved particularly useful. It also helped me to think my way into researching the cattle industry in general as an alternative to planned colonisation.

Several overseas organisations also provided information in response to specific enquires: the Moscow Archives of Ancient Record; the Japanese Foreign Office; the General Government Archives in The Hague; the Bethel College Historical Society, Kansas; the Public Archives of Canada, Ottawa; the Archives Office, Mauritius; the National Archives of India in New Delhi; the Public Record Office in London; the Arsip Nasional Republik Indonesia in Jakarta; Archives New Zealand; C.H.A. (Enrik)

Plug, Second Secretary of the Netherland's Embassy Canberra, for accessing and translating documents on the Dutch East Indies and the Northern Territory; J. Gausdal of Oslo and Olav Hodne of the Santal Mission in India; Tom Harrisson and his staff of the Sarawak Museum, Kuching; J.M. Gullick of the Malayan Division of the Royal Asiatic Society and Douglas Potter (grandson of Bloomfield Douglas) of Argyle, Scotland. In addition Edward Duyker of the Australian Mauritian Research Group provided valuable information on the Mauritius connection. As early as 1971 Douglas Pike put me in contact with D.C.S. Sissons for his work on Japanese in the Territory.

No attempt has been made to analyse the response of the indigenous peoples to the invasion of their country by rootless nomadic outsiders except at the most empirical descriptive level. No doubt they would have concurred with this statement: 'Poor bugger Whitefella got no Dreaming', i.e. he has no deep spiritual roots to do with the land.[977] Research on Aboriginal-European contacts was fraught with difficulties; many European pioneers played down the massacres (the bush code forbade mentioning the number of Aborigines killed), while others played up the massacres because they liked to see themselves as soldiers on the front line. What is certain, large numbers of indigenous people died from dispossession and introduced diseases. To quote another Aborigine in another place: 'The smell of the white man is killing us.'

For over 25 years I have worked side by side with Aboriginal colleagues from whom I have learned the hazard of trying to explain the subjective responses of one culture in terms of another. To paraphrase the film-maker Rolf De Heer: 'Ours is a cosmology of categorisation; theirs is a cosmology of connection'. In general I have tried to strike a balance between an Aboriginal presence and not taking away from Aboriginal peoples the right to write their history perhaps using other concepts of time and space as well as other ways of explaining.

I look forward to Aboriginal scholars telling their own story.

My thanks to Helen Raduntz who helped with the final typing

977 See PhD thesis: Mary-Anne Gale, *Poor Bugger Whitefella got no Dreaming: the representation and appropriation of published Dreaming narratives, with special reference to David Unaipon's writings*, University of Adelaide, 2000.

of the text. Also to my late parents whose hard-earned savings contributed to the preparation of this book.

At the publication stage my thanks to Michael Bollen, Julia Beaven, Bethany Clarke and Yvonne Miels for their careful work as editors. Also to the typesetter Michael Deves, who helped incorporate rare nineteenth-century visuals throughout the text.

Most of all my great, great thanks to Jillian B who had to live with the project for so long, to whom I dedicate this book.

INDEX

H

Wakefield Press is an independent publishing and
distribution company based in Adelaide, South Australia.
We love good stories and publish beautiful books.
To see our full range of titles, please visit our website at
www.wakefieldpress.com.au.